◀ TIM

WRITE
MALAY

By the same author:

Speak Malay!

◀ **TIMES LEARN MALAY** ▶

WRITE MALAY

Edward S King
B.A. (Hons.) (London)
Malayan Education Service (Ret.)

*An Introduction to the Modern Written
Language for English-speaking Malaysians*

TIMES BOOKS INTERNATIONAL
Singapore • Kuala Lumpur

New Edition 1986
Reprinted 1988, 1991, 1993, 1995

© 1986 TIMES EDITIONS PTE. LTD.

Published by Times Books International
an imprint of Times Editions Pte. Ltd.

Times Centre, 1 New Industrial Road
Singapore 1953.

Times Subang
Lot 46, Subang Hi-Tech Industrial Park
Batu Tiga, 40000 Shah Alam
Selangor Darul Ehsan, Malaysia.

All rights reserved. No part of this publication
may be reproduced, stored in a retrieval system,
or transmitted, in any form or by any means,
electronic, mechanical, photocopying, recording
or otherwise, without the prior permission of the
copyright owner.

Printed by JBW Printers & Binders Pte. Ltd.

ISBN 981 204 114 1

MIRI
NOV. 10, 96

TO
TED AND TOPSY
WHO MADE IT POSSIBLE

FOREWORD

This is an outstanding book written with meticulous caution and skill. The approach is highly remarkable.

The author has taken great care to analyse all the intricate problems in language structure. In fact he has made the mastery of the language easy and interesting.

His approach is practical. The students are able to assimilate the substance with ease.

I strongly recommend this book to all the aspiring students of Bahasa Malaysia.

Prof. Dr. G. Soosai
J.P., P.P.N.

PREFACE TO THE NEW EDITION

It is gratifying to know that my humble efforts to elucidate a few of the difficulties and intricacies of this fascinating and increasingly important language have met with sufficient approval to necessitate a further edition.

My thanks are due to Times Books International for preparing this new edition; to Dr. G. Soosai for so kindly writing a foreword; and above all to the people of Malaysia, who welcomed me amongst themselves and who inspired me with a great love for their beautiful country and for the Malay language. I hope that I may have made some small contribution towards promoting understanding between Malaysians and English-speaking foreigners everywhere, thereby making some small repayment towards the great debt I owe to Malaysia.

Edward S. King
October 1986

PREFACE TO FIRST EDITION

The gratifying popularity of my first radio course and of the textbook which was based upon it (*Speak Malay*) led to my being asked to write a second and more advanced course in the National Language for Radio Malaya. This second course, entitled *Gunakanlah Bahasa Kebangsaan Kita!*, went on the air early in 1960 and, to judge from the kind letters received from listeners of all races all over the Federation, was even more popular than the earlier and more elementary series. It is on the second series that the present work is based.

In this second course, which follows on from where the previous one (*Speak Malay*) leaves off, the emphasis has been shifted from the spoken language to the modern written language. This does not mean that the present course is entirely literary in content: much of the material contained in it can also be used in ordinary everyday conversation. It is rather that I have tried to give the student the equipment he needs to read and write good modern Malay of the kind that he will hear in radio broadcasts on serious subjects — news-bulletins, talks, lectures, and so on — and the kind that he will find in newspapers, magazines, modern novels and short stories, government reports, and official and commercial correspondence of all kinds. This kind of Malay, which is in some respects stiffer and more formal than the Malay of everyday conversation, is the kind of Malay that is taught in the schools under the name of National Language (*Bahasa Kebangsaan*) and it is clearly the language of the future if not of the present.

Like its predecessor, this second course is based on the sentence, and it is therefore the sentences (Section A) of each lesson which are the most important part of the course. Nevertheless, in view of the greater complexity of written Malay, considerably more grammatical explanation has been found necessary on this occasion. I have given more elaborate explanations of the various Malay affixes than most of my predecessors have given and, I believe, considerably more examples of their use. The difficulty of the Malay affixes has, to my mind, been vastly overrated in the past by both teachers and students, and this regrettable state of affairs has been largely encouraged by abortive attempts to cram all the affixes into one chapter and has given the erroneous impression that prefixes and suffixes are refinements which can be dispensed with. I have spread the teaching of these affixes over the whole course on the principle of "divide and conquer". The student thus has time to let one affix "sink in" before being brought face to face with half a dozen others.

The vocabulary of the course, amounting to almost 2,000 Malay words, has been kept as up-to-date as possible, and practically every word in the book may be heard every day on the radio or seen every day in the newspapers. While not neglecting the rural aspects of the Malay language, I have tried to show the student that Malay also possesses a perfectly adequate vocabulary for dealing with the more urban side of life. Malay is no longer the "racy idiom of peasants": it is a modern language, very much alive and developing rapidly to the stage at which it can be used for all purposes — science as well as literature, economics as well as agriculture. The only reason why Malay cannot yet be used as the medium of instruction in the University — apart from the text-book difficulty in most subjects — is that not enough people know the language well enough, not that the language is itself inadequate to its task. It is my hope, therefore, that this volume may help those Malaysians who wish to know their National Language more thoroughly in order to be able to take part in its development. A student who has worked conscientiously through *Speak Malay* and *Write Malay* should have a vocabulary of about 2,500 common Malay words and be reasonably confident of how to use them in good sentences. Once he has read his set books and studied sufficiently to be able to answer questions set in the General Paper he should be able to pass the Government Standard II, Malay Examination with ease.

My thanks are due to many Malay friends who have given me help of all kinds both during the preparation and broadcasting of the original radio course and also during the writing of the book itself. In particular I should like to thank Syed Alwi and Manaff Abdullah of Radio Malaya, who produced the original programme and made many helpful suggestions and also Abdullah bin Haji Hakim of Radio Malaya's Malay Service who not only read the Malay of the radio lessons so beautifully but also pointed out my errors in the original scripts. My greatest debt, however, is to my friend and colleague, Encik Jamaludin bin Abdul Rani, who has painstakingly gone through the whole manuscript and made many very useful suggestions in addition to weeding out numerous errors which had escaped even the vigilant eyes of Radio Malaya's Malay Section. Encik Jamaludin's profound knowledge of his own language coupled with his excellent command of English has enabled me to get rid of many inaccuracies which a lesser man than he would have missed.

My debt to previous writers on the Malay language is, of course, considerable. The works of Winstedt, Wilkinson, Brown and Lewis are too well known for me to catalogue them here and I shall confine myself to mentioning a number of books which are not as widely known as they deserve to be among British scholars. The *Pelita Bahasa Melayu* (3 vols.) by Zainal Abidin bin Ahmad (Za'ba), although intended for natives, is a veritable gold-mine of scholarly information and has been my constant guide. Of tremendous value also have been *Kaidah Bahasa Indonesia* (2 vols. Penerbit Djambatan — Djakarta 1956) by Dr Slametmuljana, and *Dasar2 Tatabahasa Indonesia* (Dinas Penerbitan Balai Pustaka — Djakarta 1956) by S. Zainuddin Gl. Png. Batuah. Also useful has been *Inleiding tot de Bahasa Indonesia* (J.B. Wolters — Groningen, 2nd Ed. 1948) by Dr M.G. Emeis. In addition to the various dictionaries of Wilkinson and Winstedt I have found the following valuable, especially for modern terminology: (1) *Istilah Jawatan dan Jabatan* published by the Dewan Bahasa dan Pustaka (Kuala Lumpur 1960); (2) *Kamus Inggeris* (2 vols. Inggeris-Indonesia and Indonesia-Inggeris—J.B. Wolters, Djakarta and Groningen — 2nd Ed. 1955) by E. Pino and T. Wittermans; and (3) *Kamus Umum Bahasa Melayu-Inggeris dan Inggeris-Melayu* (Pustaka Kathay — Singapore 1960) by Dr Suwisantoso and Dr Lee Yu-Kai. This last is an admirable pocket dictionary and apart from a few misprints, can be thoroughly recommended to the student who wants a complete dictionary for a very modest price.

May 1961

AUTHOR'S NOTE

This is not a beginner's book: a knowledge of elementary Malay such as is contained in the companion volume, *Speak Malay* is assumed. Complete beginners are advised to begin their studies with *Speak Malay* or some similar elementary primer.

CONTENTS

FOREWORD		vi
PREFACE		vii
AUTHOR'S NOTE		xi
First Week:	Lessons 1 – 3	1
Second Week:	Lessons 4 – 6	16
Third Week:	Lessons 7 – 9	36
Fourth Week:	Lessons 10 – 12	52
Fifth Week:	Lessons 13 – 15	71
Sixth Week:	Lessons 16 – 18	88
Seventh Week:	Lessons 19 – 21	105
Eighth Week:	Lessons 22 – 24	121
Ninth Week:	Lessons 25 – 27	140
Tenth Week:	Lessons 28 – 30	157
Eleventh Week:	Lessons 31 – 33	176
Twelfth Week:	Lessons 34 – 36	192
Thirteenth Week:	Lessons 37 – 39	212
Fourteenth Week:	Lessons 40 – 42	233
Fifteenth Week:	Lessons 43 – 45	252
Sixteenth Week:	Lessons 46 – 48	270
Key to the Translation and Grammatical Exercises		292
Malay-English Alphabetical Vocabulary		324
English-Malay Alphabetical Vocabulary		351

ABBREVIATIONS USED

adj.	adjective
adv.	adverb
cf.	(Latin) *confer*: compare
cl.	classifier
coll.	colloquial
conj.	conjunction
demon.	demonstrative
e.g.	(Latin) *exempli gratia*: for example
etc.	(Latin) *et cetera*: and so on
f.	feminine
gram.	grammar; grammatical
hon.	honorific
i.e.	(Latin) *id est*: that is
interrog.	interrogative
intro. *or* **intrans.**	intransitive
lb (s)	pound (s)
lit.	literary
m.	masculine
mil.	military
n.	noun
N.B.	(Latin) *Nota bene*: note well
plur.	plural
prep.	preposition
pron.	pronoun *or* pronounced
q.v.	(Latin) *quod vide*: which see
rel.	relative
sing.	singular
tr. *or* **trans.**	transitive
vb.	verb
viz.	(Latin) *videlicet*: namely

Minggu Yang Pertama
First Week

Pelajaran Yang Pertama
Lesson 1

Perbandingan 1
Comparison I

A. Sentences

Ahmad besar.	*Ahmad is big.*
Yusuf kecil.	*Yusuf is small.*
Ahmad lebih besar daripada Yusuf.	*Ahmad is bigger than Yusuf.*
Yusuf lebih kecil daripada Ahmad.	*Yusuf is smaller than Ahmad.*
Meja ini panjang.	*This table is long.*
Méja itu péndék.	*That table is short.*
Méja ini lebih panjang daripada méja itu.	*This table is longer than that table.*
Méja ini lebih péndék daripada meja ini.	*This table is shorter than this table.*
Orang ini lebih gemuk daripada orang itu.	*This man is fatter than that man.*
Pénsél ini lebih péndék daripada pénsél itu.	*This pencil is shorter than that pencil.*
Yusuf kurang berakal daripada Ahmad.	*Yusuf is less intelligent than Ahmad.*
Dia kurang tinggi daripada saya.	*He is less tall than I am.*
Bangunan itu kurang rendah daripada bangunan ini.	*That building is less low than this building; or: that building is not as low as this building.*
Ahmad lebih besar daripada Yusuf, tetapi Hamid yang besar sekali.	*Ahmad is bigger than Yusuf, but Hamid is the biggest (of all).*
Ahmad lebih berakal daripada Yusuf, tetapi Hamid yang berakal sekali.	*Ahmad is more intelligent than Yusuf, but Hamid is the most intelligent (of all).*

Johor Baharu bandar yang besar sekali di Johor.	*Johor Baharu is the biggest town in Johor.*
Bahasa Melayu bahasa yang berguna sekali di negeri ini.	*Malay is the most useful language in this country.*
Budak ini kurang berakal daripada budak itu.	*This boy is less intelligent than that boy.*
Ipoh bandar yang besar sekali di negeri Perak.	*Ipoh is the biggest town in Perak.*

B. Word List

Nouns

méja	*table*	perbandingan	*comparison*
budak	*boy, girl, youngster*	orang	*person, man*
bangunan	*building*	pénsél	*pencil*
bahasa	*language*	bandar	*town*
negeri	*country*		

Pronouns

ini	*this, these*	itu	*that, those*
dia	*he, she, him, her*	saya	*I, me*
yang	*which, who*		

Adjectives

besar	*big, large*	kecil	*small, little*
panjang	*long*	péndék	*short*
gemuk	*fat*	berakal	*intelligent*
tinggi	*tall, high*	rendah	*low*
Melayu	*Malay*	berguna	*useful*

Miscellaneous

lebih	*more*	daripada	*from, than*
kurang	*less*	tetapi	*but*

se	*one*	kali	*time, occasion*
sekali	*once*	yang ... sekali	*the ... -est, the most ...*
di	*in, at, on*		

C. Grammar

1 In this lesson we begin to study the various ways in which Malay expresses the idea of comparison, but before we do so it may not be a bad idea to consider how comparison is indicated in English and then see how the Malay system differs. Many English adjectives have three different forms – (a) the positive or normal form *big*; (b) the comparative *bigger*; and (c) the superlative *biggest*. In other words the positive is the ordinary plain form of the adjective; the comparative adds the suffix -er; and the superlative adds the suffix -est. Many adjectives, however, would sound funny to English ears if they underwent this process: for example, we do not say *intelligent*er or *intelligent*est. In such cases we prefer to use the words *more* and *most* to prevent the adjectives from becoming too long, and so we have *intelligent,* more *intelligent,* and most *intelligent.* The first method (i.e. the addition of suffixes) is unknown in Malay, the second method being used instead.

2 *Ahmad lebih besar daripada Yusuf:* This is the standard way of indicating a comparative adjective in Malay. *Lebih*, which means *more*, is placed before the adjective and the English *than* is rendered by *daripada*, the basic meaning of which is *from*. Literally, the sentence means "Ahmad is more big from Yusuf". The basic pattern is therefore,

lebih + adjective + *daripada*

Further examples are given in the sentences in Section A, which should be studied carefully.

3 *Yusof kurang berakal daripada Ahmad.* The patterns described in 1 and 2 above are used in forming what are called *comparisons of superiority*. A *comparison of inferiority* is obtained in English by using the

words *less* and in Malay by using *kurang* instead of *lebih*. The basic pattern, then, is

kurang + adjective + *daripada*

or in English

less + adjective + than

Study carefully the examples in Section A.

4 *Hamid yang besar sekali:* This is the standard pattern for the formation of superlatives in Malay. *Yang*, which in this pattern means much the same as the English *the* (notice that English superlatives nearly always have *the* in front of them), is placed in front of the adjective and *sekali*, which really means *once*, is placed after it. The basic pattern is

yang + adjective + *sekali*

Once again, study the examples in Section A of this lesson.

D. Exercises

Exercise 1   Translate into English:
1   Hamid lebih gemuk daripada saya.
2   Ahmad yang gemuk sekali.
3   Bangunan ini lebih tinggi daripada bangunan itu.
4   Bahasa Melayu yang berguna sekali.
5   Saya lebih berakal daripada dia.
6   Budak ini kurang berakal daripada Hamid.
7   Bandar ini kurang besar daripada Kuala Lumpur.
8   Méja itu yang panjang sekali.
9   Méja ini yang rendah sekali.
10 Bangunan ini tinggi, tetapi bangunan itu yang tinggi sekali.

Exercise 2   Translate into Malay:
1   Yusuf is more intelligent than his father.
2   My father is fatter than my mother.

3   Ahmad's car is less big than Hamid's car.
4   Perlis is the smallest state in Malaysia.
5   Yusuf is fatter than Ahmad, but Ali is the fattest.
6   In Kuala Lumpur Malay is more useful than French.
7   In Paris French is the most useful language.
8   This is the biggest factory in Malaysia.
9   My house is smaller than his house.
10 Yusuf's house is the smallest of all.

Exercise 3
Make up ten Malay sentences of your own using the constructions and vocabulary you have learned in this lesson.

E. Additional Word List (of new words needed for the above exercise)

bapa, ayahanda*	*father*	ibu, emak, bonda**	*mother*
keréta	*car*	negeri Perlis	*Perlis*
negeri	*state*	Malaya***	*Malaya*
Perancis	*French*	kilang	*factory*
rumah	*house*		

* *Ayah* is a more polite word than *bapa*. *Bapa* is usually pronounced as if written *bapak*. Indeed it is often spelled in that way.
** *Emak* and *ibu* are about equal in value, although the latter is more literary while the former is more colloquial. *Bonda* is a polite word and forms a pair with *ayahanda*.
*** The official name of the country is *Persekutuan Tanah Melayu* — the Federation of Malaya (lit. Federation of Malay Lands). It often used to be called *Tanah Melayu*, and this phrase is often used to-day, but the English word *Malaya* is being used more and more. It is not pronounced like the English word, however, the most normal pronunciation being (melaye).

Minggu Yang Pertama
First Week

Pelajaran Yang Kedua
Lesson 2

Perbandingan 2
Comparison 2

A. Sentences

Yang ini lebih besar daripada yang lain.	*This one is larger than the others.*
Yang ini lagi besar.	*This one is larger.*
Buku itu lebih kecil daripada buku ini.	*That book is smaller than this book.*
Buku itu lagi kecil.	*That book is smaller.*
Budak ini lebih tua daripada budak itu.	*This boy is older than that boy.*
Budak ini lagi tua.	*This boy is older.*
Keréta ini lebih besar daripada keréta itu.	*This car is bigger than that car.*
Keréta ini lagi besar.	*This car is bigger.*
Dia kurang berakal.	*He is less intelligent;* or: *he is not very intelligent;* or: *he is not intelligent (polite).*
Dia kurang tinggi.	*He is less tall; he is not very tall; he is not tall (polite).*
Makanan ini kurang sedap.	*This food is less tasty; this food is not very tasty; this food is not tasty (polite).*
Orang itu kurang ajar.	*That man is badly behaved;* or: *that man has no manners.*
Kurang periksa.	*I haven't really looked into the matter;* i.e. *I'm sorry but I don't really know.*
Bapa saya kurang tinggi.	*My father is not very tall.*
Buah durian lagi sedap.	*Durians are more tasty.*
Budak itu amat berakal.	*That boy is very intelligent.*

Budak itu sangat berakal.	*That boy is very intelligent.*
Budak itu berakal sangat.	*That boy is too intelligent.*
Budak itu berakal benar.	*That boy is very intelligent.*
Budak itu berakal sungguh.	*That boy is very intelligent.*
Kerétapi ini terlalu lambat.	*This train is too slow.*
Budak ini terlalu besar.	*This boy is too big.*
Kotak itu terlalu kecil.	*That box is too small.*

B. Word List

Nouns

buku	*book*	makanan	*food*
keréta	*car, cart, carriage, vehicle*	buah durian	*durian*
buah	*fruit*	kerétapi	*train*
bapa	*father*	kotak	*box (small)*
api	*fire*		

Adjectives

lain	*other, different*	tua	*old (people)*
sedap	*tasty*	benar	*true*
sungguh	*true*	lambat	*slow, late*
betul	*right, correct*		

Verbs

periksa	*examine, inquire*	ajar	*teach*

Miscellaneous

yang ini	*this one*	yang lain	*the other one, the others*
lagi	*more, yet, still*	amat	*very*
kurang ajar	*ill-bred*	benar	*very*
sangat	*very, too*	terlalu	*too*
sungguh	*very*	terlampau	*too*
ataupun	*or*	betul	*very*

C. Grammar

5 *Yang ini lagi besar:* In all the comparisons in Lesson 1 we were comparing two persons or things directly with each other. In other words both terms of the comparison were mentioned. Quite often, however, we want to say that something is *bigger*, or *smaller*, or *more expensive*, and so on without actually stating the other thing with which we are making the comparison. For instance, we may be looking at a number of objects all of which are the same size except for one which is larger than the others. Then, instead of saying, "This one is larger than the others", we simply say, "This one is larger". The first sentence in Malay would be . . . *yang ini lebih besar daripada yang lain*, but the second one would be . . . *yang ini lagi besar*. That is to say that when the comparison stops short after the adjective and does not continue with a *than* or *daripada*, the *lebih* must be changed to *lagi* in Malay. Study carefully the parallel examples in Section A above.

6 *Dia kurang berakal:* This is another shortened comparison, but *kurang*, unlike *lebih*, remains in such construction. Notice, however, that in this use *kurang* often has the meaning of "not very", or is even used as a weak and therefore polite form of *tidak* (not). *Dia kurang berakal*, therefore, may mean either "He is less intelligent", or "He is not very intelligent", or even "He is not intelligent".

7 *Orang itu kurang ajar; kurang periksa:* In connexion with the use of *kurang* mentioned in 6 above, notice these two expressions. *Kurang ajar* literally means something like "not very well taught", and so comes to the same thing as the English "ill-bred", "badly brought up" or "ill-mannered". *Kurang periksa*, which means roughly "I haven't really investigated the matter" is often used to mean "I'm afraid I don't know", as a polite answer to such a question as "Can you tell me where . . . etc?"

8 *very:* There are several ways of rendering the English *very* into Malay. The most commonly used words are *amat, sangat, benar, sungguh,* and *betul*. In this use (i.e. to mean *very*) *amat* and *sangat* precede the adjective. Examples:

amat besar	*very big*
amat kecil	*very small*
sangat gemuk	*very fat*
sangat kurus	*very thin*

When *sangat* follows the adjective it normally implies that the quality expressed by the adjective is possessed to excess: in other words it means the same as the English *too* or *excessively:*

gemuk sangat	*too fat*
kurus sangat	*too thin*

Benar, which means "true" or "truly", almost always follows its adjective:

berakal benar	*very (*or: *really) intelligent*
berguna benar	*very (*or: *really) useful*

Sungguh, which also means "true" or "truly", and *betul*, which means "real" or "correct", are also used to render "very" or "really". They may either precede or follow the adjective, being more emphatic when they precede:

Buku ini besar sungguh.	*This book is very big.*
Buku ini sungguh besar.	*This book is really big. (i.e. That's what I call a big book).*
Buku ini besar betul.	*This book is really big.*
Buku ini betul besar.	*This book is really big.*

9 *too:* In addition to the use of *sangat* after an adjective described in 8 above, the English *too* is often rendered by either *terlalu* or *terlampau* in Malay:

Kerétapi ini terlampau lambat.	*This train is too slow.*
Budak ini terlalu kecil.	*This boy is too small.*

D. Exercises

Exercise 4   Translate into English:
1. Yang ini lebih kecil daripada yang itu.
2. Yang ini lagi kecil.
3. Bapa Yusuf sangat berakal.
4. Ibu dia lagi berakal.
5. Bahasa Melayu bahasa yang berguna sungguh.
6. Bangunan ini sangat tinggi.
7. Bangunan itu lagi tinggi.
8. Budak ini kurang ajar.
9. Kotak itu amat kecil.
10. Keréta Ahmad terlalu lambat.

Exercise 5   Translate into Malay:
1. My father is too fat.
2. This building is taller.
3. This boy is not very intelligent.
4. That man has no manners.
5. Yusuf is more intelligent than the other boy.
6. Ahmad is fat, but Said is fatter.
7. This factory is very large; (it is) the largest in Malaysia.
8. Pahang is the largest state in Peninsular Malaysia.
9. Ipoh is large, but Kuala Lumpur is larger.
10. Is Yusuf intelligent? I'm afraid I don't know.

Exercise 6

Make up ten Malay sentences of your own using what you have learned so far in this course.

Minggu Yang Pertama
First Week

Pelajaran Yang Ketiga
Lesson 3

Perbandingan 3
Comparison 3

A. *Sentences*

Budak itu tidak berapa berakal.	*That boy is not very intelligent.*
Budak itu tak berapa berakal.	*That boy is not very intelligent.*
Kuala Lumpur lebih besar daripada Kota Baharu.	*Kuala Lumpur is bigger than Kota Baharu.*
Kapal terbang lebih deras daripapa kapal laut.	*Aeroplanes are faster than ships.*
Keréta lembu lebih lambat daripada kerétapi.	*Bullock carts are slower than trains.*
Keréta ini kurang deras daripada keréta itu.	*This car is less swift than that car;* or: *this car is not so fast as that car.*
Ali kurang pantas daripada Dolah	*Ali is less energetic than Dolah.*
Buku ini kurang berguna daripada buku itu.	*This book is less useful than that book.*
Ahmad lagi kuat.	*Ahmad is stronger.*
Makanan Cina lagi sedap.	*Chinese food is more tasty.*
Ali kurang pantas.	*Ali is less energetic;* or: *Ali isn't very energetic.*
Buku ini kurang berguna.	*This book is less useful;* or: *this book isn't much use.*
Buku ini yang berguna sekali.	*This book is the most useful.*
Hamid yang pantas sekali.	*Hamid is the most energetic.*
Bahasa kebangsaan bahasa yang merdu sekali.	*The national language is the most melodious.*
Ahmad cerdik; Hamid lagi cerdik; tetapi Noraini yang cerdik sekali.	*Ahmad is bright; Hamid is brighter; but Noraini is the brightest of all.*

Orang Cina ini amat pandai bercakap bahasa Melayu.	*This Chinese is very good at speaking Malay.*
Bahasa Inggeris bahasa yang sangat berguna.	*English is a very useful language.*
Gulai ini pedas sangat.	*This curry is too hot.*
Adik saya muda benar.	*My younger brother is very young.*

B. Word List

Nouns

kapal	*ship*	adik	*younger brother, younger sister*
kapal laut	*(sea-going) ship*	laut	*sea*
kapal terbang	*aeroplane, aircraft*	kapal api	*steamship*
keréta lembu	*bullock-cart*	lembu	*ox, cow*
gulai	*curry*		

Adjectives

ketiga	*third*	deras	*swift, fast*
pantas	*energetic, active*	kuat	*strong*
merdu	*melodious*	cerdik	*bright, quick-witted*
pandai	*clever, good at*	pedas	*hot (of curry, etc.)*
muda	*young*		

Verbs

terbang	*to fly*	bercakap	*to speak, talk*

Miscellaneous

tidak	*not*	tidak berapa	*not very*
berapa	*how much? how many?*	tak	*not*
tak berapa	*not very*		

C. Grammar

10 *Budak itu tidak berapa berakal:* In Lesson 2 (7) we saw that "not very" may be translated by *kurang* in Malay. Here is another way of rendering the same idea, viz. by using the phrase *tidak berapa,* or, more colloquially *tak berapa,* before the adjective.

D. Exercises

Exercise 7
Read aloud the following conversation and translate it into English. The conversation is between two friends shopping in the market and a fruit-stall holder in the market:

Hamid:	Kita sudah sampai ke pasar. Apa encik nak beli dahulu?
Yusuf:	Saya nak beli buah durian. Buah durian lagi sedap.
Hamid:	Bukan. Saya tidak bersetuju. Saya fikir buah manggis lebih sedap daripada buah durian, tetapi buah rambutan yang sedap sekali.
Yusuf:	Ah, itu betullah. Buah rambutan betul sedap. Saya sangat suka makan. Buah rambutan itu buah yang sedap sekali di negeri kita ini.
Hamid:	Baik kita beli buah rambutan di kedai ini.
Orang Kedai:	Apa encik-encik nak beli?
Hamid:	Kami hendak beli buah rambutan. Encik ada yang besarkah?
Orang Kedai:	Ada. Ini yang besar sekali di pasar.
Hamid:	Yang itukah? Tapi yang itu terlalu kecil. Saya mahu rambutan yang lagi besar.
Orang Kedai:	Lagi besar? Mana boléh? Lagi besar di mana-mana pun tak boléh dapat. Rambutan ini amat besar.
Yusuf:	Baiklah. Saya nak beli sepuluh biji. Ini dia duit.
Orang Kedai:	Terima kasih.

Exercise 8 Translate into English:
1. Buah rambutan ini tidak berapa sedap.
2. Hamid lebih kuat daripada Ah Chong.
3. Ah Chong kuat benar, tetapi Krishna yang kuat sekali.
4. Bonda dia lebih muda daripada ayahanda dia.
5. Bahasa Perancis bahasa yang merdu benar, tetapi bahasa Melayu yang merdu sekali.
6. Bahasa Inggeris lebih berguna daripada bahasa Perancis.
7. Adik saya kurang pantas daripada abang saya.
8. Noraini cerdik, tetapi Zainab lagi cerdik.
9. Keretapi deras, tetapi kapal terbang yang deras sekali.
10. Negeri Kedah lebih besar daripada negeri Perlis.

Exercise 9 Translate into Malay:
1. Durians are larger than rambutans.
2. My elder sister is younger than my elder brother.
3. Malay is the national language of the Federation of Malaysia.
4. What are you going to buy in the market? Mangosteens.
5. Yusuf is not very energetic.
6. Noraini is very bright.
7. Ah Kim is very good at speaking Malay, but his father is better.
8. My father is older than my mother.
9. This one is too small. I want a bigger one.
10. Kuala Lumpur is a very large town.

Exercise 10
Make up ten sentences of your own in Malay, using what you have learned so far.

E. Additional Word List
(of new words needed for the exercises in Section D above)

Nouns

pasar	*market*	buah manggis	*mangosteen*
buah rambutan	*rambutan*	kedai	*shop*

orang kedai	*shopkeeper*	biji	*seed; cl. for fruits*
duit	*money, cent*	kasih	*love*
abang	*elder brother*	kakak	*elder sister*
bahasa Inggeris	*English (language)*	orang Inggeris	*Englishman*
negeri Kedah	*Kedah*		

Pronouns

kita	*we, us, our*	apa?	*what?*
encik	*you*	encik-encik	*you (plur.)*
kami	*we, us, our*		

Verbs

sampai	*to arrive*	ingat	*to think, to remember*
bersetuju	*to agree*	makan	*to eat*
suka	*to like*	ada	*to be, to have*
mahu	*to want*	dapat	*to get, to manage to*
boléh	*to be able, can*	fikir	*to think*
terima	*to receive*	beli	*to buy*

Adjectives

betul	*right, correct*	baik	*good*
Inggeris	*English*		

Miscellaneous

sudah	*finished (perfect tense sign)*	ke	*to (place)*
nak	*to be going to*	dahulu	*first, formerly*
bukan	*no, not*	-lah	*emphatic particle*
hendak	*going to*	tapi	*but*
-kah	*question particle*	mana boléh?	*how can that be?*
mana	*which, how*	baiklah	*all right, O.K.*
di mana-mana pun tidak	*nowhere*	ini dia . . .	*here is . . . this is . . .*
sepuluh	*ten*	terima kasih	*thank you*

Minggu Yang Kedua
Second Week

Pelajaran Yang Keempat
Lesson 4

Tambahan-tambahan: Awalan Me- 1
The Affixes: The Prefix Me- 1

A. Sentences

There are no sentences for you to study in this lesson.

B. Word List

Verbs

lukis (melukis)	*to draw*
masukkan (memasukkan)	*to insert*
nantikan (menantikan)	*to wait for*
rosakkan (merosakkan)	*to damage*
wakili (mewakili)	*to represent*
ngaum (mengaum)	*to roar (like a tiger)*
nyatakan (menyatakan)	*to explain*
angkat (mengangkat)	*to lift, to pick up*
gulung (menggulung)	*to roll up*
koyakkan (mengoyakkan)	*to tear*
buka (membuka)	*to open*
baca (membaca)	*to read*
pandang (memandang)	*to look at*
pukul (memukul)	*to strike*
cari (mencari)	*to look for*
jawab (menjawab)	*to answer*
dapat (mendapat)	*to obtain, to get*
tutup (menutup)	*to close, to shut*
simpan (menyimpan)	*to put away, to keep*

C. Grammar

11 *Affixes in Malay.* The Malay language makes great use of affixes, especially in the written language, (a) for grammatical purposes, and

(b) in order to form new words from old in the process of vocabulary building. An affix is an extra syllable (sometimes more than one syllable) added either to the beginning or the end of a word. Affixes added to the beginning of words are called *prefixes* (Malay: *awalan*) and those added to the end of words are called *suffixes* (Malay: *akhiran*). English, too, makes considerable use of affixation for much the same purposes as Malay: that is English affixes may be either grammatical or lexical. Before we go on to begin our study of the Malay system of affixes, let us look at a few English examples in order to be sure of our terminology.

A common grammatical affix in English is the *-ed* suffix added to a verb to indicate the past tense, e.g. *I open the door* (present) and *I open*ed *the door* (past). Another one is the *-s* suffix added to nouns to form the plural, e.g. *the book* (singular) and *the books* (plural). A lexical (or vocabulary-building) suffix in English is the syllable *-ness*, which we add to many adjectives to form abstract nouns, e.g. *good* and *good*ness, *wicked* and *wicked*ness. Prefixes in English are usually used to change the basic meaning of the root word, e.g. per-*form*, de-*form*, re-*form*, etc., in which the basic root is *form* and the *per-*, *de-* and *re-* are prefixes giving it a different meaning in each case.

Affixation in English, especially lexical affixation, is a highly irregular process. This is because of the varied origin of the English vocabulary. It is very difficult, if not impossible, to reduce the English system to any simple set of rules. For instance, although we can add *-ness* to many adjectives to get an abstract noun we cannot add it to *every* adjective. The abstract noun from *beautiful* is *beauty*, not *beautifulness*! The past tense of *go* is *went*, not *goed*, and so on and so forth. The Malay system of affixation, however, being almost entirely *native* to the language, is subject to very few irregularities, and although many students fight shy of this subject, it is, as I hope to show you in these lessons, not nearly as difficult to understand as it is reputed to be. It is certainly much easier than anything to be found in English or any other European language.

Most Malay prefixes and suffixes are lexical. That is to say they are used to form new words from old. It would be possible to ignore the lexical system of affixation for practical purposes and treat each derivative word as a new item of vocabulary. *Pelajaran* (lesson, for instance, could be learned just as it stands without reference to the root word *ajar* (teach). Nevertheless it is worth studying the lexical affixes, because their great regularity in usage enables the student to make a scientific guess at the meaning of a new word he has not seen before, and also quite often to make up new words with a fair chance of success when he wants to.

A small number of affixes in Malay, however, are grammatical. In other words the choice of affix is conditioned by the grammatical structure of the sentence or phrase in which a particular word — especially a verb – occurs. These affixes need particular care if we are to use them correctly. On the principle of "divide and conquer" we shall consider them one by one and eliminate the difficulties gradually.

12 *The prefix* me-: I have chosen this prefix to begin with, partly because it is one of the most difficult to handle and I believe it is a good idea to get the worst over as soon as possible, and partly because it is one of the most important prefixes in the language and it is almost impossible to write more than a couple of sentences without having to use it at least once. It is the most difficult of the prefixes for two reasons: firstly, although it is called the *me*-prefix it does in fact have different forms according to the initial letter of the word to which it is added; secondly, its meaning is very difficult to express in English. We shall attempt to deal with the first difficulty – the five forms – in this lesson, but the second difficulty – that of usage – we shall deal with as we go along through the course.

First of all, study carefully the table on page 19, which shows how the five different forms are related to the initial letters of the words to which the prefix is added. Do not try to learn this table by heart, however, because we shall discuss it step by step. Afterwards you can use it for reference in cases of doubt.

FORMS TAKEN BY THE ME-PREFIX

me-	meng-	mem-	men-	meny-
L	A		C	
M	E		J	
N	E		Z*	
R	I		DZ*	
W	O		SY*	
NG	U			
NY	H			
Y	KH*			
	G	B	D	
	(K)	(P)	(T)	(S)

(Note: To find the correct form of the prefix, locate the initial letter of the basic word in the above table and prefix the form standing at the head of the column in which you find this initial letter. Letters in parentheses are *omitted* when adding the prefix. Forms marked with an asterisk are very rare and may be disregarded at this stage.)

13 *The* me-*prefix before liquid consonants:* The *me*-prefix is added as it stands to words beginning with what are often called *liquid* consonants (cf. column one in the table in 12 above). The liquid consonants are L, M, N, R, W, NG, NY and Y. If you think about the sounds which these letters represent, you will, I think, agree that *liquid* is a very good name for them. Let us have some examples. To make the process clearer I have separated the prefix from its root-word by a

hyphen, although normally, of course, they would be written together as one word:

lukis	me-lukis	*to draw*
masukkan	me-masukkan	*to insert*
nantikan	me-nantikan	*to wait for*
rosakkan	me-rosakkan	*to damage*
wakili	me-wakili	*to represent*
ngaum	me-ngaum	*to roar*
nyatakan	me-nyatakan	*to explain*

14 *The* me-*prefix before vowels and gutturals:* When the root-word begins with one of the six vowels or one of what we call *guttural* consonants, H, KH, G and K, the *me*-prefix takes the form **meng-** When the prefix is added, the K of words beginning with that letter is *left out.* Examples:

angkat	meng-angkat	*to lift*
gulung	meng-gulung	*to roll up*
koyakkan	meng-oyakkan	*to tear*

(cf. column two of the table in 12 above and note that K is put in parentheses to indicate that it disappears when the prefix is added).

15 *The* me-*prefix before labial consonants:* The labial consonants are those made, as the name implies, by closing lips together. The Malay labials are B, P and M. M, however, is also a liquid (cf. 13), and does not count as a labial for the present purpose. Before B and P the *me*-prefix takes the form *mem-*. P, like K, promptly disappears (cf. column three of the table in 12). Examples:

buka	mem-buka	*to open*
baca	mem-baca	*to read*
pandang	mem-andang	*to look at*
pukul	mem-ukul	*to strike*

16 *The* me-*prefix before palatal or dental consonants:* All the consonants in column four of the table in 12 above are pronounced in the front part of the mouth, either by placing the tongue in contact with the hard palate or by placing it in contact with the teeth or the roots of the teeth. Hence we call these consonants *palatals* or *dentals*. Before all these consonants the *me*-prefix takes the form *men*-. Like K, and P, T completely disappears when the prefix is added. Z, DZ and SY only occur in a few words borrowed from Arabic, so do not worry too much about them. The really important ones in this column are C, J, D and T. Examples:

cari	men-cari	*to look for*
jawab	men-jawab	*to answer*
dapat	men-dapat	*to obtain*
tutup	men-utup	*to close*

17 *The* me-*prefix before S:* An initial S-behaves so oddly that it ranks a column all to itself: column five in the table in 12 above. Before S the *me*-prefix takes the form *meny-* and the S disappears without trace. Examples:

| simpan | meny-impan | *to put away* |

18 *General note on the various forms of the* me-*prefix:* Let us try to summarise what we have studied in this lesson and to see if we can discover any logic in the five forms of the *me*-prefix. First of all, notice the four letters or sounds which dissappear when the prefix is added. They are K, P, T and S, and have been placed in the bottom line of the table in 12 in parentheses to help you to remember their propensity to vanish.

Having considered these four, let us next consider the remainder column by column. In the first column we have what we called earlier the liquids. All these sounds take the plain *me*-prefix just as it stands without any alteration or addition.

In the second column we find all the vowels and the four consonants H, KH and K, which may be loosely described as gutturals because they are all pronounced in the back of the mouth in, or near, the throat. Before these sounds the prefix takes the form *meng-*, that is to say we add the nasal sound NG to it. This nasal sound is also made at the back of mouth in the same place as G, and K, and I think you will agree that it is the most natural nasal sound to use in this context, if there is going to be a nasal sound at all.

Similarly, column three contains only two sounds – B and P – which we have already described as labials. In this case the prefix takes the labial nasal (or liquid) M, and thus has the form *mem-*. Here again, I think you will agree that M is the most logical nasal sound to put before B or P.

The fourth column, at first sight, appears to contain a considerable variety of unrelated sounds, but if you consider them carefully you will see that all of them are produced in the front part of the mouth and that during their pronounciation either the upper or lower teeth or the hard palate just behind the upper teeth come into play. The corresponding (or *homorganic*) nasal sounds for this part of the mouth is N, and so we should not be surprised to find that the correct form of the prefix is in this case *mem-*, which runs fairly naturally into all the sounds in column four.

The logic of column five, where the sound S disappears and the prefix takes the form *meny-* is perhaps not so easy to see, but since S is the only sound in the column it is fairly easy to remember anyway.

Now, study the table again very carefully and compare it with the words in Word List B above, all of which have been carefully chosen to exemplify the forms in the table.

D. Exercise

Exercise 11 Add the *me*-prefix to the following ten verbs:
1 lompat (jump)
2 baca (read)
3 tulis (write)
4 curi (steal)
5 susun (arrange)
6 ganti (substitute)
7 kacau (annoy; stir)
8 kupas (peel, pare)
9 daftarkan (register)
10 pukul (strike)

Minggu Yang Kedua
Second Week

Pelajaran Yang Kelima
Lesson 5

Tambahan-tambahan: Awalan Me- 2
The Affixes: The Prefix Me- 2

A. *Sentences*

Ali baca buku.	*Ali reads books.*
Ali membaca buku.	*Ali reads books.*
Ahmad membaca buku Melayu.	*Ahmad reads Malay books.*
Orang itu mewakili kerajaan Malaysia di London.	*That man represents the Malaysian government in London.*
Guru menerangkan perkataan-perkataan yang baharu.	*The teacher explains the new words.*
Orang India itu tidak membaca suratkhabar Inggeris.	*That Indian did not read the English newspapers.*
Sekarang Ali sedang membaca buku Melayu.	*Ali is now reading a Malay book.*
Ahmad sedang melukis gambar yang cantik.	*Ahmad is drawing a beautiful picture.*
Guru sedang menyatakan makna perkataan ini.	*The teacher is explaining the meaning of this word.*
Saya sedang mencari bapa saya.	*I am looking for my father.*
Ali hendak membeli barang di pasar.	*Ali is going to buy goods in the market.*
Ahmad hendak menutup pintu.	*Ahmad is going to shut the door.*
Orang itu akan mewakili kerajaan Malaysia di negeri Jepun.	*That man will represent the Malaysian government in Japan.*
Kerani akan memasukkan surat ini dalam fail.	*The clerk will insert this letter in the file.*
Saya akan menantikan encik di luar pejabat pos.	*I will wait for you outside the post office.*
Ali suka melukis gambar.	*Ali likes drawing pictures.*
Bapa saya suka membaca buku Cina.	*My father likes reading Chinese books.*

23

Orang perempuan itu suka memakai pakaian cantik.	*That woman likes wearing pretty clothes.*
Ahmad pandai melukis gambar.	*Ahmad is clever (or: good) at drawing pictures.*
Orang Cina ini pandai membaca buku Melayu.	*This Chinese is good at reading Malay books.*
Saya tidak berapa pandai menulis surat.	*I am not very good at writing letters.*

B. Word List

Nouns

kerajaan	*government*	guru	*teacher*
perkataan	*word*	surat	*letter*
khabar	*news*	suratkhabar	*newspaper*
gambar	*picture*	makna	*meaning*
barang	*goods*	pintu	*door*
negeri Jepun	*Japan*	kerani	*clerk*
fail	*file, dossier*	pejabat pos	*post office*
orang perempuan	*woman*	pakaian	*clothes*
orang India	*Indian*	orang Cina	*(a) Chinese*

Adjectives

baharu	*new*	India	*Indian*
cantik	*pretty, beautiful*	Cina	*Chinese*
Jepun	*Japanese*		

Verbs

beli (membeli)	*to buy*	pakai (memakai)	*to wear, to use*
terangkan (menerangkan)	*to explain*		

Miscellaneous

sekarang	*now*	dalam	*in*
di luar	*outside*	sedang	*sign of progressive action*
akan	*shall, will*		

C. Grammar

19 *The uses of the* me-*prefix: (a) General:* The *me*-prefix always indicates a verb — almost always a transitive verb, that is a verb which has a direct object. We can describe it therefore as a *verbal* prefix. Not all verbs, even transitive ones, can take it, however. For instance, it cannot be added to a verb which already has another prefix such as *ber-* or *ter-*. We cannot add it then to verbs like *bercakap* (to speak), *berjalan* (to walk) or *terlupa* (to forget), because they already have prefixes. The *me*-prefix, then, with the exception of one big group of verbs with which we shall deal in a later lesson, must be added only directly to basic root and never in front of another prefix. There are a few intransitive verbs which take the *me*-prefix, e.g. *tari/menari* (to dance), *nyanyi/menyanyi* (to sing) and *amuk/mengamuk* (to run amok), but most verbs with *me*-forms are transitive.

20 *The uses of the* me-*prefix: (b) Plain Statement: Ali baca buku: Ali membaca buku:* All transitive verbs which can take the *me*-prefix exist in both forms, i.e. with and without *me-*. For example, *baca* and *membaca* (to read) exist side by side. We shall indicate all such verbs in the word lists and vocabularies by giving both forms from now on. There is very little difference in English between the meanings of *baca* and *membaca*. The choice of one form or the other is largely dependent upon the form of the sentence. In some sentences we *must* have *me-* and in others not. What the circumstances are which determine our choice we shall see as we go along.

In a sentence such as "Ali reads books" it makes very little difference whether we translate "reads" by *baca* or *membaca*. The difference is here largely a matter of style and emphasis, about which we shall have a lot more to say later. For the time being the following explanation will suffice for plain statements of fact. In the written language the *me*-form is preferred in such sentences; in the spoken language the form with *me*- is more common in the southern part of Peninsular Malaysia and the form without *me*- is more common in the northern half of the country, especially in Kedah and Penang, where the *me*-forms are felt as definitely literary and bookish. Where this free choice exists, the student is advised to use the *me*-forms partly for the sake of practice, and partly because they are regarded as more desirable forms by most Malays. They should certainly normally be used in writing.

21 *The uses of the* me-*prefix: (c) after sedang: Sekarang Ali sedang membaca buku Melayu:* The word *sedang* basically means something like "during", "in the middle of (doing)", and so it has come to be used to indicate that the action in question is looked upon as still in progress. It was once very strong in meaning, rather like *to be in the act of* in English or *être en train de* in French, but in the course of time it has become much weaker and is now much the same as the various English progressive tenses (I am doing, I was doing, etc.) in meaning, although it is not used as much as these tenses are in English. It is not much used in conversation, but is becoming more and more common in writing.

Verbs which have *me*-forms always go into that form when immediately following *sedang*. Of course, if a verb has no *me*-form, then its normal form must be used:

Saya sedang menulis surat.
I am writing (*or:* I was writing) a letter.

BUT:

Saya sedang bercakap bahasa Melayu.
I am speaking Malay.

Saya sedang duduk di kerusi.
I am sitting on a chair.

because *bercakap* and *duduk* have no *me*-forms.

22 *The uses of the* me-*prefix: (d) after auxiliary verbs: Ali hendak membeli*

barang di pasar: When one verb is dependent on another in some way, the dependent verb (*i.e.* the second one) goes into the *me-*form if it has one:

Ahmad hendak menulis surat.
Ahmad is going to write a letter.

Ali suka melukis gambar.
Ali likes drawing pictures.

23 *Ali hendak membeli barang di pasar:* "Ali is going to buy goods in the market." *Hendak* (coll. *nak*) basically means "to want" and is indeed often used in that sense, but it is also very commonly used to indicate intention and is then very much the same in meaning as the English expression "to be going to". In the spoken language, it is the nearest equivalent to the English future tense. *Hendak* is followed by the *me-*prefix where appropriate.

24 *Kerani akan memasukkan surat ini dalam fail:* "The clerk will insert this letter in the file". *Akan*, followed by a *me-*prefix if possible, forms a future tense. This tense is not used much in conversation but is becoming more and more common in writing and public speaking. It is very common on the radio, for instance.

25 *Ahmad pandai melukis gambar:* "Ahmad is good at drawing pictures." Here, *melukis* is dependent on the adjective *pandai*, and is really another example of the rule given in 22 above. A verb dependent on an adjective goes into the *me-*form if it has one.

26 *Guru menerangkan perkataan-perkataan yang baharu:* "The teacher explains the new words." *Perkataan-perkataan* is the doubled or reduplicated form of *perkataan* (word). We shall have a good deal to say about reduplication later in the course, as it plays a large part in Malay grammar. For the moment remember that a word can be reduplicated to indicate a *plural of variety*. Malay nouns do not normally change to indicate the plural, but if one is thinking of several different kinds of something, as in the above sentence, then the noun in question is usually doubled. *Perkataan-perkataan*, then, really means "words of different kinds" or "all sorts of words".

Tambahan-tambahan at the head of this lesson means something like "all the various affixes". To save time and trouble reduplicated words may be written once only with the figure 2 after them, thus:

> *perkataan-perkataan* may be written *perkataan2*
> *tambahan-tambahan* may be written *tambahan2*

Sometimes the figure 2 is written smaller above or below the line instead of on it, thus:

$$\text{perkataan}^2 \text{ or perkataan}_2$$
$$\text{tambahan}^2 \text{ or tambahan}_2 \text{ *}$$

*The use of "2" (angka dua) to indicate reduplication is no longer allowed in the new spelling system, but may still be met in older books.

D. Exercises

Exercise 12   Translate into English:
1. Kakak saya tidak suka memakai pakaian cantik.
2. Dia sedang mencari bapa dia di pasar.
3. Orang Cina itu suka bercakap bahasa Melayu.
4. Encik Ali akan mewakili kerajaan kita.
5. Kerani saya akan menulis surat itu.
6. Hamid sedang melukis gambar pejabat pos.
7. Dia hendak memasukkan surat ini dalam fail yang baharu.
8. Ibu saya sedang membaca suratkhabar Melayu.
9. Sekarang bonda dia sedang menantikannya di luar pejabat pos.
10. Abang saya hendak menulis buku dalam bahasa Melayu.

Exercise 13   Translate into Malay:
1. Ali is writing a letter.
2. Ahmad is going to draw a picture.
3. The teacher will explain the meaning of that word.
4. People will stare (*pandang/memandang*) at you.

5   I am going to buy a new Malay book.
6   Your elder sister wears pretty clothes.
7   Ali is going to open the door.
8   I shall put this letter away.
9   That Indian is reading an English newspaper.
10 Our teacher is good at explaining the new words.

Exercise 14
Make up ten sentences of your own using verbs with *me*-prefixes.

Minggu Yang Kedua / Second Week

Pelajaran Yang Keenam / Lesson 6

Tambahan-tambahan: Awalan Me- 3
The Affixes: The Prefix Me- 3

A. Sentences

Ribut sudah merosakkan banyak rumah.	*The storm has destroyed many houses.*
Kerani memasukkan dua pucuk surat ke dalam fail.	*The clerk puts two letters into the file.*
Bapa saya akan mewakili kerajaan di Kahirah.	*My father will represent the government in Cairo.*
Perdana Menteri sudah menyatakan dasar kerajaan.	*The Prime Minister has explained the policy of the government.*
Harimau sedang mengaum di dalam hutan.	*The tiger is roaring in the jungle.*
Dia sedang menantikan kawannya datang.	*He is waiting for his friend to come.*
Ali sudah mengangkat kotak besar.	*Ali has picked up a large box.*
Saya akan menghantar sepucuk surat kepada dia.	*I shall send him a letter.*
Dia mengambil sebatang rokok dari dalam kotak.	*He takes a cigarette from (inside) the box.*
Ahmad sedang menggulung hamparan.	*Ahmad is rolling up the carpet.*
Anak saya sudah mengoyakkan kertas itu.	*My son has torn that paper.*
Ah Kim hendak membeli buah rambutan di pasar.	*Ah Kim is going to buy some rambutans in the market.*
Bapa saya membaca suratkhabar Melayu sahaja.	*My father only reads the Malay newspapers.*
Ali sedang memandang gambar yang cantik.	*Ali is looking at a beautiful picture.*

Ahmad sedang memukul anjingnya.	*Ahmad is beating his dog.*
Saya sedang mencari buku saya.	*I am looking for my book.*
Ahmad tidak mahu menjawab soalan itu.	*Ahmad does not want to answer that question.*
Ali hendak mendaftarkan surat ini di pejabat pos.	*Ali is going to register this letter at the post office.*
Saya akan menutup pintu.	*I will shut the door.*
Saya akan menulis surat kepada guru besar.	*I shall write a letter to the headmaster.*
Saya selalu menyimpan buku saya di dalam almari ini.	*I always keep my books in this cupboard.*

B. Word List

Nouns

ribut	*storm*	rumah	*house*
perdana	*principal*	menteri	*minister*
Perdana Menteri	*Prime Minister*	dasar	*policy, basis*
harimau	*tiger*	hutan	*jungle*
kawan	*friend*	kotak besar, tong	*large box, crate*
rokok	*cigarette*	hamparan	*carpet*
kotak kecil	*small box*	kertas	*paper*
anak	*child, son, daughter*	anjing	*dog*
soalan	*question*	guru besar	*headmaster, headmistress*
almari	*cupboard*		

Verbs

hantar (menghantar)	*to send*	datang	*to come*
ambil (mengambil)	*to take, fetch*	mahu	*to want*

Miscellaneous

sudah	*sign of perfect tense or aspect*	banyak	*a lot, much, many*
pucuk	*cl. for letters*	batang	*cl. for stick-like objects*
ke dalam	*into*	di dalam	*in, inside*
dari dalam	*from inside*	dari	*from*
kepada	*to (people)*	sahaja	*only*
selalu	*always*		

C. Grammar

27 *Ribut sudah merosakkan banyak rumah:* "The storm has destroyed (*or*: damaged) many houses." *Sudah* (colloquial: *'dah*) basically means "finished" and is often used with that meaning, but it is also used together with a verb, the latter taking the *me-*prefix where appropriate, to indicate that an action is complete. This construction corresponds more or less to the English prefect tense – *I have done,* etc., but remember that Malay strictly speaking has no real tenses and that therefore the above sentence may refer equally well to the past and future as well as the present. It all depends on the general context. The sentence might just as well have been translated by "the storm had destroyed many houses"(*e.g.* before help arrived) or by "the storm *will have* destroyed many houses", or even by "the storm *would have* destroyed many houses", depending on the general sense of the whole context in which the sentence occurs.

28 *Bapa saya membaca suratkhabar Melayu sahaja: Sahaja,* which means "only", is used differently from the English word. *Sahaja* usually follows directly the word or group of words to which it refers, whereas the English *only* normally precedes the word it refers to or goes in front of the verb as in the English translation of the above sentence: "My father only reads Malay newspapers".

D. Exercises

Exercise 15 Translate into English:
1 Hamid menyimpan rokok ke dalam kotak.
2 Abang saya sudah menggulung hamparan.
3 Perdana Menteri hendak menyatakan dasarnya kepada kita.
4 Dia tidak akan menjawab soalan ini.
5 Orang itu selalu memukul anjingnya.
6 Kami hendak membeli hamparan baharu.
7 Saya sudah menulis tiga pucuk surat kepada dia.
8 Anjing encik sudah merosakkan hamparan kami.
9 Kita hendak bercakap bahasa Melayu sahaja.
10 Kawan kita sudah membeli rumah baharu di Kuala Lumpur.

Exercise 16 Translate into Malay:
1 I am looking for my mother.
2 Yusuf puts the book away in the cupboard.
3 Ali will not answer that question.
4 He does not like waiting for people.
5 I shall send my son to Kuala Lumpur.
6 I have come to (translate "to" by using the *me*-prefix) fetch my book.
7 The Prime Minister has come to Kuala Lumpur to explain his new policy.
8 I have inserted your letter in the file.
9 My son has drawn all kinds of (use reduplication) beautiful pictures.
10 I have received only one letter.

Exercise 17 Translate into English:
Ali: Apa khabar?
Ahmad: Khabar baik.
Ali: Apa encik buat sekarang?
Ahmad: Saya sedang menulis sepucuk surat.
Ali: Encik sedang menulis surat kepada siapa?
Ahmad: Kepada anak saya. Lama dia menantikan surat saya. Tetapi saya ada banyak kerja; sampai sekarang saya tak

	sempat menulis surat kepada dia. Baharu hari ini dapat saya menulis surat yang péndék ini kepada dia.
Ali:	Encik sudah mendapat surat daripada anakkah?
Ahmad:	Sudah. Dua minggu dahulu saya sudah mendapat sepucuk surat panjang daripada dia. Dalam surat itu dia berkata dia menantikan saya menulis kepada dia, tetapi surat saya tak sampai lagi.
Ali:	Di mana dia tinggal?
Ahmad:	Dia tinggal di London. Dia sedang mewakili kerajaan Malaysia di sana.
Ali:	Baguslah. Baik encik menjawab surat dia, dan baik saya jangan mengacau encik lagi. Saya kena pergi ke pejabat pos hendak mendaftarkan dua tiga pucuk surat saya. Selamat tinggal, encik.
Ahmad:	Selamat jalan.

E. Additional Word List (for Exercise 17)

Nouns

kerja	*work*	minggu	*week*
hari	*day*	jalan	*way, road*
selamat	*peace, safety*		

Adjectives

| baik | *good* | lama | *old (of things)* |
| bagus | *fine, splendid* | | |

Verbs

buat (membuat)	*to do, to make*	sampai	*to arrive*
berkata	*to say*	kena	*must, to have to*
tinggal	*to stay, live*	dapat	*to manage to*
pergi	*to go*	boléh	*can, to be able*

Pronouns

| apa? | *what?* | siapa? | *who?* |

34

Miscellaneous

tak sempat	*have no time to*	lama	*for a long time*
baharu hari ini	*only today, today for the first time*	sampai	*until*
		dua minggu	*two weeks ago*
dua	*two*		
hari ini	*today*	daripada	*from (persons)*
di mana?	*where?*	di sana	*there*
baik (with vb.)	*had better*	baik jangan (with vb.)	*had better not*

Phrases

apa khabar?	*what's the news?*	(the usual greeting)
khabar baik	*the news is good*	(the usual answer to "apa khabar?")
selamat jalan	*peace on your road*	("good-bye" — said by one remaining)
selamat tinggal	*stay in peace*	("good-bye — said by one going away)

Minggu Yang Ketiga
Third Week

Pelajaran Yang Ketujuh
Lesson 7

Perbandingan 4
Comparison 4

A. Sentences

Ahmad besar.	*Ahmad is big.*
Yusuf besar.	*Yusuf is big.*
Ahmad sama besar dengan Yusuf.	*Ahmad is as big as Yusuf.*
Bangunan ini sama tinggi dengan bangunan itu.	*This building is as tall as that building.*
Ali sama berakal dengan Hamid.	*Ali is as intelligent as Hamid.*
Makanan ini sama sedap dengan makanan itu.	*This food is as tasty as that food.*
Buku saya sama berguna dengan buku dia.	*My book is as useful as his book.*
Surat dia sama panjang dengan surat itu.	*This letter is as long as that letter.*
Yusuf sebesar gajah.	*Yusuf is as big as an elephant.*
Ali sekecil Hamid.	*Ali is as small as Hamid.*
Gulai ini sepedas gulai itu.	*This curry is as hot as that curry.*
Ali tidak boléh membaca buku sepanjang itu.	*Ali can't read a book as long as that; or: Ali can't read such a long book.*
Orang Putih tidak suka makan gulai sepedas ini.	*Europeans do not like eating curry as hot as this; or: Europeans do not like eating such hot curry.*
Semalam di pasar saya melihat seorang yang sebesar gajah.	*Yesterday in the market I saw a man as big as an elephant.*
Rumah kita sama besar dengan rumah meréka.	*Our house is as big as their house.*
Saya tidak boléh menulis surat sepanjang itu.	*I cannot write a letter as long as that; or: I cannot write such a long letter.*

Marilah kita makan gulai di kedai itu!	*Come on! Let's have some curry in that shop!*
Encik sukakah makan gulai?	*Do you like eating curry?*
Ya. Saya suka.	*Yes, I do.*
Tetapi, encik Orang Putih; saya ingat Orang Putih tak suka makan gulai?	*But you're European; I thought Europeans didn't like curry?*
Lagi pula, gulai di kedai itu pedas benar.	*Further, the curry in that shop is very hot.*
Ramai Orang Putih suka makan gulai.	*Lots of Europeans like eating curry.*
Gulai pedas pun tak apa.	*It doesn't even matter if it's hot.*
Lagi pedas lagi baik.	*The hotter the better.*
Lagi ramai lagi seronok.	*The more the merrier.*
Lagi besar lagi berat.	*The bigger the heavier.*
Lagi dia bercakap lagi pandai dia bercakap.	*The more he speaks the better he is at speaking.*
Makin pedas makin baik.	*The hotter the better.*
Makin ramai makin seronok.	*The more the merrier.*
Makin besar makin berat.	*The bigger the heavier.*
Semakin pedas semakin baik.	*The hotter the better.*
Semakin ramai semakin seronok.	*The more the merrier.*
Semakin besar semakin berat.	*The bigger the heavier.*

B. Word List

Nouns

gajah	*elephant*	Orang Putih	*European*

Adjectives

seronok	*enjoyable, merry, having a good time*	berat	*heavy*
		putih	*white*

ramai	*many (of people)*		

Verbs

makan (memakan)	*to eat*	ingat (mengingat)	*to remember*
mari!	*come! come on!*	lihat (melihat)	*to see, look*
ingat	*to think*		

Miscellaneous

sama	*together with*	dengan	*with*
sama .. dengan	*as .. as*	kelmarin	*yesterday*
mereka	*they, them, their*	marilah kita ...	*come on let's ...*
lagi pula	*furthermore*	pun	*even*
tak apa	*it doesn't matter*	lagi .. lagi ..	*the more .. the more ..*

(*cf.* French: ca ne fait rien)

makin ... makin ...	*the more ... the more ...*
semakin ... semakin ...	*the more ... the more ...*

C. Grammar

29 *Ahmad sama besar dengan Yusuf.* "Ahmad is as big as Yusuf." Notice how comparisons of equality are made in Malay. Where English has *as* + adjective + *as*, Malay has *sama* + adjective + *dengan*. *Sama besar dengan Yusuf* is literally "same big with Yusuf".

30 *Yusuf sebesar gajah:* "Yusuf is as big as an elephant." Here we have another common way of forming a comparison of equality. The first "as" in English is translated by the prefix *se-* (which is short either for *sama* or for *satu*, "one") and the second one is left untranslated. Note that *sebesar gajah* does *not* mean "a big elephant", although it would make sense in this context. "A big elephant" would be *seékor gajah yang besar*.

31 *Buku sepanjang itu:* "Such a long book." "A book as long as that." The construction *se-* + adjective, is particularly common when following a noun as here. In this case, especially when used with *itu* or *ini*, it means much the same as the English construction with *such*.

32 *Lagi pedas lagi baik: makin pedas makin baik: semakin pedas semakin baik:* "The hotter the better." Notice these three ways of translating the English *the more ... the more ...* or *the -er ...the -er.*

33 *ingat* and *ingat/mengingat:* When *ingat* means "to think" or "to be of the opinion" it is not normally used in its *me*-form. The *me*-form is normally only used in the meaning of "to remember".

34 *makan/memakan:* Although *makan* has a *me*-form, this is not often used even in writing. This is because the *-e-* of *memakan* is practically silent except in very careful or pedantic speech. The resulting word would be *m'makan*, but Malay does not normally tolerate double consonants in pronunciation and so the *me*-form is usually realised as *makan* — the same as the root-form.

35 *kelmarin* and *semalam:* These two words form a Malay shibboleth. In North Malaysian Peninsular *kelmarin* (colloquially: *kemarin*) means "yesterday", and the expression *malam semalam* is used for "last night" or "yesterday evening". In South Peninsular Malaysia *kelmarin* is used as an adverb referring rather vaguely to past time and means something like "the other day", "a month or so ago", or even "a year or so ago". This meaning is rendered in North Peninsular Malaysia by the expression *hari itu*, literally "that day". The student should make his choice according to his location but he should also bear in mind that the Southern form of language is regarded as more acceptable in writing by most Malays. You may, however, take comfort from the fact that Malays too get mixed up with these two words and frequently one hears Malays joking about each other's alleged misuse of them. In Indonesia *kelmarin* is normal for *yesterday* and *semalam* means *last night.*

D. *Exercises*

Exercise 18   Translate into English:
1   Semakin dia makan gulai Melayu semakin dia suka makan.

2 Saya tidak suka membaca buku sepanjang itu; buku itu terlalu panjang.
3 Gulai Melayu bukan sama pedas dengan gulai India.
4 Gulai India yang pedas sekali.
5 Bapa dia sama tua dengan emak dia.
6 Hamid sebesar gajah.
7 Makin berakal makin baik.
8 Dia bukan seberakal itu.
9 Semakin lama dia tinggal di Malaysia semakin dia pandai bercakap Melayu.
10 Saya ingat dia suka memakan gulai pedas.

Exercise 19 Translate into Malay:
1 The more the merrier.
2 My father is not as tall as that.
3 My car is as big as your car.
4 Ah Kim is as lazy (*malas*) as Yusuf.
5 My crate is as heavy as his crate.
6 The heavier the better.
7 The more he talks the more he wants to talk.
8 My house is not as large as the headmaster's house.
9 My mother is not as old as my father.
10 I think he arrived yesterday.

Exercise 20

Write ten sentences in Malay using what you have so far learned during the course.

Minggu Yang Ketiga
Third Week

Pelajaran Yang Kedelapan
Lesson 8

Latihan Lagi dengan Awalan Me-
Further Practice with the Prefix Me-

A. Sentences

Saya mesti menulis sepucuk surat.	*I must write a letter.*
Kita mesti menggunakan bahasa kebangsaan kita.	*We must use our national language.*
Ali mesti mendaftarkan nama anaknya di pejabat kerajaan.	*Ali must register his child's name at the government office.*
Ibu saya sama gemuk dengan bapa saya.	*My mother is as fat as my father.*
Ali bekerja di ibu pejabat.	*Ali works at the head office;* or: *at the secretariat.*
Di depan Ibu Pejabat Kerajaan ada jalan raya.	*In front of the Government Secretariat is a main road.*
Di tengah jalan raya itu ada isyarat dengan perkataan "ikut kiri".	*In the middle of the main road is a sign with the words "ikut kiri".*
Apa makna perkataan "ikut kiri"?	*What is the meaning of the words "ikut kiri"?*
Kalau kita hendak tahu makna perkataan "ikut kiri" kita mesti melihat dalam Panduan Jalan Raya.	*If we want to know the meaning of the words "ikut kiri" we must look in the Highway Code.*
Di dalam Panduan Jalan Raya kita boléh melihat semua isyarat-isyarat jalan raya.	*In the Highway Code we can see all the road signs.*
Ah! Ini dia isyarat "ikut kiri". Makna isyarat itu "keep left".	*Ah! Here's the "ikut kiri" sign. The meaning of the sign is "keep left".*
Dia datang ikut sini.	*He came this way.*
Dia pergi ikut situ.	*He went that way.*

Sila ikut sini, encik.	*Please come this way, sir.*
Sila masuk!	*Please come in!*
Sila duduk, tuan!	*Please sit down, sir!*
Ali suka memandu kereta.	*Ali likes driving a car.*
Ali telah membaca Panduan Jalan Raya.	*Ali has read the Highway Code.*
Semua orang yang membawa kereta mesti membaca Panduan Jalan Raya.	*All people who drive cars must read the Highway Code.*
Kalau kita melihat isyarat "ikut kiri", makna isyarat itu kita mesti mengikut sebelah kiri.	*If we see a "keep left" sign, that means that we must keep to the left-hand side.*
Di negeri Perancis orang yang membawa kereta mesti mengikut sebelah kanan.	*In France people driving cars must keep to the right.*
Saya telah mendaftarkan nama anak saya dalam daftar sekolah menengah.	*I have registered my child's name in the secondary school list.*
Buku ini tak berapa menarik hati.	*This book is not very interesting.*
Apa makna isyarat "berhenti – lihat – jalan"?	*What is the meaning of the sign "berhenti – lihat – jalan"?*
Makna isyarat itu "stop – look – go".	*The meaning of that sign is "stop – look – go".*

B. Word List

Nouns

latihan	*practice*	nama	*name*
pejabat	*office*	ibu pejabat	*head office, secretariat*
jalan raya	*main road, highway*	isyarat	*sign*
panduan	*guide*	Panduan Jalan Raya	*Highway Code*

tuan	*lord, sir, Mr*	sebelah	*side*
daftar	*list*	sekolah	*school*
sekolah rendah	*primary school*	sekolah menengah	*secondary school*
sekolah tinggi*	*university*	negeri Perancis	*France*
hati	*liver*		

*more usually nowadays: *universiti*

Adjectives

raya	*public*	kiri	*left*
kanan	*right, senior*	menengah	*secondary*
rendah	*low, primary*	menarik hati	*interesting*
kedelapan	*eighth*		

Verbs

mesti	*must*	gunakan (menggunakan)	*to use*
bekerja	*to work*	masuk	*to enter, to go in, to come in*
ikut (mengikut)	*to follow*	bawa (membawa)	*to take, carry,*
memandu	*to drive*	tarik (menarik)	*to pull*
tahu	*to know*	berhenti	*to stop*

Miscellaneous

di depan	*in front of*	di tengah	*in the middle of*
ikut	*by way of, via*	kalau	*if*
semua	*all*	ini dia . . .	*here's . . .*
ikut sini	*this way*	ikut situ	*that way*
sila	*please (invitation)*	telah	*sign of perfect or past tense*

C. Grammar

36 *Saya mesti menulis surat:* "I must write a letter." *Mesti* is a very strong word for "must". It is normally, as here, followed by a *me-*prefix if the verb in question has a *me-*form available.

37 *Di pejabat kerajaan:* "At the government office." Instead of pejabat, "office", the English word, spelt *ofis*, is quite commonly used, especially in conversation.

38 *Ibu pejabat:* "Head office" or "secretariat". Literally, of course, this picturesque phrase means "mother of offices".

39 *Ikut kiri:* "Keep left." Basically, *ikut* and its *me-*form *mengikut* mean "to follow" or "to go by way of". *Ikut* (without *me-*) has, however, come to be used as a preposition meaning "by way of" or "via". Notice the two phrases *ikut sini* and *ikut situ*, which mean "this way" and "that way" respectively.

40 *Sila masuk!:* "Please come in." *Sila* is used to indicate a polite invitation to do something, and so corresponds to the English "please" in such contexts.

41 *Ali telah membaca Panduan Jalan Raya:* "Ali has read the Highway Code." *Telah* is the classical equivalent of *sudah*, and is more common than *sudah* in writing. It is used, like *sudah*, to indicate perfected or completed action, but is also being used more and more in modern prose writing to indicate a simple narrative past tense in imitation of English usage.

42 *Menarik hati:* "Interesting." *Tarik (menarik)* means "to pull" or "to attract". *Hati* means "liver", which the Malays, like the Elizabethans, believe to be the seat of the emotions, and so in figurative usage *hati* is used like the English "heart" or "mind". *Menarik hati*, then, is a set expression meaning "attracting the mind", and so "interesting".

43 *Berhenti – lihat – jalan:* "Stop – look – go." Strictly speaking *jalan* should only be used as a noun meaning "road" or "way", but in vulgar or bazaar Malay it is often used as a verb meaning of "to go". This usage begun to creep back into standard Malay, although more correctly the verb form is *berjalan*. *Jalan* is also quite often seen in public notices in the sense of "to go" or "to proceed". The student is advised, however, not to imitate this usage, but to keep *jalan* as a noun and *berjalan* as the corresponding verb.

D. Exercises

Exercise 21   Translate into English:
1. Anak saya telah masuk sekolah tinggi (or: *universiti*) di Kuala Lumpur.
2. Saya mesti membaca buku itu.
3. Di depan pejabat saya ada isyarat "ikut kiri".
4. Gunakanlah bahasa kebangsaan!
5. Bahasa Perancis sangat menarik hati.
6. Encik sukakah memandu keréta?
7. Semalam saya telah membaca Panduan Jalan Raya.
8. Keréta dia berhenti di luar Ibu Pejabat Kerajaan.
9. Kalau encik hendak mendaftarkan nama anak encik, encik mesti pergi ke pejabat pelajaran.
10. Adik saya belajar di sekolah rendah Melayu.

Exercise 22   Translate into Malay:
1. The Highway Code is a very useful book.
2. Where do you work? I work in the secretariat.
3. If we drive a car in France, we must keep to the right.
4. Please come in, sir.
5. What is the meaning of that sign?
6. In the middle of the road is a "stop-look-go" sign.
7. My father does not like driving a car.
8. You must register this letter at the post office.
9. Ah Kim always writes letters in the national language.
10. Come on, let's speak Malay today!

Exercise 23
Write down ten sentences in Malay using what you have so far learned during the course.

Minggu Yang Ketiga / Third Week

Pelajaran Yang Kesembilan / Lesson 9

Latihan Lagi dengan Cara-cara Perbandingan dan Awalan Me-
Further Practice on the Methods of Comparison and the Prefix Me-

A. Sentences

Zahrah sama cerdik dengan Aminah.	*Zahrah is as bright as Aminah.*
Bapa Ahmad sama kurus dengan bapa Ariffin.	*Ahmad's father is as thin as Ariffin's.*
Yusuf sama berakal dengan Awang.	*Yusuf is as intelligent as Awang.*
Buku ini sama berguna dengan buku itu.	*This book is as useful as that one.*
Ali sebesar gajah.	*Ali is as big as an elephant.*
Bangunan ini setinggi bangunan itu.	*This building is as tall as that one.*
Saya tak boléh mengangkat kotak seberat itu.	*I can't lift such a heavy box.*
Saya tak boléh berjalan kaki sejauh itu.	*I can't walk as far as that.*
Lagi besar lagi baik.	*The bigger the better.*
Makin pedas makin sedap.	*The hotter it is the more tasty it is.*
Semakin dia menggunakan bahasa kebangsaan, semakin pandai dia bercakap.	*The more he uses the national language, the better he is at speaking it.*
Semakin lama dia mewakili kerajaan, semakin baik.	*The longer he represents the government, the better.*
Semakin lama dia tinggal di negeri China, semakin pandai dia bercakap bahasa Cina.	*The longer he stayed in China, the better he was at speaking Chinese.*
Ahmad selalu menutup pintu	*Ahmad always closes the door of the*

pejabat pada pukul lima.	office at five o'clock.
Guru kita belum menyatakan perkataan ini.	Our teacher has not yet explained this word.
Dia akan menyatakan perkataan itu ésok.	He will explain that word tomorrow.
Orang itu selalu mengacau saya.	That man always annoys me.
Siapa akan mewakili kerajaan Malaysia di sana?	Who will represent the Malaysian government there?
Encik Ali bin Yusuf akan mewakili kerajaan di negeri itu.	Encik Ali bin Yusuf will represent the government in that country.
Ali sedang mengupas buah rambutan.	Ali is peeling a rambutan.
Aminah sedang menyusun buku dalam almari.	Aminah is arranging the books in the cupboard.
Orang itu telah mencuri wang Ali.	That man has stolen Ali's money.
Ahmad sudah menggulung hamparan.	Ahmad has rolled up the carpet.
Dia hendak mencuci bilik saya.	He's going to clean my room (i.e. wash the floor etc.).
Dia hendak membersihkan bilik saya.	He's going to clean my room.
Dia hendak mengemas bilik saya.	He's going to tidy my room.
Yusuf tidak suka menjawab soalan yang sesusah itu.	Yusuf doesn't like answering such difficult questions.
Dia suka menjawab soalan yang senang sahaja.	He only likes answering easy questions.

B. Word List

Nouns

cara	*method, fashion*	kaki	*foot, leg*

negeri China	*China*	bahasa Cina	*Chinese (language)*
wang	*money*	bilik	*room*

Adjectives

kurus	*thin*	jauh	*distant, far*
susah	*difficult*	senang	*easy*

Verbs.

berjalan kaki	*to walk*	bersihkan (membersihkan)	*to clean (dry)*
cuci (mencuci)	*to clean (with water), to wash*	kemas (mengemas)	*to tidy*

Miscellaneous

pada	*at, on*	pukul	*o'clock*
belum	*not yet*		

C. Grammar

44 *Berjalan kaki*: *Berjalan* means "to go" in the sense of "to proceed", "to be under way", "to be in motion" and also "to go" or "to function" of a machine, for instance. It corresponds pretty well to *marcher* in French. It is also used to mean "to walk", but because of possible ambiguity in meaning the word *kaki*, "foot", is usually added to it when there is any emphasis on the idea of walking.

45 *Pada pukul lima*: "At five o'clock". *Pada* is the usual preposition used to indicate a point in time; it corresponds to the English "at" or "on" in such contexts. *Pukul* literally means "strike" or "stroke", and is the usual word for *o'clock*. For more details on how to tell the time in Malay, see "Speak Malay!", Lesson 31-35, pp. 104-122.

D. Exercises

Exercise 24 Translate into English:
1. Abang saya hendak memandu keréta dia ke Kuala Lumpur.
2. Di mana saya mesti mendaftarkan nama saya? Di ibu pejabat.
3. Bahasa Cina itu bahasa yang sangat menarik hati.
4. Dia akan membuka pejabat pada pukul sembilan.
5. Siapa akan membersihkan bilik ayah?
6. Semakin senang semakin baik.
7. Encik sudah belajar semua isyarat-isyarat jalan rayakah?
8. Saya belum belajar semua isyarat-isyarat itu.
9. Ahmad belum menggulung hamparan dalam bilik saya.
10. Bangunan yang besar itu Ibu Pejabat Kerajaan.

Exercise 25 Translate into Malay:
1. I shall follow the main road to Kuala Lumpur.
2. What is the meaning of this difficult word?
3. He is driving the car.
4. Yusuf is as intelligent as his father.
5. If we want to drive a car, we must learn all the road signs first.
6. If your child is going to enter a primary school, you must register his name at the Education Office first.
7. Where is the Education Office? The Education Office is in the Government Secretariat.
8. I cannot drive a car as far as that.
9. I have not yet read the newspaper today.
10. Come on, let's go to the post office; I must send this letter to Ali.

Exercise 26 Translate into English:
- A: Apa encik baca?
- B: Saya sedang membaca "Panduan Jalan Raya".
- A: "Panduan Jalan Raya"? Apa itu?
- B: "Panduan Jalan Raya" itu sebuah buku yang berguna benar. Kerajaan sudah menyusun buku itu hendak menolong kita

menggunakan jalan raya dengan selamat. Orang yang membawa keréta pun, orang yang naik basikal pun, orang yang berjalan kaki pun, tak apa. Kita semua mesti membaca "Panduan Jalan Raya".

A: Gambar itu gambar apa?
B: Ini gambar isyarat-isyarat jalan raya. Gambar ini gambar isyarat "ikut kiri". Bila kita melihat isyarat "ikut kiri", kita mesti membawa keréta kita ke sebelah kiri isyarat itu.
A: Isyarat ini isyarat apa? Ada perkataan "berhenti–lihat–jalan".
B: Bila kita melihat isyarat itu, maknanya kita hendak masuk jalan raya dari jalan kecil. Pertama, kita mesti berhenti. Lepas itu kita mesti melihat; maknanya kita mesti menantikan keréta-keréta di jalan raya lalu dahulu. Baharulah boléh kita berjalan semula.
A: Buku itu sangat berguna. Di mana saya boléh beli?
B: Di kedai mana-mana pun boléh beli. Harganya lima puluh sén sahaja. Belilah, hari ini juga. Kalau encik tak tahu makna semua isyarat-isyarat jalan raya, tentulah encik tak lulus dalam peperiksaan membawa keréta.

E. Additional Word List (for Exercise 26)

Nouns

basikal	*bicycle*	harga	*price*
sén	*cent*	peperiksaan	*examination, test*
pelajaran	*education*		

Adjectives

tentu	*certain, sure*

Verbs

tolong (menolong)	*to help*	naik	*to go up, come up, rise, to ride*

lalu	*to pass by*	lulus	*to pass (an examination)*

Miscellaneous

buah	*cl. for large objects*	bila	*when*
harganya	*it costs*	maknanya	*it means (that)*
lepas itu	*then, next, afterwards*	lepas	*after, beyond*
lima puluh	*fifty*	baharulah	*only then*
hari ini juga	*this very day*	mana-mana pun	*any (at all)*
semula	*again (as before)*	satu	*one*
dengan selamat	*safely*		

Minggu Yang Keempat
Fourth Week

Pelajaran Yang Kesepuluh
Lesson 10

Ganti Nama Diri 1
Personal Pronouns I

A. Sentences

Saya hendak membaca suratkhabar.	I *am going to read the newspaper.*
Dia mengajar *saya* membaca bahasa kebangsaan.	*He teaches* me *to read the national language.*
Tolong bagi *saya* buku itu.	*Please give* me *that book.*
Di mana buku *saya?*	*Where is* my *book?*
Aku hendak menulis surat.	I *am going to write a letter.*
Dia sudah menulis surat kepada *aku.*	*He has written a letter to* me.
Di mana sapu tangan *aku?*	*Where is* my *handkerchief?*
Kita mesti menggunakan bahasa kebangsaan kita.	*We must use our national language.*
Marilah kita pergi ke Kuala Lumpur.	*Come on, let's go to Kuala Lumpur.*
Ke mana encik-encik pergi semalam?	*Where did you all go yesterday?*
Kami pergi menengok wayang gambar.	*We went to the pictures.*
Buku kami ada di dalam almari itu; di mana buku encik?	*Our books are in that cupboard; where are yours?*
Kami hendak keluar sekarang; encik mesti tinggal di sini.	*We are going out now; you must stay here.*
Ibu kami gemuk; ibu encik kurus.	*Our mother is fat; yours is thin.*
Di mana encik-encik belajar bahasa Melayu?	*Where do you gentlemen learn Malay?*
Di mana tuan tinggal?	*Where do you live, sir?*
Dari mana puan datang?	*Where do you come from, madam?*

Tuankah yang menulis surat ini?	*Was it you who wrote this letter, sir?*
Tolong saudara menulis surat kepada dia.	*Please write to him.*
Kalau saudara belum menulis surat kepada dia, tolong tulislah hari ini.	*If you have not yet written to him, please write today.*

B. Word List

Nouns

ganti nama	*pronoun*	ganti nama diri	*personal pronoun*
tangan	*hand*	sapu tangan	*handkerchief*
wayang	*puppet, puppet show*	wayang gambar	*film, picture*
saudara	*colleague, you*	puan	*Madam, Mrs, you*

Pronouns

aku	*I, me, my*	kami	*we, us, our*
diri	*self*		

Verbs

sapu (menyapu)	*to sweep, wipe*	ajar (mengajar)	*to teach*
keluar	*to go out, to come out*	bagi	*to give (coll.), for*
téngok (menéngok)	*to see, look at*		

Miscellaneous

tolong	*please*	di sini	*here*
ke mana?	*(to) where?, whither?*	dari mana?	*where from?, whence?*

C. *Grammar*

46 *Personal pronouns:* The correct use of the personal pronouns is more difficult in Malay than it is in English because of the Malay tendency to grade pronouns in politeness. For this reason, we have restricted ourselves so far in this course (and throughout "Speak Malay!", q.v.) to what may be called the *safe* pronouns, that is to say we have only used those words which are reasonably safe in all contexts and which can be used without much danger of giving offence to the person we are addressing. There are, however, quite a lot of other words which can be used in certain circumstances instead of these "safe" pronouns, and although you may not need to use them yourself, you will have to know them in order to understand them when you hear them in conversation or see them in writing. In the next few lessons, therefore, we shall try to cover the whole ground of personal pronouns, learning these new words and at the same time revising the pronouns you have already learned.

47 *Invariability of pronouns:* The first thing to be borne in mind when dealing with pronouns in Malay is that they are invariable: that is, they do not change their form to show whether they are being used as the subject or the object of a verb, and only the word order shows us if a pronoun is being used as possessive. In English, however, we use "I" for instance only as the subject of a verb, "me" as the direct or indirect object, and "my" as a possessive. In Malay, however, the word *saya* does the job of all these three English words, and generally speaking, it is the word order which tells us the function of the word, e.g.

Saya hendak membaca suratkhabar.

I am going to read the newspaper. (*I* and *saya* are subjects)

Dia mengajar saya membaca bahasa kebangsaan.
He teaches me to read the national language. (*me* and *saya* are direct objects)
Tolong bagi saya buku itu.
Please give me that book. (*me* and *saya* are indirect objects)
Di mana buku saya?
Where is my book? (*my* and *saya* are possessives)

48 *Saya hendak membaca suratkhabar:* "I am going to read the newspaper." *Saya* is the "safe" pronoun for "I", "me" and "my". It is a polite word and is definitely the best word for a non-Malay to use when talking to anybody at all.

49 *Aku hendak menulis surat:* "I am going to write a letter." *Aku* is a common word for "I", "me" and "my", but it is not as polite as *saya*. It is normally used only between close friends, or by a superior to an inferior, for example by parents talking to children, or by a teacher addressing a pupil in school. The student is advised not to use it himself, except in exercises for practice, but to be prepared to hear it or, more commonly, see it in books.

50 *Kita mesti menggunakan bahasa kebangsaan kita:* "We must use our national language." *Kita* is, of course, the "safe" word for "we", "us" and "our", but strictly speaking it should only be used when we *include* the person addressed. For this reason grammarians usually call *kita* an *inclusive pronoun*. In other words *kita* is not just the plural of *saya* but means "I and you" or "we and you". Study the examples in Section A above and you will see that the sentences in which *kita* occurs include the person or persons addressed by the speaker or writer of the sentence.

51 *Kami pergi menéngok wayang gambar:* "We went to the pictures." This sentence is an answer to the question *Ke mana encik-encik pergi semalam?* – "Where did you go yesterday?" The questioner is clearly excluded from the reply, and so the word *kami* is used for "we" instead of *kita*. *Kami*, then, is the true plural of *saya* or *aku*, and means "we", "us" or "our" *excluding* the person addressed. Grammarians call it an *exclusive pronoun*. Study the examples in Section A above and you will see that, in the sentences in which *kami* occurs, the person

addressed is not included in the action.

52 *Di mana encik-encik belajar bahasa Melayu?* "Where do you (gentlemen) learn Malay?" The English word which really causes trouble when we try to translate it into Malay is, however, the second person pronoun "you". The Malays are world-famous for their politeness and courtesy to other people and this has resulted in the fact that there is no single word which is always safe for the word "you". The word *encik*, which we have been using up to now, is fairly safe in most contexts, especially since His Late Majesty the First Yang Dipertuan Agung recommended its wider use in place of the English "mister", but, although it is polite, it may sometimes not be polite enough. *Encik* is really a Malay title roughly equivalent to Mr, Mrs or Miss in English, but it is much more widely used than those English words. It is more like *Herr* in German or *Monsieur* in French. Normally it is singular in meaning and is reduplicated—*encik-encik*—when we address more then one person.

53 *Di mana tuan tinggal?* "Where do you live, sirs?" *Tuan* is much more polite than *encik* and should always be used when addressing a Haji or someone with the prefix *Syed* to his name. It would normally be used by a junior employee to his boss, and is roughly equivalent in politeness value to the English word "sir". It is also, by courtesy, usually extended to foreign visitors to Malaysia.

54 *Dari mana puan datang?:* "Where do you come from, madam?" *Puan* is the feminine equivalent of *tuan* and is being used more and more as a title with much the same meaning as *Mrs* or *madam* in English.

55 *Tolong saudara menulis surat kepada dia:* "Please write to him." Another word which has been coming into use as a polite equivalent for "you" is the word *saudara*, which is often abbreviated in writing as *sdr*. This word was originally a Sanskrit word meaning "brother" and it has this meaning in Malay too, but is also often used to mean "a close friend". Its use to mean "you" originated in Indonesia, but it is now quite often used in Malaysia especially in writing and especially between colleagues working in the same department or office, or between teachers or lecturers on the staff of the same school or college.

56 *Tuankah yang menulis surat ini?:* "Was it you who wrote this letter, sir?" Notice this construction. Just as Malay does not need the verb "to be" in a sentence like "this is my book" (*ini buku saya*), neither does it need it here. The addition of *-kah* to the subject is sufficient to call attention to it, especially when the word *yang* is inserted after the group. In this construction any verb which has a *me-*form *must* be used in it.

57 *Tolong tulislah hari ini:* "Please write today." *Tolong* is very often used nowadays to render the English "please". It always stands at the head of the sentence unlike "please", which can come almost anywhere in an English sentence.

D. Exercises

Exercise 27   Translate into English:
1. Aku sudah membaca buku itu.
2. Kami hendak pergi ke Singapura (*Singapore*).
3. Tolong saudara datang ke pejabat saya pada pukul sepuluh.
4. Pukul berapa tuan sampai ke sini (*hither, here*)?
5. Marilah kita pergi menengok wayang gambar.
6. Ke mana puan pergi? Saya pergi ke Ipoh.
7. Siapa hendak mengajar aku?
8. Bila saudara hendak menulis surat kepada dia?
9. Saudarakah yang pandai bercakap bahasa Cina?
10. Encikkah yang telah membuka pintu itu?

Exercise 28   Translate into Malay:
1. Where are you going, gentlemen? We're going to the market.
2. We must learn Malay.
3. We must learn English, but you must learn French.
4. Please give me the newspaper.
5. Our car is here; where's yours? (say: your car).
6. Please go to the headmaster's office at nine o'clock.
7. I am the one who wants to learn Malay.

8 Where's my bicycle? I am afraid I don't know.
9 Was it Ali who sent the letter to the Prime Minister?
10 You are very good at speaking Malay, madam.

Exercise 29
Write down ten Malay sentences of your own using what you have learned so far.

Minggu Yang Keempat
Fourth Week

Pelajaran Yang Kesebelas
Lesson 11

Ganti Nama Diri 2
Personal Pronouns 2

A. Sentences

Ia melihat saya.	*He sees me.*
Saya melihat dia.	*I see him.*
Ia mendengar kami.	*She hears us.*
Kami mendengar dia.	*We hear her.*
Buku dia.	*His book; or her book.*
Keréta dia.	*His car; or: her car.*
Ibu dia.	*His mother; or: her mother.*
Hari ini Perdana Menteri negeri Ruritania telah sampai di lapangan terbang.	*Today the Prime Minister of Ruritania arrived at the airport.*
Beliau berkata sudah lama beliau hendak melawat Malaysia Barat.	*He said he had been wanting for a long time to visit West Malaysia.*
Ésok beliau akan melawat Menteri Pelajaran.	*Tomorrow he will visit the Minister of Education.*
Lepas itu beliau akan pergi ke Maktab Perguruan Harian.	*After that he will go to the Day Training College.*
Meréka hendak melawat kami ésok.	*They are going to visit us tomorrow.*
Kami sudah menjemput meréka ke rumah kami.	*We have invited them to our house.*
Meréka akan datang dengan bas, sebab keréta meréka rosak.	*They will come by bus, because their car has broken down.*
Meréka nak belajar bahasa kebangsaan.	*They're going to learn the national language.*
Guru kita nak mengajar meréka bercakap bahasa Melayu.	*Our teacher is going to teach them to speak Malay.*

Di mana murid-murid itu belajar?	*Where do those pupils study?*
Meréka belajar di sekolah Melayu Kampung Bahagia.	*They study in the Kampung Bahagia Malay school.*
Meréka belajar menulis bahasa Melayu dan lagi meréka belajar ilmu hisab.	*They learn to write Malay and also they study arithmetic.*
Apa lagi meréka belajar di sekolah itu?	*What else do they learn in that school?*
Meréka belajar ilmu alam dan tawarikh.	*They learn geography and history.*
Di mana anak lelaki engkau belajar?	*Where does your son study?*
Anak lelaki aku pun belajar di sekolah itu juga.	*My son studies in that school too.*
Adakah anak lelaki engkau belajar ilmu sains?	*Does your son study science?*
Tidak. Tak boléh belajar ilmu sains di sekolah rendah.	*No, you can't learn science in the primary school.*
Bila anak perempuan engkau nak masuk sekolah menengah?	*When's your daughter going to the secondary school?*
Ia nak masuk sekolah menengah tahun depan.	*She is going to the secondary school next year.*
Saya dengar kerajaan akan membangunkan maktab di bandar kita.	*I hear that the government is going to build a college in our town.*
Ya, Maktab Perguruan Harian.	*Yes, a Day Training College (for teachers).*
Siapa akan menjadi pengetua maktab itu?	*Who will be the principal of the college?*
Saya tak tahu lagi.	*I don't know yet.*

B. Word List

Nouns

lapangan	*field*	lapangan terbang	*airport*
bas	*bus*	Menteri Pelajaran	*Minister of Education*
Maktab Perguruan Harian	*Day Training College*	maktab	*college*
ilmu	*knowledge*	perguruan	*teacher training*
ilmu hisab	*arithmetic*		
ilmu alam	*geography*	murid	*pupil*
ilmu sains	*science*	hisab	*calculation*
sains	*science*	alam	*world*
		bumi	*Earth*
tawarikh	*history*	anak perempuan	*daughter*
tahun	*year*		
kampung	*village*	pengetua	*principal*
		bahagia	*happiness*

Adjectives

rosak	*broken down, damaged*	harian	*daily*

Pronouns

ia	*he, she*	beliau	*he, she*
meréka	*they, them, their*	engkau	*you*

Verbs

dengar (mendengar)	*to hear, listen (to)*
lawat (melawat)	*to visit*
jemput (menjemput)	*to invite*
bangunkan (membangunkan)	*to build, to erect*
jadi (menjadi)	*to become*

Miscellaneous

apa lagi?	*what else?*	dan	*and*
adakah?	*(question phrase like French est-ce que)*	dan lagi	*and also*
pun . . . juga	*also*	tahun depan	*next year*
ya	*yes*		

C. Grammar

58 *Ia melihat saya:* "He (or: she) sees me." *Ia,* which means "he" or "she", is an exception to the rule of invariability mentioned in 47 above. *Ia* may be used only as the subject of a verb or of a sentence, and cannot be used either as an object or as a possessive. The objective and possessive form of *ia* is *dia*. In speech, and quite often in writing too, *dia* can also be used as the subject form. In writing, however, it is regarded as more correct to reserve *ia* for the subject and to use *dia* for the object or the possessive. We should write, therefore:

Ia melihat saya.	*He sees me.*
Saya melihat dia.	*I see him.*
Saya membaca buku dia.	*I read his book.*

59 *Beliau berkata:* "He said." The word *beliau,* which comes from Indonesia, is a very polite word for "he" or "she". It is being used more and more today when we are referring to people to whom we owe a certain respect, such as heads of state or public figures of some importance. In the newspapers it is used even more widely out of politeness.

60 *Meréka hendak melawat kami ésok:* "They are going to visit us tomorrow." *Meréka* is the most usual word in writing, and often in conversation, for "they", "them" or "their". It often has the words *ini* or *itu* tacked on to it, thus *meréka ini* (referring to people close by) and *meréka itu* (referring either to people some distance away, or to people already mentioned previously).

61 *BUMI/ALAM:*

Bumi is "the Earth"; *alam* is "the world". Both *ilmu alam* and *ilmu bumi* are used for "geography", but be careful: in Indonesia *ilmu alam* means "physics" (Malay: *ilmu fizik*), *ilmu bumi* is the only word for "geography", and *ilmu bumi alam* means "physical geography".

62 *Di mana anak engkau belajar?:* "Where does your child study?" *Engkau* which means "you" or "your", is much less polite than *encik*. It is used only between very intimate friends and relations rather like *tu* in French or *du* in German. The non-Malay who uses it runs the risk of giving grave offence and so the student is advised not to use it himself, although he will certainly hear it in conversation and read it in books. We shall have more to say about *engkau* in a later lesson (see below, Lesson 13).

63 *Anak aku pun belajar di sekolah itu juga:* "My child studies in that school too." *Pun*, combined with *juga*, means "also" or "too". For further details and examples see "Speak Malay!", Lesson 53, pp. 178-180.

64 *Ilmu sains:* "Science" (as a school subject). *Ilmu* is an Arabic word meaning "knowledge" or "science" and is used in Malay to form the names of most sciences or fields of study, rather as we use the Greek suffix *-ology* in English. *Sains* is, of course, merely an attempt to spell the English word phonetically.

65 *Maktab Perguruan Harian:* "Day Training College." *Harian*, "daily" or "daytime", is an adjective formed from *hari*, "day". *Maktab* is a "college" or "institute". The Malay name of the Language Institute in Pantai Valley is *Maktab Perguruan Bahasa*, or "Institute for the Training of Teachers of Languages". Do not confuse the Language Institute, by the way, with the Language and Literature Agency, which has an entirely different function and is called in Malay — *Déwan Bahasa dan Pustaka* or "the Council for Language and Books".

D. *Exercises*

Exercise 30   Translate into English:
1   Hari ini saya sudah melihat Perdana Menteri di lapangan terbang.

2   Beliau sudah melawat maktab kita.
3   Bapa aku mengajar ilmu alam di sebuah sekolah menengah.
4   Aku sedang belajar bahasa kebangsaan di sekolah itu.
5   Bila kerajaan akan membangunkan sebuah Maktab Perguruan Harian di bandar kita?
6   Orang itu pengetua sebuah Maktab Perguruan.
7   Engkaukah yang mahu masuk sekolah ini?
8   Anak saya sangat suka mengajar tawarikh.
9   Kita mesti belajar tawarikh Malaysia kita ini.
10 Ésok Menteri Pelajaran akan melawat Universiti Kebangsaan di Pulau Pinang.

Exercise 31   Translate into Malay:
1   In the secondary school we learn science, geography and English.
2   They must go by bus because they have no car.
3   I think arithmetic is more difficult than geography.
4   Yes, but science is as difficult as arithmetic.
5   Next year my daughter is going to the Language Institute; she wants to be (*menjadi*) a teacher of Malay.
6   If you want to be a primary school teacher you'd better get into the Day Training College.
7   I see him, but he doesn't see me.
8   At the airport the Prime Minister of Ruritania said he wanted to visit the University.
9   My village is small; your village is small too.
10 Please give me that book; I want to read it too.

Exercise 32
Write ten sentences in Malay using what you have so far learned.

Minggu Yang Keempat — Pelajaran Yang Kedua Belas
Fourth Week — Lesson 12

Ganti Nama Diri 3
Personal Pronouns 3

A. *Sentences*

Dia melihatku.	*He sees me.*
Cikgu Ahmad akan mengajarku bercakap bahasa Melayu.	*Cikgu Ahmad will teach me to speak Malay.*
Di mana bukuku?	*Where is my book?*
Aku hendak menjual kerétaku.	*I'm going to sell my car.*
Aku nampak kau di pekan pagi tadi.	*I saw you in the town this morning.*
Ia akan melawat kau ésok.	*He will visit you tomorrow.*
Bukalah buku kau!	*Open your book!*
Di mana tinggal bapa kau?	*Where does your father live?*
Perdana Menteri akan melawat maktabmu minggu depan.	*The Prime Minister will visit your college next week.*
Di mana bapamu bekerja?	*Where does your father work?*
Kalau kamu jahat, bapamu akan memukulmu.	*If you are naughty, your father will beat you.*
Guru kamu akan mengajarmu bercakap bahasa Melayu.	*Your teacher will teach you to speak Malay.*
Meréka hendak membaca bukunya.	*They are going to read their books.*
Emak saya sedang bekerja di dalam biliknya.	*My mother is working in her room.*
Bapa saya pensyarah di Maktab Perguruan; syarahannya sangat menarik hati.	*My father is a lecturer in a Teacher Training College; his lectures are very interesting.*
Buka almari dan simpan bukumu di dalamnya.	*Open the cupboard and put your books away in it.*
Maktab itu besar; penuntut-penuntutnya ramai.	*That college is big; its students are many (or: it has a lot of students).*

Pensyarah kanan akan bersyarah darihal perguruan.	*The senior lecturer will lecture about teacher training.*
Di dalam Maktab Perguruan Harian ini ada seorang pengetua dan dua orang pensyarah kanan.	*In this Day Training College there are a principal and two senior lecturers.*
Seorang pensyarah kanan bersyarah darihal teori pendidikan dan seorang pensyarah kanan bersyarah darihal bahasa Melayu.	*One senior lecturer lectures on educational theory and one senior lecturer lectures on the Malay language.*
Syarahan-syarahannya sangat menarik hati.	*Their lectures are very interesting.*
Pelajar-pelajarnya sangat suka mendengarnya.	*Their students very much enjoy listening to them.*
Pelajar-pelajarnya belajar banyak daripadanya.	*Their students learn a great deal from them.*
Tiap-tiap minggu semua penuntut mesti menulis satu karangan bagi pengetua maktab.	*Every week all the students must write an essay for the principal of the college.*
Meréka mesti menulis karangannya dalam bahasa kebangsaan.	*They must write their essays in the national language.*
Kerajaan Malaysia sedang menjalankan banyak maktab-maktab.	*The Government of Malaysia is running many colleges.*
Tahun depan kerajaan akan membangunkan sebuah Maktab Perguruan lagi di bandar kita.	*Next year the government is going to build another Teacher Training College in our town.*
Seorang kawan saya akan menjalankannya.	*A friend of mine will run it.*
Ia akan menjadi pengetuanya.	*He will become the principal of it.*

B. Word List

Nouns

cikgu	*teacher*	pekan	*town*
pagi	*morning*	pensyarah kanan	*senior lecturer*
pensyarah	*lecturer*	penuntut	*student*
syarahan	*lecture*	pengetua	*principal*
pelajar	*student*	karangan	*essay, composition*
téori pendidikan	*educational theory*		

Adjectives

jahat	*bad, naughty, wicked, evil*	ramai	*many (people), crowded*

Pronouns

-ku	*(I), me, my*	kau	*you, your*
-mu	*you, your (plur.)*	-nya	*him, his, her, its, it, them, their*
kamu	*you, your (plur.)*		

Verbs

jalankan (menjalankan)	*to set in motion, to run (something)*	jual (menjual)	*to sell*
bersyarah	*to lecture*		

Miscellaneous

tadi	*just now*	pagi tadi	*this morning (only used of the past)*
minggu depan	*next week*	tiap-tiap	*each, every*
ésok	*tomorrow*		
darihal	*about, concerning*		

C. Grammar

66 . *Dia melihatku:* "He sees me." *Aku,* "I" or "me", may take the form *-ku* or *ku-* when there is no particular emphasis on it; that is to say, *ku* is a weak form of *aku*. This can happen when it is the subject of a verb–in English "I"–but I want to leave this aside for the time being as this use of *ku-* introduces further complications which we shall not be ready for until a later lesson. For the moment let us confine ourselves to its use as a suffix. In this case it may be either the object (direct or indirect) of a verb, the "object" of a preposition, or a possessive adjective meaning "my". Study the first batch of examples in Section A above to see how it works.

67 *Aku sudah melihat kau di pekan pagi tadi:* "I saw you in town this morning." *Kau* is the short or weak form of *engkau,* "you" or "your" (singular). Like *-ku-*(cf. 66)–it may be subject, object or possessive in meaning. We shall, however, not bother about its subjectival use for the moment. The second batch of sentences in Section A above gives examples of its use as an object or a possessive.

68 *Di mana bapamu bekerja?:* "Where does your father work?" *-Mu* is the weak form of *kamu,* "you" or "your" (plural), about which we shall have more to say later. For the moment remember that *kamu* is the plural form of *engkau*. Its short form *-mu* is used only as an object or a possessive and never as a subject except in dialect. The third batch of examples in Section A above illustrates its uses.

69 *Meréka hendak membaca bukunya:* "They are going to read their books." The most useful of all the short or weak forms of pronouns is that of the third person *-nya*, which takes the place not only of *dia* but also of *mereka* and *beliau*. *-Nya* cannot be used as a subject, but as an object it may mean "him", "her", "it" or "them", and as a possessive it may mean "his", "her", "its", or "their". In addition, *-nya* also has many other uses as a suffix and we shall have a lot more to say about it in later lessons. For the moment, however, we shall confine ourselves to its use as a pronoun. Study the examples of *-nya* in the sentences in Section A above and you will see how it works.

70 *Cikgu Ahmad:* "Mr (Schoolmaster) Ahmad." *Cikgu* is a very popular abbreviation of *Cik Guru*, and is the normal title accorded to

Malay school teachers, where in English we should just say the simple *Mr.* Where English schoolboys would call their teacher "sir", Malay children address their teachers, both male and female, as *Cikgu*.

71 *Pagi tadi:* "This morning." This expression is only used when "this morning" refers to the past. "I saw him this morning" would be *Saya telah melihatnya pagi tadi*, but "I shall see him this morning" would be *Saya akan melihatnya pagi ini*.

72 *Ilmu pendidikan:* Note that this expression means "education" as a subject of study, as in a teacher training college, for example as opposed to education as a service or commodity, which is *pelajaran*.

73 *Pensyarah kanan:* "Senior lecturer." Notice the use of the word *kanan*, "right", to mean "senior" in official designations. This usage is becoming more and more common every day.

D. Exercises

Exercise 33   Translate into English:
1. Ia sudah menyuruhku membuka pintu. (*suruh/menyuruh:* to order)
2. Perdana Menteri sedang menantikan keréta beliau.
3. Penuntut-penuntut pensyarah itu suka mendengar syarahannya.
4. Pelajar-pelajar mesti menulis karangannya sebelum hari Sabtu. (*Sebelum:* before, by; *hari Sabtu:* Saturday)
5. Kotak kau sangat berat; apa ada di dalamnya?
6. Boléhkah encik mengajarku bercakap bahasa Melayu?
7. Syarahannya tidak berapa menarik hati.
8. Maktab ini amat besar; siapa akan menjalankannya?
9. Di mana buku-bukumu? Di dalam almari, Cikgu.
10. Engkau hendak menjual keréta kau kepadanya?

Exercise 34   Translate into Malay:
1. Where is my car? Your car is waiting for you outside the post office.

2. Where does your father work? He's a senior lecturer at the University.
3. He lectures on the Malay language; his lectures are very interesting.
4. My elder brother lectures on educational theory at the Day Training College.
5. Before you listen to his lectures, you must read this book.
6. His elder brother is a teacher in a national school.
7. Where did he buy his new car? He bought it in Singapore.
8. They are reading their new books.
9. Where is your college? It is in Kuala Lumpur.
10. My father works in the Government Secretariat.

Exercise 35
Write down ten sentences of your own, using what you have learned so far in this course.

Minggu Yang Kelima
Fifth Week

Pelajaran Yang Ketiga Belas
Lesson 13

Ganti Nama Diri 4: Awalan Ber- 1
Personal Pronouns 4: The Prefix Ber- 1

A. Sentences

Ahmad, di mana awak tinggal?	*Ahmad, where do you live?*
Saya tinggal di Bukit Tinggi, Cikgu.	*I live at Bukit Tinggi, sir.*
Murid-murid! Di mana telah kamu simpan buku-bukumu?	*Children! Where have you put your books?*
Kami telah menyimpannya dalam almari besar, Cikgu.	*We have put them in the big cupboard, sir.*
Yusuf, di mana buku engkau?	*Yusuf, where is your book?*
Buku saya di rumah, Cikgu.	*My book is at home, sir.*
Emak nak ke mana?	*Where are you going?* or: *where are you going, mother?*
Ahmad nak ke mana?	*Where are you off to, Ahmad?*
Ahmad nak ke pasar. Ke mana Yusuf?	*I'm off to the market. Where are you going, Yusuf?*
Tukang masak nak masak apa hari ini?	*What are you going to cook today, cookie?*
Di mana Cikgu mengajar?	*Where do you teach?*
Nak ke mana? Nak ke pasar.	*Where are you going? I'm going to the market.*
Di mana beli? Beli di Singapura.	*Where did you buy it? I bought it in Singapore.*
Orang ini bertopi, tetapi orang itu bersongkok.	*This man has a hat but that man has a songkok;* or: *this man is wearing a hat but that man is wearing a songkok.*
Kapal terbang itu berkipas, tetapi Concorde tak ada kipas.	*That aeroplane has propellers but the Concorde hasn't any propellers.*

Keréta sudah rosak; kita mesti bermalam di sini.	*The car has broken down; we must spend the night here.*
Bapa saya berkedai.	*My father has a shop;* or: *my father keeps a shop;* or: *my father is a shopkeeper.*
Kapal terbang itu berkipas dua.	*That aeroplane has two propellers.*
Orang Melayu itu bersongkok hitam.	*That Malay is wearing a black songkok.*
Gadis itu berbaju sutera.	*That girl is wearing a silk blouse.*
Méja itu berkaki enam.	*That table has six legs.*

B. Word List

Nouns

bukit	*hill*	topi	*hat*
tukang masak	*cook-boy*	kipas	*fan, propeller*
songkok	*Malay cap*	baju	*coat, jacket, shirt, blouse, dress*
malam	*night*	gadis	*girl, young woman*
sutera	*silk*		

Pronouns

awak	*you, your (sing.)*

Adjectives

hitam	*black*

Verbs

masak (memasak)	*to cook*	bermalam	*to spend the night*

Miscellaneous

di rumah	*at home*	nak ke	*to be off to*
enam	*six*		

C. Grammar

74 *Di mana awak tinggal?:* "Where do you live?" *Awak* and *engkau* are equal in value. Both mean "you" or "your" (singular) and both use *kamu* as their equivalent plural form. Now, *awak* and *engkau* are not very polite words for "you". They are used between very intimate friends who, in English, might address each other by their Christian names or with some such expression as "chum" or "old man", although, unlike "chum" and "old man", *awak* and *engkau* are not at all slangy; they are in fact practically identical in meaning with *tu* in French, *du* in German, or *nii* in Chinese. The plural form (i.e. the form used to address more than one person), *kamu*, is much the same as German *ihr* or Chinese *nümen*. Non-Malays should avoid using these three words to address anybody — even servants — to be on the safe side. One common place in which they may be used, however, is in school, where a teacher would address a single pupil as *engkau* or *awak* and the whole class as *kamu*. In replying, on the other hand, a single pupil would refer to himself as *saya* and the whole class would refer to themselves as *kami* (i.e. excluding the teacher) out of deference to the teacher. They would address the teacher as *Cikgu*. Study carefully the brief dialogue at the beginning of Section A above between a teacher and his pupils to see how this works. Although my advice is to avoid the use of these words until you are much more sure of yourself, you will have to know them because they are very common in written Malay — especially in the literature — both classical and modern.

75 *Emak nak ke mana?* "Where are you going (mother)?" The Malays often have the feeling that it is rude to use pronouns, and that it is better to use a person's name, title, or rank than to refer to him by a blunt "you" or "he". English people sometimes have the same feeling. I remember being scolded, when I was a small child, by my father for referring to my mother as "she" with a strong stress — something like *"she* did it". I was told to refer to my mother as "mother" or "mummy" and that to call her "she" was rude. In English, however, this really depends on the tone of voice in which the pronoun is uttered but a Malay would normally jib at calling his mother "engkau" or "awak", or even "encik". When referring to his mother in either the second or the third person, he would more normally call her *emak*, or, really politely, *bonda*. Now, this courtesy is extended in all directions and people are referred to by their names, titles or jobs, and in fact often use their own names instead of saying *saya* or *aku*. Study carefully the examples in Section A above.

76 *The* ber-*prefix — General:* The *ber*-prefix, like the *me*-prefix, is used to form verbs, but unlike the latter, which almost always forms transitive verbs, it normally forms *intransitive* verbs, although there are some important exceptions to this. The *ber*-prefix is usually added to nouns to turn them into verbs of a special kind and it has *two forms*. Firstly, if the root word either begins with *r*- or contains an *r*- in the first syllable, the prefix drops its own -*r*- and becomes simply *be*-, e.g.

rumah	*house*
berumah	*to own a house,* or *to live in a house*
kerja	*work*
bekerja	*to work*

In front of almost all other words, with one important exception, the full form *ber*- is used, e.g.

topi	*hat*
bertopi	*to wear a hat*
kipas	*propeller*
berkipas	*to have propellers*
malam	*night*
bermalam	*to spend the night*
kedai	*shop*
berkedai	*to keep a shop*

The important exception mentioned above is the root *ajar*. *Ajar* and its *me*-form *mengajar* mean "to teach". With the *ber*-prefix the word becomes *belajar* and then means "to learn". In other words, with this root the -*r*- of the *ber*-prefix is changed to -*l*-.

77 *The uses of the* ber-*prefix—General:* It is difficult to find a single way in English of rendering the *ber*-prefix, but its general function appears to be to reflect back to the subject of the word to which it is attached and to involve that subject personally in whatever action or state is being discussed. For futher details see the notes which follow in this lesson and those which follow it.

78 *Orang ini bertopi tetapi orang itu bersongkok:* "This man has a hat but that one has a songkok." When added to many nouns the *ber*-prefix denotes straightforward possession and is in fact one way of rendering the English verb "to have" into Malay. These possessive forms, however, cannot always be rendered by "to have" in English, and indeed the present example would be better translated by, "This man is wearing a hat but that one is wearing a songkok." Once again, study carefully the examples in Section A above to see how these various possessive *ber*-forms are to be translated into English.

79 *Bersongkok hitam: berkipas dua: berbaju sutera:* This possessive *ber*- can be added to phrases as well as to single words. The phrases are usually composed of (a) a noun with an adjective, (b) a noun with a numeral, or (c) a noun with another noun.

The examples above mean:

bersongkok hitam	*wearing a black songkok (noun + adjective)*
berkipas dua	*having two propellers (noun + numeral)*
berbaju sutera	*wearing a silk blouse (noun + noun)*

This structure of *ber*- plus a phrase is very common indeed both in speech and writing.

D. *Exercises*

Exercise 36 Add the correct form of the *ber*-prefix to the following words and phrases and try to guess the meaning of the result before checking your answer in the key:

(1) Kuda (horse)
(2) Jalan (road)
(3) Kasut (shoe)
(4) Pagar (fence)
(5) Tingkat tiga (three storey)
(6) Kain biru (blue sarong)

Exercise 37 Translate into English:
1. Gadis itu berbaju hitam dan berkasut putih.
2. Seorang berkuda telah masuk ke dalam kampung.
3. Di mana ia bekerja? Ia berkedai di pasar.
4. Bangunan ini bertingkat sepuluh.
5. Saya sangat suka belajar bahasa kebangsaan.
6. Semalam saya telah melihat seorang Melayu bersongkok putih.
7. Semalam kita bermalam di Kuala Langat.
8. Ia sangat suka berjalan kaki.
9. Concorde itu sebuah kapal terbang yang tidak berkipas.
10. Méja ini berkaki tiga.

Exercise 38 Translate into Malay:
1. He is wearing a green (*hijau*) songkok.
2. That table has four legs.
3. They are on horseback.
4. We shall spend the night in Singapore.
5. My elder sister will be wearing a white blouse and a blue sarong.
6. My house has two storeys.
7. That boy has no shoes on.
8. This aeroplane has six propellers.
9. Ahmad is learning English at school.
10. He walked from Ipoh to Kuala Kangsar.

Minggu Yang Kelima
Fifth Week

Pelajaran Yang Keempat Belas
Lesson 14

Awalan Ber-2
The Prefix Ber-2

A. Sentences

Siapa orang bertopi itu?	*Who's that man in the hat?*
Siapa orang berjanggut itu?	*Who's that man with the beard?*
Sebuah kapal terbang yang berkipas empat sudah sampai di lapangan terbang.	*A four-engined aircraft has arrived at the airport.*
Pesawah padi hendak menanam padinya minggu depan.	*The padi-planters will plant their rice next week.*
Orang yang berpedang itu seorang pegawai.	*That man with the sword is an officer.*
Orang berkeris itu seorang Melayu.	*That man with the kris is a Malay.*
Orang yang bersenapang itu seorang askar.	*That man with the gun is a soldier.*
Menteri Pelajaran sudah berkata bahawa kerajaan akan membangunkan sebuah Maktab Perguruan di bandar kita.	*The Minister of Education has said that the government will build a Teacher Training College in our town.*
Di dalam maktab itu semua penuntut akan belajar bercakap bahasa kebangsaan.	*In that college all the students will learn to speak the national language.*
Perdana Menteri sangat suka berjalan kaki.	*The Prime Minister is very fond of walking.*
Hari ini Perdana Menteri negeri Ruritania sudah tiba di lapangan terbang Kuala Lumpur.	*Today the Prime Minister of Ruritania arrived at Kuala Lumpur airport.*
Sebelum pergi ke Istana Teta-	*Before going to the Visitor's Palace,*

77

mu, Perdana Menteri Ruritania bercakap dua tiga minit dengan wartawan-wartawan.

the Ruritanian Prime Minister spoke for two or three minutes with journalists.

Beliau berkata bahawa beliau berharap perhubungan di antara dua buah negeri kita akan bertambah érat pada masa yang akan datang.

He said that he hoped that relations between our two countries would become even closer in the future.

Lepas itu beliau naik keréta pergi ke Istana Tetamu.

Afterwards he got into the car and went to the Visitor's Palace.

Sebab ramai orang menunggu menyambut beliau, keréta itu berjalan perlahan-lahan.

Because there were crowds of people waiting to welcome him, the car went slowly.

Pagi tadi saya lambat bangun; saya tak bercukur.

This morning I got up late; and I didn't have time to shave.

Sudah sampai pejabat, kerja tak banyak; jadi saya pergi ke kedai tukang cukur.

When I got to the office, there wasn't much work; so I went to a barber's shop.

Tukang cukur itu mencukur saya; lepas itu saya balik ke pejabat.

The barber shaved me and after that I went back to the office.

Ahmad sedang menjemur hamparan.

Ahmad is airing the carpets; or: *Ahmad is putting the carpets in the sun.*

Saya sangat suka berjemur di pantai.

I am very fond of sunbathing on the beach.

B. *Word List*

Nouns

janggut	*beard*	wartawan	*journalist*
sawah	*rice-field*	masa	*time*
padi	*rice (growing)*	pedang	*sword*
beras	*rice (uncooked)*	senapang	*gun*
nasi	*rice (cooked)*	pegawai	*officer, official*

keris	*kris (Malay dagger)*	istana	*palace*
askar	*soldier*	minit	*minute*
tetamu	*guest, visitor*	perhubungan	*relation, communication*
tukang	*workman*	tukang cukur	*barber*
pantai	*beach*	bendang	*rice-field*

Adjectives

erat	*close, tight, firm*

Verbs

berjanggut	*to have a beard*	bersawah	*to have a rice-field*
tanam (menanam)	*to plant*	berpedang	*to have a sword*
berkeris	*to have a kris*	bersenapang	*to have a gun*
berkata	*to say*	sambut (menyambut)	*to welcome*
berharap	*to hope*	bercukur	*to shave (intrans.)*
tunggu (menunggu)	*to wait*	balik	*to return*
bangun	*to get up*	berjemur	*to sunbathe*
cukur (mencukur)	*to shave (trans.)*	bertambah	*to increase*
jemur (menjemur)	*to dry in the sun*	tiba	*to arrive*

Miscellaneous

bahawa	*that (conj.)*	di antara	*between*
yang akan datang	*future (adj.)*	sebab	*because*
perlahan-lahan	*slowly*		
jadi	*so (conj.)*		

C. Grammar

80 *Siapa orang bertopi itu?:* The possessive *ber-*form dealt with in Lesson 13 (78-79) may be used adjectivally and will then have to be rendered differently into English. *Orang itu bertopi* means "that man is wearing a hat", i.e. the *bertopi* is being used as a verb; but *orang bertopi itu* means "that hat-wearing man" or rather "that man in the hat", i.e. the *bertopi* is being used as an adjective. *Janggut* is a noun meaning "beard" and so *berjanggut* as a verb means "to have a beard" but as an adjective it means "bearded". Similarly *berkipas empat* as a verb means "to have four propellers (or engines)", while as an adjective it means "four-engined". Study the first batch of examples in Section A above and notice the various ways in which these *ber-*forms are rendered into English.

81 *Beliau berkata...:* "He said that..." The word *bahawa* is being used more and more today to introduce a noun clause like the English conjunction *that*. It is not used much in speech, except in public speaking, but is very common in writing.

82 *Istana Tetamu:* "The Visitor's Palace." This is the palace in Kuala Lumpur which is normally placed at the disposal of very important personages when they make an official visit to Malaysia. *Istana* is the ordinary word for palace. His Majesty the *Yang Dipertuan Agung* lives in the *Istana Negara* (State Palace), which is also in Kuala Lumpur. *Tetamu* is a very polite or honorific word for *guest* or *visitor*.

83 *Wartawan:* This word, which means "journalist", comes from the Sanskrit *varttavan*, which means "one who has the news". The word for "news" in the newspaper or radio sense of the word is *warta berita,* which again comes from two Sanskrit words–*vartta* "event" and *vritta* "happening". From *berita* comes another Malay word– *pemberita* which means "a reporter."

84 *cukur/mencukur* and *bercukur: jemur/menjemur* and *ber-jemur:* There are some verbs which may have either the *me-*prefix or the *ber-*prefix with a slight difference in meaning according to which one is chosen. In some verbs the difference is the same as that between transitive and intransitive in English, although Malay is much more fussy about this distinction than English is. With the above two pairs, the *ber-*

forms are intransitive, i.e. the action is performed by the subject upon himself, and for this reason some people would call them reflexive verbs. *Bercukur*, then is "to shave oneself" and *berjemur* is to "sun oneself" and so "to sunbathe". *Cukur* and *mencukur* mean "to shave someone else", while *jemur* and *menjemur* mean "to sun someone else" or "to dry something in the sun". Study carefully the last batch of examples in Section A above.

85 *jadi*: *jadi* and *menjadi* are normally verb-forms meaning "to become", but the simple root *jadi* is also very commonly used nowadays in both speaking and writing to point out the result of some previous action, like the English conjunction "so".

D. *Exercises*

Exercise 39   Translate into English:
1. Perdana Menteri akan bercakap dengan pemberita-pemberita pada pukul sembilan.
2. Siapa wartawan yang bertopi hitam itu?
3. Ia telah tiba dengan kapal terbang yang berkipas dua.
4. Esok pagi kita hendak berjemur di pantai.
5. Ahmad mesti menjemur pakaian saya.
6. Beliau hendak pergi ke lapangan terbang menyambut Perdana Menteri.
7. Kereta-kereta berjalan perlahan-lahan.
8. Semalam di lapangan terbang saya telah melihat seorang pemberita yang berjanggut panjang.
9. Kalau dia tidak ada wang, tukang cukur tidak akan mencukurnya.
10. Di Kuala Lumpur ada sebuah bangunan yang bertingkat empat belas.

Exercise 40   Translate into Malay:
1. I always shave in the morning.
2. My father is ill; he wants me to shave him.
3. I sunbathed on the beach.
4. Ahmad has put the carpets in the sun.

5   The reporter said that the Prime Minister's aeroplane would arrive at five o'clock.
6   Last night I saw a picture called (*yang bernama*) "The Man in the White Suit".
7   I work in a seven-storeyed building in Kuala Lumpur.
8   Who is the pretty girl in the green dress?
9   Officers carry swords; but soldiers carry guns.
10 Who is that old Malay with the long kris?

Exercise 41
Write ten Malay sentences of your own using what you have already learned up to now.

Minggu Yang Kelima
Fifth Week

Pelajaran Yang Kelima Belas
Lesson 15

Awalan Ber- 3 dan Ulangkaji
The Prefix Ber- 3 and Revision

A. Sentences

Orang Melayu menanam padi pada musim hujan.	*The Malays plant rice in the rainy season.*
Orang itu bertanam padi.	*That man plants rice (i.e. for his living); or: that man is a rice-planter.*
Bapa saya berjual keréta.	*My father sells cars; or: my father is a car dealer; or: my father is a car salesman.*
Hari ini ia sudah menjual sebuah keréta besar kepada seorang taukéh Cina.	*Today he sold a big car to a Chinese towkay.*
Apa kamu belajar di sekolah ini?	*What do you learn in this school?*
Kami belajar menulis dan membaca, Cikgu.	*We learn to read and write, sir.*
Yusuf, apa lagi awak belajar?	*Yusuf, what else do you learn?*
Saya belajar ilmu hisab dan ilmu alam, Cikgu.	*I learn arithmetic and geography, sir.*
Di mana buku kau, Yusuf?	*Where is your book, Yusuf?*
Buku saya di rumah, Cikgu; saya lupa membawanya.	*My book is at home, sir; I forgot to bring it.*
Kalau kau tak membawa buku kau ke sekolah, bagaimana kau hendak belajar?	*If you don't bring your book to school, how are you going to learn?*
Orang itu bertopi hitam.	*That man has (or: wears) a black hat.*
Gadis cantik itu berbaju kuning.	*That pretty girl is wearing a yellow dress.*

Gadis berbaju sutera itu penuntut Maktab Perguruan Harian.	*That girl in the silk dress is a student of the Day Training College.*
Tiba-tiba seorang pegawai yang berpedang masuk ke bilik dia.	*Suddenly an officer with a sword entered his room.*
Saya hendak bercakap dengan dia esok.	*I will speak to him tomorrow.*
Saya berharap bahawa perhubungan di antara negeri kami dan negeri tuan akan bertambah érat pada masa yang akan datang.	*I hope that the relations between our country and yours will be even closer in the future.*
Dia berkata dia mesti menyambut bapanya di lapangan terbang.	*He said he had to meet his father at the airport.*
Bapa saya sangat suka berjalan kaki.	*My father is very fond of walking.*
Pagi tadi saya tak sempat bercukur.	*This morning I didn't have time to shave.*
Tukang cukur akan mencukur saya.	*The barber will shave me.*
Pada hari Sabtu yang lalu saya berjemur di pantai.	*Last Saturday I sunbathed on the beach.*
Hari-hari saya menjemur hamparan.	*Every day I dry the carpet in the sun.*
Saya berjual keréta di Kuala Lumpur.	*I sell cars in Kuala Lumpur;* or: *I am a car dealer in Kuala Lumpur.*
Semalam saya menjual sebuah keréta kepada seorang taukéh.	*Yesterday I sold a car to a towkay.*

B. Word List

Nouns

ulangkaji	*revision*	taukéh	*towkay; Chinese businessman*
musim hujan	*rainy season*	hujan	*rain*
musim	*season*		

Adjectives

kuning	*yellow*	yang lalu	*last, past*

Verbs

berjual	*to sell* (86)	bertanam	*to plant* (86)
lupa	*to forget*		

Miscellaneous

tiba-tiba	*suddenly*	bagaimana	*how*
		hari-hari	*every day*

C. Grammar

86 *Orang itu bertanam padi:* "That man is a rice-planter." There are a certain number of verbs which normally take the *me-*prefix and which are all transitive, but which remain transitive when the *me-*prefix is changed to *ber-*. In this case the *ber-*prefix indicates that the action mentioned is performed by the subject to *earn his living*, in other words he is personally involved in the action (cf. 77) to the extent that without it he might starve. In the other sentence—*Orang Melayu menanam padi pada musim hujan*—"The Malays plant rice in the rainy season"—however, we are speaking of the Malays in general, many of whom plant rice without it being their sole means of support; they may also grow rubber or work in an office, for instance. In such a sentence the *ber-*prefix would be out of place on *tanam*, and so the *me-*prefix is used instead. Compare the following pair of examples:

Bapa saya berjual keréta.
My father sells cars (*i.e.* that is his job).

Hari ini ia sudah menjual sebuah keréta besar kepada seorang taukéh Cina.
Today he sold a big car to a Chinese towkay.

The point here is that in the first sentence *berjual keréta* implies that if my father did not sell cars fairly regularly the whole family would find themselves on short commons! In the second sentence *menjual* is used because we are thinking of only one sale on one particular day, and although the manager of the car firm might have been displeased with my father for failing to sell that particular car to that particular towkay, my father is not likely to lose his job unless he starts making a habit of it!–Be careful with this construction, however, as not all verbs can indulge in this luxury of having what we might call "an ordinary" and "a professional" form. It is best just to learn such verbs as we go along. Where they occur in future lessons we shall point them out to you.

D. Exercises

Exercise 42   Translate into English:
1   Di mana dia bekerja? Dia bertanam padi di negeri Kedah.
2   Bila orang Melayu menanam padinya?
3   Meréka menanam padinya pada musim hujan.
4   Saya hendak menjual keréta saya kepada abang dia.
5   Saya hendak berjual keréta di Ipoh.
6   Kalau awak tidak bekerja, bagaimana awak hendak lulus dalam peperiksaan?
7   Pagi tadi ia lambat bangun; tak sempat bercukur.
8   Tukang cukur telah mencukurnya.
9   Siapa pegawai yang berpedang itu? Dia adik saya.
10 "Vickers Viscount" itu sebuah kapal terbang yang berkipas empat.

Exercise 43   Translate into Malay:
1   We are going to move to Ipoh ("to move", "to be transferred" is *berpindah*).

2 The bird (*burung*) perched (*hinggap*) on the fence.
3 He is very well off ("well off", "rich": *berada*).
4 My father is a horse-dealer.
5 Did you shave this morning? No, the barber will shave me.
6 Did you see the four-engined aircraft which (*yang*) arrived at the airport at six o'clock this morning?
7 Yes, I did. It was the Prime Minister's plane. I went to the airport to welcome him.
8 The Prime Minister told the reporters that he would speak to them tomorrow.
9 I am very fond of sunbathing.
10 Please put my clothes out in the sun.

Minggu Yang Keenam
Sixth Week

Pelajaran Yang Keenam Belas
Lesson 16

Bentuk Pasif dan Awalan Di- 1
The Passive Construction and the Prefix Di- 1

A. Sentences

Buku itu dibaca oléh Ahmad.	*That book is read by Ahmad.*
Surat ini ditulis oléh saya.	*This letter was written by me.*
Keréta itu dibeli oléh bapanya.	*That car was bought by his father.*
Pertunjukan itu akan diadakan minggu depan.	*The exhibition will be held next week.*
Maktab ini dijalankan oléh kerajaan.	*This college is run by the government.*
Saya telah dijemput oléh kerajaan bersyarah kepada penuntut-penuntut.	*I have been invited by the government to lecture to the students.*
Buku ini ditulis oléhnya.	*This book was written by him.*
Buku ini ditulisnya.	*This book was written by him.*
Calon ini sudah dipilih rakyat.	*This candidate has been elected by the people.*
Ia sudah dipilihnya.	*He has been elected by them.*
Encik Polan tidak dipilihnya.	*Mr So-and-So was not elected by them.*
Tahun lepas suatu pilihanraya telah diadakan kerajaan di seluruh negeri.	*Last year a general election was held by the government throughout the country.*
Sebab orang tidak percayakan ia, ia tidak dipilihnya.	*Because people did not trust him, he was not elected by them.*
Calon itu akan dipilih nampaknya.	*That candidate will be elected by the looks of it;* or: *it looks as if that candidate will be elected.*
Nampaknya, pertunjukan itu tidak akan diadakan.	*It looks as if the exhibition will not be held.*

Encik Anu seorang calon bébas agaknya.	*Apparently Mr So-and-So is an independent candidate;* or: *I think Mr So-and-So is an independent candidate.*
Ia sudah dijemput kerajaan agaknya.	*It seems he was invited by the government.*
Surat itu telah ditulis oléh Encik Ahmad.	*The letter has been written by Encik Ahmad.*
Buku itu telah dibacanya.	*The book has been read by him;* or: *the book was read by him.*
Buku itu belum dibacanya.	*The book has not been read by him.*
Buku itu tidak dibacanya.	*The book was not read by him.*

B. Word List

Nouns

bentuk	*form, shape*	rakyat	*the people*
calon	*candidate*	pilihanraya umum	*general election*
pilihanraya	*election*	pertunjukan	*exhibition*

Adjectives

pasif	*passive (gram.)*	bébas	*free, independent*
lepas	*last, previous*		

Verbs

adakan (mengadakan)	*to hold (e.g. a meeting)*	pilih (memilih)	*to elect, to choose*
percayakan	*to trust*	percaya	*to believe*

Miscellaneous

oléh	*by*	Encik Anu	*Mr So-and-So*

anu	*such-and-such (things)*	Si Polan	*So-and-So (persons)*
Si Anu	*So-and-So (persons)*	Encik Polan	*Mr So-and-So*
suatu	*one*	agaknya	*apparently*
nampaknya	*it seems*	di seluruh	*throughout*

C. Grammar

87 *The passive construction:* In this lesson we begin to deal with a grammatical feature which, in English grammar, goes by the name of "the passive voice", and for want of a better term we can use this expression for a certain Malay construction too, although the passive voice is not always used in Malay in exactly the same circumstances as it is in English. I shall, however, try to explain the differences in usage between the two languages later on in the course, and so for the moment you can take it that the usage is much the same.

First of all, let us get clear in our minds what the passive voice is. In such a sentence as "Ahmad reads the book" we have a subject– Ahmad – acting upon an object – the book. In other words the subject of such a sentence is the agent or active participant in the action. The form which the verb takes – "reads" in English and "membaca" in Malay – is said to be the active form or "voice" of the verb. Now, sometimes we turn the sentence round and say "the book is read by Ahmad" and in this sentence the original object – the book – has become the *grammatical* subject of the verb, while the original subject – Ahmad – has been shifted out of line as it were and is now neither the object nor the subject. The preposition "by" is placed in front of it instead, and this word "by" simply indicates that "Ahmad" is the agent of the action. In such a sentence the (original or logical) object is thought of as more important and the agent is added later, almost as an afterthought. Now, this kind of sentence is said to be *passive*, that is the object becomes the subject and the verb changes from the active form "reads" to what is called the passive form, which in English happens to be "is read" in this case.

The main difference between the active and the passive is that the active form tends to lay some emphasis on the subject, while the passive form pushes the real subject into the background and transfers the emphasis to the object. In fact the passive form enables us to avoid mention of the true subject altogether, as for example in such sentences as "this book is read everywhere" or "an exhibition will be held next week", where the important things are the book and the exhibition and nobody cares who does the reading or who will sponsor the exhibition. Such forms are particularly common in newspapers and official writing where the writer is, say, a public servant and has to express views which may not in fact be his own but those of his employers. For instance, instead of saying "I request you to pay your income tax within seven days", the tax collector is more likely to write *"You are requested* to pay your income tax within seven days". By doing so he is not necessarily being pompous, but rather he is keeping himself out of the quarrel, which is after all not his private war but a struggle between "you" and "the department". In such letters, too, the passive form is felt to be more polite, just because the matter is kept impersonal.

88   *Buku itu dibaca oléh Ahmad:* "That book is read by Ahmad." The passive form (*bentuk pasif*) in Malay is much easier to make than the corresponding English. Normally, only verbs which *can* take the *me-* prefix can be used in the passive, which is formed by prefixing *di-* to the *simple form* of the verb. The English preposition "by" is expressed by the Malay word *oléh*. The normal word order in such constructions is.—

*subject (*or *logical object) + di-verb + oleh + agent*

Of course, as in English, the agent (the *oléh*-phrase) can be omitted as in:

Suatu pertunjukan akan diadakan.
An exhibition will be held.

Calon kita sudah dipilih.
Our candidate has been elected.

89 *Calon ini dipilih rakyat:* "This candidate is elected by the people." The preposition *oléh* may be left out in the construction, although "by" in English cannot be so omitted. If *oléh* is left out, the agent must follow the verb *immediately* and no words may be inserted in between.

90 *Buku ini ditulisnya:* "This book was written by him." Notice that when the agent is a third person pronoun (masculine, feminine or neuter; or singular or plural) it may be expressed quite adequately by tacking the ubiquitous *-nya* on to the *di-*form of the verb. *Ditulisnya* can therefore mean "written by him, by her, (by it), by them" according to the context.

91 *Nampaknya:* "By the looks of it." This is a very useful idiomatic expression which can be tacked on to the end or the beginning of a sentence to express the English "it looks as if" or "to judge from appearances" and so on.

92 *Agaknya:* Literally "(by) the guess of it". Another expression like *nampaknya* (91). *Agaknya* means much the same as the English "it seems", or "I think" or "apparently".

93 *telah/belum* and *telah/tidak:* We said earlier (41) that *telah* was the classical form of *sudah* and was therefore used to form what might be described as a perfect tense, but we also said that it was commonly used in the modern written language to indicate a simple narrative past. When *telah* stands for *sudah* its negative form is *belum*, but when it merely forms a simple past tense its negative form is *tidak*. Study the examples in Section A above, and see "Speak Malay!", Lesson 36, pp. 123-125, for further details about *sudah* and *belum*.

D. Exercises

Exercise 44 Translate into English:
1 Ia tidak akan dipilih nampaknya.
2 Suatu pertunjukan gambar-gambar sedang diadakan sekarang di Kuala Lumpur.

3 Siapa orang yang bersongkok itu? Dia tidak dijemput.
4 Encik Polan akan dipilih rakyat nampaknya.
5 Si Anu seorang calon bebas agaknya.
6 Maktab kita akan dijalankan oléh kerajaan pada masa yang akan datang.
7 Agaknya suatu pilihanraya akan diadakan tahun depan.
8 Ahmad telah dicukur oléh tukang cukur.
9 Perdana Menteri telah disambut oléh Menteri Pelajaran.
10 Semua hamparan sedang dijemur.

Exercise 45 Translate into Malay:
1 This candidate has been elected.
2 A general election will be held throughout Malaysia.
3 Mr So-and-So will not be elected; people do not trust him.
4 This book will be read throughout the country.
5 This car cannot be sold before tomorrow.
6 This letter must be sent to him this very day.
7 He was chosen by them.
8 This letter was written by her.
9 This door was opened by Yusuf.
10 My room is being cleaned.

Exercise 46
Write down ten Malay sentences of your own using what you have so far learned.

Minggu Yang Keenam
Sixth Week

Pelajaran Yang Ketujuh Belas
Lesson 17

Bentuk Pasif 2
The Passive Construction 2

A. Sentences

Buku itu telah dibaca oléhku.	*That book has been read by me.*
Buku itu telah kubaca.	*That book has been read by me.*
Buku itu telah dibaca oléh kau.	*That book has been read by you.*
Buku itu telah kaubaca.	*That book has been read by you.*
Orang itu sudah kulihat.	*That man I have seen;* or: *that man has been seen by me.*
Orang itu sudah saya jemput.	*That man I have invited;* or: *that man has been invited by me.*
Keréta itu di mana encik beli?	*That car — where did you buy it?*
Sudah saya beli di Singapura.	*I bought it in Singapore.*
Encik mahukah membaca buku ini?	*Do you want to read this book?*
Tidak, buku itu sudah saya baca.	*No, I've read that book.*
Encik Polan telah dijemput oléh kerajaan melawat negeri ini.	*Mr So-and-So has been invited by the government to visit this country.*
Surat ini telah kutulis; surat itu tidak kutulis.	*This letter I wrote; that letter I did not write.*
Kertas ini telah saya pakai; kertas itu telah saya buang.	*This paper I have used; that paper I have thrown away.*
Hikayat Hang Tuah telah digambar; Hikayat Abdullah belum digambar.	*The Story of Hang Tuah has been filmed; the Story of Munshi Abdullah has not been filmed.*
Sebab dia tidak mendapat cukup undi, calon bébas tidak dipilih.	*Because he did not get enough votes, the independent candidate was not elected.*
Pertunjukan itu akan dibuka	*The exhibition will be opened by the*

oléh pengarah jabatan.	*director of the department.*
Encik Anu telah dipilih sebagai pengarah.	*Mr So-and-So has been chosen as director.*
Saya hendak menunjukkan rumahnya kepada encik.	*I'll point his house out to you.*
Sudah encik tunjukkan semalam.	*You pointed it out yesterday.*

B. Word List

Nouns

hikayat	*story, epic, romance*	undi	*vote*
pengarah	*director*		

Verbs

buang (membuang)	*to throw away, to discard*
gambar (menggambar)	*to photograph, to film*
undi (mengundi)	*to vote (for)*
tunjukkan (menunjukkan)	*to show, to point out*

Miscellaneous

cukup	*enough*	sebagai	*as*

C. Grammar

94 *Buku itu telah kubaca:* "That book has been read by me." (Alternative form: *buku itu telah dibaca oléhku.*) In Lesson 12 (66-67) we learned the abbreviated forms of the personal pronouns *aku* (*ku-* and *ku-*) and *engkau* (*kau* and *kau-*), but until now we have confined ourselves to using them as suffixes, that is as objectival and possessive pronouns. Now, *ku-* and *kau-* (meaning "I" and "you"), but *not -mu*, which is short for *kamu* "you", can also be used as *subject* pronouns in a construction, which, for practical purposes is best lumped together with the passive construction which we studied in Lesson 16.

Now, this is one of the places in which the Malay use of the passive is different from the English usage. In English, sentences like "that book has been read by me" and "that book has been read by you" sound rather stiff and unnatural, but in Malay the equivalent *"buku itu telah kubaca"* and *"buku itu telah kaubaca"* are perfectly normal in writing and even in colloquial Malay as *"buku tu dah kubaca"* and *"buku tu dah kaubaca"* they sound quite natural.

In English we should more naturally say something like "*that* book I have *read*" or "*that* book you have *read*". (The italic type indicates heavy stress.) In other words, in order to put emphasis upon the object rather than upon the subject or agent we bring the object to the beginning of the sentence and make use of an emphatic intonation in order to push the real subject or agent into the background. In the sentence "I have read that book" there is no special emphasis on any of the words, but in "that book has been read by me" and even more so in "*that* book I have *read*" the stress goes very definitely on the logical object and perhaps on the action too, but is taken away from the logical subject or agent. In English this kind of inverted sentence is rather unusual, especially in writing, but in Malay it is very common indeed.

When a Malay wants to emphasise any word or group of words, he frequently places them at the beginning of the sentence. Now, if the word so treated happens to be the object of some verb or other — and this is very common — then that object finds itself standing where the subject would normally be, and almost automatically the passive construction is called into use.

You will remember that we said in the last lesson that the main function of the passive in both English and Malay is to push the agent or true subject into the background: this, then, is the effect of using forms like *kubaca* and *kaubaca*. Notice that in such forms the verb has neither the *di-*prefix nor *me-*prefix when the true subject is first or second person — that is when it is "I", "we" or "you". Instead of *ku-* and *kau* we may use the longer forms *aku* and *engkau* and even any other words meaning "I", "we" or "you". E.g.

Buku itu sudah engkau baca.
That book you have read.

Buku itu sudah tuan baca.
That book you have read, sir.

Buku itu sudah kita baca.
That book we have read.

95 *Orang itu sudah saya jemput:* "That man I have invited" or "that man has been invited by me" or "I have *invited that man*". If you prefer it, you may consider these forms as active instead of passive: it is indeed merely a matter of opinion what we should call them. Whatever we decide to call them, the forms remain and they carry the same meaning; and since that meaning is much the same as that of the passive — *i.e.* they push the subject into the background — then I personally think that they are better thought of as passive.

Now, *ku-* and *kau-* are joined in writing to the words to which they are prefixed, and this shows us that nothing can be inserted between *ku-* and *kau-* and their verb: not even *tidak* meaning "not". The same applies in this construction to the other first and second person pronouns *saya, kita, kami, kamu* and so forth, so that strictly speaking just as we cannot say, for example, *orang itu ku-tidak kenal* but should rather say *orang itu tidak kukenal* ("that man I don't know"), neither can we say *orang itu saya tidak kenal* but rather we should say *orang itu tidak saya kenal*. This is the rule in writing at least, although in conversation it is frequently not adhered to. In writing, if we want to put something in between the agent and the verb, the verb must have the *me-*prefix, assuming it is one of the verbs which can have it. We must say, therefore, either *saya tidak membaca buku itu* or *buku itu tidak saya baca*, according to the type of emphasis we want the sentence to have.

96 *Di mana keréta encik? Sudah saya jual:* "Where's your car? I've sold (it)." The passive construction is always preferred in Malay if the object comes in front of the verb, even if it is not actually expressed in the sentence, but has perhaps been mentioned earlier in the

conversation, say, one or two sentences before, as in the above example. In the above example — *sudah saya jual* — the word "it" is not expressed by any *word* in the Malay sentence, but it is *implied by that choice of the passive construction*. If the original question has been, say, *siapa yang menjual kereta encik?* ("Who was it who sold your car?"), the answer would have needed a stressed subject because it is the subject or agent of the action of selling which is being questioned and the passive construction would have been out of place. Furthermore the English "it" in such an answer as *"my brother* sold it" would have to be *expressed* by a *word* — *-nya* — in the Malay, viz. *abang saya yang menjualnya.*

This probably seems rather complicated, but I think that if you study the examples in Section A above carefully and compare the Malay sentences with the English translations given, you will at least see how the construction *works*. As you become more familiar with the language you will begin to see when to choose between the active and the passive forms. Let me just remind you here that the basic difference is that the active forms lay stress on the subject — if at all; while the passive forms lay the emphasis either on the action itself, or on the object, or upon both. For the time being you will be fairly safe if you use the Malay passive in more or less the same contexts as English uses its own passive forms, and also use it when the object is strongly emphasised and comes first in the sentences. Very often the difference is very slight and amounts to little more than a matter of style or of personal taste.

D. Exercises

Exercise 47 Translate into English:
1. Di mana buku saya? Sudah saya simpan dalam almari besar.
2. Calon itu orang jahat. Tidak akan kita pilih.
3. Perdana Menteri telah kulihat; Menteri Pelajaran belum kulihat.
4. Kereta besar ini — di mana tuan beli?

5 Sudah saya beli di Singapura.
6 Buku setebal itu tidak boléh saya baca.
7 Ahmad telah kujemput; Hamid belum kujemput.
8 Sudahkah tuan membeli buah rambutan? Sudah, sudah saya beli pagi tadi.
9 Bila saudara hendak menulis surat itu? Sudahlah saya tulis; ini dia.
10 Sudahkah encik melawat pertunjukan gambar-gambar di Dewan Tunku Abdul Rahman? Ya, sudah saya lawat semalam.

Exercise 48   Translate into Malay:
1 This car I have sold to Ahmad's father.
2 This book you have read; that book you have not read.
3 The exhibition has been filmed by Mr So-and-So.
4 An independent candidate will not be voted for by me.
5 When are you going to buy the rice, mother? I have bought it.
6 When did you buy it? I bought it this morning.
7 I don't think he will be elected (use *agaknya*).
8 Who wrote this letter? I wrote it, sir.
9 Who visited the exhibition? The Prime Minister visited it.
10 Next week an exhibition will be held by the government in the Tunku Abdul Rahman Hall in Kuala Lumpur.

Exercise 49
Make up ten sentences of your own in Malay using what you have so far learned during the course.

Minggu Yang Keenam / Sixth Week

Pelajaran Yang Kedelapan Belas / Lesson 18

Bentuk Pasif 3
The Passive Construction 3

A. Sentences

Perdana Menteri telah dijemput melawat negeri Ruritania.	*The Prime Minister has been invited to visit Ruritania.*
Perdana Menteri negeri Ruritania yang menjemputnya.	*It is the Prime Minister of Ruritania who invited him.*
Di negeri Ruritania beliau akan melawat Présiden Polan.	*In Ruritania he will visit President So-and-So.*
Lepas melawat Présiden, beliau akan membuka suatu pertunjukan.	*After visiting the President, he will open an exhibition.*
Pertunjukan itu pertunjukan gambarfoto.	*It's an exhibition of photographs.*
Pertunjukan itu akan diadakan oléh Kerajaan Malaysia.	*The exhibition will be run by the Malaysian Government.*
Calon kita tak mendapat banyak undi; ia tidak dipilih.	*Our Candidate did not get many votes; he was not elected.*
Tetapi kita berharap bahawa dalam pilihanraya umum yang akan diadakan tahun depan ia akan dipilih oléh rakyat.	*But we hope that in the general election to be held next year he will be elected by the people.*
Pengarah pilihanraya telah berkata bahawa suatu pilihanraya akan diadakan di bandar kita pada bulan depan.	*The director of elections has said that an election will be held in our town next month.*
Kalau calon kita dipilih oléh rakyat, tentulah ia hendak bekerja kuat.	*If our candidate is elected by the people, he will certainly work hard.*
Bahasa kebangsaan mesti di-	*The national language must be used*

gunakan di seluruh tanahair kita.	*throughout our native land.*
Semua surat mesti ditulis dalam bahasa kebangsaan.	*All letters must be written in the national language.*
Gambar itu belum kulihat.	*That film — I haven't seen (it) yet.*
Ia membuka buku lalu dibacanya.	*He opened the book and read it.*
Ia belajar bahasa kebangsaan lalu digunakannya.	*He learned the national language and then used it.*
Saya membuka buku lalu membacanya.	*I opened the book and read it.*
Ia memasak nasi lalu dimakannya.	*She cooked the rice and (then) ate it.*
Ia membeli hadiah lalu diberinya kepada anak perempuannya.	*He bought a present and (then) gave it to his daughter.*
Ia melihat gambar lalu ditunjukkannya kepada kawannya.	*He looked at the picture and (then) showed it to his friends.*
Ia menutup buku lalu disimpannya dalam almari.	*He closed the book and (then) put it away in the cupboard.*
Ia membuat téh lalu diminumnya.	*He made tea and (then) drank it.*
Ia mengoyakkan kertas lalu dibuangnya.	*He tore up the paper and threw it away.*
Saya menutup buku saya lalu menyimpannya dalam almari.	*I closed my book and put it away in the cupboard.*
Saya membeli hadiah lalu memberinya kepada dia.	*I bought a present and gave it to him.*
Buku ini sedang dibaca oléh semua penuntut kita.	*This book is being read by all our students.*
Buku itu belum dibacanya.	*That book has not yet been read by him;* or: *he hasn't read* that *book.*

Surat itu mesti tuan tulis hari ini.	*That letter must be written by you today, sir;* or: *you must write that letter today, sir.*

B. Word List

Nouns

présiden	*president*	air	*water*
tanahair	*native land*	hadiah	*present, prize*
téh	*tea*		

Verbs

beri (memberi)	*to give*	minum	*to drink*

Miscellaneous

lalu	*and then*

C. Grammar

97 *Ia membuka buku lalu dibacanya:* "He opened the book and read it." Here we have a useful and common construction in which the active and passive forms are combined in one sentence. The same subject or agent is performing two *consecutive* actions upon the same object. The Malay structure, however, is totally different from the English. In English we simply use two main verbs (*opened* and *read*) and join them together with the conjunction "and". If the object is a noun, it is placed after the first main verb and is repeated by means of a suitable pronoun (in this case "it") after the second verb. The Malay structure begins with *subject + active verb + noun-object* (*ia membuka buku*); this is then joined to the second part by the conjunction *lalu*, which means "and then" or "and next" (*dan*, "and", would be wrong in this construction). The main verb in the second part of the Malay sentence, however, goes into the passive form, to which the suffix *-nya* is added to repeat the *subject* or *agent* and the object remains unexpressed, although it is implied by the choice of the passive

form. As we saw in Lesson 17 (96) the passive form of the verb is preferred if the object precedes the verb, and this construction is a good example of this. In the first half of the sentence the object (*buku*) follows the verb (*membuka*) and so the verb is normally in the active form with a *me*-prefix where applicable, but by the time we get to the second verb the object has already been mentioned and therefore this time *precedes* the verb. The passive form is therefore the appropriate one.

This construction is very common indeed when the subject is a noun or a third person pronoun (he, she, it, they), but, although possible, it is less common when the subject is a first or second person pronoun (I, you, we). In the latter case the more normal structure is:

subject + active verb + object + lalu + active verb + -nya

for example:

Saya membuka buku lalu membacanya.
I opened the book and read it.

Study carefully the examples in Section A above.

98 *Perdana Menteri negeri Ruritania yang menjemputnya:* "It is (was) the Prime Minister of Ruritania who invited him." Notice how the subject can be emphasised in Malay by following it with *yang*. The verb in such a sentence *must* have the *me*-prefix if possible. In English we achieve the same degree of emphasis by using the structure "it is (was etc.) *the subject* who ... "

D. Exercises

Exercise 50 Translate into English:
1 Ia mengupas buah rambutan itu lalu dimakannya.
2 Ia membaca surat itu lalu dimasukkannya ke dalam fail.
3 Ahmad menulis surat lalu dihantarnya kepada Hamid.
4 Ia mencuci bajunya lalu disimpannya dalam almari.
5 Ia mengambil baju lalu dipakainya.

6   Saya membaca surat lalu menunjukkannya kepada Ahmad.
7   Saya menyambut Encik Hamid di lapangan terbang lalu membawanya ke rumah saya.
8   Ia berjumpa dengan Ali lalu dibawanya ke rumahnya.
9   Ia melihat sebuah buku baharu lalu dibelinya.
10   Meréka membuat kopi lalu diberinya kepada kawannya.

Exercise 51   Translate into Malay:
1   By the look of it an election will be held next year.
2   I think Mr So-and-So will be the Minister of Education.
3   Three cars are sold by him every day.
4   He has been invited to lecture to the students of our college.
5   Dollah rolled up the carpet and picked it up.
6   He drew a picture and showed it to me.
7   Afterwards I drew a picture and showed it to him.
8   She looked for her blouse and put it on.
9   It was Hamid who wrote the letter to the Minister of Education.
10   It is Encik Ali's father who sells cars in Singapore.

Exercise 52
Write ten Malay sentences using what you have learned so far.

Minggu Yang Ketujuh
Seventh Week

Pelajaran yang Kesembilan Belas
Lesson 19

Awalan Ter- 1
The Prefix Ter- 1

A. Sentences

Ia telah terjatuh tangga.	*He has fallen downstairs.*
Saya terlupa membawa buku saya.	*I forgot to bring my book.*
Ia sudah masuk "Foreign Legion" hendak melupakan isterinya.	*He has joined the Foreign Legion to forget his wife.*
Tiba-tiba teringatlah ia.	*Suddenly he remembered.*
Gadis cantik itu tersenyum kepada dia.	*The pretty girl smiled at him.*
Terkejutlah dia!	*He did get a fright!*
Malam semalam saya duduk di rumah mendengar radio.	*Last night I stayed at home and listened to the radio.*
Tiba-tiba saya terdengar bunyi suaranya.	*Suddenly I heard the sound of his voice.*
Saya mendengar semuanya menyanyi.	*I heard them all sing.*
Saya terdengar semuanya menyanyi.	*I heard them all singing.*
Bila saya terjatuh tangga, ia pun tertawa.	*When I fell down the stairs, he burst out laughing.*
Pagi tadi kerétanya terlanggar kereta orang lain.	*This morning his car collided (with) someone else's.*
Kerétanya tersimpang.	*His car went off at a tangent (i.e. it ran off the road,* or: *swerved).*
Tiba-tiba saya terlihat seorang kawan saya.	*Suddenly I saw a friend of mine;* or: *suddenly I caught sight of a friend of mine.*
Saya tidak terangkat tong ini.	*I can't lift this box.*

105

Tong ini tidak terangkat.	*This box can't be lifted.*
Tandatangannya tiada terbaca.	*His signature cannot be read;* or: *his signature is illegible.*
Ramailah orang di sana — tiada terbilang.	*There were crowds of people there — they could not be counted;* or: *there were countless crowds of people there.*
Ia mencuba hendak mencabut tiang itu, tetapi tiada tercabut.	*He tried to pull out the pole, but it couldn't be pulled out.*
Masa ia memotong daging, jarinya terluka.	*While he was cutting the meat, he cut his finger.*
Gulai sebanyak itu encik tidak termakan.	*You cannot eat as much curry as that;* or: *you'll never eat all that curry.*
Masa dia makan itik yang ditembaknya, termakanlah ia sebiji peluru.	*While he was eating the duck which he had shot, he (accidentally) ate a piece of shot.*

B. Word List

Nouns

tangga	*ladder, stairs*	**isteri**	*wife*
radio	*radio*	**bunyi**	*sound*
suara	*voice*	**tanda**	*sign, mark*
tandatangan	*signature*	**tiang**	*pole, post, pillar*
daging	*meat, flesh*	**jari**	*finger*
itik	*duck*	**peluru**	*bullet, shot*
simpang	*crossroads*		

Verbs

jatuh	*to fall*	**bilang** (membilang)	*to count*
lupa	*to forget*		
lupakan (melupakan)	*to forget (deliberately)*	**cuba** (mencuba)	*to try*

tertawa	*to laugh*	potong (memotong)	*to cut (off)*
langgar (melanggar)	*to run into, to ram*	lukakan (melukakan)	*to injure*
témbak (menémbak)	*to shoot*	tersimpang	*to swerve, to go off at a tangent, to run off (the road)*
terjatuh	*to fall*	terlupa	*to forget*
tersenyum	*to smile*	cabut (mencabut)	*to pull out, to extract*
terkejut	*to be startled*	terlanggar	*to collide with, to run over*
terluka	*to be injured, to be cut (wounded)*		

Miscellaneous

semuanya	*all of them, all of it*	orang lain	*other people, someone else*
tiada	*not*	masa (conj.)	*while*

C. Grammar

99 *Ia telah terjatuh tangga:* "He has fallen downstairs." In this lesson we begin the study of another useful and important prefix — the prefix *ter-*. Like the prefix *ber-* (q.v. Lesson 13 (76) above), the *ter-* prefix loses its *-r-* if the root to which it is added either begins with *-r-* or contains an *-r-* in the first syllable. Like the *ber-*prefix, too, the *ter-*prefix usually forms verbs and also participles or verbal adjectives. The *ter-*prefix varies in meaning according to the kind of sentence or phrase it occurs in, and also according to the whole situational context.

Most of the verbs which we have had so far have described what we may call "deliberate" actions, like "reading", "buying", "selling", "going", and so on. Such actions are nearly always performed with conscious thought and rarely happen by accident. Some actions, however, like "falling", "forgetting", "remembering" and so forth are usually either accidental or involuntary. Nobody falls on purpose, for instance. Such verbs in Malay almost always have the *ter*-prefix, one of whose functions is to show that an action is either accidental or involuntary. *Jatuh* (to fall), for example, does occur in its simple form — especially in speech — but, in writing at least, it usually has the *ter*-prefix, thus: *terjatuh*. Similarly *lupa* (to forget) *can* occur by itself, but is better with the *ter*-prefix — *terlupa*, because forgetting is usually involuntary. (See below, however, 100).

100 *Ia sudah masuk "Foreign Legion" hendak melupakan isterinya:* "He has joined the Foreign Legion to forget his wife." In this sentence the forgetting is obviously deliberate. The man has joined the Foreign Legion with the declared intention of forgetting his wife, and this is emphasised in the Malay version (a) by using *hendak* and (b) by using another derivative of *lupa* — *lupakan* with its *me*-form *melupakan*. *Terlupa* would be quite wrong in this sentence.

101 *Tiba-tiba teringatlah ia:* "Suddenly he remembered." Perhaps because such involuntary actions often cause surprise, it frequently happens that *ter*-verbs are emphasised in Malay by inverting the verb and its subject and adding the emphatic particle -*lah* to the verb as in this sentence and several others in Section A above.

102 *Saya duduk di rumah mendengar radio: Saya terdengar bunyi suaranya:* "I stayed at home and listened to the radio" and "I heard the sound of his voice." Here the difference between the *ter*-verb and the ordinary verb is brought out very clearly. *Listening* is normally deliberate while *hearing* is usually accidental (but see below 103). While "I" was listening (*mendengar*) to the radio, I suddenly heard or caught (*terdengar*) the sound of his voice. In this context *mendengar* implies a continuous process which, to some extent at least, must have been deliberate, while *terdengar* implies a *sudden* and *involuntary* awareness of "his voice".

103 *Saya mendengar semuanya menyanyi: Saya terdengar semuanya menyanyi:* "I heard them all sing" and "I heard them all singing". In the first sentence deliberateness is implied by the choice of the *me*-form of *dengar*. The sentence might be said, for instance, by an

impresario who had been auditioning a number of singers, or, perhaps, a choir. He deliberately sat down and said, "Right! Start singing." and then listened. The sentence could equally well be rendered in English by "I listened to them all sing(ing)." In the second sentence, however, the implication is that, while I was in the middle of doing someting else, I suddenly became aware that there were a lot of people singing and this has forced the choice of the *ter*-form, *terdengar*.

104 *Kerétanya terlanggar keréta orang lain:* "His car crashed into someone else's." Cars do not normally crash on purpose and so this word usually has the *ter*-prefix, especially when the accidental nature of the crash is uppermost in the speaker's mind. The *ber*-form, *berlanggar* can also be used, but in this case the preposition *dengan* must be used, thus:

> *Kerétanya berlanggar dengan keréta orang lain:*
> His car collided with someone else's (the implication being that the blame was equally shared by both drivers).

The *me*-form of *langgar* would imply a deliberateness and hostility out of place in a decent law-abiding motorist! *Langgar* and *melanggar* would, however, be appropriate in wartime when describing, say, an attack by a destroyer on a submarine, thus:

> *Kapal pembinasa itu melanggar kapal selam lalu dikaramkannya.*
> The destroyer *rammed* the submarine and sank it.

Note: *kapal pembinasa:* destroyer; *kapal selam:* submarine; *karamkan* and *mengaramkan:* to sink (transitive).

105 *Tandatangannya tiada terbaca:* "His signature is illegible". Another use of the *ter*-form is to indicate possibility, or rather, since in this usage the verb is usually negative, impossibility. Often such forms, combined with *tidak* or *tiada,* correspond roughly to English adjectives beginning with *in-* or *un-* and ending with *-able* or *-ible*. *Tiada terbaca* may mean therefore, according to the word order and context, either *cannot read* or *illegible (unreadable)*. Similarly, *tiada terbilang* means *cannot be counted, uncountable* or *countless*.

D. Exercises

Exercise 53   Translate into English:
1. Tiba-tiba terdengarlah saya suara orang menyanyi.
2. Ia terlanggar seorang budak lalu melukannya.
3. Orang jahat itu melanggar mata-mata lalu dibunuhnya (*mata-mata:* policeman; *bunuh:* to kill, murder).
4. Dua buah kapal laut telah berlanggar di Singapura.
5. Kerétanya tersimpang lalu terjatuh ke dalam parit (ditch).
6. Sebuah kapal pembinasa telah dikaramkan oléh kapal selam.
7. Banyaklah makanan ini! Tiada termakan.
8. Janganlah kita melupakan tanahair kita ini.
9. Di mana buku kau, Yusuf? Terlupalah saya membawanya, Cikgu.
10. Tiba-tiba saya terlihat Ahmad bekerja di bendangnya.

Exercise 54   Translate into Malay:
1. He smiled at me.
2. I was startled by hearing the voice.
3. I cannot walk any further.
4. Be careful (*hati-hati*)! You'll (*awak nanti*) fall down the stairs!
5. He was killed by a car which ran off the road and fell into the ditch.
6. The two cars collided and ran off the road.
7. Ahmad shot the officer and wounded him.
8. This letter is illegible.
9. This book is unreadable, but I *must* read it before the examination.
10. The officer was startled to see the Prime Minister's signature at the bottom of (*di bawah*) the letter.

Exercise 55
Write ten sentences in Malay using what you have learned so far.

Minggu Yang Ketujuh
Seventh Week

Pelajaran Yang Kedua Puluh
Lesson 20

Awalan Ter- 2
The Prefix Ter- 2

A. *Sentences*

Buku ini tertulis oléh anak lelaki saya.	*This book was written by my son.*
Ia terpaksa pergi ke Singapura.	*He was forced to go to Singapore.*
Pegawai itu sedang membawa pedang terhunus.	*That officer is carrying a drawn sword.*
Buku ini ditulis oléh anak lelaki saya.	*This book was written by my son.*
Ia dipaksa pergi ke Singapura.	*He was forced to go to Singapore.*
Pegawai itu sedang membawa pedang yang dihunusnya.	*That officer is carrying the sword which he drew.*
Saya sudah membuka pintu; pintu itu sekarang sudah terbuka.	*I have opened the door; the door is now opened.*
Ia sudah menutup pintu; pintu itu sekarang tertutup.	*He has closed the door; the door is now closed.*
Lakonan "Macbeth" itu tertulis oléh William Shakespeare.	*The play "Macbeth" was written by William Shakespeare.*
Kita akan menéngok sebuah lakonan yang tertulis oléh Bernard Shaw.	*We are going to see a play written by Bernard Shaw.*
Buku ini terkarang oléh Encik Ismail.	*This book was compiled by Encik Ismail.*
Makna ayat ini tersembunyi.	*The meaning of this sentence is hidden.*
Ia seorang pengarang yang masyhur.	*He is a famous author.*
Ia seorang pengarang yang termasyhur sekali di dalam dunia.	*He is one of the most famous authors in the world.*

Rumah itu rumah yang terbesar sekali.	*That is an extremely large house.*
Ia datang lambat.	*He came late.*
Ia datang terlambat.	*He came too late.*

B. Word List

Nouns

lakonan	*play, drama*	ayat	*sentence (gram.)*
pengarang	*author, writer*	dunia	*world*

Adjectives

tertulis	*written*	terhunus	*drawn, unsheathed*
terbuka	*open*	tertutup	*closed*
terkarang	*compiled, composed*	tersembunyi	*hidden*
masyhur	*famous*	termasyhur	*very famous*
terbesar	*extremely large*	terlambat	*too late*

Verbs

terpaksa	*to be forced, to be compelled*	paksa	*to force*
karang (mengarang)	*to compile, to write (books)*	hunus (menghunus)	*to draw (sword) to unsheath*
sembunyikan (menyembunyikan)	*to hide (trans.)*	bersembunyi	*to hide (intrans.)*

C. Grammar

106 *Buku ini tertulis oleh anak lelaki saya:* "This book was written by my son." Here we have what we may call the "participial" or "adjectival" use of the *ter*-prefix. In English we make great use of what is called the *past participle* of verbs — that is the form which usually has some part of the verb *to have* in front of it; for instance: "I

have *written*", "I have *sung*", "we have *broken*", "he has *taken*", and so on, where *written, sung, broken,* and *taken* are called *past participles*. A participle is that part of a verb which can also be used as an adjective: for instance in English we can talk of a *written* report or a *broken* cup. In Malay there are not true participles and almost any verb form is capable of being used adjectivally if it makes sense and the circumstances warrant it. Many verbs with the *ter-*prefix, however, correspond very often to English past participles. For examples see the sentences in Section A and the word list in Section B of this lesson.

107 *Buku ini ditulis* (or: *tertulis*) *oléh anak lelaki saya:* "This book was written by my son." Here we have (apparently) two ways of saying the same thing. There is, however, a slight difference between them. The *di-*verb lays great emphasis on the action itself, while the *ter-*verb is more concerned with the result of the action than with the action itself. In such a sentence as *buku ini tertulis oléh anak lelaki saya* we are more interested in the fact that the book is there in front of us than in the great labour of writing it. In the other sentence — *buku ini ditulis oléh anak lelaki saya* — we are more interested in the energy and industry of the writer of the book than in the book itself. "Look at my son and see how clever he is! He's actually written a book!" There is, however, not such a great difference in the Malay as is suggested by the English, which I have exaggerated in order to show the direction in which the two forms tend; we might equally well find either *tertulis* or *ditulis* on the title page of the book.

108 *Ia terpaksa* (or: *dipaksa*) *pergi ke Singapura:* "He was compelled to go to Singapore." Cf. 107 above: the difference here is greater. If we use *terpaksa*, all we are interested in is the fact that, for some reason or other unknown to us, "he" finds himself in the position of having to go to Singapore. If we use *dipaksa*, on the other hand, we are putting great emphasis on the compulsion — that is the act of compelling — rather that upon the result of it. In this particular case we can almost see someone sticking a pistol in the poor fellow's back and saying, "You will go to Singapore — *or else!*"

A similar difference of emphasis exists also between *pegawai itu sedang membawa pedang terhunus* and *pegawai itu sedang membawa pedang yang dihunusnya*. In the first sentence the use of *terhunus* focuses attention on the sword itself: we are not interested in who drew the sword; all we care about is that the sword is there before our eyes *out of its scabbard*. In other words we are thinking about the nakedness of the sword, and the action which led to it. In the second sentence, however, the use of *dihunusnya* suggests that we are more interested in the action than in the result; the sentence suggests that we actually witnessed the drawing of the sword, and that action has impressed us more than the fact that the man is now parading about with a naked sword.

Such subtle differences of emphasis are, of course, more a matter of style and personal feeling than of grammar and the student need not worry too much about them until he feels much more sure of himself.

109 *Ia seorang pengarang yang termasyhur:* "He is a very famous author." When prefixed to an adjective *ter-* often indicates a strengthening or intensifying of the meaning of the adjective and amounts, roughly, to the English "very" or "extremely". Study the examples in Section A and Section B above.

D. *Exercises*

Exercise 56   Translate into English:
1. Encik Ali sedang mengarang sebuah buku dalam bahasa kebangsaan.
2. Buku yang saya beli kelmarin itu terkarang oléh seorang pengarang Melayu yang termasyhur.
3. Pegawai yang membawa pedang terhunus itu masuk ke dalam bilik Yusuf lalu dibunuhnya.
4. Ia menghunus pedangnya lalu membunuh musuhnya (*musuh:* enemy).
5. Ia membunuh musuhnya dengan pedang yang baharu dihuhusnya.

6. Ia hendak menengok lakonan di Kuala Lumpur, tetapi terlambatlah ia.
7. Ia mencari makna tersembunyi di dalam surat itu, tetapi tidak didapatinya (*dapati/mendapati:* to find).
8. Tertawalah ia melihat buku tertulis oleh anak lelakinya.
9. "Hikayat Hang Tuah" itu sebuah karangan yang termasyhur di dalam kesusasteraan Melayu (*kesusasteraan:* literature).
10. Pintu sudah tertutup sekarang; kita tidak boleh masuk.

Exercise 57   Translate into Malay:
1. The senior officer carries a drawn sword.
2. His writing (*tulisan*) is almost (*hampir-hampir*) illegible.
3. He arrived too late.
4. He is a very famous journalist.
5. The officer compelled him to write a letter.
6. He was forced by the officer to write a letter.
7. I was forced to shoot because he was going to kill me.
8. My father has bought a great big car.
9. This letter was written by a friend of mine; it was a friend of mine who wrote it.
10. This book was written by my old teacher.

Exercise 58
Write down ten Malay sentences of your own.

Minggu Yang Ketujuh
Seventh Week

Pelajaran Yang Kedua Puluh Satu
Lesson 21

Awalan Ter- 3
The Prefix Ter- 3

A. Sentences

Dia bersembunyi; saya tak nampak dia.	*He is hiding; I can't see him.*
Tiba-tiba saya ternampak seorang kawan saya datang.	*Suddenly I saw one of my friends coming.*
Semalam saya sedang mendengar radio; tiba-tiba terdengarlah saya bunyi senapang.	*Yesterday I was listening to the radio; suddenly I heard the sound of a rifle.*
Marilah kita melupakan perkara itu.	*Come on — let's forget about that matter.*
Di mana buku kau, Ahmad? Sudah saya terlupa, Cikgu.	*Where's your book, Ahmad? I forgot it, sir.*
Saya mencuba mengingat nama dia.	*I am trying to remember his name.*
Ah! Teringatlah saya! Nama dia Abdullah.	*Ah! Now I remember! His name is Abdullah.*
Saya tidak terbaca buku sepanjang itu.	*I can't read such a long book.*
Salahnya tiada terbilang.	*His faults are countless.*
Satu langkah pun saya tiada terjalan lagi.	*I can't walk another step.*
Kasut ini tidak terpakai lagi.	*These shoes cannot be used any more.*
Kasut ini terlalu kecil; saya tidak terpakai.	*These shoes are too small; I can't get them on.*
Karangan ini tertulis oléh seorang penuntut saya.	*This essay was written by one of my students.*
Karangan itu mesti ditulis sebelum hari Jumaat.	*That essay must be written before Friday.*
Pintu ini dibuka pada pukul lapan pagi.	*This door is opened at eight o'clock in the morning.*

Pintu ini terbuka sekarang, tetapi lima minit lagi orang akan menutupnya.	*This door is opened now, but in five minutes' time someone will shut it.*
Masa pintu tertutup, kita tak boléh masuk.	*When the door is closed we cannot get in.*
Dia tak mahu pergi, tetapi saya akan memaksanya pergi.	*He doesn't want to go, but I will force him to go (or: make him go).*
Kerana bapanya sakit teruk, terpaksalah ia pergi ke Singapura.	*Because his father was seriously ill he was forced to go to Singapore.*
Sudah melukis gambar, ditunjukkannya kepada ibunya.	*Having drawn a picture, he showed it to his mother.*
Gambar ini terlukis oléh Rembrandt.	*This picture was drawn by Rembrandt.*
Sungguhpun ia datang lambat, tetapi kerétapi belum bertolak.	*Although he came late, the train had not yet left.*
Ia datang terlambat; kerétapi sudah bertolak.	*He came too late; the train had gone.*
Calon kita seorang wartawan yang termasyhur di dalam dunia.	*Our candidate is a world-famous journalist.*
Tong itu terbesar; saya tiada terangkatnya.	*That crate is too big; I can't lift it.*

B. Word List

Nouns

salah	*mistake, error fault, guilt*	perkara	*matter, affair, case (court)*
jumaat	*community, congregation*	langkah	*step*
hari Jumaat	*Friday*		

Adjectives

teruk	*acute, severe*	sakit	*ill, sick*
sakit teruk	*seriously ill*	tidak terpakai	*unwearable, unusable*
terlukis	*drawn, painted*		

Verbs

nampak	*to see, to be able to see, to be visible*	bertolak	*to start, to set off, to leave, depart*
ternampak	*to catch sight of*		

Miscellaneous

kerana	*because*	sungguhpun	*although*

C. Grammar

110 *Sungguhpun ia datang lambat, tetapi kerétapi belum bertolak:* "Although he came late, the train had not yet left." The English *although* can be rendered by *sungguhpun* in Malay. Notice, however, that the main clause must begin with *tetapi*. For more details see Lesson 22 and also see "Speak Malay!" Lesson 48, p. 160 ff.

111 *terlalu* and *terlampau: Lalu* is basically a verb meaning "to pass". It can, however, also be used adjectivally with the meaning of "past", or adverbially to mean "and next", "and then". Its meaning is strengthened by the addition of the *ter-*prefix to something like "well past", or "beyond the limit of need or endurance". It comes to mean, then, "too much" or "excessively", and is the normal way of rendering the English "too" before an adjective: *terlalu besar*, "too big". *Lampau* and *terlampau* mean the same as *lalu* and *terlalu* respectively, but are less commonly used.

These two words are really "crystallised" forms. That is to say that the prefix has become so much part of the word that we can consider the two forms (prefixed and unprefixed) as different word altogether. There are quite a lot of these crystallised *ter-*forms in Malay; that is words with a special meaning which either mean something quite different if we remove the prefix, or never occur at all without the *ter-*. Many common verbs come in the latter category: for instance *tertawa*, "to laugh", and *tersenyum*, "to smile", never occur without the prefix. Such words are best learnt with the prefix on the front and treated as separate items of vocabulary.

D. Exercises

Exercise 59   Translate into English:

1 Masa saya hendak tidur semalam, terdengarlah saya suara seorang menyanyi di luar tingkap (*tingkap:* window).
2 Kalau kita hendak belajar bahasa kebangsaan, baik kita membaca buku-buku yang terkarang oléh pengarang-pengarang Melayu yang termasyhur.
3 Lagi pula, kita mesti mendengar lakonan-lakonan Melayu di radio.
4 Masa bertolak dari pangkalan di Singapura kelmarin sebuah kapal api yang terbesar terlanggar sebuah kapal pembinasa Ruritania, lalu dikaramkannya.
5 Orang yang mengamuk itu berkeris terhunus.
6 Ia mengambil kerisnya lalu dihunusnya hendak membunuh mata-mata yang menantikannya di luar rumah.
7 Tetapi mata-mata itu terlihat dia datang lalu dibunuhnya dengan senapangnya.
8 Ia memotong sekeping roti (a piece of bread) lalu dimakannya dengan mentéga (*mentéga:* butter).
9 Buku ini terlalu panjang; saya tidak terbaca lagi.
10 Ahmad mengambil sekeping kertas lalu menulis surat kepada ayahnya.

Exercise 60   Translate into Malay:
1 This road is too narrow (narrow: *sempit*).
2 His car collided with a bus.
3 He caught sight of his father coming out of the house.
4 There is a hidden meaning in these words.

5   The submarine sank two enemy ships, but in the end (*akhirnya*) it was itself (*sendiri*) rammed by a destroyer and sunk.
6   Ahmad hid outside the window and saw Yusuf hiding his money in a cupboard.
7   Ali could not find the hidden meaning in the sentence.
8   Who opened this door? I'm afraid I don't know; I found it open when I arrived just now.
9   I hope it wasn't Hamid who opened it because I told him yesterday not to open the door before I came.
10 I don't think it was Hamid. He's not (here) today because his wife is seriously ill. She was run over by a car last night and Hamid spent the night at the hospital (*hospital*).

Exercise 61
Write ten Malay sentences of your own.

Minggu Yang Kedelapan — Pelajaran Yang Kedua Puluh Dua
Eighth Week — Lesson 22

Sendikata Penambat dan Ayat-ayat Berkait 1
Subordinating Conjunction and Complex Sentences 1

A. Sentences

Kalau awak pergi ke sana, tentulah awak akan mendapat duit itu.	*If you go there, you will certainly get the money.*
Jika dia tidak bekerja kuat, tentulah dia tidak lulus dalam peperiksaannya.	*If he does not work hard, he will certainly not pass his examination.*
Jika ia mendapat peluang, tentulah ia akan menyokong cadangan saya.	*If he gets the opportunity, he will certainly support my proposal.*
Jikalau cadangan kita akan dibangkang oléh pihak pembangkang, tentulah ia tidak boléh menyokongnya.	*If our proposal is opposed by the opposition, he will certainly not be able to support it.*
Jikalau boléh, kami akan mengadakan mesyuarat agung.	*If possible, we shall hold a general meeting.*
Sekiranya tuan pengerusi sakit, tuanlah yang mesti mengadakan mesyuarat khas itu.	*If the chairman is ill, it is you who must hold the special meeting.*
Jikalau sekiranya tuan tidak boléh mengadakannya sendiri, saya pun boléh mengadakannya.	*If by any chance you can't hold it yourself, I can hold it.*
Walaupun awak pergi ke rumahnya, tentulah ia tidak ada.	*Even if you go to his house, he is sure not to be there.*
Walaupun cadangan itu disokongnya, nampaknya tidak akan diluluskan mesyuarat.	*Even if the motion is supported by him, it doesn't look as if it will be accepted by the meeting.*
Sungguhpun ia bekerja kuat, tetapi ia tidak maju.	*Although he works hard, he gets nowhere.*

Sungguhpun saya menyokong cadangannya, tetapi tidak diluluskan mesyuarat.	*Although I supported his proposal, it was not accepted by the meeting.*
Meskipun cadangannya baik sekali, tetapi ditolak kerajaan.	*Although his proposal was extremely good, it was rejected by the government.*
Meskipun ucapannya tidak berapa terang, tetapi kami semua faham maknanya.	*Although his speech was not very clear, we all understood his meaning.*
Teranglah bahawa ia tidak akan menyokong cadangan tuan.	*It is clear that he will not support your proposal.*
Teranglah bahawa kita mesti membeli sebuah keréta yang baharu.	*It is clear that we must buy a new car.*
Nyatalah bahawa kita patut menyokongnya.	*It is clear that we ought to support him.*
Perdana Menteri telah berkata bahawa kita patut menggunakan bahasa kebangsaan.	*The Prime Minister has said that we should use the national language.*
Tuan pengerusi berkata bahawa cadangan itu tidak boleh dirudingkan oléh mesyuarat.	*The chairman said that the proposal could not be discussed by the meeting.*
Ia berkata bahawa cadangannya telah ditolak oléh kerajaan.	*He said that his proposal had been rejected by the government.*

B. Word List

Nouns

duit	*money*	peluang	*opportunity*
cadangan	*proposal, suggestion*	pihak	*side (in a contest)*
pembangkang	*opposer*	pihak pembangkang	*the opposition*

mesyuarat	*meeting*	pengerusi	*chairman*
ucapan	*a speech*		

Adjectives

tentu	*certain, sure*	agung	*general*
khas	*special*	maju	*progressive, making progress*
terang	*clear, bright*	nyata	*clear*

Verbs

sokong (menyokong)	*to support*	tolak	*to push, to reject*
bangkang (membangkang)	*to oppose*	rundingkan (merundingkan)	*to discuss*
luluskan (meluluskan)	*to accept, to pass*	faham	*to understand*
patut	*ought, should*		

Miscellaneous

kalau	*if*	jika	*if*
jikalau	*if*	sekiranya	*if*
walaupun	*even if*	sungguhpun	*although*
meskipun	*although*	nyatalah bahawa...	*it is clear that...*
teranglah bahawa..	*it is clear that...*		

C. Grammar

112 *Complex sentences (Ayat-ayat berkait):* So far in this course we have, in the main, contented ourselves with fairly straightforward statements and questions, and, although some of our sentences have been quite long, very few of them have been at all complicated. Now in both speech and writing we frequently join two or more sentences together by making one or more of them dependent in some way upon the others. This is done in English by using words like "if",

"although", "when", "until", and so on. Such words are called in English *conjunctions* (Malay: *sendikata*), and the ones which we have just mentioned as well as many more are called *subordinating conjunctions* (Malay: *sendikata penambat*) because they subordinate the clause which they introduce and make it dependent on the main clause of the sentence. Malay, too, has its conjunctions although in Malay they are more common in writing than they are in speech: in spoken Malay the tendency is to keep sentences as short as possible. Nevertheless, conjunctions are very much used in written Malay and are becoming more and more common in the modern language. People are beginning to use them more often nowadays in speech as well.

113 *Kalau awak pergi ke sana . . . :* "If you go there . . ." *Kalau* is the commonest word for "if" and is as much used in speech as in writing. We have, of course, used it many times before.

114 *Jika dia tidak bekerja kuat . . .:* "If he does not work hard . . ." *Jika* is also very commonly used to introduce *if*-clause.

115 *Jikalau cadangan kita akan dibangkang . . . :* "If our proposal is opposed . . . " *Jikalau* is a "telescoped" form of *jika* and *kalau* together. All three words, *kalau, jika* and *jikalau,* are equal in value, and all three are direct borrowing from Arabic.

116 *Sekiranya tuan pengerusi sakit . . . :* "If the chairman is (or: should be) ill . . . " *Sekiranya* is very much used to mean "if". It carries just a slight suggestion that the statement in the clause is not altogether likely to be true — something like "if, by any chance . . . "

117 *Jikalau sekiranya tuan tidak mengadakannya sendiri . . . :* "If by any chance you don't hold it yourself . . . " *Sekiranya* is frequently combined with any of the other words for *if* and adds the suggestion of improbability mentioned in 116 above. *(ji)ka(lau) sekiranya* could be translated as "Just supposing . . ." or "If (he) should by any chance . . .", etc.

118 *Walaupun awak pergi ke rumahnya . . . :* "Even if you do go to his house . . . " *Walaupun,* which can be used to render the English "even if" can also be used for "although" and, like *sungguhpun* (cf. below 119), often requires the clause on which it depends to begin

with *tetapi*, "but".

119 *Sungguhpun ia bekerja kuat, tetapi ia tidak maju:* "Although he works hard, (but) he makes no progress." *Sungguhpun* is the commonest way of rendering the English "although" in written Malay, but notice that the Malay usage differs from the English in one respect: in English it is incorrect to follow up "although" with a "but" at the beginning of the main clause. In Malay, however, the word *tetapi must* be used at the beginning of a main clause which has a *sungguhpun*-clause dependent upon it.

120 *Meskipun cadangannya baik sekali, tetapi...:* "Although his proposal was extremely good, (but)..." *Meskipun* is a frequently used alternative to *sungguhpun*. *Meskipun* also requires *tetapi* to introduce the main clause, cf. 119 above.

121 *Teranglah bahawa...:* "(It is) clear that..." Note this construction: there is no need for "it is" in Malay in such a sentence. The adjective with the emphatic suffix *-lah* is quite sufficient. *Bahawa* is being used more and more in modern Malay to introduce a noun clause and therefore corresponds to the English conjunction "that".

122 *Nyatalah bahawa kita patut menyokongnya:* "It is clear that we ought (or: should) support him." *Patut* is used as an auxiliary verb indicating obligation or duty. Literally, *patut* means something like "fitting" or "right and proper".

D. *Exercises*

Exercise 62   Translate into English:

1 Kalau sekiranya ia tiada di rumah, hendaklah kita mencarinya di pekan.
2 Meskipun kapal pembinasa itu melanggar kapal selam, tetapi tidak dikaramkannya.
3 Jikalau cadangan kita ditolak oléh kerajaan, hendaklah kita mengadakan mesyuarat khas.
4 Sekiranya saudara mendapat peluang, tolong sokong cadangan saya.

5   Walaupun ia belajar sepuluh tahun, tentulah ia tidak akan bercakap bahasa kebangsaan sebagai seorang Melayu.
6   Nyatalah bahawa kita patut bercakap bahasa Melayu hari-hari dengan kawan-kawan Melayu.
7   Sungguhpun ia sampai pada pukul sembilan, tetapi kerétapi sudah bertolak.
8   Jika ayah membeli keréta baharu, boléhlah kita pergi ke Singapura bulan depan hendak melawat Encik Ali.
9   Sungguhpun cadangan kerajaan itu dibangkang oléh pihak pembangkang, tetapi diluluskan oléh Déwan.
10 Sungguhpun perkara itu dirundingkan tiga jam setengah oléh Dewan Rakyat (*House of Representatives*), tetapi satu perkataan pun tidak saya faham.

Exercise 63   Translate into Malay:
1   Even if you buy that book, you will not read it.
2   Although the proposal was opposed by the opposition, it was passed by the meeting.
3   Even if you support the proposal, it will be rejected.
4   It is clear that we ought to support this proposal.
5   If the chairman is not present (present: *hadir*), the meeting will be held by the secretary (secretary: *setiausaha*).
6   The chairman told the reporters that a special meeting would be held next week.
7   He hoped that the government's proposals would be supported by the people even if they were rejected by the opposition.
8   Although this affair has been discussed by the House of Representatives, it has not been explained to the people.
9   If by any chance he is not at home, give this letter to his wife.
10 It is clear that you must register your son's name at the Education Office if he is going to get into a secondary school next year.

Exercise 64
Write down ten Malay sentences of your own.

Minggu Yang Kedelapan
Eighth Week

Pelajaran Yang Kedua Puluh Tiga
Lesson 23

Sendikata Penambat dan Ayat-ayat Berkait 2
Subordinating Conjunction and Complex Sentences 2

A. *Sentences*

Sebelum ia naik kerétapi, ia membeli tikétnya.

Before he got into the train, he bought his ticket.

Sebelum ia tidur, ia menghisap sebatang rokok.

Before he went to sleep, he smoked a cigarette.

Sebelum cadangan kita ditolak oléh mesyuarat, ia telah dirundingkan dahulu.

Before our proposal was rejected by the meeting, it was first of all discussed.

Setelah cadangan kita dibentangkan, mesyuarat agung telah merundingkannya.

After our motion was tabled, the general meeting discussed it.

Setelah kita berunding tiga jam, tuan pengerusi menamatkan mesyuarat.

After we had had a discussion of three hours, the chairman closed the meeting.

Setelah mesyuarat ditamatkan, tuan pengerusi berkata kepada wartawan-wartawan bahawa cadangan Encik Polan telah dibangkang lalu ditolak oléh kerajaan.

After the meeting had been closed, the chairman told journalists that Mr So-and-So's proposal had been opposed and then rejected by the government.

Kita akan berunding dengan Perdana Menteri Ruritania.

We shall have discussions (or: talks) with the Ruritanian Prime Minister.

Perkara itu akan kita rundingkan minggu depan di London.

We shall discuss that matter next week in London.

Berkenaan dengan perkara ini kita akan berunding ésok.

In connexion with this matter we shall have talks tomorrow.

Meréka sudah berunding tentang perkara itu.

They have had talks about that matter.

127

Dalam ucapannya ia telah mengucapkan terima kasih kepada tuan pengerusi di atas cadangannya.	*In his speech he said thank you to the chairman for his suggestion.*
Patutlah kita mengucapkan banyak-banyak terima kasih kepada tuan pengerusi.	*We should express our great gratitude to the chairman;* or: *we ought to make a vote of thanks to the chairman.*
Berkenaan dengan cadangan encik, akan saya tulis kepada encik.	*With reference to your suggestion, I shall write to you.*
Setelah mesyuarat dibuka oléh pengerusi, butir-butir mesyuarat yang lepas telah dibacanya.	*After the meeting had been opened by the chairman, the minutes of the last meeting were read.*
Butir-butir telah dibaca lalu diluluskan oléh mesyuarat.	*The minutes were read and accepted by the meeting.*
Tuan pengerusi akan mengadakan satu mesyuarat khas berkenaan dengan surat yang diterimanya daripada Perdana Menteri.	*The chairman will hold a special meeting in connexion with the letter which he has received from the Prime Minister.*

B. Word List

Nouns

tikét	*ticket*	butir	*grain, pellet, particle*
jam	*hour*		
butir-butir	*minutes (of a meeting)*		

Verbs

hisap (menghisap)	*to suck, to smoke*	tamatkan (menamatkan)	*to terminate (trans.), to close (proceedings, etc.)*
bentangkan (membentangkan)	*to spread out (trans.), to table a motion*	bacakan (membacakan)	*to read aloud*
ucapkan (mengucapkan)	*to pronounce, express, utter*		
berunding (dengan)	*to have discussions (with), to have talks (with) (intrans.)*		

Miscellaneous

sebelum	*before (conj.)*	berkenaan dengan	*in connexion with, with reference to, with regard to*
setelah	*after (conj.)*	tentang	*about, regarding*

C. Grammar

123 *before:* As a conjunction the English "before" may be translated by *sebelum* in Malay. "Before" as an adverb, however, is *dahulu,* and "before" as a preposition of place (e.g. "before the class" etc.) is *di depan* or *di hadapan. Sebelum* is, however, used as preposition of time, e.g.:

sebelum hari Sabtu	before Saturday
sebelum pukul tiga suku	before 3.15
ia berdiri di depan rumah	he stood before the house
dahulu ia tinggal di Ipoh	before (*i.e.* formerly), he lived in Ipoh

but *sebelum ia tinggal di Ipoh, ia* before he lived in Ipoh, he
   tinggal di Kuala Lumpur lived in Kuala Lumpur

124 *after:* "After", as a conjunction, is rendered by *setelah*, which like *sebelum* (before) may also be used as a preposition of time but not of place. "After" meaning "behind" is rendered by *di belakang*. As an adverb "after" (i.e. afterwards) is *lepas itu. Lepas* and *selepas* may be used also instead of *setelah*, e.g.:

selepas hari Jumaat	after Friday
selepas pukul empat	after four o'clock
lepas itu kita makan nasi	after(wards), we had dinner
setelah kita makan nasi, ayah pun membaca bukunya	after we had had dinner, father read his book

Another common equivalent or synonym for *setelah* and *selepas* is *sesudah:*

Sesudah itu kami pun baliklah.
After that we went home.

Sesudah surat itu diterima, kerani memasukkannya dalam fail.
After the letter was received, the clerk put it in the file.

125 *rundingkan (merundingkan)* and *berunding: Rundingkan* with its *me-* form *merundingkan* is a transitive verb and corresponds to the English "to discuss", which takes a direct object without any preposition. *Berunding* is an intransitive verb and means roughly "to have a discussion" or "to have talks". If *berunding* is to be given an object, then the preposition *tentang* (about) or some such phrase as *berkenaan dengan* (in connexion with) must be used between it and its object, e.g.:

Kita sedang merundingkan perkara itu sekarang.
We are discussing that matter now.

Kita akan berunding tentang perkara itu esok.
We shall have a talk about that matter tomorrow.

Kita sedang berunding sekarang.
We are now in conference (*or:* we are now having talks).

126 *Terima kasih* di atas *cadangan tuan:* "Thank you *for* your suggestion." Notice that *di atas* is the correct preposition to use in such contexts as this. This usage probably comes from Dutch (*dank U* over *uw voorstel*) via Indonesian, but it is now quite normal in Malaysia. Notice also that "to thank" is translated by *mengucapkan terima kasih kepada*.

D. Exercises

Exercise 65   Translate into English:
1 Setelah kapal selam dikaramkan, kapal pembinasa itu pun menamatkan rondaannya (*rondaan:* patrol) lalu kembali (*kembali:* to return) ke pangkalannya.
2 Berkenaan dengan surat encik yang saya terima semalam itu saya akan menjawab setelah merundingkannya dengan tuan pengarah.
3 Selepas butir-butir dibacakan oléh setiausaha, mesyuarat merundingkan cadangan-cadangan yang dibentangkan oléh pihak pembangkang.
4 Kerja ini mesti ditamatkan sebelum tahun 1982.
5 Dahulu pintu-pintu pejabat selalu ditutup sebelum pukul empat setengah, tetapi sesudah Encik Ahmad menjadi pengarah pintu-pintu tidak ditutup sebelum pukul lima.
6 Patutlah kita mengucapkan banyak-banyak terima kasih kepada setiausaha di atas butir-butir yang baharu dibacakannya.
7 Setelah membaca butir-butir mesyuarat khas, setiausaha menjemput Encik Jamaluddin menyatakan perkara-perkara yang patut dirundingkan pada hari itu.
8 Mesyuarat agung tidak akan ditamatkan sebelum pukul sepuluh malam.
9 Kalau sekiranya mesyuarat agung tidak ditamatkan sebelum pukul dua belas malam, bagaimanakah kita hendak balik?

10 Sungguhpun perkara itu telah dirundingkan di London, tetapi pihak pembangkang di negeri ini tidak bersetuju dengan tindakan (*tindakan:* action) kerajaan.

Exercise 66   Translate into Malay:
1 We shall have a discussion about your proposal tomorrow.
2 We shall discuss your proposal tomorrow.
3 Before the meeting was closed he made a vote of thanks to the chairman.
4 In his speech he said that a general meeting ought to be held.
5 Although the chairman closed the meeting at 10 p.m. we did not leave the House before half past eleven.
6 In his speech to the House of Representatives the Minister of Education said that fifty new schools would be opened before the end (*akhir*) of (the year) 1980.
7 The opposition said that they would support the government's action in this matter.
8 Before going out he closed his book and put it away in the cupboard; after that he looked for the key of the car and found it in his wife's room.
9 Before finishing its patrol the submarine sank a large enemy ship which was carrying troops (*askar-askar*) to Ruritania.
10 Suddenly the officer spotted (*ternampak*) some enemy soldiers hiding in the rice-field but he was too late and was killed by a hand grenade (*bom tangan*) which fell in front of him.

Exercise 67
Write down ten Malay sentences of your own composition using what you have learnt so far in this course.

Minggu Yang Kedepalan / Eighth Week

Pelajaran Yang Kedua Puluh Empat
Lesson 24

Sendikata Penambat dan Ayat-ayat Berkait 3
Subordinating Conjunctions and Complex Sentences 3

A. Sentences

Oléh kerana ia tidak ada duit, ia tidak pergi ke pasar.
Because he had no money, he did not go to the market.

Oléh sebab ia berasa sakit, emaknya menghantarnya ke doktor.
Because he felt ill, his mother sent him to the doctor.

Sehingga ia pergi ke sana, ia tidak mendapat gajinya.
Until he went there, he did not get his salary.

Sehingga saya menerima surat encik, saya akan menunggu di rumah.
Until I get your letter, I shall wait at home.

Sehingga ia bermula bekerja kuat, pelajarannya tidak maju.
Until he began working hard, his education made no progress.

Ia pergi ke pejabat untuk mendapat gajinya.
He went to the office in order to get his salary.

Ia hendak berpindah ke Ipoh supaya menjadi pegawai daérah.
He is going to move to Ipoh in order to become a district officer.

Perdana Menteri telah dijemput melawat maktab kita untuk bersyarah kepada kita.
The Prime Minister has been invited to visit our college in order to lecture to us.

Supaya bercakap bahasa Melayu semacam orang Melayu, patutlah kita duduk lama di sebuah kampung Melayu.
In order to speak Malay like a Malay we should live for a long time in a Malay village.

Asalkan ia bekerja kuat, tentulah ia boléh lulus dalam peperiksaan.
Provided that he works hard, he can certainly pass the examination.

Lamun kita menggunakan bahasa kebangsaan, senanglah kita mendapat kerja.	*Provided we use the national language it is easy for us to get work.*
Asalkan pindaan ini dikemukakan sebelum ésok, boléhlah kami rundingkan dalam mesyuarat agung yang akan datang.	*Provided that this amendment is put forward before tomorrow, we can discuss it in the coming general meeting.*
Lamun pindaan saya akan dirundingkan dalam mesyuarat agung, saya suka hati.	*Provided that (or: as long as) my amendment is discussed at the general meeting, I am happy.*
Jikalau sekiranya pindaan saya ditolak oléh mesyuarat khas, saya akan mengemukakannya sekali lagi dalam mesyuarat agung.	*If by any chance my amendment is rejected by the special meeting, I shall put it forward again at the general meeting.*
Walaupun pindaan saya ditolak oléh mesyuarat agung, saya hendak mengucapkan banyak-banyak terima kasih kepada tuan pengerusi.	*Even if my amendment is rejected by the general meeting, I am going to make a vote of thanks to the chairman.*
Jika surat tuan tidak sampai sebelum ésok, saya mesti pergi seorang.	*If your letter does not arrive by tomorrow, I shall have to go alone.*
Sungguhpun saya menantikan dia dua jam setengah, tetapi ia tidak datang.	*Although I waited for her for two and a half hours, she didn't come.*
Meskipun ia tidak berada, tetapi ia sudah membeli sebuah keréta yang baharu.	*Although he is not well-off, he has bought a new car.*
Oléh sebab duitnya sudah habis, dia tidak makan nasi dua hari.	*Because his money was all gone, he didn't eat for two days.*

Oléh kerana kerétanya terlanggar keréta orang lain, ia pergi ke balai polis untuk melaporkan perkara itu.	*Because his car collided with somebody else's, he went to the police station to report the matter.*
Sehingga bapanya datang, ia mesti menantikannya di rumah.	*Until his father came, he had to wait for him at home.*
Ia telah pergi ke England untuk menjadi pensyarah dalam bahasa Melayu di Universiti.	*He has gone to England in order to become a lecturer in Malay at the University.*
Supaya negeri kita boléh maju dan kuat, kita mesti bekerja kuat.	*In order that our country may be progressive and strong, we must work hard.*
Setelah kita berunding tentang pindaan tuan, mesyuarat telah ditamatkan oléh pengerusi.	*After we had had a discussion on your amendment, the meeting was closed by the chairman.*
Lamun dia datang ésok!	*If only he comes tomorrow!*
Asalkan butir-butir itu dibacakan dahulu, boléhlah kita merundingkan perkara-perkara itu.	*Provided that the minutes are read first, we can discuss those matters.*

B. Word List

Nouns

doktor	*doctor*	gaji	*salary, pay, wages*
daérah	*district*	pindaan	*amendment*
pegawai daérah	*district officer*	polis	*police*
balai	*(official) building*	negeri Inggeris	*England*
balai polis	*police station*		

Adjectives

berada	*well-off, wealthy*	suka hati	*pleased, happy*
habis	*finished, all gone*		

Verbs

berasa	*to feel*	pergi	*to go*
berpindah	*to move (house)*	bermula	*to begin*
kemukakan (mengemukakan)	*to bring forward, to put forward*	laporkan (melaporkan)	*to report (trans.)*
duduk	*to sit, to stay*		

Miscellaneous

oléh kerana	*because*	oléh sebab	*because*
sehingga	*until*	untuk	*for, in order to*
supaya	*in order to*	asalkan	*provided that*
lamun	*provided that, if only*	semacam	*like (prep.)*

C. Grammar

127 *Oléh kerana ia tidak ada duit: oléh sebab ia berasa sakit:* "Because he had no money: because he felt ill." *Kerana* and *sebab*, which we have had before (cf. also "Speak Malay!" Lesson 56 (154), p. 181), and which both mean "because", frequently also occur with the word *oléh* in front of them. This *oléh* makes no difference to the meaning. *Kerana* and *sebab*, with or without *oléh*, can also be used as prepositions meaning "because *of*", e.g.:

Oléh kerana itu ia pun kembalilah ke rumahnya.
Because of that (*or:* for that reason) he went home to his house.

Oléh sebab tindakan kerajaan kilang taukéh itu sudah ditutup.
Because of the government's action that towkay's factory has been closed.

Kerana kemangkatan Sultan meréka, songkok meréka berpita putih.
Because of the demise of their Sultan, their caps have white ribbons (round them).

Note: *Mangkat:* to die (used of sultans, kings, and other high ranking persons); from this is derived the abstract noun:
Kemangkatan: death, decease, demise (For the method of deriving such words see below, Lesson 32).
Pita: ribbon, tape. A Malay wears a white band round his songkok as sign of mourning (*Berpita putih*, of course, means "having a white ribbon": cf. Lesson 13 (79).)

128 *Sehingga ia pergi ke sana:* "Until he went there." *Sehingga* is the normal way of rendering the English "until".

129 *Untuk mendapat gajinya:* "(In order) to get his salary." *Untuk* followed by a verb means "in order to" or "to" used to indicate purpose. It can also be used as a preposition, in which case it means "for" and is interchangeable with *bagi*, e.g.:

Ini dia sepucuk surat untuk tuan pengarah.
Here is a letter for the director.

130 *Supaya menjadi pegawai daérah:* "In order to become a district officer." *Supaya* also means "in order to", but, unlike *untuk*, it is not used as a preposition.

131 *Asalkan ia bekerja kuat:* "Provided that he works hard." *Asalkan* is a useful conjunction meaning "provided that".

132 *Lamun kita menggunakan bahasa kebangsaan:* "Provided that we use the national language." *Lamun* is a synonym of *asalkan*, and means "provided that", but it is also used to introduce a wish or desire rather like the English "if only . . . !", e.g.:

Lamun dia datang!
If only he would come (*or:* I wish he would come!)

133 *laporkan* and *melaporkan*: Laporkan and *melaporkan* are used transitively to mean "to report".

D. *Exercises*

Exercise 68   Translate into English:
1. Supaya pindaannya diluluskan oléh mesyuarat khas, ia merundingkan perkara itu dengan tuan pengerusi.
2. Kerana kemangkatan Sultan, semua pejabat-pejabat kerajaan akan ditutup pada hari Rabu (*hari Rabu:* Wednesday).
3. Setelah kerétanya terlanggar isyarat "ikut kiri" itu, seorang mata-mata menulis nama dia dalam bukunya lalu dilaporkannya di balai polis.
4. Asalkan dia tahu bercakap bahasa kebangsaan, senanglah dia boléh mendapat kerja di sebuah sekolah kebangsaan.
5. Ia berkata kepada gurunya, "Lamun saya bercakap bahasa Melayu semacam orang Melayu!"
6. Supaya anaknya boléh masuk sekolah menengah, ia pergi ke Pejabat Pelajaran Negeri untuk mendaftarkan namanya.
7. Setelah nama anaknya didaftarkan, pegawai pelajaran itu bertanya (*bertanya:* to ask) anak dia hendak masuk sekolah manakah.
8. Sesudah ia menunggu dua jam di luar pejabat, ia menerima gajinya daripada kerani wang itu.
9. Sekiranya encik tidak boléh membeli buku yang kita rundingkan tadi, cubalah mendapatkannya di kedai Hong Tai.
10. Meskipun kerétanya tersimpang lalu terjatuh ke dalam parit di sebelah jalan, tetapi seorang pun tidak terluka pula.

Exercise 69   Translate into Malay:
1. If by any chance you can't buy the book today, buy it tomorrow before you come to school.
2. If our car should crash into someone else's, we must report the matter at the nearest police station (near: *dekat*).

3   After falling downstairs, I felt dizzy (dizzy: *pening*); so my wife called the doctor (to call: *panggil/memanggil*).
4   Before he finished his lecture, the lecturer told the students to buy a new book.
5   Because the second amendment was brought forward too late, the chairman said that it could not be discussed until the next meeting.
6   In his speech the Prime Minister said that it was clear that the opposition's amendment should be rejected.
7   Until the senior lecturer returns from England, the principal of the college will lecture to the students about Malay literature.
8   The district officer will hold a meeting today in order to explain the general election to the people of his district.
9   Provided that you speak slowly, I understand every word.
10 Today, in the House of Representatives, the Prime Minister said that he had been invited to visit Ruritania.

Exercise 70
Write down ten Malay sentences of your own composition, using what you have learnt so far.

Minggu Yang Kesembilan
Ninth Week

Pelajaran Yang Kedua Puluh Lima
Lesson 25

Awalan Pe- dan Akhiran -An 1
The Prefix Pe- and the Suffix -An 1

A. *Sentences*

Ia sedang membuka botol ini.	*He is opening this bottle.*
Dengan apa ia membukanya?	*What is he opening it with?*
Ia sedang membukanya dengan *pembuka botol.*	*He is opening it with a* bottle opener.
Orang itu telah mencuri wang saya; ia seorang *pencuri.*	*That man has stolen my money; he is a thief.*
Ia sedang menyapu lantai; ia menyapunya dengan *penyapu.*	*She is sweeping the floor; she is sweeping it with a* broom.
Saya memegang penyapu; saya memegangnya dengan *pemegang.*	*I am holding the broom; I am holding it by the* handle.
Orang itu ketua kampung kita.	*That man is the chief of our village;* or: *that man is our village headman.*
Orang itu *pengetua* maktab kita.	*That man is the* principal *of our college.*
Nasihat tuan sangat berguna.	*Your advice is very useful.*
Orang itu bekerja di negeri kita sebagai *penasihat.*	*That man is working in our country as an* adviser.
Buah ini buah rambutan.	*This fruit's a rambutan.*
Ia sangat suka makan *buah-buahan.*	*He is very fond of eating* fruit.
Ia sangat suka duduk di pantai menéngok laut.	*He loves to sit on the beach and look at the sea.*
Kapal laut itu akan menyeberang *lautan.*	*That ship will cross the ocean.*
Semenanjung Malaysia itu sebuah negeri di *Gugugusan Pulau* Melayu.	*Malaysian Peninsular is a country in the Malay* Archipelago.

Di negeri kita ada banyak *gali-galian*.	*In our country there are many* minerals.
Ia suka makan *sayur-sayuran*.	*He likes eating* vegetables.

B. Word List

Nouns

akhiran	*suffix*	nasihat	*advice*
lantai	*floor*	penasihat	*adviser*
penyapu	*broom*	botol	*bottle*
pemegang	*handle*	pembuka	*opener*
buah-buahan	*fruit (in general)*	pencuri	*thief*
gugusan	*a cluster*	ketua	*chief headman*
pulau	*island*	lautan	*ocean*
gugusan pulau	*archipelago*	gali-galian	*minerals*
sayur-sayuran	*vegetables (in general)*		

Verbs

pegang (memegang)	*to hold*	menyeberang	*to cross*

C. *Grammar*

134 *General remarks on word-building affixes:* In the first half of this course we have dealt with almost all the "grammatical" affixes, that is those suffixes and prefixes which either affect or are affected by the structure of the sentence in which they occur. These affixes have mostly been "detachable"; that is to say that words occur sometimes with them and sometimes without them according to the circumstances. There are, however, quite a lot more prefixes and suffixes in Malay which do not affect the sentence structure and which are used almost entirely for forming new words from old ones. We have quite a few of this kind of affix in English too. For instance, we add -*ation* to form all kinds of abstract nouns: *embark* and *embarkation*, *destine* and *destination*, and many others. We add -*ness* to adjectives to form nouns of quality: *big* and *bigness*, *careful* and *carefulness* and so on.

English has many other such suffixes and a lot of prefixes too. They are used mainly to extend the *vocabulary* of the language and a knowledge of how they work will often enable us to guess the meaning of an unfamiliar English word we may meet in a book, but which we may never have seen before. In English the application of these affixes is often highly irregular and unpredictable, but in Malay the system of word-building is much more regular — although there are some exceptions to many of the rules — and in fact even the foreigner can often construct new Malay words for himself with about an eighty per cent chance of being right. It is clearly worth while, then, making at least a brief study of how Malay extends its vocabulary by means of its system of affixation. It will help us to understand long new words when we see them and will often help us to guess at the correct Malay word for some English one which we want to express in Malay.

135 *buka/membuka* and *pembuka:* One of the most useful word-building prefixes is the prefix *pe-*. It is added to words in much the same way as the *me-*prefix and almost always demands the same phonetic changes at the beginning of the word to which it is added as the *me-*prefix does (cf. the table in Lesson 4 (12)). There are a few common exceptions to this, but we shall point them out as we go along, and so for the moment you should just remember that *pe-* and *me-* require the same phonetic changes in the word to which they are added.

The *pe-*prefix can be added to almost any part of speech, but particularly to nouns and verbs. The resulting word usually expresses either the *agent* or *instrument* normally associated with the meaning of the root word. Thus the *pe-*prefix often corresponds to the English suffix *-er* in such pairs as *keep* and *keeper*, *hold* and *holder*. E.g.:

buka (membuka)   *to open*   pembuka   *opener*

pegang (memegang)	*to hold*	pemegang	*holder, handle*
curi (mencuri)	*to steal*	pencuri	*"stealer", i.e. thief*
sapu (menyapu)	*to sweep*	penyapu	*broom*
nasihat	*advice*	penasihat	*adviser*

136 *ketua: pengetua:* "headman: principal". In this case the *pe-*prefix has been added to the noun *ketua*, which already indicates a person and means "the man in charge" or "the man at the head" (e.g. *ketua jabatan* "head of department" and *ketua menteri* "chief minister"). The addition of the *pe-*prefix merely gives us another word with a similar but shifted meaning: *pengetua* means "the head of an educational establishment" and the best English word for it is therefore "principal".

137 *buah: buah-buahan:* "a fruit: fruits". It is difficult to predict what part of speech a word ending in the *-an* suffix will be, but generally speaking it is used to form nouns from verbs and from other nouns. When the *-an* suffix is added to many nouns it gives the idea of a large collection of similar things all crowded together into one and looked at as a whole. In this case the noun to which the suffix is added is often doubled (or reduplicated) first, e.g.:

buah	*(a single fruit)*	buah-buahan	*fruit (of all kinds)*
laut	*sea*	lautan	*a collection of seas, and so "ocean"*
gugus	*cluster of small things like fruit etc.*	gugusan	*cluster of larger or more important objects, e.g.*
		gugusan pulau	*archipelago*
gali (menggali)	*to dig*	gali-galian	*things which are dug up, and so "minerals"*
sayur	*(green) vegetables*	sayur-sayuran	*all kinds of green vegetables*

143

D. Exercises

Exercise 71
Try to guess the meanings of the following Malay words:
1. penyokong
2. pembunuh
3. pemeriksa
4. penunjuk
5. pemilih
6. pencukur
7. pendengar
8. pembaca
9. penulis
10. pengikut

Exercise 72
Use the *pe*-prefix to make up Malay words for the following:
1. visitor
2. salesman
3. draughtsman
4. planter
5. spectator
6. assistant
7. buyer
8. spade
9. hammer
10. instructor

Exercise 73 Translate into English:
1. Saya tidak berapa suka makan buah-buahan.
2. Di mana pembuka botol?
3. Kalau saya tak ada penyapu, macam mana saya nak menyapu lantai?
4. Dia pergi ke pasar buah-buahan untuk membeli buah durian.
5. Pencuri itu menggali lubang besar dengan penggali lalu menanamkan wang yang dicurinya itu.*
6. Dekat pejabat pos ada seorang penjual buah-buahan.
7. Pemegang pintu ini sudah rosak. Siapa yang merosakkannya?
8. Esok ketua pemeriksa akan mengadakan mesyuarat semua penolong pemeriksa.
9. Bahasa Melayu itu bahasa yang berguna sekali di seluruh Gugusan Pulau Melayu.
10. Pengarang ini termasyhur; ramailah pembaca-pembacanya.

*New Words: *lubang:* hole; *tanamkan (menanamkan):* to bury.

Exercise 74 Translate into Malay:
1   Malaysian minerals are famous throughout the world.
2   Among (*di antara*) Malaysian fruits the durian is the most tasty.
3   The Prime Minister has many followers throughout Malaysia (say: Many are the followers . . .).
4   He arrived in Malaya to become a rubber-planter. Now he plants rubber in Kedah near Sungai Patani. (rubber: *getah*).
5   After sweeping the floor of the office, Ali picked up the broom and put it away in the cupboard under the stairs.
6   The opposition candidate was not elected because he was not trusted by the voters.
7   The murderer was arrested by the police and hanged in Pudu Gaol (to arrest, to catch: *tangkap (menangkap)*; to hang: *gantung (menggantung)*; gaol, prison: *penjara*).
8   The thief stole the money and buried it in a hole behind his house.
9   He dug a hole with a spade and buried the money in it.
10 After the thief had been arrested, the police looked for the money and found it in a hole in the garden (*kebun*).

Exercise 75
Write down ten Malay sentences of your own composition.

Minggu Yang Kesembilan
Ninth Week

Pelajaran Yang Kedua Puluh Enam
Lesson 26

Awalan Pe- dan Akhiran -An 2
The Prefix Pe- and the Suffix -An 2

A. Sentences

Encik sukakah makan gulai?

Do you like eating curry?

Suka. Saya sangat suka makan *makanan* pedas.

Yes, I do. I am very fond of eating hot food.

Encik sukakah minum *minuman* manis?

Do you like (drinking) sweet drinks?

Suka juga; tetapi saya lagi suka *minuman* yang pahit.

I don't mind them; but I prefer bitter drinks.

Di mana kapal kita berlabuh?

Where does our ship anchor?

Kapal kita akan berlabuh di *labuhan* besar dekat pulau itu.

Our ship will anchor in a large anchorage close to the island.

Siapa yang mengatur mesyuarat ini?

Who arranged this meeting?

Encik Rashid yang mengaturnya; *aturannya* baik sekali.

It was Encik Rashid who arranged it; his arrangements are excellent.

Kerjanya melatih guru-guru mengajar bahasa kebangsaan

His work is to train teachers to teach the national language.

Latihan ini berguna sungguh.

This training is very useful.

Suratkhabar ini suratkhabar *harian*.

This newspaper is a daily newspaper.

Suratkhabar ini sampai tiap-tiap hari dari Singapura.

This newspaper arrives daily (or: every day) from Singapore.

Majalah ini majalah *mingguan*.

This magazine is a weekly.

Mesyuarat *bulanan* akan diadakan minggu depan.

The monthly meeting will be held next week.

Mesyuarat agung *tahunan* akan diadakan pada akhir bulan ini.

The annual general meeting will be held at the end of this month.

Pihak pembangkang akan menolak cadangannya.	The opposition (party) will reject his proposal.
Beri dia wang pembeli daging.	Give him the money intended (set aside) for buying meat.
Tolong bagi saya pisau pembuka surat.	Please give me the knife for opening letters.
Orang itu guru pelawat.	That man is a visiting teacher.
Guru yang dilawatnya itu guru pelatih.	The teachers whom he visits are teachers in training (or: trainee teachers).
Pegawai yang membawa pedang itu orang muda.	The officer carrying the sword is a young man.
Pegawai pembawa pedang itu orang muda.	The officer who carries the sword is a young man: or: the sword-bearer is a young man.

B. Word List

Nouns

labuhan	anchorage	minuman	(a) drink
latihan	training, practice, exercise		
akhir	end	aturan	arrangement, organisation
pembawa	bearer	majalah	magazine
pelatih	trainee		

Adjectives

pahit	bitter	manis	sweet
mingguan	weekly		
tahunan	yearly, annual	bulanan	monthly
		muda	young

Verbs

berlabuh	*to anchor (intrans.)*	atur (meng-atur)	*to arrange, to organise*
latih (melatih)	*to train*		

Miscellaneous

tiap-tiap hari   *daily (adv.), every day*

C. Grammar

138 *Saya sangat suka makan makanan pedas:* "I am very fond of (eating) hot food." The suffix *-an* is particularly common when added to verbs to form nouns which are connected in some way or other with the action or state expressed by the verb. Thus, from the verb *makan (memakan)* "to eat" we get the noun *makanan*, which means "what we eat", that is "food". Note that the suffix is usually added to the simple root form of the verb, any prefix being removed first. Further examples:

minum (meminum)	*to drink*	minuman	*(a) drink*
(ber)labuh	*to drop anchor*	labuhan*	*anchorage*
atur (mengatur)	*to arrange, to organise*	aturan	*arrangement, organisation*
latih (melatih)	*to train*	latihan	*training, practice, exercise*

In this case the suffix *-an* is particularly prolific and every day we can see more and more new examples of its application to form nouns from verbs or from other parts of speech.

139 *Suratkhabar harian:* "A daily newspaper". When added to certain nouns indication periods of time, the suffix *-an* forms adjectives. The following are the most commonly used of these:

hari	*day*	harian	*daily*
minggu	*week*	mingguan	*weekly*
bulan	*month*	bulanan	*monthly*
tahun	*year*	tahunan	*yearly, annual*

Be careful, however, when trying to render these English words in Malay. *Daily, weekly, monthly* and *yearly* may be adverbs in English, in which case they would be rendered differently in Malay. As adverbs they would be translated as follows in Malay:

daily	*tiap-tiap hari* or *hari-hari*
weekly	*tiap-tiap minggu*
monthly	*tiap-tiap bulan*
yearly, annually	*tiap-tiap tahun*

140 *Pihak pembangkang akan menolak cadangannya:* "The opposition (or: the opposing party) will reject his proposal." We have had *bangkang* and its *me*-form *membangkang* meaning "to oppose" and here we have the same root with the *pe*-prefix. Strictly speaking, *pembangkang* is a noun and means "opposer" or "one who opposes", but in the phrase *pihak pembangkang* (literally, "opposing side") it is being used as an adjective or, if you prefer, as a present participle. The *pe*-form of a verb is very often used in this way to denote "someone or something whose *purpose* is to do whatever is denoted by the verb". Notice the following examples taken from Section A above:

wang pembeli daging	*money intended for buying meat*
pisau pembuka surat	*knife for opening letters*
guru pelawat	*teacher whose purpose is to visit teachers in training*
guru pelatih	*teacher whose purpose is to be trained, i.e. trainee teacher*

141 *Pegawai yang membawa pedang: pegawai pembawa pedang:* "The officer carrying the sword: the sword-bearer." This pair of examples brings out the function of the participial use of the *pe*-prefix quite well. The first of the two expressions has no special implications: this may be *any* officer carrying *any* sword either on parade or off. The second expression, however, implies that the officer concerned has as one of his duties the task of carrying some special sword connected with a special ceremonial parade, say, trooping the

colour, and that, probably, he is always the one who carries out this task, which, very likely, is regarded as a special honour. "A man carrying an umbrella" would be *"seorang yang membawa payung"*, but the royal umbrella bearer so often seen at state functions in Malaysia is more likely to be described as *"seorang pembawa cetera"*.

N.B. *payung* is an ordinary umbrella or sunshade, but the elaborate yellow umbrella used as a mark of royalty is given a Sanskrit name, viz. *cetera* (Sanskrit *chattra*).

D. Exercises

Exercise 76
Try to guess the meanings of the following Malay words:
1. gambaran
2. jemputan
3. pandangan
4. sokongan
5. panggilan
6. jualan
7. bilangan
8. tolongan
9. lukisan
10. bacaan

Exercise 77
Try your hand at putting the following into Malay:
1. national dance
2. a command
3. a commander
4. in the world market
5. daily news
6. the cut of his clothes
7. a reading book
8. discussion
9. an old acquaintance
10. memory

Exercise 78   Translate into English:
1. Kita tak ada wang pembeli suratkhabar.
2. Di pelabuhan mana kapal kita akan berlabuh?
3. Majalah ini majalah bulanan.
4. Bila mesyuarat agung tahunan hendak diadakan?
5. Gali-galian Malaysia termasyhur di pasaran dunia.

6 Wang pembeli buku-buku belum diterima daripada kerajaan.
7 Patutlah kami mengucapkan terima kasih di atas jemputan tuan.
8 Murid-muridnya menggunakan dua buah buku: sebuah buku bacaan dan sebuah buku tulisan.
9 Guru mereka seorang guru pelatih. Ia diperiksa tiap-tiap bulan oléh seorang guru pelawat.
10 Tarian-tarian kebangsaan Malaysia sangat menarik hati.

Exercise 79   Translate into Malay:
1 This is the first number of a new weekly magazine called "The Weekly News".
2 An exhibition of my father's drawings will be held next month in the Dewan Tunku Abdul Rahman.
3 He bought a cold drink and drank it before the train left.
4 When you have written this exercise, you ought to write exercise eighty.
5 He sat in the reading room and read the history book which he had found in the college library (library: *perpustakaan* or *khutubkhanah*).
6 I must thank you for your support in connexion with our proposal.
7 Encik Ibrahim has been ordered by the chairman to arrange a special meeting at the end of this month in order to discuss the amendments which have been put forward by the opposition.
8 After the two ships had collided outside the harbour (*labuhan*), they dropped anchor and waited until the government inspector could inspect them.
9 The train leaves daily at nine o'clock.
10 The murderer killed his victim (*mangsa*) with a knife for opening letters.

Exercise 80
Write down ten sentences of your own composition in Malay.

Minggu Yang Kesembilan
Ninth Week

Pelajaran Yang Kedua Puluh Tujuh
Lesson 27

Awalan Pe- (Per) dengan Akhiran -An
The Prefix Pe- (Per) together with the Suffix -An

A. Sentences

Ia memulakan ucapannya dengan *perkataan* "tuan-tuan dan puan-puan".	*He began his speech with the words "Ladies and Gentlemen".*
Permulaan ucapannya sangat menarik hati.	*The beginning of his speech was very interesting.*
Kerjanya menyapu lantai.	*His work is to sweep the floor.*
Pekerjaannya pekerjaan doktor.	*His profession is that of a doctor.*
Tolong tunjukkan buku itu kepada saya.	*Please show me that book.*
Pertunjukan buku-buku sangat menarik hati semua pelawat.	*The exhibition of books greatly interested all the visitors.*
Ucapannya sudah habis.	*His speech is finished.*
Pada *penghabisan* ucapannya ia mengucapkan terima kasih kepada tuan pengerusi.	*At the end of his speech he said thank you to the chairman.*
Saya berasa sakit.	*I feel ill.*
Perasaan dia bahawa kita patut menyokong cadangan ini.	*His feeling is that we should support this proposal.*
Pada *perasaan* saya, cadangan itu patut ditolak.	*In my opinion, that proposal ought to be rejected.*
Budak-budak di Malaysia sangat suka main sepak raga.	*Malaysian boys are very fond of playing sepak raga.*
Sepak raga itu satu *permainan* Melayu.	*Sepak raga is a Malay game.*
Anak lelaki saya suka main dengan *permainannya*.	*My son likes playing with his toys.*
Pekerjaannya mengajar bahasa kebangsaan.	*His profession is teaching the national language.*

Pada *permulaan pelajarannya* ia menyatakan dua tiga *perkataan* yang baharu.	*At the* beginning *of his* lesson *he explained two or three new* words.
Pertunjukan itu sangat menarik hati orang ramai.	*The* exhibition *is of great interest to the public.*
Pada *penghabisan pertunjukan* ia mengucapkan terima kasih kepadanya.	*At the end of the show she said thank you to him.*
Suruh kanak-kanak menyimpan semua *permainan-permainan-nya.*	*Tell the children to put all their* toys *away.*

B. Word List

Nouns

pekerjaan	*profession, occupation, employment*	perasaan	*feeling, opinion*
permulaan	*beginning*	kanak-kanak	*children*
penghabisan	*end, conclusion*	sepak raga	*Malay kickball*
raga	*basket*	orang ramai	*the public*
permainan	*game, toy*		

Verbs

mulakan (memulakan)	*to begin (trans.)*	sepak (menyepak)	*to kick*
main *or* bermain	*to play*		

C. *Grammar*

142 *The prefix* pe- *(or* per-*) together with the suffix* -an: In the last two lessons we studied the two word-building affixes *pe-* and *-an,* but so far we have kept the two quite separate from each other. These two affixes, however, are frequently both added at the same time to a root word to produce nouns which are usually abstract but may also

sometimes be concrete. The only difficulty which arises is that there is another prefix, *per-*, which in this combination (*pe*-root-*an*) appears to be confused with *pe-*, with the result that we may find either of them used in the same way. Some words take *pe-* and some take *per-*, and there is unfortunately no way of knowing in advance which to choose. This does not matter very much, however, as these affixes are *derivational* rather than *functional* or *grammatical:* that is to say that they simply form new words and never have any effect on the actual construction of the sentence in which they occur. In other words, a knowledge of these derivational affixes is more useful in helping us to form new words for ourselves. They aid our *passive* rather than our *active* knowledge of the language.

The *pe*-root-*an* or *per*-root-*an* structure, then, gives a noun which denotes either the activity connected with the verbal root involved or the result or product of that activity; sometimes the structure indicates the implement (e.g. *permainan*, "toy" from *main*, "to play") with which the activity is carried on. Study the following examples carefully:

(ber)	kata	*to say*	per-kata-an	*what is said, i.e. word*
(be-)	kerja	*work*	pe-kerja-an	*profession*
(ber-)	mula	*to begin*	per-mula-an	*beginning*
	habis	*finished*	peng-habis-an	*end, conclusion*
(be-)	rasa	*to feel*	pe-rasa-an	*feeling*
	main	*to play*	per-main-an	*games or toy*
(bel-)	ajar	*to learn*	pel-ajar-an	*lesson or education*

This combination of *pe*-root-*an* or *per*-root-*an* is very prolific and is being used every day to form new words for new ideas.

143 *Pertunjukan:* "Exhibition." Notice the way this word is pronounced. The most common way of pronouncing it is as if it were spelled *per-tunjuk-kan*, that is to say the final *-k* of the root *tunjuk*, which represents a glottal stop (*tunju'*), retains that pronunciation

but is joined to the suffix *-an* by the insertion of a pronounced, but unwritten *k*. This is the normal pronunciation for any word ending in *-k* to which the suffix *-an* is added. Two other pronunciations are possible but not recommendend: such words may be pronounced exactly as spelled (i.e. *per-tunju-kan*) or the *-k* may be pronounced as a glottal stop without the extra *-k* of the liason (i.e. *per-tunju'-an*).

D. Exercises

Exercise 81

Try to guess the meanings of the following Malay words:

1. pembunuhan
2. penerangan
3. pendapatan
4. percakapan
5. pencurian
6. persatuan
7. pendaftaran
8. pendengaran
9. permusuhan
10. penyeberangan

Exercise 82

Using the *per*-root-*an* structure, try to work out Malay equivalents for the following:

1. a deed (action)
2. development
3. shelter (hiding place)
4. journey (trip)
5. shipping, navigation
6. cross-roads
7. destruction
8. station, (bus) stop
9. question, inquiry
10. attention

Exercise 83

Using the *pe*-root-*an* structure, try to work out Malay equivalents for the following:

1. restoration, restitution
2. scene, scenery, view
3. construction
4. substitution
5. removal
6. enlargement
7. aviation, flight
8. formation
9. store, depot
10. opening

Exercise 84   Translate into English:
1. Pada perasaan penasihat-penasihat saya, cadangan tuan mesti ditolak.
2. Saya tidak berapa suka minum minuman sejuk.
3. Penyapu ini tidak ada pemegang.
4. Pencuri itu ditangkap oléh polis.
5. Pendaftaran budak-budak sekolah akan dimulakan minggu depan.
6. Semalam saya bercakap dengan Perdana Menteri; percakapan kami sangat menarik hati.
7. Bahasa kebangsaan itu bahasa persatuan.
8. Selepas pembukaan bangunan yang baharu itu, Perdana Menteri telah kembali ke pejabat beliau.
9. Ahmad sedang menantikan ayahnya di perhentian bas.
10. Ia telah menunjukkan pembesaran gambar itu kepada isterinya.

Exercise 85   Translate into Malay:
1. His income is five hundred dollars a month.
2. He likes buying toys for his children.
3. The construction of the new Parliament Building commenced last month.
4. After the lesson was finished the children went out and began to play "*sepak raga*".
5. In my opinion Mr So-and-So's drawings and pictures are not very interesting.
6. In this letter there are two words which I do not understand.
7. With your assistance I am going to force him to discuss this matter.
8. The development of Bahasa Malaysia as the national language of Malaysia is of great interest to the people of this country.
9. I am sending this letter for your attention.
10. An exhibition of school-books will be opened tomorrow by the Minister for Education.

Minggu Yang Kesepuluh
Tenth Week

Pelajaran Yang Kedua Puluh Delapan
Lesson 28

Akhiran -Kan 1
The Suffix -Kan 1

A. Sentences

Saya mengharapkan sebuah keréta yang baharu.	*I am hoping for a new car.*
Saya berharap bahawa dia akan datang.	*I hope that he will come.*
Ia telah membelanjakan semua gajinya.	*He has spent all his salary.*
Wang pembeli buku-buku sudah dibelanjakan.	*The money for buying books has been spent.*
Saya akan menamakan anak lelaki saya Ahmad.	*I will call my son Ahmad.*
Buku ini dinamakan "Hikayat Hang Tuah".	*This book is called "The Story of Hang Tuah".*
Ia telah dirajakan oléh rakyat.	*He was made king by the people.*
Guru kami hendak menceritakan kami kisah Hang Jebat.	*Our teacher is going to tell us the story of Hang Jebat.*
Ia akan membesarkan gambar ini.	*He will enlarge this picture.*
Gambar ini terlalu kecil; hendaklah kita besarkan.	*This picture is too small; we shall have to enlarge it.*
Jalan kami terlalu sempit; kami mesti melébarkannya.	*Our road is too narrow; we must widen it.*
Semua jalan-jalan di bandar kita akan dilébarkan oléh Jabatan Kerja Raya.	*All the roads in our town will be widened by the Public Works Department.*
Parit ini mesti didalamkan.	*This ditch (or: drain) must be made deeper.*
Jabatan Parit dan Tali Air akan mendalamkannya.	*The Drainage and Irrigation Department will deepen it.*

157

Bumbung bangunan ini mesti direndahkan.	*The roof of this building must be lowered.*
Ia selalu merendahkan diri(nya).	*He's always humbling himself.*
Gambar itu hendak saya besarkan sendiri.	*I'll enlarge that photograph myself.*
Ia selalu membesarkan diri(-nya).	*He's always "magnifying" himself, i.e. he's always boasting.*
Pelita sudah padam; siapa yang memadamkannya?	*The lamp is out; who put it out?*
Ahmad yang memadamkannya.	*It was Ahmad who put it out.*

B. Word List

Nouns

belanja	*outlay, expense*	perbelanjaan	*expenditure*
harap	*hope*	raja	*king*
cerita (*or* ceritera)	*story*	kisah	*story*
Jabatan Kerja Raya	*Public Works Department*	jabatan	*department*
Jabatan Parit dan Tali Air	*Drainage and Irrigation Department*	J.K.R.	*P.W.D.*
tali air	*canal*	tali	*line, cord, string*
bumbung	*roof*	pelita	*lamp*

Adjectives

dalam	*deep, profound*	sempit	*narrow*
padam	*extinguished, out*	lébar	*wide, broad*

Verbs

berharap	*to hope (intrans.)*
harapkan (mengharapkan)	*to hope for, to set one's hopes on, to bank on*
belanjakan (membelanjakan)	*to spend*
namakan (menamakan)	*to name, to call*
rajakan (merajakan)	*to make a king of*
ceritakan (menceritakan)	*to tell (a story), to narrate*
ceriterakan (menceriterakan)	*to tell (a story), to narrate*
besarkan (membesarkan)	*to enlarge, to magnify*
besarkan diri (membesarkan diri)	*to boast*
lébarkan (melébarkan)	*to widen (trans.)*
dalamkan (mendalamkan)	*to deepen (trans.)*
rendahkan (merendahkan)	*to lower (make lower)*
rendahkan diri (merendahkan diri)	*to humble oneself*
padamkan (memadamkan)	*to extinguish, to put out*

Miscellaneous

diri *or* dirinya	*oneself*	sendiri	*self*

C. Grammar.

144 *Saya mengharapkan sebuah kereta yang baharu:* "I am hoping for a new car." The suffix *-kan* is added to almost any part of speech to form various kind of verbs, all of which are *transitive*, that is they can take a direct object. Furthermore, with the exception of a special construction whereby the suffix *-kan* is added to verbs which already have the prefix *ber-*, and which we shall discuss later in the course, all verbs formed with the suffix *-kan* also take the *me-*prefix when required to do so by the sentence structure. We have already used several of these "*-kan* verbs" without bothering to analyse them into roots and suffixes; for example, *masukkan* and *memasukkan* "to insert" which are derived from *masuk* "to go in" by adding the suffix *-kan* to the root. Similarly, from *harap* "hope" we get the transitive verb *harapkan* with its *me-*form *mengharapkan* meaning "to hope for". The other form, *berharap* with the *ber-*prefix, is only used intransitively.

(Compare the first two sentences in Section A above.) Study carefully the following examples and also the sentences in Section A above in which they occur:

belanja	*expense*	(mem-) belanjakan	*to spend*
nama	*name*	(me-) namakan	*to name, call*
raja	*king*	(me-) rajakan	*to make king*
cerita	*story*	(men-) ceritakan	*to narrate*

Note: cerita and its alternative form *ceritera*, both meaning "story", come from the Sanskrit pair *carita* and *caritera* respectively. Both Sanskrit words also mean "story". *Hikayat*, "story", "romance" comes from the Arabic *hikayah* and *kisah* comes from the Arabic word *qisah*.

145 *Ia akan membesarkan gambar ini:* "He will enlarge this picture." Almost any adjective may be turned into a special kind of verb by adding to it the suffix *-kan*. In this case the function of the suffix *-kan* is much the same as the function of the English prefix *en-* in words like *enlarge* (from *large*) or the suffix *-en* in a word like *deepen* (from *deep*). *Enlarge* means *make larger* and *deepen* means *make deeper;* in the same way *besarkan* (from *besar*) means "to make *lagi besar*". Study the following examples carefully:

besar	*big, large*	(mem-) besarkan	*to enlarge, to magnify*
lébar	*wide, broad*	(me-) lébarkan	*to widen, broaden*
dalam	*deep*	(men-) dalamkan	*to deepen, make deeper*
rendah	*low, humble*	(me-) rendahkan	*to lower, to humble*
padam	*extinguished, out*	(mem-) (p)adamkan	*to put out, to extinguish*
panjang	*long*	(mem-) (p)anjang-kan	*to lengthen*

| kurang | *less* | (meng-) (k)urang-kan | *to decrease, to diminish* |

146 *diri* and *sendiri: Diri* is used as a reflexive pronoun-object and in this form may be used for any person (first, second or third) or number (singular or plural). It may, therefore, have many translations in English. Study the following examples carefully:

Ia telah membunuh diri.
He has killed himself.

Saya hendak minta diri.
I want to excuse myself (said by someone wishing to break off an interview and go away).

Mereka itu menyerahkan diri.
They surrendered (themselves). (*serahkan* and *menyerahkan*, to surrender (trans.)

If it is for any reason important to distinguish *person*, then the suffixed short forms of the personal pronouns may be added, thus: *diriku* "myself", *dirimu* "yourself" or "yourselves", and *dirinya* "himself", "herself", "itself", "oneself", "themselves". Examples:

Ia telah membunuh dirinya.
He has killed himself.

Awak selalu membesarkan dirimu.
You are always boasting.

Aku tidak akan menyerahkan diriku.
I will not surrender.

Sendiri is used to strengthen the subject like the English non-reflexive "myself", "himself", etc. Examples:

Saya sendiri hendak menulis surat kepada dia.
I myself will write a letter to him.

Buku itu sudah saya baca sendiri.
I have read that book myself.

Tiba-tiba pintu terbuka sendiri.
Suddenly the door opened (by) itself.

Sendiri can also be used as a possessive to indicate "one's own", e.g.:

Semua pelawat-pelawat membawa makanan sendiri.
All the visitors brought their own food.

Kita hendak pergi dengan keréta sendiri.
We're going in our own car.

Note also the phrases *sama sendirinya* "between or among ourselves etc.", and *dengan sendirinya* "of its own accord" or "automatically". Examples:

Mereka berunding sama sendirinya tentang perkara itu.
They had a discussion among themselves on the matter.

Pintu bilik saya terbuka dengan sendirinya.
The door of my room opened of its own accord.

Kalau tuan tidak hadir, cadangan tuan akan ditolak dengan sendirinya.
If you are not present, your suggestions will be automatically rejected.

D. Exercises

Exercise 86
Try to guess the meanings of the following:

1. menghabiskan
2. memendekkan
3. menérangkan
4. menghisabkan
5. membebaskan
6. membetulkan
7. menguatkan
8. memaniskan
9. menyatukan
10. membenarkan

Exercise 87
Add the *me-*prefix and the *-kan* suffix to the following words and say what you think the resulting word means:

1	kubur (tomb, grave)	6	hangat (hot)
2	terus (straight on, direct)	7	utama (eminent, important)
3	sebab (cause, reason)	8	sedia (ready)
4	saksi (witness)	9	selesai (finished, done)
5	tetap (permanent, definite)	10	pecah (broken, smashed)

Exercise 88   Translate into English:
1. Saya telah dijemput untuk menyaksikan pembukaan bangunan baharu.
2. Utamakanlah bahasa kebangsaan!
3. Hendaklah kita meneruskan belajar bahasa kebangsaan kita.
4. Orang yang dibunuh itu akan dikuburkan ésok pagi.
5. Karangan encik mesti dipendekkan; karangan yang sepanjang ini saya tidak terbaca.
6. Orang yang ditangkap semalam oléh polis itu akan dibébaskan pada hari Jumaat.
7. Setelah ucapannya diselesaikan Perdana Menteri pun duduklah.
8. Pelajar-pelajar maktab ini tidak dibenarkan keluar selepas pukul sepuluh malam.
9. Semua pelita-pelita mesti dipadamkan pada pukul sebelas malam.
10. Sebelum menceritakan kisah Sang Kancil, guru kami menerangkan perkataan-perkataan yang baharu.

Exercise 89   Translate into Malay:
1. This picture must be enlarged.
2. Our road is going to be widened.
3. Your letter has been put into a new file.
4. The lamp is out; who put it out?
5. The murder of the old man was witnessed by two policemen.
6. I haven't got time to correct your essay right now.
7. Before he could be hanged the murderer commited suicide.
8. This food must be heated before eating.
9. The national language will unite all Malaysians.

10 The Prime Minister said that he wanted to explain the matter himself.

Exercise 90
Write down ten Malay sentences using what you have learned so far.

Minggu Yang Kesepuluh
Tenth Week

Pelajaran Yang Kedua Puluh Sembilan
Lesson 29

Akhiran -Kan 2
The Suffix -Kan 2

A. Sentences

Kapal terbang telah menjatuhkan tiga biji bom.	*The aircraft dropped three bombs.*
Hakim itu menjatuhkan hukum ke atas orang salah.	*The judge pronounced sentence upon the guilty man.*
Perbuatan-perbuatan ini akan mendatangkan banyak kedukaan kepada rakyat.	*These acts will bring much unhappiness to the people.*
Tolong turunkan tong besar itu dari tingkat yang kelima.	*Please bring down that big crate from the fifth floor.*
Kucing itu tak boléh turun; saya hendak memanjat pokok lalu menurunkannya.	*That cat can't get down; I'll climb the tree and get him down.*
Harga getah sudah diturunkan oléh kerajaan.	*The price of rubber has been lowered by the government.*
Kerajaan hendak menaikkan harga getah.	*The government is going to raise the price of rubber.*
Bendéra akan dinaikkan pada waktu matahari terbit.	*The flag will be raised at sunrise.*
Tolong naikkan barang-barang tuan ini ke tingkat yang keempat.	*Please take this gentleman's luggage up to the fourth floor.*
Orang itu malas benar; kita akan mengeluarkannya.	*That man is very lazy; we are going to "put him out" (i.e. sack him).*
Buku ini akan dikeluarkan pada akhir bulan depan.	*This book will be put out (i.e. issued) at the end of next month.*
Budak jahat itu telah dikeluarkan oléh guru besar.	*That naughty boy was expelled by the headmaster.*
Tolong tutupkan pintu.	*Please close the door.*

Malay	English
Butir-butir mesyuarat telah dibacakan.	The minutes of the meeting were read.
Tolong buatkan saya dua helai baju keméja.	Please make me two shirts.
Saya hendak memberikan tuan sedikit nasihat.	I'm going to give you a piece of advice.
Berikan dia secawan téh.	Give him a cup of tea.
Saya membelikan dia sebuah buku yang baharu sampai dari England.	I bought him a book which had just arrived from England.
Tolong tuliskan saya sepucuk surat.	Please write me a letter.
Saya hendak menghantarkan dia buku yang awak pinjamkan saya.	I am going to send him the book which you lent me.
Ia membacakan anak lelakinya cerita Hang Tuah.	He read his son the story of Hang Tuah.

B. Word List

Nouns

bom	*bomb*	hakim	*judge*
hukum	*sentence, judgement*	kedukaan	*unhappiness*
pokok	*tree*	harga	*price*
bendéra	*flag*	kucing	*cat*
matahari	*sun*	waktu	*time*
baju keméja	*shirt*	barang-barang	*luggage*
cawan	*cup*		

Adjectives

patah	*broken, fractured*	salah	*guilty*
malas	*lazy*		

Verbs

jatuhkan (menjatuhkan)	*to let fall, to drop*
jatuhkan (menjatuhkan) hukum	*to pronounce sentence*
datangkan (mendatangkan)	*to bring, to cause*
turunkan (menurunkan)	*to bring down, to take down, to lower.*
naikkan (menaikkan)	*to raise, to take up, to bring up*
keluarkan (mengeluarkan)	*to expel, to dismiss, to issue*
pinjamkan (meminjamkan)	*to lend*
panjat (memanjat)	*to climb*
terbit	*to rise (of the sun), to be issued, published*

Miscellaneous

helai	*cl. for items of clothing, sheets of paper, etc.*
patah	*cl. for words and phrases*
sedikit	*a little*

C. Grammar

147 *Kapal terbang telah menjatuhkan tiga biji bom:* "The aircraft dropped three bombs." Another common function of the suffix -*kan* is to form transitive verbs from intransitive ones. *Jatuh* and *terjatuh* mean "to fall", and so *jatuhkan* and *menjatuhkan* mean "to make fall" or "to fell" or "to drop"; *menjatuhkan hukum* means "to make the sentence fall" and so "to pronounce sentence". Similarly, from *datang* "to come" we get *datangkan* and *mendatangkan* which really mean "to make (someone) come" but are rarely used in this concrete sense: they are more usually used figuratively in the meaning of "to bring about" or "to cause to happen". Further examples:

turun	*to descend*	turunkan menurunkan	*to bring down, to lower*
naik	*to go up*	naikkan menaikkan	*to raise, to take up*
masuk	*to go in*	masukkan memasukkan	*to put in, to insert*

167

keluar	*to go out*	keluarkan mengeluarkan	*to put out, to sack, to issue*

148 *Tolong tutupkan pintu:* "Please shut the door." The suffix *-kan* may be added to almost any transitive verb with little difference to the meaning except that it perhaps adds just a suggestion that the action is being performed for the benefit of someone other than the subject. For this reason the suffix *-kan* is quite often added to a verb when it is used to give an order — that is to say when the verb is in what we should call the imperative mood in English. The addition of *-kan* to an imperative tends to soften it and thereby make it slightly more polite. In the sentence *butir-butir mesyuarat telah dibacakan* — "the minutes of the meeting were read" — the implication is that they were read aloud for the benefit of the members of the committee.

149 *Tolong buatkan saya dua helai baju keméja:* "Please make me two shirts." The suffix *-kan* is frequently added to verbs when the idea of *giving* or *handing over* is suggested. In such sentences *-kan* corresponds very closely with the English prepositions "to" and "for". Further examples:

Saya hendak memberikan tuan sedikit nasihat.
I am going to give (to) you a piece of advice.

Berikan dia secawan téh.
Give (to) him a cup of tea.

Saya membelikan dia sebuah buku.
I bought (for) him a book.

D. *Exercises*

Exercise 91   Translate into English:
1   Bukunya yang baharu belum dikeluarkan lagi.
2   Pada waktu matahari turun, bendéra diturunkan oléh seorang mata-mata.

3 Ia dijemput membacakan butir-butir rancangannya kepada ahli jawatankuasa (*rancangannya:* his plans; *ahli:* member; *jawatankuasa:* committee).
4 Kedukaan ini sudah disebabkan (caused) oléh tindakan-tindakan kerajaan.
5 Tolong pinjamkan saya seratus ringgit.
6 Kerajaan patut menaikkan harga getah.
7 Semalam saya mendengar seorang Cina membacakan cerita péndék di dalam bahasa Melayu.
8 Buatkan dia secawan téh lalu suruh dia tidur.
9 Di dalam surat ini ada dua patah perkataan yang tidak saya faham; cuba encik terangkan kepada saya.
10 Majalah ini dikeluarkan tiap-tiap hari Sabtu.

Exercise 92   Translate into Malay:
1 Please close the door.
2 This student will be expelled.
3 He is going to give you a new book.
4 He is going to call his daughter Rahmah.
5 Don't raise the flag before the sun rises.
6 Tell Ahmad to bring down my luggage before ten o'clock.
7 Before my father went to Singapore, he gave me a piece of advice.
8 He took a sheet of paper and wrote a letter to the chairman of the committee.
9 This coffee is cold; please warm it up.
10 My father did not allow me to give Yusuf a hundred dollars.

Exercise 93
Make up ten Malay sentences of your own using what you have learned so far in the course.

Minggu Yang Kesepuluh
Tenth Week

Pelajaran Yang Ketiga Puluh
Lesson 30

Akhiran -I
The Suffix -I

A. Sentences

Dia berdiri di luar rumah lima minit; lepas itu dia masuk.	*He stood outside the house for five minutes; then he went in.*
Ia memasuki rumahnya.	*He went into his house.*
Rumahnya telah dimasuki oléh empat orang pencuri.	*His house was entered by four thieves.*
Dua jam lagi kami telah mendatangi bandar Kuala Lumpur.	*Two hours later we came to (or: we attacked) the town of Kuala Lumpur.*
Negeri Kelantan telah didatangi oléh askar-askar Jepun pada tahun 1941.	*Kelantan was attacked by Japanese troops in 1941.*
Ia menuruni tebing sungai lalu terjun ke dalam air.	*He went down the river-bank and jumped into the river.*
Ia berlari kuat lalu melompat pagar.	*He ran fast and jumped over the fence.*
Ia melompati pentas lalu mulai bercakap kepada orang ramai.	*He jumped on the platform and began to speak to the crowd.*
Ia mengikut jalan yang menaiki bukit.	*He followed the road which led up the hill.*
Mengikut Radio Peking, Gunung Everest telah dinaiki oléh tiga orang Cina.	*According to Radio Peking, Mount Everest has been climbed by three Chinese.*
Perlahan-lahan kami mendekati sungai yang lébar.	*Slowly we approached the wide river.*
Saya akan menamai anak lelaki saya Yusuf.	*I shall call my son Yusuf.*
Kerusi ini sudah rosak; Ahmad yang merosakkannya.	*This chair is broken; it was Ahmad who broke it.*

Hendaklah kita baikkan.	*We must mend it.*
Hendaklah kita baiki.	*We must mend it.*
Tukang kayu akan membaikkannya.	*The carpenter will mend it.*
Tukang kayu akan membaikinya.	*The carpenter will mend it.*
Ia memasuki rumah.	*He entered the house.*
Ia memasukkan surat ke dalam fail.	*He put the letter in the file.*
Ia menaiki bukit.	*He went up the hill.*
Ia menaikkan tangannya.	*He raised his hand.*
Kapal terbang sudah mendekatkan negeri-negeri jauh.	*The aeroplane has brought distant countries nearer.*
Kapal terbang mendekati negeri Jepun.	*The aircraft approached Japan.*
Ia menuruni bukit lalu memasuki rumahnya.	*He came down the hill and went into his house.*
Turunkan barang-barang saya lalu masukkan ke dalam keréta.	*Bring down my luggage and put it into the car.*

B. Word List

Nouns

sungai	*river*	pentas	*platform, stage*
tebing	*(river-) bank*	kayu	*wood (material)*
panggung	*stage, theatre*	gunung	*mountain*
tukang kayu	*carpenter*		

Verbs

berdiri	*to stand*
terjun	*to jump down*
lompat (melompat)	*to jump up, over*
masuki (memasuki)	*to enter*

datangi (mendatangi)	*to come to, to arrive at, to attack*
turuni (menuruni)	*to descend (trans.), to go down (trans.)*
lompati (melompati)	*to jump on, to jump on to*
mulai (memulai)	*to begin (trans. and intrans.)*
naiki (menaiki)	*to ascend, to go up, to climb*
dekati (mendekati)	*to approach*
dekatkan (mendekatkan)	*to bring near*
namai (menamai)	*to name, to call*
baikkan (membaikkan)	*to mend, to repair*
baiki (membaiki)	*to mend, to repair*

Miscellaneous

hendaklah ...	*it is necessary to (that) ...*	mengikut	*according to*

C. Grammar

150 *Ia memasuki rumahnya:* "He entered his house." The suffix *-i* like the suffix *-kan*, is used mostly to form transitive verbs from other words. Verbs ending with the suffix *-i*, like those ending in *-kan*, may also take the prefix *me-* when the sentence structure demands it. We have already used one of these verbs in *-i*, viz. *wakili* and *mewakili* "to represent", which are derived from the noun *wakil* "representative". The suffix *-i* is not used quite as freely as the *-kan* suffix nowadays to form new verbs and most of the verbs in which it is used are now really "crystallised" forms. Nevertheless some of these verbs are very common and so we must spend a little time on them here. In the majority of cases the suffix *-i* implies that the action denoted by the verbs takes place *in* or *on* or *near* the thing (or person) denoted by the direct object. For example, from the intransitive verb *masuk* "to enter" we get a corresponding transitive form *masuki* (and *memasuki*) which also means "to enter" but must have an object.

Notice the pronunciation of forms like *masuki*. The *-k* of *masuk* represent a glottal stop (*masu'*) and this glottal stop must be retained in the derived form. The suffix -*i* is joined to words ending in -*k* by a pronounced but unwritten -*k; masuki*, then, is normally pronounced as if written *masu'ki* or *masuk-ki*. (Cf. the note on the pronunciation of the -*an* suffix in similar circumstances — Lesson 27 (143) above).

151 *Ia mulai bercakap:* "He began to speak." *Mulai* and *memulai* mean "to begin" and may be used both transitively and intransitively in place of *mulakan (memulakan)* and *bermula* respectively. When used intransitively (instead of *bermula*) *mulai* does not take the *me*-prefix. *Mulai* is derived from the word *mula* which may be either a verb ("to begin") or a noun ("beginning") by the addition of the suffix -*i*. In careful writing the -*i* suffix is written with the diaeresis (two dots) when it is added to a word ending in a vowel. This is to show that it forms a separate syllable which is joined to the root word by a glottal stop. *Mulai*, therefore, is pronounced with three syllables as if written *mula'i*.

152 *pentas* and *panggung:* Originally the word *panggung* meant "a platform", especially the platform or stage on which a dramatic performance took place. The early Malay theatre, however, was a temporary or makeshift affair which was carried about by strolling players and set up wherever it was intended to give a performance. This is still done in country districts by itinerant *wayang kulit* companies and is still quite a common sight in Kedah, for instance. The *panggung* is a kind of covered shed mounted on stakes and is occupied by the actors and others connected with the performance. The audience at such a show sits on the grass around the *panggung*. With the development of the western-style theatre and cinema, however, the word *panggung* has come to be used to mean the whole theatre including the auditorium — in fact the whole building. It is now the most usual word for *theatre* or *cinema*. For *stage* or *platform* (any kind of platform, including a railway platform*) the word *pentas* is now used in Malaysia. In Indonesia, however, the word *pentas* appears to be unknown, and *panggung* means stage as opposed to

---

*nowadays the word *"platfom"* (i.e. English "platform") is usually used for a "railway platform."

auditorium and also means stage or theatre in the abstract (e.g. "my daughter is on the stage" or "he is very interested in the theatre"). In Indonesia a theatre-building is called either *gedung komedi* or *rumah panggung*. Even in Malaysia *panggung* is sometimes used for "stage".

153 *namai* and *namakan; dekati* and *dekatkan:* Notice that in some cases it makes no difference whether we add the *-i* suffix or the *-kan* suffix to a word: *namai* and *namakan* are merely alternatives with the same meaning "to name". In other cases, however, the *-i* suffix produces a different meaning from that given by the *-kan* suffix: when added to the adjectives *dekat* "near" the suffix *-i* produce *dekati* and *mendekati* which means "to get near to" and so "to approach". The *-kan* suffix on the other hand gives *dekatkan* and *mendekatkan*, which are causative in sense and mean "to make or bring near together". Further examples:

	mem-baik-i	*to repair* } *(no difference)*
	mem-baik-kan	*to repair*
but		
	turunkan (menurunkan)	*to bring down*
	turuni (menuruni)	*to descend*
	masukkan (memasukkan)	*to insert*
	masuki (memasuki)	*to enter*
	naikkan (menaikkan)	*to raise*
	naiki (menaiki)	*to ascend, to climb*

D. Exercises

Exercise 94   Translate into English:
1   Bila kapal terbangnya mulai turun, ia pun takutlah.
2   Wayang itu akan bermula (*or:* mulai *or:* dimulakan) pada pukul sembilan setengah malam.
3   Setelah menaiki pentas ia memulakan ucapannya dengan perkataan-perkataan "tuan-tuan dan puan-puan".

4 Kita akan pergi ke panggung Cathay untuk melihat gambar Melayu yang baharu.
5 Ia mendekati panggung lalu berdiri di luar sehingga kawan-kawannya datang.
6 Ahmad telah menurunkan tong besar itu lalu disimpannya di dalam bilik guru besar.
7 Malam semalam rumah saya telah dimasuki oléh seorang pencuri.
8 Meja ini mesti dibaiki oléh tukang kayu.
9 Kerajaan kita akan diwakili oléh Tuan Haji Ahmad.
10 Perlahan-lahan kapal selam itu mendekati pulau kecil itu.

Exercise 95   Translate into Malay:
1 The house was entered by four officers carrying drawn swords.
2 The minutes of the last meeting have not yet been read.
3 My car is damaged; it must be repaired.
4 He approached the river and jumped into the water.
5 The Public Works Department has begun to build a new five-storey building behind the secretariat.
6 He went up on the stage and began his speech.
7 Slowly the enemy troops approached the river.
8 We shall have to repair this building before next year.
9 He sat on the river-bank and watched the children playing in the water.
10 The carpenter began to repair the broken chair with the wood which Ahmad had bought in the market.

Exercise 96
Write down ten Malay sentences of your own using what you have learnt so far in the course.

Minggu Yang Kesebelas
Eleventh Week

Pelajaran Yang Ketiga Puluh Satu
Lesson 31

Awalan Ke-
The Prefix Ke-

A. Sentences

Siapa orang tua itu?	*Who is that old man?*
Dia ketua kampung kita.	*He is our village headman.*
Apa kehendaknya?	*What is his wish?*
Kehendaknya ialah pergi ke negeri Jepun untuk berniaga.	*His wish is to go to Japan to trade.*
Emaknya berkata: "Janganlah menangis lagi, sayangku".	*His mother said: "Don't cry any more (my) darling".*
Di atas méja ada dua buah buku; buku yang kedua buku saya.	*On the table there are two books; the second book is mine.*
Pelajaran ini pelajaran yang ketiga puluh satu.	*This lesson is the thirty-first.*
Naikkan barang-barang saya ke tingkat yang kelima.	*Take my luggage up to the fifth floor.*
Menteri yang pertama ialah Perdana Menteri.	*The first minister is the Prime Minister.*
Ada tiga perkara yang hendak saya kemukakan.	*There are three matters which I must bring up.*
Pertama: dari mana dia datang?	*Firstly: where did he come from?*
Kedua: di mana dia sekarang?	*Secondly: where is he now?*
Ketiga: ke mana dia nak pergi?	*Thirdly: where is he going to?*
Kedua orang itu akan belajar bahasa kebangsaan.	*Both those people will learn the national language.*
Ketiga adik-beradik bersekolah di Ipoh.	*All three brothers and sisters are at school in Ipoh.*
Dua orang sudah datang; keduanya orang Melayu.	*Two people have come; both of them are Malays.*

Dalam almari ada dua buah buku; kedua-duanya dalam bahasa kebangsaan.	*In the cupboard are two books; both of them are in the national language.*
Tiga orang sudah lulus dalam peperiksaan; ketiga-tiganya kawanku.	*Three people have passed the examination; all three of them are friends of mine.*
Ketiganya orang India.	*The three of them are Indians.*
Di pelabuhan ada lima buah kapal perang; kelimanya kapal India.	*In the harbour are five warships; all five are Indian.*

B. *Word List*

Nouns

kehendak	*wish, desire*	ketua	*chief*
adik-beradik	*brothers, sisters, brothers and sisters*	ketua kampung	*village headman*
pelabuhan	*harbour*	kekasih, sayang	*darling, beloved*
perang	*war*	kapal perang	*warship*

Verbs

tangis (menangis)	*to weep, to cry*
berniaga	*to trade*
bersekolah	*to be at school, to go to school*

Miscellaneous

ialah	*to be (used as a copula)*

C. *Grammar*

154 *Dia ketua kampung kita:* "He is our village headman." The prefix *ke-* is mainly used to form new words, normally nouns, from other parts of speech. Such words are for the most part "crystallised"

forms and the prefix is not used so much today as it used to be to form new words. Examples of nouns formed with the prefix *ke-*:

tua	old	ketua	chief, headman (cf. English: elder, alderman)
hendak	to want	kehendak	wish, desire
kasih	love	kekasih	darling

155 *Buku yang kedua buku saya:* "The second book is mine." The prefix *ke-* is frequently added to numbers and when the resulting word has *yang* before it the group forms an ordinal number. This is, of course, the regular method of forming ordinal numerical adjectives and was dealt with fully in "Speak Malay!" (q.v. Lesson 31 (93a) pp. 106). Remember, however, that "first" is usually *(yang) pertama* from the Sanskrit *prathama* "first". *Yang kesatu* is sometimes seen and heard nowadays for "first", but this is still frowned upon by most Malay speakers. Examples:

satu	one	yang pertama	(the) first
dua	two	yang kedua	(the) second
tiga	three	yang ketiga	(the) third
empat	four	yang keempat	(the) fourth
dua puluh	twenty	yang kedua puluh	(the) twentieth
seratus	a hundred	yang keseratus	(the) hundredth
seribu	a thousand	yang keseribu	(the) thousandth
sejuta	a million	yang kesejuta	(the) millionth

156 *Pertama: dari mana dia datang?:* "Firstly, where did he come from?" The ordinal numerals given in (155) above may be used without the prefix *yang* as ordinal adverbs, i.e. those ordinal forms which would end in *-ly* in English. Examples:

pertama	*firstly*
kedua	*secondly*
ketiga	*thirdly*
keempat	*fourthly*

157 *Ketiga adik-beradik bersekolah di Ipoh:* "All three brothers and sisters are at school in Ipoh." The *ke*-forms of the numerals are used when the number is definite, i.e. when it refers to a definitely known group. The same effect is achieved in English by placing *the* or *all the* in front of the number. Note, however, that in English *kedua* is rendered either by "the two" or by "both". Examples:

| dua orang | *two people* | kedua orang | *the two people* or *both people* |
| tiga buah buku | *three books* | ketiga buah buku | *the three books* or *all three books* |

158 *Keduanya orang Melayu:* "Both (of them) are Malays." With the addition of the suffix *-nya* the *ke*-forms of the numerals become pronouns. In this case the root numeral is often reduplicated as well. Examples:

keduanya (kedua-duanya)	*both of them*
ketiganya (ketiga-tiganya)	*all three of them*
keempatnya (keempat-empatnya)	*all four of them*
kelimanya (kelima-limanya)	*all five of them*

159 *Menteri yang pertama ialah Perdana Menteri:* "The first minister is the Prime Minister." The phrase *ialah*, which literally means "he indeed", is often used in written Malay simply as a copula, that is to say it is used where English would have some part of the verb "to be" — "am", "is", "are", "was", "were", and so on. Examples:

Bahasa kebangsaan negeri ini ialah bahasa Melayu.
The national language of this country is Malay.

Perkara itu ialah perkara yang sangat menarik hati.
That matter is a very interesting one.

Bangunan ini ialah Pejabat Kerajaan.
This building is the Government Secretariat.

D. Exercises

Exercise 97   Translate into English:
1. Kehendakku yang besar sekali ialah belajar bahasa Melayu.
2. Bapa saya akan menjadi ketua pejabat.
3. Kita hendak membaca cerita yang pertama dalam buku ini.
4. Kelima-limanya pegawai polis.
5. Tentang bangunan baharu itu ada dua perkara yang hendak kita rundingkan: pertama, di mana akan kita bangunkan; kedua, dari mana akan kita mendapat wangnya?
6. Keempat-empat buah buku itu telah dibelinya semalam.
7. Keempat-empatnya tertulis dengan tulisan Jawi.
8. Ketujuh-tujuh orang Cina itu baharu sampai di negeri ini.
9. Ketua pejabat kita akan memeriksa pejabat pada pukul tiga.
10. Ketiga orang Jepun itu pandai bercakap bahasa Melayu.

Exercise 98   Translate into Malay:
1. All four sisters are in school in Kuala Lumpur, but next year all four will enter the University of Malaya.
2. His desire is to build a new building near the post office.
3. This big house is the fifth that he has built in this road.
4. Having come out of the theatre, the three brothers went into a coffee shop.
5. *Ronggeng* is a Malay dance which we can see throughout Malaysia.
6. Malay is the most useful language in the whole Southeast Asia *(Asia Tenggara)*.
7. Bahasa Malaysia is the official *(rasmi)* language of Malaysia.
8. Ramaswami and Krishnan are two Indians; both of them work in the District Office.
9. These five students did not pass the examination.
10. My father has just *(baharu)* become the headman of our village.

Exercise 99
Write down ten Malay sentences of your own using what you have learnt.

Minggu Yang Kesebelas
Eleventh Week

Pelajaran Yang Ketiga Puluh Dua
Lesson 32

Awalan Ke- dengan lain-lain Tambahan 1
The Prefix Ke- with other Affixes 1

A. Sentences

Buku ini tidak diketahui di negeri ini.	*This book is not known in this country.*
Saya tidak mengetahui perkataan itu.	*I don't know those words.*
Apa yang dikehendakinya tidak saya tahu.	*What he wants I don't know.*
Ia selalu menghendaki apa-apa yang baharu.	*He is always wanting something new.*
Orang itu sangat jahat; kejahatannya tidak tertahan lagi.	*That man is very wicked; his wickedness cannot be tolerated any longer.*
Pelajaran ini susah benar; kesusahannya akan dinyatakan oléh Cikgu.	*This lesson is very difficult; its difficulties will be explained by the teacher.*
Sekarang Malaysia sudah merdéka; kemerdékaannya telah diterima pada tahun 1957 (seribu sembilan ratus lima puluh tujuh).	*Malaysia is now independent; she received her independence in 1957.*
Sekarang Malaysia maju benar; kemajuannya akan berkembang lagi.	*Malaysia is now very progressive; her progress will still increase.*
Ramai orang hendak datang; kebanyakannya orang Cina.	*Many people will come; most of them will be Chinese.*
Eh! Kebodohan orang itu!	*Oh dear! The stupidity of that man!*
Keputusan-keputusan peperiksaan belum dikeluarkan lagi.	*The results of the examination have not yet been issued.*
Keputusannya telah ditolak oléh pihak pembangkang.	*His decision was rejected by the opposition.*

Tali ini sudah putus.	*This string has snapped.*
Perkara itu telah diputuskan oléh ketua pejabat.	*That matter has been decided by the head of department.*
Dengan suara terputus-putus ia berkata bahawa anaknya sakit teruk.	*With a break in his voice he said that his child was seriously ill.*
Ucapannya tidak berkeputusan; kebanyakan pendengarnya pun tidurlah.	*His speech was interminable and the majority of his listeners went to sleep.*
Sidang pendengar yang dihormati sekalian!	*Hullo, listeners!* (lit. *"session of honoured listeners"*).
Para penuntut tidak dibenarkan keluar selepas makan malam.	*Students are not allowed to go out after dinner.*
Para tetamu dipohon memasuki bilik makan.	*Guests are requested to go into the dining-room.*

B. Word List

Nouns

kejahatan	*wickedness*	kesusahan	*difficulty*
kemerdekaan	*independence*	kemajuan	*progress*
kebanyakan	*majority*	kebodohan	*stupidity*
keputusan	*result, decision*	sidang	*session*
pendengar	*listener*	bilik makan	*dining-room*
makan malam	*dinner*		

Adjectives

merdeka	*independent*	bodoh	*stupid*
putus	*severed, snapped*	terputus-putus	*broken, interrupted*
tidak berkeputusan	*endless, interminable*		

Verbs

ketahui (mengetahui)	*to know*
kehendaki (menghendaki)	*to want, to require*
tahan (menahan)	*to bear, to endure*
tertahan	*to be able to bear*
tidak tertahan	*to be unable to bear*
putuskan (memutuskan)	*to decide*
putusi (memutusi)	*to break off, to snap, to sever*
hormati (menghormati)	*to honour, to respect*
pohon (memohon)	*to request*

Miscellaneous

sekalian	*all*	para	*all (plural prefix)*

C. Grammar

160 *Buku ini tidak diketahui:* "This book is not known." There is a small number of verbs formed by adding the prefix *ke-* together with the suffix *-i*. These verbs are all transitive and also take the prefix *me-* whenever necessary. Example:

tahu	*to know*	ketahui (mengetahui)	*to know*
hendak	*to want*	kehendaki (mengehendaki)	*to want, to require*

In connexion with *ketahui*, notice also the noun *pengetahuan*, "knowledge", which is formed from *tahu* by adding to it the suffix *-an* together with the prefixes *pe-* and *ke- (penge-)*.

161 *Kejahatannya tidak tertahan lagi:* "His wickedness can no longer be tolerated." Perhaps the most common use of the prefix *ke-* is together with the suffix *-an*. This combination is added to almost any adjective to form the corresponding abstract noun. Examples:

jahat	*wicked*	kejahatan	*wickedness*
susah	*difficult*	kesusahan	*difficulty*
merdeka	*independent*	kemerdékaan	*independence*

bébas	*free*	kebébasan	*freedom*
maju	*progress*	kemajuan	*progress*
bodoh	*stupid*	kebodohan	*stupidity*

162 *Sidang pendengar yang dihormati sekalian!:* "Hullo, listeners!" (Literally: All honoured listeners!) The word *sidang* means "session" or "gathering" and so *sidang pendengar* means "session of listeners", i.e. "radio audience", but *sidang* is often used in modern Malay simply to indicate that the following noun is to be plural. Another plural-former is the word *para* as in *para penuntut* (students) and *para tetamu* (guests). Both *sidang* and *para* are very commonly used like this nowadays, especially in writing.

Note that *dihormati* (honoured) must be distinguished from *berhormat* (honourable). Both words are derived from *hormat* (honour), but *dihormati* is just a polite expression which may be used of anyone, whereas *berhormat* is only used in official titles, e.g. *yang berhormat menteri pelajaran* "the honourable the minister for education", and so forth.

Note also the word *sekalian*, a more literary word for *semua* "all". *Sekalian* is normally pronounced *skelian* or *sklian*, i.e. with the stress on the last syllable.

D. Exercises

Exercise 100
Try to guess the meanings of the following:

1. kesungguhan
2. kesenangan
3. kejauhan
4. kebaikan
5. kemalasan
6. kesatuan
7. kepahitan
8. kecantikan
9. kebenaran
10. kepandaian

Exercise 101
Try to work out Malay equivalents for the following:

1. dizziness
6. damage

2 narrowness
3 clarification
4 strength
5 depth
7 guilt
8 certainty
9 heaviness
10 sweetness

Exercise 103 Translate into English:
1. Kemajuan Malaysia dan Singapura sangat menarik hati orang di seluruh dunia.
2. Kebanyakan penuntut di maktab ini belajar bahasa kebangsaan.
3. Ramai orang yang menakuti (*takut/menakuti:* "to fear") kematian.
4. Kesusahannya yang besar sekali ialah menulis surat dalam bahasa kebangsaan.
5. Kemalasan budak ini tidak tertahan lagi.
6. Ahmad minta kebenaran untuk keluar selepas makan malam.
7. Guru kami bercakap tidak berkeputusan; akhirnya saya pun tidurlah.
8. Perkara ini tidak boleh kita putuskan sebelum mesyuarat agung.
9. Ia menarik tali lalu diputuskannya.
10. Keterangan perkara-perkara ini tidak dikehendaki lagi.

Exercise 103 Translate into Malay:
1. This officer is very stupid; his stupidity cannot be tolerated any longer.
2. His knowledge is not very profound.
3. The majority of the Chinese in my office are learning the national language.
4. My father has been honoured by the government.
5. That is the word which he did not know.
6. After the results had been issued, he said with a break in his voice that his son had not passed the examination.
7. This matter will be decided by the Prime Minister himself.
8. This string is broken; who broke it?
9. Students are not permitted to bring their own food into the dining-room.

10 Today we shall discuss the progress of the two students who did not pass the examination.

Exercise 104
Write down ten sentences of your own composition in Malay, using what you have learnt so far.

Minggu Yang Kesebelas
Eleventh Week

Pelajaran Yang Ketiga Puluh Tiga
Lesson 33

Awalan Ke- dengan lain-lain Tambahan 2
The Prefix Ke- and other Affixes 2

A. Sentences

Keadaan perékonomian di negeri Ruritania sangat merbahaya.	*The economic situation in Ruritania is very dangerous.*
Urusan Kerajaan.	*(On) Government Service.*
Kawan saya kehilangan ibu bapanya.	*My friend has lost his parents.*
Orang kampung itu kekurangan air.	*The people of that village are short of water.*
Gunung itu kelihatan dari sini.	*The mountain is visible from here.*
Rumahnya kemasukan polis.	*His house was entered by the police.*
Saya sudah meninggalkan buku saya di sekolah.	*I have left my books at school.*
Buku saya tertinggal di sekolah.	*I have left my books at school.*
Buku saya ketinggalan di sekolah.	*I have left my books at school.*
Tiba-tiba kedengaranlah oléh meréka suara orang menyanyi.	*Suddenly they heard the voice of someone singing.*
Ucapannya tidak kedengaran oléh orang di belakang.	*His speech was inaudible to the people at the back.*
Kejadian-kejadian minggu lepas akan dirundingkan oléh para menteri.	*The events of last week will be discussed by the ministers.*
Ramailah orang mati kelaparan.	*Many people died of hunger.*
Kerana kejahatannya ia pun telah dimasukkan ke dalam penjara.	*Because of his wickedness he was put in gaol.*

Kerana kekurangan air keadaan penduduk-penduduk kampung ini kurang baik.	Because of the water shortage the condition of the inhabitants of this village is not very good.
Dua orang kawanku akan pergi ke negeri Jepun; kedua-duanya hendak belajar bahasa Jepun.	Two friends of mine are going to Japan: both of them are going to learn Japanese.
Sebelum kemerdékaan Perdana Menteri Persekutuan dinamakan Ketua Menteri.	Before independence the Prime Minister of the Federation was called the Chief Minister.
Pada bulan Ogos kita akan merayakan ulang tahun Kemerdékaan Malaysia.	In August we shall celebrate the anniversary of the Independence of Malaysia.

B. Word List

Nouns

keadaan	condition, situation	perékonomian	economy, economics
kehilangan	loss	urusan	business
kekurangan	shortage	ibu bapa	parents
kelaparan	hunger	kejadian	event
Seri Paduka Baginda	His Majesty	penduduk	inhabitant
		ulang tahun	anniversary
Ketua Menteri	Chief Minister		

Adjectives

hilang	lost	mati	dead
lapar	hungry	merbahaya	dangerous
kelihatan	visible	kedengaran	audible

Verbs

takutkan (menakutkan)	to frighten

urus (mengurus)	*to manage, to arrange*
uruskan (menguruskan)	*to manage, to arrange*
tinggalkan (meninggalkan)	*to leave (behind)*
tertinggal	*to leave behind, to get left behind*
rayakan (merayakan)	*to celebrate*

Verbals

kehilangan	*to lose*	kemasukan	*to be entered*
kekurangan	*to be short of*	ketinggalan	*to get left behind*
kelihatan	*to be seen*	kedengaran	*to be heard*

Miscellaneous

di belakang   *behind, at the back*

C. Grammar

163 *Keadaan perékonomian sangat merbahaya:* "The economic situation is very dangerous." The prefix *ke-* and the suffix *-an* may be added to other parts of speech as well as to adjectives to form abstract nouns. *Keadaan* is formed from the verb *ada*, "to be" or "to exist", and so means "something which exists", i.e. "situation" or "condition".

Perékonomian is derived from the root-*ékonomi-* (borrowed from the English "economy") by the addition of the prefix *per-* and the suffix *-an*. It may be used either as a noun meaning "economy" or "economics" or as an adjective meaning "economic".

164 *Urusan Kerajaan:* "(On) Government Service." Another phrase which is frequently used nowadays on the envelopes of letters sent out by government departments is *Urusan Seri Paduka Baginda* — "(On) His Majesty's Service". *Seri* is from the Sanskrit word *sri* meaning "glory" and in Malay just as in Sanskrit it is frequently used as an honorific prefix to a name or title (especially names of kings); *paduka* means "excellency" and *baginda* means "majesty". The whole phrase *Seri Paduka Baginda*, then, means "His Majesty" and is the standard way of referring to the Paramount Ruler: *Seri Paduka Baginda Yang Dipertuan Agong Malaysia* means "His Majesty the Paramount Ruler of Malaysia". The word *baginda*, by the way, is used

as pronoun meaning "he" when referring to a king. *Ia* or *dia* would be quite out of place in such contexts and even *beliau* would not be polite enough.

165 *Kawan saya kehilangan ibu bapanya:* "My friend has lost his parents." (Literally: "my friend — loss of parents".) A certain number of *ke*-root-*an* forms can be used in a curious construction in which they appear to be acting as verbs. At the same time, however, they are not basically verbs and seem to retain something of noun idea in them. For this reason, and for want of a better term, I prefer to call them *verbals* in order to remind you that they cannot always be used as verbs. The commonest of them are those given in the list in Section B above. Study the examples in Section A of the lesson carefully and you will see how they work. The use of verbals in such sentences implies that the action is outside the subject's control. This is certainly the difference between *ketinggalan* and *tinggalkan*. *Saya sudah meninggalkan buku saya di sekolah* implies that I left my books at school *on purpose*, whereas the sentences with *ketinggalan* and *tertinggal* (cf. Section A above), which have more or less the same meaning, imply that I left my books at school because I *forgot* to put them in my bag and bring them home.

D. Exercises

Exercise 105   Translate into English:
1   Tiba-tiba kedengaranlah oleh meréka bunyi senapang di dalam hutan.
2   Tolong tinggalkan pintu itu terbuka! Jangan tutup!
3   Keputusan-keputusan peperiksaannya kurang baik.
4   Ia telah kehilangan semua wangnya.
5   Ia menghendaki kemerdékaan perékonomian.
6   Sidang pendengar yang dihormati sekalian! Pelajaran kita sudah dihabiskan bagi minggu ini.
7   Rumahnya tidak kelihatan dari sini.
8   Oléh kerana kekurangan air di sini, sekalian penduduk kampung kita akan berpindah ke tempat lain.

9   Kedua-duanya telah mati kelaparan.
10 Tiba-tiba kerétapi bertolaklah. Saya pun tertinggallah.

Exercise 106   Translate into Malay:
1   After independence had been received, the Chief Minister became the first Prime Minister.
2   The Prime Minister will have discussions with the ministers in the Tunku Abdul Rahman Hall in Kuala Lumpur.
3   Respected readers! I hope that this book will help you to learn our national language.
4   In August we celebrate the anniversary of independence.
5   The majority of my friends are learning the national language.
6   Yesterday the principal of the college told us to write an essay about the exhibition which was held last week.
7   All three of them are going to England to learn English.
8   The events of last month have frightened the government of Ruritania. The situation there now is very dangerous.
9   Don't be afraid to write your letters in the national language.
10 They will celebrate their twenty-fifth wedding anniversary next year (wedding: *perkahwinan*).

Exercise 107
Write down ten Malay sentences of your own composition using what you have learnt so far during the course.

Exercise 108
Write a short composition (about 150 words) on one of the following topics:
   a   Rumah Saya
   b   Bahasa Kebangsaan Kita
   c   Makanan Melayu
   d   Mendengar Radio
   e   Pejabat Tempat Tuan Bekerja

Minggu Yang Kedua Belas / Twelfth Week

Pelajaran Yang Ketiga Puluh Empat / Lesson 34

Pergandaan 1
Reduplication 1

A. Sentences

Bubuh bunga raya itu dalam jambangan.	*Put those hibiscus in a vase.*
Di dalam kebun bapa saudaraku ada banyak bunga-bunga yang cantik.	*In my uncle's garden there are many beautiful flowers.*
Tolong pergi ke kedai bunga-bungaan belikan saya bunga melur.	*Please go to the flower-shop and buy me some jasmine.*
Semalam saya pergi ke pasar buah-buahan membeli buah rambutan.	*Yesterday I went to the fruit market to buy some rambutans.*
Ia sangat suka makan buah-buahan.	*He is very fond of eating fruit.*
Ia sangat suka makan buah ini.	*He is very fond of eating this fruit.*
Buah ini buah apa?	*What fruit is this?*
Buah ini buah cempedak.	*This fruit is a jackfruit.*
Dalam perpustakaan maktab kita ada banyak buku-buku.	*In our college library there are many books.*
Buku itu boléh dibeli di kedai buku itu.	*That book can be bought in that bookshop.*
Tidak ada siapa-siapa dalam rumah itu.	*There isn't anybody in that house.*
Ada apa-apa saya boléh belikan encik di pekan?	*Is there anything I can buy for you in town?*
Buku ini di kedai mana-mana pun tak dapat dibeli.	*You can't buy this book in any shop.*
Ia bertanya boléhkah ia pergi menéngok wayang.	*He asked whether he could go to the theatre.*

Sepanjang hari itu ia bertanya-tanya boléhkah ia pergi menéngok wayang.	*All that day he kept on asking if he could go to the theatre.*
Marilah kita berbual!	*Come on! Let's have a chat!*
Meréka selalu berbual-bual.	*They are always chattering.*
Apa kau buat di sini? Aku sedang menantikan bapaku datang.	*What are you doing here? I am waiting for my father to come.*
Saya tidak boléh menanti-nanti sepanjang hari.	*I can't go on waiting all day long.*
Dia datang pagi-pagi ke rumah saya.	*He came to my house early in the morning.*
Tiap-tiap pagi kita pergi ke sekolah pada pukul tujuh setengah.	*Every morning we go to school at half past seven.*

B. Word List

Nouns

bunga	*flower*	bunga raya	*hibiscus*
bunga melur	*jasmine*	pasu	*flower-vase*
kebun	*garden*	jambangan	*vase*
kedai bunga-bungaan	*flower-shop*	bapa saudara	*uncle*
buah cempedak	*jackfruit*	perpustakaan	*library*
		pergandaan	*reduplication*
kedai buku	*bookshop*	beranda	*verandah (European-style)*
wayang	*play, show*		
serambi	*verandah (Malay-style)*		

Verbs

berbual	*to chat*	nanti (menanti)	*to wait*
bertanya	*to ask, to enquire*	bubuh (membubuh)	*to put*

Miscellaneous

siapa-siapa	*anyone, anybody*	tiap-tiap pagi	*every morning*
mana-mana	*any*	apa-apa	*anything*
sepanjang	*the whole length of, as long as*	di pekan	*in town*
sepanjang hari	*all day long*	pagi-pagi	*early in the morning*

C. Grammar

166 *Banyak bunga-bunga yang cantik:* "Many beautiful flowers." The student will have noticed from previous lessons that Malay makes a great deal of use of what the grammar books call reduplication (*pergandaan*): that is doubling of words. We must now begin to study the various functions of reduplication more systematically.

One of the commonest uses of reduplication in Malay is to indicate a kind of plural, but not the sort of plural we have in English and many other languages. In English the plural simply indicates that there are more than one of something or other, but the Malays do not normally bother to express plurality unless there is some emphasis on *variety*. We say, for instance, *sekuntum bunga* for "one flower", but we should not normally say *lima kuntum bunga-bunga* for "five flowers", which is *lima kuntum bunga* in correct Malay. It would be most unusual to reduplicate a noun when a numeral is present, because the numeral shows quite clearly whether the noun is singular or plural. The English word "flowers" by itself, however, may be either *bunga* or *bunga-bunga* in Malay. There would be certainly no reduplication if the flowers were all of the same kind — all jasmine, say. The doubled form *bunga-bunga* is only used when the flowers are of several different kinds — say, jasmine, frangipanni, bougainvillea and hibiscus, for example — all collected together.

In the sentence *bubuh bunga raya itu dalam jambangan*, "put those hibiscus in a vase", all the flowers are hibiscus and so there is no need to reduplicate the word *bunga*, but in the sentence *di dalam kebun . . . . . ada banyak bunga-bunga yang cantik*, "in the garden there are many beautiful flowers", the implication is that there are many different kinds of flowers in the garden and since there is consequently emphasis on *variety* we must reduplicate *bunga*. Words reduplicated in this way frequently add the suffix *-an* to the whole group, e.g. *bunga-bungaan*. This addition of *-an* emphasises the collectiveness or "uncountableness" of the varied group. Examples:

(a) *Dalam jambangan ada bunga (melur)*.
In the vase are some (jasmine) flowers (i.e. all the flowers are the same).
(b) *Dalam kebun ada banyak bunga-bunga yang cantik.*
In the garden are many beautiful flowers (i.e. all different kinds with emphasis on the variety).
(c) *Dalam kebun ada banyak bunga-bungaan.*
In the garden are many (different) flowers (giving a single map of colour, say; i.e. the emphasis is on the single combined effect of the different kinds of flowers).

167 *Tidak ada siapa-siapa dalam rumah itu:* "There is no-one (or: there isn't anyone) in that house." When the interrogative words *siapa, apa, mana* are reduplicated they often correspond to the English indefinite pronouns "anyone (anybody)", "anything" and "any". Like the English words they are used only in questions and negative statements; in positive statements they are usually still interrogatives. (For further details cf. "Speak Malay!", Lesson 45 (128), p. 146.)

168 *Ia bertanya-tanya bolêhkah ia pergi:* "He kept on asking whether he could go." When a verb is reduplicated is usually indicates continual or continuous repetition of the action. Notice that, if the verb has a prefix or a suffix (or both), only the root is repeated although any phonetic changes caused by the prefix are retained in the second part. For examples, the reduplicated form of *memukul* (from *pukul*) is *memukul-mukul*, or *bertanya-tanya*, and so on. Study the pairs of examples in Section A above very carefully.

169 *Pagi-pagi* means "early in the morning". "Every morning" is *tiap-tiap pagi*.

D. Exercises

Exercise 109   Translate into English:
1. Pagi-pagi bapa saudara saya tiba melawat kami.
2. Di dalam pasu itu sekuntum bunga pun tak ada.
3. Sepanjang hari dia duduk di kebun menengok-nengok bunga-bungaan.
4. Dia bercakap-cakap tiga jam tidak berkeputusan.
5. Buku-bukunya telah disimpan di dalam almari besar.
6. Tiap-tiap hari ia duduk menangis-nangis sahaja kerana kematian anaknya.
7. Sebuah majalah yang dikeluarkan tiap-tiap bulan ialah majalah bulanan.
8. Ia bertanya-tanya boléhkah saya menolongnya; akhirnya saya berkata, "boléh juga."
9. Saya menanti-nantikannya sepanjang hari itu; dia tak sampai juga.
10. Di jalan raya kelihatan banyak keréta-keréta.

Exercise 110   Translate into Malay:
1. He kept on asking whether his father had come.
2. I could not buy anything in the market this morning because I did not have a cent left.
3. The shops in Kuala Lumpur are very interesting.
4. His friends are going to France to learn French.
5. Is anyone sitting on the verandah?
6. The flowers in his garden are very beautiful.
7. He got up early in the morning and went to the office.
8. He kept on asking if he could go to the pictures.
9. Every morning I get up at seven o'clock and drink a cup of tea.
10. The wicked man kept on beating the dog until it died.

Exercise 111
Write down ten Malay sentences of your own composition using what you have learnt so far.

Exercise 112
Write a short composition (about 150 words) on one of the following topics:
    a Bunga-bunga di Kebun Saya
    b Kerani-kerani di Pejabat Saya
    c Seorang Budak Yang Jahat Sekali
    d Askar-askar Malaysia
    e Kedai-kedai Singapura

Minggu Yang Kedua Belas
Twelfth Week

Pelajaran Yang Ketiga Puluh Lima
Lesson 35

Pergandaan 2: Bilangan-bilangan
Reduplication 2: Numerals

A. Sentences

Kalau mata kita tidak tajam, kita tak boleh menjadi mata-mata.	*If our eyes are not sharp, we cannot become policeman.*
Orang itu bukan mati; dia buat-buat sahaja.	*That man is not dead; he's only shamming.*
Budak ini bukan sakit; dia buat-buat sahaja.	*This boy isn't ill; he's only pretending to be.*
Meja panjang itu disokong oleh empat buah kuda-kuda.	*That long table is supported by four trestles.*
Anak saya sangat suka bermain dengan anak-anak patungnya.	*My daughter is very fond of playing with her dolls.*
Pakaian ini mahal-mahal.	*These clothes are terribly expensive.*
Budak-budak itu jahat-jahat; guru besar patutlah bercakap dengan mereka.	*Those children are very naughty; the headmaster ought to speak to them.*
Hendaklah tuan membaca suratkhabar baik-baik.	*You must read the newspaper very carefully.*
Gadis-gadis ini cantik-cantik.	*These girls are very pretty.*
Ia telah minum dua cawan setengah.	*She has drunk two and a half cups.*
Pada pukul sebelas setengah saya pun tidurlah.	*At half past eleven I went to bed.*
Setengah orang tidak suka makan buah durian.	*Some people do not like eating durian.*
Ramailah orang di sini; separuhnya bercakap bahasa Jepun.	*There are crowds of people here; some of them are speaking Japanese.*

Pada pukul tiga suku bapa saya akan sampai.	*At a quarter past three my father will arrive.*
Tiga suku penduduk-penduduk kampung kita bertanam padi.	*Three-quarters of the inhabitants of our village plant padi.*
Dua perlima penduduk penoréh getah.	*Two-fifths of the inhabitants tap rubber.*
Dua perlimanya penoréh getah.	*Two-fifths of them are rubber-tappers.*
Lima perenamnya berugama Islam.	*Five-sixths of them are Muslim by religion.*
Lima puluh peratus penduduk kampung itu orang Cina.	*Fifty per cent of the inhabitants of that village are Chinese.*
Keputusan peperiksaannya baik sekali; ia mendapat lapan puluh peratus.	*His examination results are very good; he got eighty per cent.*
Tiga perpuluhan lima.	*Three point five (3.5).*
Satu perpuluhan sembilan.	*One point nine (1.9).*
Kebanyakan orang itu penoréh getah di kebun getah bapaku.	*Most of those people are rubber-tappers on my father's rubber-estate.*
Tetapi setengahnya peladang.	*But some of them are farmers.*
Saya ingat lima peratus sahaja yang bertanam padi.	*I think only five per cent are padi-planters.*
Siapa orang perempuan yang berdiri dekat telaga itu?	*Who is that woman standing near the well?*
Dia isteri seorang peladang yang bertanam padi di luar kampungku.	*She is the wife of a farmer who plants padi outside my village.*
Dia sedang bercakap dengan isteri pegawai daérah.	*She is talking to the district officer's wife.*
Suaminya akan menjadi penghulu kita.	*Her husband will become our district headman.*

B. *Word List*

Nouns

bilangan	*number*	kuda-kuda	*trestle clothes-horse*
kuda	*horse*	penoréh getah	*rubber-tapper*
anak-anak patung	*doll*	ugama Islam	*Islam*
getah	*rubber, latex*	peladang	*farmer*
ugama	*religion*	penghulu	*district headman*
kebun getah	*rubber-estate*		
		mata	*eye*
telaga	*well*		
suami	*husband*		

Adjectives

tajam	*sharp*	mahal	*dear, expensive*

Verbs

buat-buat	*to sham, to pretend*	berugama Islam	*be Muslim by religion*
toréh (menoréh)	*to tap (rubber)*		

Miscellaneous

dengan baik; or baik-baik	*carefully, properly*	suku	*quarter*
(se) perenam	*(a) sixth*	separuh	*half, some*
perpuluhan	*(decimal) point*	setengah	*half, some*
seperlima	*(a) fifth*	peratus	*per cent*

C. *Grammar*

170 *mata* and *mata-mata*: "eye(s)" and "policeman (-men)". There are a great many reduplicated words in which the doubling indicates a kind of similarity with some other thing the name of which is *not* a doubled word. For instance, although *mata* means "eye", *mata-mata* does not mean "eyes", or at least not literally. *Mata-mata*, of course, means a "policeman", but originally it means a "spy", the idea presumably being that "spies" are the "eyes" of the king. (Cf. the English use of "eye" in detective story slang — "private eye", i.e. "private detective"). Further examples:

kuda	*horse*	kuda-kuda	*trestle* or *clothes-horse*
buat	*to do*	buat-buat	*to pretend to do*
anak	*child*	anak-anak patung	*doll*

171 *Pakaian ini mahal-mahal:* "These clothes are terribly expensive." Often an adjective is reduplicated; this has the effect, usually, of intensifying the adjective and is rather like putting "very" in front of it in English. Study the examples in Section A above. (*N.B.* a reduplicated adjective always suggests the plural or variety.)

172 *Fractions: Setengah* and *separuh* are both used to mean "a half", but *separuh* is only used by itself and never in conjunction with other numerals. Both expressions are also used inexactly to indicate an indefinite number less than the whole; in this use they correspond to the English stressed "some", as in "*some* people like it, but *others* do not". "Two and a half" etc. are expressed by *dua setengah* and so on, but notice that if a noun is used it must come between the whole number and the fraction, e.g.:

dua jam setengah	*two and a half hours*
lima batu setengah	*five and half miles*
tiga kaki setengah	*three and a half feet*

Suku is used for "a quarter" and "three quarters" is *tiga suku**. The other fractions are obtained by adding the prefix *per-* to the basic

---

Note:
Be careful when using *tiga suku*, "three quarters", as it is used colloquially to mean "only three quarters there", i.e. "not all there" or "crazy", "crackers", "nuts"!

cardinal numeral. Examples:

setengah	*a half*
separuh	*a half*
suku	*a quarter*
sepertiga	*a third*
seperlima	*a fifth*
seperenam	*a sixth*
sepertujuh	*a seventh*
seperdelapan	*an eighth*

etc. etc.

The word *perpuluhan* is used to render the English "point" when dealing with decimals, e.g.:

tiga perpuluhan tiga	*three point three*
enam perpuluhan empat	*six point four*
lapan perpuluhan tujuh	*eight point seven*

D. Exercises

Exercise 113   Translate into English:
1 Separuh orang tidak suka makan gulai pedas.
2 Setengahnya bertanam padi di luar kampung itu.
3 Isteri pegawai daérah sangat cantik.
4 Dua buah kuda-kuda tidak cukup untuk menyokong méja sebesar itu.
5 Dua puluh peratus orang kampung saya bertanam padi.
6 Tiga sukunya penoréh-penoréh getah.
7 Surat itu hendaklah tuan tulis baik-baik.
8 Ia duduk dekat telaga kampung berbual dengan isteri penghulu.
9 Dalam peperiksaan yang akhir ia mendapat enam puluh tiga peratus.
10 Semua penduduk-penduduk kampung saya berugama Islam.

Exercise 114   Translate into Malay:
1. Both of them are rubber-tappers on my uncle's rubber-estate.
2. Two-thirds of the inhabitants of our village are farmers.
3. Twenty-five per cent of these people did not vote in the last general election.
4. The women like standing near the well and chatting.
5. My daughter's new doll was terribly expensive.
6. He has failed the examination; he only got thirty-one per cent.
7. He waited for an hour and a half but his friend didn't come.
8. He stayed in China for four and a half years in order to learn Chinese.
9. The time (*waktu*) now is 4.45 p.m.
10. The train will leave at a quarter past eleven in the morning.

Exercise 115

Write a short composition in Malay (about 150 words) on one of the following topics:
   a Sebuah Kebun Getah
   b Telaga Kampung
   c Seorang Mata-mata
   d Kampung Saya
   e Kerja Saya

Minggu Yang Kedua Belas
Twelfth Week

Pelajaran Yang Ketiga Puluh Enam
Lesson 36

Latihan Lagi dengan Pergandaan
Further Practice on Reduplication

A. Sentences

Saya duduk di sebuah kampung besar dekat Sungai Anu.

I live in a large village near the River Such-and-Such.

Ramailah penduduk-penduduk di kampung saya: lebih kurang lima ribu orang.

There are many people living in my village: about five thousand.

Separuhnya berkedai; separuhnya bertanam padi.

Some of them are shopkeepers and some of them plant padi.

Tetapi kebanyakannya bekerja di kebun-kebun getah di keliling kampung itu.

But most of them work on the various rubber-estates around the village.

Saya ingat lapan puluh peratus penduduk kampung kita penoréh getah.

I think eighty per cent of the inhabitants of our village are rubber-tappers.

Bapa saya berkebun getah lebih kurang tiga batu setengah dari kampung.

My father is a rubber-planter about three and a half miles from the village.

Lebih kurang dua ratus orang kampung itu bekerja di kebunnya.

About two hundred of the villagers work on his estate.

Pagi-pagi penoréh-penoréh getah bangun lalu pergi menoréh getah.

Early in the morning the rubber-tappers get up and go tap the rubber.

Mangkuk-mangkuk kecil digantung kepada pokok-pokok getah untuk menerima getah yang mengalir ke dalamnya.

Little cups are hung on the trees to receive the latex which flows into them.

Getah itu diambil oléh penoréh-penoréh getah lalu dimasukkannya ke dalam timba.

The latex is taken by the rubber-tappers and put into buckets.

Selepas itu timba-timba itu dikandarnya balik ke kilang.	After that the buckets are carried on a pole back to the factory.
Ada orang yang membimbit timba dengan tangan, tetapi kebanyakanya mengandarnya selepas memenuhinya dari mangkuk-mangkuk kecil.	There are people who carry the buckets in their hand, but most of them carry them on a pole after filling them from the little cups.
Selepas memungut getah, penoréh-penoréh getah, berhenti dari kerjanya lalu balik makan.	After collecting the latex, the tappers stop work and go home for lunch.
Pada hari Jumaat meréka berhenti awal sedikit lalu balik mandi.	On Fridays they stop a bit earlier and go home for a bath.
Lepas mandi kebanyakannya pergi sembahyang di mesjid ataupun di surau-surau yang kelihatan di dalam kebun-kebun getah.	After having a bath most of them go for prayers in the mosque or in the chapels which can be seen in the various rubber-estates.
Ugama kebanyakan penduduk-penduduk kita ugama Islam; oléh kerana itu empat lima tahun dahulu sebuah mesjid yang cantik telah dibangunkan di tengah-tengah kampung.	The religion of the majority of our inhabitants is Islam; for this reason, about four or five years ago a very beautiful mosque was built right in the centre of the village.
Pada hari Jumaat bapa saya selalu pergi ke mesjid.	On Fridays my father always goes to the mosque.
Bapa saudara saya pun selalu pergi sama.	My uncle always goes with him.
Kedua-duanya suka sembahyang bersama-sama dengan orang gajinya.	Both of them like to pray together with their employees.

Kadang-kadang abang saya pun pergi juga, tetapi saya dan adik saya masih kecil lagi; kami selalu tinggal di rumah.

Emak saya memang tidak pergi ke mesjid bersama-sama bapa; ia selalu tinggal di rumah memasak nasi tengah hari.

Kakak dan adik perempuan saya suka menolong emak masak nasi.

Datuk saya sudah meninggal dunia dua tahun dahulu, tetapi nenek saya masih hidup; ia duduk di rumah kami selepas kematian suaminya.

Masa emak masak nasi dengan pertolongan kakak, adik perempuan pun mendukung bayi yang berumur enam bulan sahaja.

Rumah kami rumah cara Melayu; bukan besar-besar, tetapi bukan kecil-kecil pula.

Masa emak bekerja di dapur, saya pun duduk di serambi.

Perkakas-perkakas di serambi bukan banyak, tetapi cukup pada kehendak kami.

Rumah kami ada dua buah bilik mandi; lagipun di dalam tiap-tiap bilik mandi ada jamban.

Sometimes my elder brother goes too, but my younger brother and I are still too young, and we always stay at home.

My mother, of course, does not go to the mosque along with father; she always stays at home to cook the midday meal.

My elder and younger sisters like helping mother with the cooking.

My grandfather died two years ago but my grandmother is still alive; she has been living in our house since the death of her husband.

While mother cooks the rice with the help of my elder sister, my younger sister carries the baby who is only six months old.

Our house is a Malay-style house; it is not particularly big, but it is not very small either.

While mother works in the kitchen, I sit on the verandah.

The furniture on the verandah is not much in quantity but it is enough for our needs.

Our house has two bathrooms; and in each bathroom there is a toilet.

| Rumahtangga kami sangat bahagia. | Our home is a very happy one. |
| Lamun semua rumahtangga di tanahair kita ini boleh menjadi begitu bahagia! | If only all the homes in this motherland of ours could be as happy! |

B. Word List

Nouns

batu	*stone, mile*	mangkuk	*bowl, cup (without handles)*
mesjid	*mosque*	pokok getah	*rubber tree*
orang gaji	*employee*	surau	*chapel (Muslim)*
kakak	*elder sister*	tengah hari	*midday*
nenek	*grandmother*	datuk	*grandfather*
umur	*age*	kematian	*death*
perabot	*furniture*	dapur	*kitchen*
jamban	*lavatory, toilet*	bilik mandi	*bathroom*
tanahair	*motherland*	rumahtangga	*home*
timba	*bucket, pail*	sukacita	*happiness, joy*

Verbs

gantung (menggantung)	*to hang*	bangkit	*to get up*
bimbit (membimbit)	*to carry in the fingers*	alir (mengalir)	*to flow*
sembahyang	*to pray*	kandar	*to carry on a pole*
hidup	*to live, to be alive*	penuhi (memenuhi)	*to fill*
berumur	*to be ... years old*	pungut (memungut)	*to collect*
		meninggal dunia	*to die*

bahagia	to be happy	dukung (mendukung)	to carry (a child astride on the hip)

Miscellaneous

lebih kurang	about, more or less, approximately	begitu	so, thus
oléh kerana itu	for this reason, therefore	di keliling	around
		awal	early
kadang-kadang	sometimes	sama	same, as well
memang	of course, as you know		
		masih	still, yet
bersama-sama (dengan)	together with		
lagipun	furthermore		

C. Grammar

173 *Kebanyakannya bekerja di kebun-kebun getah:* "Most of them work on the rubber-estates." Notice how a compound word is reduplicated: the normal way is to double the first element only. Examples:

kebun getah	*rubber-estate*	kebun-kebun getah
orang kampung	*villager*	orang-orang kampung
penoréh getah	*rubber-tapper*	penoréh-penoréh getah
Perdana Menteri	*Prime Minister*	Perdana-perdana Menteri

Sometimes, however, the whole phrase may be reduplicated as if it were a single word. Example:

Perdana Menteri	*Prime Minister*	Perdana-menteri Perdana-menteri

The first method is far more common than the second.

174 *Datuk saya sudah meninggal dunia:* "My grandfather has passed away" (lit. has left the world). The expression *meninggal dunia* is a euphemism for *mati*, which some Malays feel to be too brutally frank for ordinary use. There are several similar expressions used for the English "die". Examples:

mati	*"to die" — this is the ordinary word and can be used for both people and animals.*
meninggal dunia	*"to leave the world" — a euphemism used of people; the word* dunia *is often left out, although some Malays do not understand the expression unless the* dunia *is included.*
mangkat	*"to die" — the word normally used of kings, sultans, and other very high ranking personages.*
kembali ke *rahmahtullah*	*"to return to the mercy of God — a very polite expression which can be used of anyone.*
kembali ke alam baka	*"to return to the house of the Eternal" — another polite expression used of people.*

There are many other religious and semi-religious expressions but those given above will suffice for practical purposes. Note also that when one mentions the name of a dead person it is regarded as proper to follow the name immediately with the Arabic sentence *rahimahu'llah*, "may God have mercy upon him".

D. *Exercises*

Exercise 117   Translate into English:
1   Ia mengandar dua timba getah balik ke kilang.
2   Awak mesti memenuhi timba ini dengan getah yang sudah mengalir ke dalam mangkuk-mangkuk.
3   Pada hari Jumaat di mesjid-mesjid dan di surau-surau ramailah orang Melayu sembahyang.
4   Ramailah orang India yang bekerja sebagai penoréh getah di kebun-kebun getah Malaysia.

5 Datuk saya *rahimahu'llah,* telah meninggal dunia pada tahun 1948.
6 Sebelum kembali ke *rahmatullah* ia pun memberi nasihat kepada isterinya.
7 Seri Paduka Baginda Yang Dipertuan Agong yang pertama telah mangkat pada tahun 1960.
8 Setelah mesyuarat ditamatkan, Ahmad memungut semua kertas-kertas yang tertinggal di atas méja besar itu.
9 Ia menggantung sebiji mangkuk kecil kepada pokok getah itu untuk memungut getah.
10 Ayahnya masih hidup lagi, tetapi ibunya telah meninggal.

Exercise 118   Translate into Malay:
1 Last Friday Ahmad prayed in the chapel on the rubber-estate where (*tempat*) he works as a rubber-tapper.
2 Ahmad's elder brother, as you know, is a padi-planter.
3 Although my grandfather is still alive, he is seriously ill.
4 Ah Chong is twenty years old and his elder sister is twenty-three.
5 Mother is preparing the midday meal in the kitchen.
6 Around our house are many rubber-trees.
7 While my elder sister carries the baby (*kanak-kanak*), my younger sister is cooking the rice.
8 Carry this bucket back to the factory.
9 The latex must be collected early in the morning.
10 People who love their motherland (they) ought to learn its national language.

Exercise 119
Write down ten Malay sentences of your own composition, using what you have learnt so far.

Exercise 120
Write a short composition (about 150 words) in Malay on one of the following topics:

a Menoréh Getah
b Ugama-ugama di Malaysia
c Hari Jumaat di Kampung
d Rumahtangga Saya
e Bangun Pagi

Minggu Yang Ketiga Belas
Thirteenth Week

Pelajaran Yang Ketiga Puluh Tujuh
Lesson 37

Menulis Surat dalam Bahasa Melayu 1
Writing Letters in Malay 1

A. Sentences

Saudaraku Ahmad	*My dear Ahmad*
Saudariku Fatimah	*My dear Fatimah*
Sahabatku Ahmad	*My dear Ahmad*
Sahabatku Fatimah	*My dear Fatimah*
Saudaraku yang diingati	*My very dear friend*
Yang benar	*Yours sincerely, yours truly, yours faithfully*

Pagi tadi saya menerima sepucuk surat daripada kawan saya Ahmad di Ipoh.
This morning I received a letter from my friend Ahmad in Ipoh.

Dalam suratnya ia berkata: Sahabatku yang diingati.
In his letter he said: My very dear friend.

Sekarang sudah lama kita tak berjumpa.
It is now a long time since we saw each other.

Oléh kerana itu saya menulis surat ini untuk menjemput saudara melawat kami di Ipoh, dan tinggal di sini dua tiga hari.
For this reason I am writing this letter to invite you to visit us in Ipoh, and to stay two or three days here.

Tolong saudara membalas surat memberitahu kami bila saudara boléh datang.
Please reply and let us know when you can come.

Yang benar, Ahmad.
Yours sincerely, Ahmad.

Sangat suka hati saya menerima surat itu.
I was very pleased to receive this letter.

Dengan lekas saya mengambil kertas lalu memenuhi kalam saya dengan dakwat.
I at once took some paper and filled my pen with ink.

Lepas itu saya mulai menulis surat balasan kepada Ahmad.	*Then I began writing a reply to Ahmad.*
Saya menulis: Saudaraku Ahmad yang diingati.	*I wrote: My very dear Ahmad.*
Dengan sukacita saya menerima surat saudara pagi tadi.	*I was very pleased to receive your letter this morning.*
Terlebih dahulu, saya hendak mengucapkan terima kasih di atas jemputan saudara melawat saudara sekalian di Ipoh.	*Firstly, I must thank you for your invitation to visit you all in Ipoh.*
Pada akhir bulan ini saya hendak bercuti dua tiga hari; oléh sebab itu tentulah saya boléh datang ke Ipoh.	*At the end of this month I shall be taking two or three days' leave and so I shall certainly be able to come to Ipoh.*
Saya hendak menulis sekali lagi bila hari cuti saya sudah tetap. Yang benar, Dolah.	*I will write again when the date of my leave is definite. Yours sincerely, Dolah.*
Lepas itu saya masukkan surat ke dalam sampul surat lalu melekatkannya dengan perekat.	*Then I put the letter into an envelope and stuck it down with gum.*
Sesudah itu saya pergi ke pejabat pos membeli setém.	*After that I went to the post office to buy a stamp.*
Saya menjilat setém dengan lidah saya untuk melembapkannya.	*I licked the stamp with my tongue to moisten it.*
Lepas itu saya memasukkan surat saya ke dalam peti surat di luar pejabat pos.	*Then I put the letter into the post-box outside the post office.*
Setelah saya mengirim surat itu saya pun baliklah.	*After I had posted the letter, I went home.*
Agaknya Ahmad akan menerima surat saya ésok.	*Probably Ahmad will receive my letter tomorrow.*

B. Word List

Nouns

saudara	*friend (male)*	saudari	*friend (female)*
sahabat	*friend*	dakwat	*ink*
kalam	*pen*	surat balasan	*reply, answer*
sampul surat	*envelope*	cuti	*leave, holiday*
pos	*post, mail*	perekat	*gum*
lidah	*tongue*	setem	*stamp*
peti surat	*letter-box*		
peti	*box, case*		

Adjective

lekas	*quick, swift*	tetap	*definite*
lembap	*moist, damp*		

Verbs

ingat (mengingati)	*to remember, to think of*
balas (membalas)	*to return, to give back*
beritahu (memberitahu)	*to tell, to inform*
lekatkan (melekatkan)	*to stick (trans.)*
jilat (menjilat)	*to lick*
lembapkan (melembapkan)	*to moisten*
kirim (mengirim)	*to send, to post*
berjumpa (dengan)	*to meet with*
jumpa	*to meet, to find*
bercuti	*to take leave, to be on leave, to have a holiday*

Miscellaneous

lekas	*at once, immediately*	oleh sebab itu	*for this reason*

C. Grammar

175 *Letter writing in Malay:* One of the most common uses most of us are going to find for the National Language in the immediate future is to write letters. Now, to master the art of Malay letter-writing is probably beyond most of us, as the style of writing differs greatly according to the rank and position of both the receiver and the sender of the letter. Love letters to sweethearts, for instance, are often couched in extremely decorative and poetic language, while letters to a king or a sultan have to observe a great many dignified courtesies involving a lot of quite difficult Malay expressions and often Arabic ones as well. Most of us, however, are not going to write love letters in Malay, nor are we going to address personal petitions to the reigning monarch! All of us, though, at some time or other are going to have to write a short note in Malay to a friend — issuing or accepting an invitation, for example — or to an employee —giving an order or granting a request, say — and also we shall want to be able to write letters to, and answer letters from, government departments and commercial firms. This sort of letter-writing is fortunately fairly straightforward in Malay provided that we take the trouble to learn a handful of stereotyped phrases or cliches of the kind to be found in English commercial correspondence or in letter-writing in almost any other language for that matter. Now, these set expressions are used in modern letter-writing mainly at the beginning and end of letters, the text in between being written in the simplest and clearest language possible. The opening and closing of the letter are usually statements of politeness or friendliness according to the relationship between the writer and the addressee. Out of courtesy to the addressee the writer should however, make the body of the letter — that is the part that carries the message — as easy to understand as possible. This applies as well in Malay as in English.

As for the general layout of the letter, the English system is widely used among the Malays today, especially when they write in Roman script: that is, the sender's address (and sometimes his name as well) in the top right-hand corner, and, if the letter is an official or commercial one, the addressee's name and address below this but over against the left-hand margin.

176 *Saudaraku Ahmad:* "My Dear Ahmad" (literally: "my friend

Ahmad"). This is a common way of opening a letter to a close friend. Slightly more polite is *saudara saya*. *Saudara* is one of the few Malay words which shows *gender:* it has a feminine form *saudari*. Also used instead of *saudara* and *saudari* is the Arabic word *sahabat*, which does duty for both sexes. (Note that *kamu, awak* and *engkau* are never used in letter-writing.)

177 *Saudaraku yang diingati:* "My very dear . . . " This is a more affectionate from than the one given in 176 above. *Diingati* is the passive form of the verb *ingati (mengingati)*, which is derived from *ingat (mengingat)*, "to remember", by the addition of the suffix *-i*. *Ingati* has two meanings: it normally means "to remind" or "to admonish" but in this context (letter-writing) it means "to think about" and so the expression *saudaraku yang diingati* literally means "my friend who is thought about" and so comes to much the same as the English "my very dear friend".

178 *Yang benar:* "Yours faithfully" or "yours sincerely". This phrase, which means literally "the true one", is the best way of ending any letter, official or friendly.

D. Exercises

Exercise 121   Translate into English:

> 27, Jalan Bukit,
> Kampung Bahagia,
> Negeri Sembilan.
> 15 hb[1] Julai 1961

Saudaraku Yusuf yang diingati,

Baharu pagi tadi sudah saya menerima surat yang dikirim saudara kepadaku dari Pulau Pinang. Oléh sebab itu lambat saya mengirim surat balasan. Tolong maafkan saya.

---

[1] hb: an abbreviation for *hari bulan*.

Saya sangat suka hati membaca dalam surat saudara bahawa saudara boléh datang melawat kami di Kampung Bahagia pada akhir bulan ini. Tolong saudara menulis sepucuk surat lagi memberitahu kami pukul berapa dan hari apa saudara akan sampai di sini. Saya akan menantikan saudara di perhentian kerétapi.

Yang benar,
AHMAD.

Exercise 122   Translate into Malay:
1. Ahmad licks the stamp and sticks it on the envelope.
2. I must post this letter to my father before five o'clock.
3. My dear Ahmad: I am writing to invite you to dinner on the 28th of August.
4. Please let me know if you can come. Yours sincerely, Yusuf.
5. Please go to the post office and buy stamps.
6. When the letter arrived Ahmad immediately opened it and read it.
7. The letter which you sent to me on the 16th of August has not yet arrived.
8. In his letter he informed his father that he had started learning the national language.
9. He has written to inform me that his father has just died.
10. Ahmad filled his pen with ink and then wrote a letter to his friend.

Exercise 123
Write ten Malay sentences of your own composition using what you have learnt so far in the course.

Exercise 124
Write a short letter on one of the following topics:
   a   Kepada seorang kawan mengucapkan terima kasih kepadanya di atas hadiah yang diterima daripada dia.

b   Kepada seorang kawan menjemputnya makan nasi di rumah tuan.

c   Memberitahu seorang kawan bahawa tuan akan melawat dia dan meminta kebenaran tinggal dua tiga hari di rumahnya.

d   Menghantar sebuah buku yang menarik hati kepada seorang kawan.

e   Tuan telah menerima sepucuk surat daripada seorang kawan; dalam surat itu tuan dijemput makan nasi di rumah kawan itu; tulislah surat balasan.

Minggu Yang Ketiga Belas
Thirteenth Week

Pelajaran Yang Ketiga Puluh Delapan
Lesson 38

Menulis Surat dalam Bahasa Melayu 2
Writing Letters in Malay 2

A. Sentences

Tuan: Dengan hormatnya dimaklumkan adalah surat tuan telah diterima.

Sir: I have the honour to inform you that your letter has been received.

Dengan hormatnya dipersilakan tuan bersyarah kepada penuntut-penuntut maktab kami.

I have the honour to invite you to lecture to the students of our college.

Dengan sukacitanya dimaklumkan adalah cadangan tuan telah diluluskan oléh jawatankuasa.

I am pleased to inform you that your suggestion has been accepted by the committee.

Dengan dukacita dimaklumkan adalah tuan tidak lulus dalam peperiksaan.

I regret to inform you that you have not passed the examination.

Dengan sukacita dimaklumkan adalah keputusan-keputusan Sijil Persekolahan baharu tiba dari England.

I am pleased to inform you that the School Certificate results have just arrived from England.

Dengan dukacita dimaklumkan adalah perkhidmatan tuan di pejabat ini tidak dikehendaki lagi.

I regret to inform you that your services in this office are no longer required.

Bersama-sama ini saya hantarkan butir-butir mesyuarat bulan lepas.

I enclose herewith the minutes of last month's meeting.

Bersama-sama ini saya hantarkan balik butir-butir yang belum ditandatangani.

Herewith I return the minutes which have not yet been signed.

Bersama-sama ini saya sertakan sepucuk surat daripada seorang kakitangan saya.	*I forward herewith a letter from one of my staff.*
Bersama-sama ini saya kirimkan contoh-contoh tandatangan saya.	*I send herewith specimens of my signature.*
Surat ini mesti dialamatkan kepada setiausaha.	*This letter must be addressed to the secretary.*
Surat itu telah saya alamatkan kepada Setiausaha Tetap.	*That letter I addressed to the Permanent Secretary.*
Tidak patut tuan mengalamatkannya kepada tuan pengarah.	*You should not address it to the director.*
Patut kita mengirim surat itu dengan pos udara.	*We ought to send that letter by airmail.*
Kita mesti mengirim bungkusan ini sebelum pukul empat.	*We must post this parcel before four o'clock.*
Pegawai pos yang tinggi sekali dinamakan Ketua Pos Negara.	*The highest postal official is called the Postmaster General.*
Kerani duduk di belakang kisi-kisi tingkap dan mengeluarkan setém.	*The clerk sits behind the grille and issues stamps.*
Lésén-lésén pun dikeluarkannya juga.	*He also issues various kinds of licences.*
Surat tuan yang bertarikh lima hari bulan Jun belum kami terima lagi.	*We have not yet received your letter dated the fifth of June.*

B. Word List

Nouns

hormat (-nya)	*honour, respect*	jawatan	*office, position*

kuasa	*power*	jawatankuasa	*committee*
dukacita	*sadness, regret*	perkhidmatan	*service*
kakitangan	*employees, staff*	contoh	*example, specimen*
setiausaha	*secretary*	Setiausaha Tetap	*Permanent Secretary*
sijil	*certificate*	udara	*air, sky*
Sijil Persekolahan	*School Certificate*	persekolahan	*schooling*
		pos udara	*airmail*
bungkusan	*parcel*		
		Ketua Pos Negara	*Postmaster General*
negara	*(the) state*		
kisi-kisi tingkap	*grille*	kisi-kisi	*trellis, lattice*
		lésén	*licence*
tarikh	*date*		

Verbs

maklumkan (memaklumkan)	*to inform*
persilakan (mempersilakan)	*to invite, to request*
hantarkan (menghantarkan)	*to send*
hantarkan balik (menghantarkan balik)	*to send back, to return*
tandatangani (menandatangani)	*to sign*
sertakan (menyertakan)	*to forward*
kirimkan (mengirimkan)	*to send*
arahkan (mengarahkan)	*to direct*
alamatkan (mengalamatkan)	*to address*
bertarikh	*to be dated*

Miscellaneous
adalah   *that (conj.)*

C. Grammar

179   *Tuan: Dengan hormatnya dimaklumkan adalah . . . .* : "Sir: I have the

honour to inform you that..." In Lesson 37 we confined our attention to friendly letter-writing. Most of us at some time or other, however, have to write or receive letters of a more formal kind, and in this kind of letter-writing most languages have special phrases and expressions, especially at the beginning of the letter. Malay is no exception to this, and so let us consider some of the most common openings which are used in official letter-writing in Malay.

The safest way to address someone officially is to use the word *Tuan* all by itself. *Tuan*, then, corresponds, more or less to the English "Sir" or "Dear Sir". The feminine equivalent is *Puan*, which corresponds to "Madam" or "Dear Madam".

The phrase *dengan hormatnya* means literally "with respect" or "with honour". *Hormat* means "respect" or "honour" and the addition of *-nya* makes no real difference. We shall have more to say about this use of *-nya* in a later lesson. (cf. Lesson 46); for the moment just accept it as it stands in this phrase; it could equally well be left out.

Maklum is from the Arabic word *ma'lum*, which means "known" and from it is derived the verb *maklumkan (memaklumkan)* meaning "to inform" or "to make known". *Dimaklumkan*, therefore, is the passive form and means "it is made known" or, in this context, "you are informed".

Adalah is used a great deal in classical Malay to introduce a new topic of discussion, and in this context it has the same meaning as *bahawa*, which also is used in the classical literature to introduce a new topic: both *bahawa* and *adalah* are often used in the modern written language to introduce a *noun clause*, like the English conjunction *that*.

The whole sentence *dengan hormatnya dimaklumkan adalah surat tuan telah diterima,* therefore, means literally: "with respect it is made known that your letter has been received". Notice that the Malay version is more impersonal than the English. The writer, who represents a department, has managed to keep himself out of it altogether.

Note the following common opening phrases which can be used in formal correspondence:

dengan hormatnya dimaklumkan adalah . . .	*I have the honour to inform you that . . .*
dengan hormatnya dipersilakan tuan . . .	*I have the honour to request (or: invite) you to . . .*
dengan sukacitanya dimaklumkan adalah . . .	*I am pleased to inform you that . . .*
dengan dukacitanya dimaklumkan adalah . . .	*I regret to inform you that . . .*
bersama-sama ini saya hantarkan . . .	*I enclose herewith . . .*
bersama-sama ini saya hantarkan balik . . .	*I return herewith . . .*
bersama-sama ini saya sertakan . . .	*I forward herewith . . .*
bersama-sama ini saya kirimkan . . .	*I send herewith . . .*

180 *Dipersilakan tuan bersyarah . . .:* "You are requested (or invited) to lecture." The verb *persilakan* is derived from *sila* (please) by the addition of the suffix *-kan* and the prefix *per-*. Its *me-*form is an exception to the rules given in Lesson 4 in that the *p-* of *per-* does not diappear when *me-* is added: the *me-*form is *mempersilakan*. *Persilakan* is one of a large group of such verbs about which we shall have more to say later (cf. Lesson 42).

181 *Tandatangani:* "To sign." This verb is a good example of the flexibility of the Malay language: here the suffix *-i* has been added to a phrase — *tandatangan* — to give a new verb *tandatangani* with a *me-*form *menandatangani*, meaning "to sign". *Tanda* means "sign" and *tangan* means "hand"; *tandatangan*, therefore, means "signature". In the spoken language the word *sain* (from English "sign") is perhaps more common than *tandatangani*. Example:

Surat itu saya tak sain lagi (colloquial)
Surat itu belum saya tandatangani lagi (written)
That letter I haven't signed yet.

182 *Kakitangan:* "Employees" or "staff". Note this picturesque phrase which literally means "hands and feet". A great man's hands and feet are often those of his employees, who do his fetching and carrying for him. *Kakitangan*, then, first came to mean "servants" and then "employees" or "staff". A common notice which may be seen in offices anywhere is KAKITANGAN PEJABAT SAHAJA — (OFFICE) STAFF ONLY.

D. *Exercises*

Exercise 125   Translate into English:

1. Hendaklah pintu ini digunakan oléh kakitangan pejabat sahaja.
2. Dengan hormatnya tuan dipersilakan membayar cukai tuan sebelum akhir bulan ini (*cukai:* tax).
3. Bersama-sama ini saya sertakan dua buah buku yang baharu diterima dari Negeri Perancis.
4. Ahmad menandatangani surat itu lalu dimasukkannya ke dalam sampul surat.
5. Surat yang ditulis semalam oléh tuan pengarah itu hendaklah kita kirimkan dengan pos udara.
6. Dengan dukacita dimaklumkan adalah cadangan tuan telah ditolak oléh jawatankuasa kerana kekurangan wang.
7. Dengan sukacita dimaklumkan adalah tuan telah lulus dalam peperiksaan akhir.
8. Berkenaan dengan surat tuan yang bertarikh 13 hb Mei dengan dukacita dimaklumkan adalah kebenaran yang dipohon oléh tuan tidak boléh diberikan pada masa ini.
9. Jangan kirimkan surat ini sebelum ditandatangani oléh tuan pengerusi.

10 Bersama-sama ini saya hantarkan balik wang sebanyak lima puluh ringgi (*sebanyak:* as much as, to the extent of).

Exercise 126   Translate into Malay:
1 Sir: I have the honour to inform you that your letter dated the 18th of June has been received.
2 Letters should be addressed to the Permanent Secretary.
3 This parcel is too big; it cannot be sent by airmail.
4 I regret to inform you that your proposal has been rejected by the Minister.
5 With reference to your letter dated the 15th of September I have pleasure in informing you that the sum of $600 will be returned to you by the end of this month (the sum: *wang sebanyak*).
6 The director read the letter and then signed it.
7 In connexion with your undated letter I regret to inform you that your son cannot enter a secondary school until he is twelve years old.
8 I have the honour to inform you that the official national language course will begin on the 25th of August.
9 I send all my letters by air mail.
10 All parcels must be sent by sea (*dengan kapal laut*); airmail is too expensive.

Exercise 127
Write down ten Malay sentences of your own composition using what you have learnt so far.

Exercise 128
Tulislah sepucuk surat rasmi yang péndék (lebih kurang 75 perkataan) tentang *satu* daripada perkara-perkara yang berikut (*following*) ini:
  a tuan tidak mahu membayar cukai tuan sebelum akhir tahun ini;
  b tuan bertanya sudahkah tuan lulus dalam peperiksaan bahasa Melayu;

c   seorang kakitangan tuan hendak mendapat kerja di pejabat lain;
d   tuan hendak mendaftarkan nama anak tuan supaya ia boléh masuk sebuah sekolah menengah tahun depan;
e   tulislah surat balasan untuk *satu* daripada perkara *(a) — (d)* di atas.

Minggu Yang Ketiga Belas
Thirteenth Week

Pelajaran Yang Ketiga Puluh Sembilan
Lesson 39

Menulis Surat dalam Bahasa Melayu 3
Writing Letters in Malay 3

A. Sentences

Apa encik nak buat malam ini?	*What are you going to do this evening?*
Saya nak menulis surat kepada seorang sahabat saya di Raub.	*I'm going to write a letter to a friend of mine in Raub.*
Ceritakan saya dalam bahasa Melayu macam mana encik menulis surat.	*Tell me in Malay how you write a letter.*
Baiklah. Mula-mula saya mengambil sehelai kertas tulis.	*All right. First of all I take a sheet of writing-paper.*
Lepas itu saya memenuhi kalam saya lalu menulis alamat saya sendiri di atas.	*Then I fill my pen and write my own address at the top.*
Oléh kerana saya hendak menulis kepada seorang kawan saya memulakan surat dengan perkataan "Saudaraku Ahmad yang diingati."	*Because I am going to write to a friend, I begin my letter with the words "My very dear Ahmad."*
Selepas surat itu ditulis saya melipatnya lalu memasukkannya ke dalam sampul surat.	*After the letter has been written, I fold it up and insert it into an envelope.*
Selepas itu saya menjilat perekat sampul surat dengan lidah lalu melekatkannya.	*After that I lick the gum on the envelope with my tongue and stick it down.*
Kemudian saya menulis alamat penerima surat pada sampul surat.	*Then I write the address of the receiver of the letter on the envelope.*

Kalau saya tak ada setém, saya mesti pergi ke pejabat pos membeli setémnya.

Dalam pejabat pos ada seorang kerani yang menjual setém; ia duduk di belakang kisi-kisi tingkap.

Saya minta setém lima belas sen daripadanya.

Setelah saya mendapat setém, saya melekatkannya pada sampul surat, lalu memasukkan surat ke dalam peti surat.

Di mana encik bekerja?

Di Kementerian Pelajarankah?

Bukan. Saya bekerja di Kementerian Pengangkutan.

Bapa saya bekerja di Kementerian Kerja Raya, Pos dan Telekom; dia seorang Timbalan Pengawal telekom.

Bapa saya pun Pengawal juga; tetapi dia Penolong Pengawal Cukai Pendapatan.

Saya tahu! Dua hari dahulu saya menerima sepucuk surat daripadanya berkenaan dengan cukai saya!

Dia berkata: Tuan dengan hormatnya dimaklumkan adalah cukai pendapatan tuan belum dibayar lagi.

Itu bukan bapa saya yang bercakap; itu jabatan.

*If I haven't got any stamps, I have to go to the post office to buy a stamp for (*lit. "of") *it.*

In the post office there is a clerk who sells stamps; he sits behind the grille.

I ask him for a 15 cent stamp.

After I get the stamp, I stick it on the envelope and put the letter in the box.

Where do you work?

At the Ministry of Education?

No. I work in the Ministry of Transport.

My father works in the Minstry of Public Works, Posts and Telecommunications; he is a Deputy Controller of the telecoms.

My father's a Controller too; but he's an Assistant Comptroller of Income Tax.

I know! Two days ago I received a letter from him in connexion with my tax!

He said: Sir, I have the honour to inform you that your income tax has not been paid.

That is not my father talking; that is the department.

Lamun saya boléh mendapat hadiah loteri kebajikan masyarakat, senanglah saya membayar cukai pendapatan!	*If only I could win a prize in the social welfare lottery, I could easily pay my income tax!*
Di mana bapa saudara encik bekerja?	*Where does your uncle work?*
Dia sudah menjadi hakim; dia bekerja dalam mahkamah pengadil di Ipoh.	*He has become a magistrate; he works in the magistrate's court in Ipoh.*
Kerja adik saya pun berkenaan dengan undang-undang juga; dia kerani di Kementerian Keadilan.	*My younger brother's work is connected with the law too; he is a clerk in the Ministry of Justice.*
Tetapi harapannya ialah menjadi Hakim Besar!	*But his hope is to become Chief Justice!*
Ia mesti lulus dalam peperiksaan undang-undang dahulu.	*He will have to pass his law examination first.*

B. Word List

Nouns

kertas tulis	*writing-paper*	alamat	*address*
penerima	*receiver, recipient*	kementerian	*ministry*
timbalan	*deputy*	pengangkutan	*transport*
penolong	*assistant*	telekom	*telecommunications*
pendapatan	*income*	pengawal	*controller, comptroller*
loteri	*lottery*	cukai pendapatan	*income tax*
masyarakat	*society, community*	kebajikan	*welfare*

hakim	*magistrate, judge*	kebajikan masyarakat	*social welfare*
undang-undang	*law*	mahkamah	*court*
		keadilan	*justice*
harapan	*hope*		
Hakim Besar	*Chief Justice*		

Adjective

adil   *just, fair*

Verbs
lipat (melipat)   *to fold*
minta (meminta)   *to ask for*
angkut (mengangkut)   *to lift (heavy objects)*
bayar (membayar)   *to pay*

Miscellaneous

macam mana	*how*	mula-mula	*first of all, to begin with*
kemudian	*then, next*		

C. Grammar

183 *Kementerian Pelajaran:* "The Ministry of Education." *Kementerian* is derived from *menteri*, "minister", by the addition of the prefix *ke-* and the suffix *-an*. The following list of ministries with their Malay titles is given for reference:

Ministry of Agriculture and Rural Development.	Kementerian Pertanian dan Pembangunan Luar Bandar.
Ministry of Trade and Industry.	Kementerian Perdagangan dan Perusahaan.
Ministry of Defence.	Kementerian Pertahanan.
Ministry of Foreign Affairs.	Kementerian Luar Negeri.
Ministry of Finance.	Kementerian Kewangan.

Ministry of Health and Social Services.	Kementerian Kesihatan dan Kebajikan Awam.
Ministry of Home Affairs.	Kementerian Dalam Negeri.
Ministry of Labour and Manpower.	Kementerian Buruh dan Tenaga Rakyat.
Ministry of Transport and Works.	Kementerian Pengangkutan dan Kerja Raya.
Ministry of Culture, Youth and Sports.	Kementerian Kebudayaan, Belia dan Sukan.
Ministry of Primary Industries.	Kementerian Perusahaan Utama.

D. Exercises

Exercise 129   Translate into English:

1. Tulislah alamat tuan di kertas ini lalu berikan kepada kerani yang duduk di belakang kisi-kisi tingkap.
2. Di mana pejabat pos yang dekat sekali? Di sebelah Kementerian Kewangan.
3. Oléh sebab ia tidak lulus dalam peperiksaan undang-undang, tidaklah ia menjadi hakim.
4. Oléh kerana suratnya tidak dialamatkan kepada Setiausaha Tetap, surat itu dihantarkan balik kepada penulis.
5. Tolong pergi ke pejabat pos beli setem lima belas sen untuk surat ini.
6. Surat-surat mesti ditulis dalam bahasa kebangsaan.
7. Ayahnya seorang pegawai pelajaran; ia bekerja di Kementerian Pelajaran.
8. Pagi tadi saya menerima sepucuk surat daripada Menteri Dalam Negeri.
9. Satu sén pun tak ada lagi; macam mana kita hendak membayar cukai pendapatan sebelum bulan depan?
10. Loteri-loteri akan dijalankan oléh Jabatan Kebajikan Masyarakat supaya mendapat wang untuk orang-orang miskin (*miskin:* poor).

Exercise 130   Translate into Malay:
1   This new building will be opened next week by the Director of Public Works.
2   In the magistrate's court he was sentenced to three months' imprisonment.
3   Sir: I have the honour to request you to pay your income tax by the end of this month.
4   The Treasury (*Jabatan Perbendaharaan*) has rejected our request for money to build a new ten-storey building.
5   He signed the letter and posted it to his brother at the nearest post office.
6   He bought a ten-cent stamp and stuck it on the envelope.
7   He is hoping to get work as a clerk in the Ministry of Labour.
8   After he had read the letter he wrote a reply.
9   In Malaysian economy the most important (*penting*) matter is rural development.
10 Rubber-planting is one of Malaysia's most important industries.

Exercise 131

Write down ten Malay sentences of your own composition using what you have learnt so far during the course.

Exercise 132

Tuliskan satu karangan pendek (lebih kurang 150 perkataan) darihal *satu* daripada perkara-perkara yang berikut ini:

   a   Sepucuk surat kepada seorang kawan tuan di luar negeri menjemputnya melawat bandar tempat tuan tinggal.
   b   Satu percakapan (*percakapan:* conversation) di antara kerani di pejabat dan seorang yang hendak mengirim surat ke luar negeri.
   c   Kalau sekiranya tuan mendapat hadiah yang pertama dalam loteri kebajikan masyarakat, apakah hendak tuan buat dengan wangnya?
   d   Pada fikiran tuan, senang atau susah belajar bahasa kebangsaan?
   e   Siaran-siaran Melayu Radio Malaysia (*siaran:* programme, broadcast).

Minggu Yang Keempat Belas
Fourteenth Week

Pelajaran Yang Keempat Puluh
Lesson 40

Yang

A. Sentences

Orang yang membaca buku itu bapa saya.	*The man who is reading the book is my father.*
Orang yang membawa keréta itu seorang kawan saya.	*The man who is driving the car is a friend of mine.*
Budak yang menulis surat ini adik saya.	*This boy who is writing a letter is my younger brother.*
Orang yang bercakap bahasa kebangsaan itu orang Cina.	*That man who is speaking the national language is a Chinese.*
Buku yang saya baca itu sangat menarik hati.	*The book which I am reading is very interesting.*
Buku yang saya beli semalam tak berapa menarik hati.	*The book which I bought yesterday is not very interesting.*
Nasi yang dimasaknya tadi sedap benar.	*The rice which she cooked just now is very tasty.*
Keréta yang dijualnya semalam keréta yang sangat lama.	*The car which he sold yesterday is a very old one.*
Orang *yang* saya memberi duit *kepadanya* seorang kawan saya.	*The man to whom I gave the money is a friend of mine.*
Orang *yang* saya menerima surat *daripadanya* tuan pengarah.	*The man from whom I received a letter was the director.*
Orang *yang* saya menghantar buku *kepadanya* ialah bapa saya.	*The person to whom I sent the book was my father.*
Rumah *tempat* saya duduk rumah kecil.	*The house in which I live is a small one.*
Méja *tempat* dia menulis surat itu meja yang berkaki tiga.	*The table on which he wrote the letter is a three-legged one.*

Rumah *yang* saya duduki itu rumah yang kecil.	*The house in which I live is a small one.*
Bilik *yang* dimasukinya ialah bilik saya.	*The room into which he went was mine.*
Rumah *di mana* saya duduk ialah rumah besar.	*The house in which I live is a big house.*
Orang *kepada siapa* saya memberi duit ialah bapa saya.	*The man to whom I gave the money is my father.*
Orang *daripada siapa* saya mendapat duit itu seorang guru.	*The man from whom I got the money is a teacher.*

B. Word List

There are no new words in Section A of this lesson.

C. Grammar

184 *Orang yang membaca buku itu bapa saya:* "The man who is reading the book is my father." Here we have a complex sentence (Malay: *ayat berkait*) consisting of a main clause (*orang itu bapa saya*, "the man is my father") and an adjectival clause (*yang membaca buku*, "who is reading the book"). When the English "who", "whom", "whose", "which" and "that" are used to introduce adjectival clauses they are called *relative pronouns,* and, when used in this sense, are mostly rendered by the one word *yang* in Malay. We have often used *yang* in this way already and generally it works quite well. There are, however, a number of important points about *yang* which need to be mentioned if we are to use it properly.

In the sentence *orang yang membaca buku itu bapa saya* the word *yang* is the *subject* of its own clause (*yang membaca buku*), and when *yang* is the subject of its own verb like this the verb itself will always take the *me-* prefix if possible. This does not apply, of course, to verbs which either never take the *me-*prefix at all or to verbs which already have some other prefix such as *ber-* or *ter-* for example.

Examples:

orang yang membawa kereta	*the man who drives the car*

budak yang menulis surat	*the boy who writes the letter*

but

orang yang datang	*the man who came*
orang yang bercakap bahasa Melayu	*the man who speaks Malay*

185 *Buku yang saya baca itu sangat menarik hati:* "The book which I am reading is very interesting." In this complex sentence the subordinate (relative) clause is *yang saya baca*, "which I am reading". In this case the subject of the verb (*baca*) is *saya* and *yang* is this time the *object* of the verb in its own clause. Notice, then, that when *yang* is the *object* of its own clause, verbs which have *me-*forms only occur in the simple form without the prefix *me-*. In other words, when *yang* is the object, the following verb goes into what we earlier called the *passive form*. Examples:

buku yang kubeli semalam	*the book which I bought yesterday*
nasi yang dimasaknya tadi	*the rice which she cooked just now*
kereta yang dijualnya semalam	*the car which he sold yesterday*

186 *Orang yang saya memberi duit kepadanya:* "The man to whom I gave the money". In English we often put a preposition in front of a relative pronoun (here: "*to* whom") but Malay has no really neat and tidy way of doing this and even in the past has had to borrow a construction from another language — Arabic — to express this kind of sentence. This construction is as common in the older literature as it is today: the *yang* is retained with no preposition in front of it, but ceases to have any effect on the following verb (cf. 184 and 185 above), and the preposition comes later in the sentence with a *pronoun* attached to it (usually *-nya*). This construction in Arabic and Malay is incidentally the cause of a common error in English spoken and written by Malays: the above sentence means literally "the man who I gave the money to *him*" — perfectly all right in Malay and Arabic, but unacceptable in English. (cf. Arabic: *ar rajulu 'lladhi ra'aituhu* — "the man whom I saw (him)" or *al-baitu 'lladhi askunu*

fihi — "the house which I live in (it)".) Examples:

orang yang saya menerima surat daripadanya	*the man from whom I received the letter*
orang yang saya menghantar buku kepadanya	*the man to whom I sent the book*

187 *Rumah tempat saya duduk rumah kecil:* "The house in which I live is a small one." *In which* or *on which* — meaning *where* — are usually rendered by the word *tempat*, "place". Examples:

pejabat tempat ia bekerja	*the office in which he works*
meja tempat ia menulis surat	*the table on which he writes*

This idea can also be expressed by using one of the verbs which take the suffix *-i*, in which case *yang* simply becomes the object of a transitive verb in Malay, whatever the English may be. In this case, of course, the rule given in 185 above applies:

rumah yang saya duduki itu	*the house in which I live*
kertas yang ditulisinya	*the paper on which he wrote*
bilik yang dimasukinya	*the room into which he went*

188 *Rumah di mana saya duduk ialah rumah besar:* "The house in which I live is a big one." In modern Malay writing we often see the words *mana* and *siapa* used in imitation of the English "which" and "who", as if they were relative pronouns. Strictly speaking, *mana,* and *siapa* are only used to ask questions and many scholars would throw up their hands in horror at the idea of using them as relatives. But "which" and "who" in English were originally only question words and came to be used as relative pronouns purely in imitation of a Latin construction. The English usage has now been hallowed and sanctioned by a thousand years of use, and no Englishman today feels that there is anything at all odd about it. We should therefore not, perhaps, be too ready to condemn what is after all an attempt to get out of a difficulty in Malay — a difficulty which badly needs to be got out of. Whatever one's view on this construction in Malay, it can

be seen more and more every day in books and newpapers, and so it must be known at least even if it is advisable for students not to use it themselves for the time being.

Examples:

kedai dari mana saya membelinya	*the shop from which I bought it*
orang kepada siapa saya memberinya	*the man to whom I gave it*

D. *Exercises*

Exercise 133

Choose the correct form from those given in brackets:
1. Buku yang (dibelinya; ia membeli) tadi ialah sebuah buku Melayu.
2. Orang yang (aku melihat; kulihat) semalam ialah seorang guru.
3. Budak yang (ditulisnya; menulis) surat ini ialah adik saya.
4. Orang yang (datang; mendatang; didatangnya) pagi tadi ialah tuan pengarah.
5. Cerita yang (diceritakannya; ia menceritakan) itu cerita Hang Tuah dan Hang Jebat.

Exercise 134 *Translate into English:*
1. Bangunan tempat ayahnya bekerja itu sebuah bangunan baharu.
2. Bangunan yang ia terjun dari atas bumbungnya ialah bangunan bertingkat sebelas.
3. Orang yang saya bercakap dengannya itu ayah dia.
4. Orang-orang miskinlah yang saya memberikan duit kepada mereka.
5. Bunyi yang kudengar itu ialah bunyi suaranya.
6. Orang yang hendak membeli keretaku itu akan datang lagi sekali pada pukul tujuh setengah.

7 Kedai di mana encik boleh membeli buku itu tidak dibuka hari ini.
8 Kerusi yang didudukinya tadi sudah rosak.
9 Orang yang dijemputnya itu ialah seorang kawan lama.
10 Buku yang saya baca semalam tidak berapa menarik hati.

Exercise 135 Translate into Malay:
1 The book which you gave me yesterday is no use.
2 The house in which he lives is a big one.
3 The man to whom I was talking is an Indian.
4 When I lived in England, I always spoke English.
5 Where is the shop in which you bought this book?
6 Where did you post the letter which I wrote yesterday?
7 The man from whom I bought this car has gone to Japan.
8 The paper on which I wrote your address is lost.
9 Here is the file into which I put your letter.
10 This is the school in which I am learning Malay.

Exercise 136

Write down ten sentences of your own composition in Malay using what you have so far learnt during the course.

Exercise 137

Tulislah sebuah karangan yang ringkas (*ringkas:* brief) darihal *satu* daripada perkara-perkara yang berikut ini:
 a Pembangunan Luar Bandar
 b Loteri Kebajikan Masyarakat
 c Ceritakanlah cerita sebuah buku yang baharu tuan baca
 d Menjual Kereta Lama
 e Pertanian Malaysia

Minggu Yang Keempat Belas
Fourteenth Week

Pelajaran Yang Keempat Puluh Satu
Lesson 41

Sendikata Penambat dan Ayat-ayat Berkait 4
Subordinating Conjunctions and Complex Sentences 4

A. Sentences

Masa saya bersekolah, saya belajar ilmu alam.	*When I was at school I learnt geography.*
Masa dia bercakap, saya pun menulis surat.	*When (or: while) he was speaking, I wrote a letter.*
Masa ia di London, dilawatnya bapa saya.	*When he was in London, he visited my father.*
Waktu ia sampai, saya tak ada di rumah.	*When he arrived I wasn't at home.*
Waktu ia masuk, saya pun sedang menulis surat.	*When he came in I was writing a letter.*
Waktu saya bertolak, ia pun belum sampai lagi.	*When I started out, he had not yet arrived.*
Bila dia sampai, berikan surat ini.	*When he arrives, give him this letter.*
Bila encik pergi ke pasar, tolong belikan saya rokok.	*When you go to the market, please buy me some cigarettes.*
Bila kawan kau datang, beritahu aku.	*When your friend comes, let me know.*
Apabila dia datang, selalulah ia membawa hadiah.	*When he comes he always brings a present.*
Apabila ia bercakap dengan saya, selalulah ia bercakap bahasa Melayu.	*Whenever he speaks to me, he always speaks Malay.*
Apabila kawanku datang, selalulah kami pergi menéngok wayang.	*When my friend comes, we always go to the theatre.*
Tatkala ia masuk, saya pun keluarlah.	*When he came in, I went out.*

Tatkala ia duduk di negeri China, ia belajar bahasa Cina.	*When he was in China, he learnt Chinese.*
Sementara ia bercakap, saya pun tidurlah.	*While he was talking, I fell asleep.*
Sementara saya tidur, ia pun bangkitlah lalu keluar.	*While I was asleep, he got up and went out.*
Sementara rumah kami yang baharu sedang dibangunkan, kami tinggal di hotel.	*While our new house is being built we are staying in a hotel.*
Sedang saya bercakap, ucapan saya itu dirakamkan.	*While I was speaking my speech was recorded.*
Sedang ucapan saya dirakamkan, seorang pun tak bercakap.	*While my speech was being recorded, nobody spoke.*
Semenjak ia duduk di sini, ia sangat suka hati.	*Since he has been living here, he has been very happy.*
Semenjak bapa saya meninggal dunia setahun dahulu, kami sudah miskin.	*Since my father died a year ago, we have been poor.*
Selama ia duduk di sini, ia suka hati.	*As long as he lives here, he is happy.*
Selama saya duduk di England, saya belajar bahasa Inggeris.	*All the time I was in England, I studied English.*
Dia bercakap semacam dia sudah mabuk.	*He talks as if he were drunk.*
Dia berjalan semacam kakinya sakit.	*He walks as if his foot were hurting.*
Dia bercakap seumpama dia tak tahu apa hendak buat.	*He spoke as if he did not know what to do.*
Dia menangis-nangis seumpama dia masih kecil lagi.	*He kept on crying as if he were still quite young.*
Dia bercakap seolah-olah dia akan meninggal dunia pada waktu itu juga.	*He spoke as if he were going to die at any moment.*

B. Word List

Adjectives

| miskin | *poor* | mabuk | *drunk* |

Verbs

| rakamkan (merakamkan) | *to record* |

Miscellaneous

masa	*when, while*	apabila	*whenever, when*
waktu	*when*	bila	*when*
tatkala	*when*	sementara	*while*
sedang	*while*	semenjak	*since*
selama	*as long as, all the time that*	semacam	*as if*
pada waktu itu juga	*at that very moment*	seumpama	*as if*
seolah-olah	*as if*		

C. Grammar

189 *Masa saya bersekolah...:* "When (while) I was at school...". "When", as a question, is *bila?* but as a conjunction introducing adverbial clauses of time it may be rendered in several different ways in Malay according to the sense. A simple rule which holds good for the spoken language was given in "Speak Malay!" — q.v. Lesson 34, Note (105), p. 113; in the written language, however, there are several other words of which account must be taken. Generally speaking, the student will be safe if he keeps to the following system:

(a) In questions "when?" is *bila?* in Malay. Examples:

> *Bila ayahnya hendak sampai?*
> When will his father arrive?

> *Bila encik mulai belajar bahasa Melayu?*
> When did you start learning Malay?

(b) When the word "when" in English really means "while" or "during the time that — that is to say, when it refers to a period and not a point of time — the most usual word in Malay is *masa*. Examples:

> *Masa saya membaca buku, Ahmad pun masuklah.*
> While I was reading, in came Ahmad.
>
> *Masa dia di Kuala Lumpur, keretanya pun rosaklah.*
> When he was in Kuala Lumpur, his car was damaged.

(c) When the word "when" refers to a point of time in the past, the most usual Malay word is *waktu* (from the Arabic *waqt*, "time"). Examples:

> *Waktu saya singgah di rumahnya, ia pun tiadalah.*
> When I called in at his house, he was not there.
>
> *Waktu saya membuka radio, warta berita sedang dibacakan.*
> When I switched on the radio, the news was being read.

(d) When the word "when" refers to a point of time in the future, the most usual Malay word is *bila*. Examples:

> *Bila dia sampai, suruh dia masuk.*
> When he arrives, tell him to come in.
>
> *Bila saya pergi ke Singapura, saya hendak membeli keréta.*
> When I go to Singapore, I am going to buy a car.

(e) When the word "when" really means "whenever", the most usual Malay word is *apabila*. Examples:

> *Apabila dia bekerja, dia bekerja kuat.*
> When(ever) he works, he works hard.
>
> *Apabila ia bercakap, ia bercakap dalam bahasa Cina.*
> When(ever) he speaks, he speaks in Chinese.

(f) The word *tatkala* (from the Sanskrit *tat kalam*, "that time") may be used in almost any of the above senses. Examples:

> *Tatkala mereka sampai, saya pun bertolaklah.*
> When they arrived, I set off.
>
> *Tatkala saya duduk di London, saya melawat mesjid di Woking.*
> When I lived in London, I visited the mosque at Woking.

(g) When there is special emphasis on the duration of a period of time, that is when English uses "while" instead of "when", then *sementera* or *sedang* should be used in Malay. Examples:

> *Sementara saya bercakap, dua orang India pun masuklah.*
> While I was talking, two Indians came in.
>
> *Sedang saya menulis surat kepadanya, ia pun masuklah sendiri.*
> Just as I was writing him a letter, he came in himself.

190 *Semenjak ia duduk di sini . . . :* "since he has been living here . . . " *Semenjak* is the normal way of translating the English "since" when referring to time. Remember, however, that "since" often means "because" in English, and in this meaning must be rendered by *kerana* or *sebab* in Malay.

191 *Selama ia duduk di sini . . . :* "As long as he lives here . . . " "As long as", meaning "all the time (or all the while) that" is usually translated by *selama*. When "as long as" means "provided that", however, it must be translated by *asalkan* in Malay.

192 *Dia bercakap semacam dia sudah mabuk:* "He talks as if he were drunk." Note the three common ways of translating "as if" into Malay: *semacam, seumpama* or *seolah-olah*. Study the examples in Section A above.

D. Exercises

Exercise 138 Translate into English:
1 Masa ia mewakili kerajaan di Mesir (Egypt), ia mulai belajar bahasa Arab.

2 Bila ia pergi ke negeri Jepun tahun depan, ia akan belajar bahasa Jepun.
3 Waktu saya masuk ke dalam biliknya, ia pun duduk menangis-nangis.
4 Apabila saya tinggal di hotel itu, selalulah saya makan makanan Cina.
5 Ia memandang saya, seolah-olah saya sudah mabuk.
6 Waktu keretanya sampai di perhentian Kuala Lumpur, bapa saya sedang menantikan saya di platfom*.
7 Semenjak ayah mereka meninggal dunia, mereka pun miskinlah.
8 Selama ia duduk di negeri Perancis, dia belajar bahasa Perancis di Sorbonne.
9 Waktu dia balik dari pasar, satu sén pun tak ada lagi.
10 Bila encik hendak menjual kereta itu?

Exercise 139 Translate into Malay:
1 While I was writing a letter, in came my father.
2 He speaks Malay as if he had been studying it for a long time.
3 We are going to speak Malay as long as we are in Malaysia.
4 This programme was recorded in the Kuala Lumpur studios (*studio*) of Radio Malaysia.
5 When the letter arrived, Ahmad opened it and read it to his wife.
6 When I visit my parents every year, I always take them a present.
7 When are you going to start learning Malay?
8 When he arrives, tell him that I have gone to the market.
9 When I was in London, I always ate English food.
10 As long as you work hard, you are sure to pass the examination

---

*platfom: (railway) platform

Exercise 140
Write down ten sentences of your own composition in Malay using what you have learnt so far during the course.

Exercise 141
Tulislah satu karangan yang ringkas di atas *satu* dari antara perkara-perkara yang berikut ini:
- a Universiti Malaya di Kuala Lumpur
- b Ulang Tahun Kemerdékaan
- c Menonton Wayang Gambar
- d Makanan Orang Melayu
- e Permainan-permainan Malaysia

Minggu Yang Keempat Belas
Fourteenth Week

Pelajaran Yang Keempat Puluh Dua
Lesson 42

Awalan (Mem)per-
The Prefix (Mem)per-

A. *Sentences*

Patutlah kita memperhatikan keadaan perékonomian.

We should take note of the economic situation.

Hendaklah pelajar-pelajar mempergunakan perpustakaan maktab.

Students should make use of the college library.

Ia akan memperisterikan anak seorang sahabatnya.

He will marry the daughter of one of his friends.

Permintaannya tidak diperkenankan oléh Hakim Besar.

His request was not granted by the Chief Justice.

Kedudukan kita tidak boléh dipertahankan lagi.

Our position can no longer be defended; or: *our position is now untenable.*

Mesin taip ini mesti kita perbaiki.

We must repair this typewriter.

Orang ini dipekerjakan oléh majlis bandaran.

This man is employed by the town council.

Témbok-témbok bangunan ini mesti diperkuatkan.

The walls of this building must be reinforced.

Selepas mata-mata menaikkan tangan, ia pun memperhentikan kereta di tepi jalan.

After the policeman raised his hand, he stopped the car at the side of the road.

Untuk memajukan negeri ini, semua bangsa-bangsa mesti dipersatukan.

In order to make this country prosper, all the various races must be united.

Ia selalu memperkatakan keadaan perékonomian.

He is always talking about the economic situation.

Saya selalu memperlakukan dia sebagai seorang yang berakal.

*I always regard (*or: *treat) him as an intelligent man.*

Dalam makmalnya ia mempertunjukkan cara pekerjaannya.	*In his laboratory he demonstrated his method of working.*
Gambar ini akan dipertunjukkan dalam déwan seni lukis.	*This picture will be exhibited in the art gallery.*
Sekarang ini ia bekerja kuat mempelajari bahasa Jepun.	*At the moment he is working hard studying Japanese.*
Calon ini kami semua percayai.	*This candidate is trusted by all of us.*
Tetapi kami tidak mempercayai calon itu.	*But we don't trust that candidate.*
Ia selalu memperbudakkan rakyat.	*He always treats the people as children.*
Ia selalù memperdéwakan wang.	*He always makes money his god.*
Ia hendak memperisterikan jurutaipnya.	*He is going to marry his typist.*
Siaran ini telah dirakamkan pada pita.	*This programme was recorded on tape.*

B. Word List

Nouns

pelajar	*student*	permintaan	*request*
kedudukan	*situation, position*	mesin	*machine*
mesin taip	*typewriter*	majlis	*council, assembly*
bandaran	*municipality*	majlis bandaran	*town council*
témbok	*wall*	makmal	*laboratory, workshop*
bangsa	*race, a people*	seni lukis	*painting*
seni	*fine art*	déwan seni lukis	*art gallery*
pita	*tape*	jurutaip	*typist*

Verbs

(mem-) perhatikan	*to take note of, to pay attention to*
(mem-) pergunakan	*to make use of*
(mem-) peristerikan	*to marry (of a man)*
(mem-) perkenankan	*to grant, to agree to, to allow*
(mem-) pertahankan	*to defend*
(mem-) perbaiki	*to repair*
(mem-) pekerjakan	*to employ*
(mem-) perkuatkan	*to reinforce*
(mem-) perhentikan	*to stop (trans.)*
(mem-) persatukan	*to unite*
(mem-) perkatakan	*to talk about*
(mem-) perlakukan	*to regard, to treat (as)*
(mem-) pertunjukkan	*to demonstrate, to exhibit*
(mem-) pelajari	*to study*
(mem-) percayai	*to trust*
(mem-) perbudakkan	*to treat as a child*
(mem-) perdéwakan	*to make a god of, to deify, to idolise*
majukan (memajukan)	*to prosper (trans.), to make prosperous*

C. Grammar

193 *Verbs formed with the prefix* per-: The prefix *per-* is often used to form new verbs from almost any other part of speech, and when used by itself without any additional suffixes it has much the same meaning as the suffixes *-kan* or *-i*: that is to say, it gives the idea of making somebody do something or of making somebody into something. In Kedah especially, a form like *perbaik*, "to repair", is often preferred to the more usual *baikkan* or *baiki*. The Paramount Ruler of Malaysia is called His Majesty the *Yang Dipertuan Agung*. *Yang* here means "the one who" and *agung* means "general" (e.g. *mesyuarat agung*, "general meeting"). *Dipertuan* is actually the passive form of the verb *pertuan*, which means "the one who has been made the general lord", and expresses the democratic idea of election very well. The ruler of Negri Sembilan, who is also chosen democratically from among a number of possible candidates, has a similar title. He is called His Highness the *Yang Dipertuan Besar*: literally, "he who has been made the great lord."

Sometimes we find both the simple form and the *per*-form side by side; for instance, we find both *buat* and *perbuat*. There is usually very little difference in meaning between such pairs, except perhaps that the *per*-form is a little more intensive: *buat* means "to do" with no special emphasis, but *perbuat* implies sometimes that the doing is carried through to a successful completion — something like "to do properly" perhaps, although that is really too strong. Classical scholars may be reminded of the difference between *facio* and *conficio* in Latin.

Mostly, however, the prefix *per-* is used together with the suffixes *-kan* or *-i* simply to form new verbs, which are being created in great profusion at present. The resulting word can then take the prefix *me-* as well, and this often gives a word of considerable length. The newness of this formation is perhaps shown by the fact that, although the prefix *me-* in this set-up takes the form *mem-* as we should expect in front of a *p-*, the *p-* itself does not vanish as it would, for instance, in a root-word like *pukul*. For examples of such verbs study the word list in Section B above as well as the sentences in Section A. Notice particularly that such verbs are the only words in the language which are permitted to take *two* prefixes at once.

194 *Notes on the derivation of a few* memper-*verbs:*

(a) memperhatikan: mem-per-hati-kan is derived from *hati*, "mind" or "heart", and means something like "to apply the mind to" and so "to take care of" or "to pay attention to".

(b) memperdewakan: mem-per-dewa-kan is derived from *dewa*, "god" or "idol", and means therefore "to make a god of" and so "to deify" or "to idolise".

(c) mempelajari: mem-pel-ajar-i is derived from *ajar*, "to teach". As usual with this root, the *-r* of a prefix is changed to *-l* (cf. *belajar* and *pelajaran*). In *mempelajari* there is something of the intensive idea mentioned in 193 above: the verb implies a thorough and serious

249

study of the subject of tuition. *Mempelajari bahasa Jepun* is likely to be much harder work than *belajar bahasa Jepun*.

195 *Ia hendak memperisterikan jurutaipnya:* "He is going to marry (lit: make a wife of) his typist." *Jurutaip* is a modern word made up from Malay *juru*, "expert", and the English word *type* spelled phonetically. The verb "to type" is in Malay *taip* with a *me*-form *menaip*. Here are a few other useful words in which the first element is *juru*.

jurutaip	*typist*
jurubahasa	*interpreter*
jurucakap	*spokesman*
jurutera	*engineer*
jururawat	*nurse*

D. Exercises

Exercise 142 Translate into English:
1 Selama ia di Kuala Lumpur ia mempelajari bahasa Melayu.
2 Kalau tuan tidak tahu bercakap bahasa Melayu, hendaklah tuan mempergunakan seorang jurubahasa sementara tuan tinggal di Malaysia.
3 Bahasa kebangsaan kita ini hendak mempersatukan rakyat.
4 Orang itu tidak dipercayai oléh rakyat; selalu ia memperbudakkan orang ramai.
5 Setelah surat itu ditaip oléh jurutaipnya, ditandatangani oléh Ahmad lalu dikirimnya dengan pos udara.
6 Setelah ia mempelajari bahasa Perancis lima tahun, ia menjadi jurubahasa di Paris.
7 Fatimah menaip surat itu lalu dibawanya kepada tuan pengarah.
8 Orang yang berugama Islam tidak patut memperdéwakan wang.
9 Janganlah kita memperbudakkan rakyat.
10 Seorang jurucakap kerajaan berkata pagi tadi bahawa bangunan baharu akan dibuka oléh Perdana Menteri minggu depan.

Exercise 143 Translate into Malay:
1. We must make use of the new laboratory.
2. He stopped his car at the side of the road.
3. This building must be reinforced; otherwise (if not), it will collapse (*runtuh*).
4. This man will not be elected because he treats the people as children.
5. My father is an interpreter in the magistrate's court in Ipoh.
6. My son wants to be an engineer but my daughter wants to be a nurse.
7. We must record this programme on tape.
8. He wanted to record the Prime Minister's speech but his request was not granted.
9. I don't like going to Encik Ahmad's house because he's always talking about the economic situation in South-east Asia.
10. He got the medicine (*ubat*) from the nurse and drank it.

Exercise 144
Make up ten Malay sentences of your own using what you have learnt so far in the course.

Exercise 145
Tuliskan satu karangan ringkas darihal *satu* daripada perkara-perkara yang berikut:
a Cerita seorang yang memperdéwakan wang
b Cukai Pendapatan
c Perdana Menteri Kita
d Kuala Lumpur
e Cerita sebuah buku Melayu yang telah tuan baca.

Minggu Yang Kelima Belas
Fifteenth Week

Pelajaran Yang Keempat Puluh Tiga
Lesson 43

"Akan" dan Awalan Ber- dengan Akhiran -Kan
"Akan" and the Prefix Ber- with the Suffix -Kan

A. Sentences

Ia tidak hirau lagi akan keputusan peperiksaan.	*He thought no more about the examination results.*
Akan perbuatan tuan tidak saya perhatikan.	*I am paying no attention to your action;* or: *as for your action, I am taking no notice.*
Dilihatnya akan bapanya meninggal dunia.	*He saw his father die.*
Dilihatnya dengan matanya sendiri akan kedatangan Perdana Menteri.	*He saw with his own eyes the arrival of the Prime Minister.*
Ia pergi ke pekan akan membeli beras.	*He went to town to buy rice.*
Ia pergi ke pejabat pendaftar akan mendaftarkan nama anaknya.	*He went to the registrar's office to register his child's name.*
Saya berharap bahawa Bapa hendak memberikan saya sebuah basikal yang baharu.	*I hope that Father is going to give me a new bicycle.*
Saya berharapkan sebuah basikal yang baharu.	*I have set my hopes on a new bicycle.*
Saya bertanya: Siapa nama tuan?	*I asked: What is your name, sir?*
Saya bertanyakan namanya.	*I asked his name;* or: *I inquired about his name.*
Tiap-tiap malam ia bermimpi.	*Every night he dreams.*
Tiap-tiap malam ia bermimpikan anaknya.	*Every night he dreams about his son.*

Dasar kursus ini ialah bahasa Melayu bertulis.	*The basis of this course is the Malay written language.*
Kursus ini berdasar bahasa Melayu bertulis.	*This course has as its basis the Malay written language.*
Kursus ini berdasarkan bahasa Melayu bertulis.	*This course is based on the Malay written language.*
Kita mesti melengkapkan tentera kita dengan senjata-senjata yang baharu.	*We must equip our army with new weapons.*
Saya hendak berlengkap untuk menyerang bandar itu.	*I am going to equip myself (or: prepare) to attack that town.*
Ia hendak berlengkapkan senapang.	*He is going to equip himself (or: arm himself) with a rifle.*
Ia bertongkatkan sebatang besi.	*He used an iron bar as a stick.*
Mereka bersenjatakan tongkat-tongkat dan batu-batu.	*They used sticks and stones as weapons;* or: *they armed themselves with sticks and stones.*
Ia berbajukan kain guni.	*He used sackcloth for a jacket.*

B. Word List

Nouns

kedatangan	*arrival*	basikal	*bicycle*
pendaftar	*registrar*	tentera	*army*
mimpi	*dream*	tentera laut	*navy*
kursus	*course*	tongkat	*stick*
tentera udara	*air force*	sebatang besi	*an iron bar*
senjata	*weapon*	kain	*cloth*
besi	*iron*		
batu	*stone*		
guni	*sack*		

Adjectives

lengkap	*complete, ready*	bertulis	*written, in writing*

Verbs

berharapkan	*to set one's hope on*
bertanyakan	*to ask about, to inquire about*
bermimpi	*to dream*
bermimpikan	*to dream about*
berangan-angan	*to day-dream*
berdasar	*to have a basis*
berdasarkan	*to be based on*
berlengkap	*to equip oneself, to get ready, to prepare*
berlengkapkan	*to equip oneself with*
bersenjata	*to be armed*
bersenjatakan	*to be armed with, to arm oneself with*
bertongkatkan	*to use as a stick*
berbajukan	*to make a jacket out of*
lengkapkan (melengkapkan)	*to equip, to prepare*
serang (menyerang)	*to attack*
hirau	*to heed, to care*

C. *Grammar*

196 *Note on the connexion between the suffix* -kan *and the preposition* akan: It is believed that originally the suffix *-kan* was not a suffix at all but a preposition used to connect a verb with its object. At first this preposition is supposed to have been felt as a separate word, but was so often used after certain verbs to indicate the object that it became eakened in pronunciation and, having lost the stress accent, began to be felt as part of the preceding word; it thus came to be regarded as a suffix. This *kan* is probably connected with the word *akan*, which we have so far used only to indicate the future tense, and may, indeed, be simply a weakened form of it. Now, in classical Malay, and sometimes in modern Malay too, the word *akan* is used as a preposition the meaning of which is difficult to define in English. Probably the nearest we can get to it in English is the phrase "as for" or "with regard to", or perhaps the preposition "towards". It is used to indicate the object, especially in a longish sentence where there

may otherwise be some doubt about which word or group of words *is* the object. Examples:

Ia tidak ingat lagi akan tanahairnya.
As for his native land, he thought no more about it.

Akan permintaan tuan tidak boléh saya perkenankan.
I cannot accede to your request.

Akan may also be used to single out the *subject* of a *passive* verb; that is to say, it indicates the *logical* object. Examples:

Didengarnya akan suara isterinya memanggil namanya.
He heard his wife's voice calling his name.

Dibacakan oleh Ahmad akan butir-butir mesyuarat agung.
Ahmad read out the minutes of the general meeting.

Akan may also be used like *untuk* to introduce a clause expressing purpose. Examples:

Fatimah pergi ke pasar akan membeli sayur-sayuran.
Fatimah went to the market in order to buy vegetables.

Ia singgah di pejabat pos akan mengirim dua pucuk surat.
He stopped off at the post office to post two letters.

197 *Saya berharapkan sebuah basikal yang baharu:* "I have set my hopes on a new bicycle." The vast majority of *ber-*verbs are intransitive and cannot, therefore, normally take an object. There are some *ber-*verbs, however, which may be connected with an object by means of the suffix *-kan*, and in these cases the addition of *-kan* does not cause the verb to reject the prefix *ber-* and take the prefix *me-* instead: these verbs have both *ber-* and *-kan* at the same time. This special use of the suffix *-kan* has almost certainly grown out of the usage of *akan* to connect a verb with its object (cf. 196 above). Study carefully the parallel pairs of examples in Section A above and note also the various meanings of the following derivatives of the adjective *lengkap*, which give a good idea of how the whole system works:

Sekarang tentera kita sudah lengkap.
Our army is now equipped (*or:* our army is now ready).

Kita hendak melengkapkan tentera udara kita dengan kapal-kapal terbang yang baharu.
We are going to equip our air force with the new aircraft.

Tentera laut kita sedang berlengkap akan mempertahankan tanahair kita ini.
Our navy is preparing to defend this motherland of ours.

Mereka sedang berlèngkapkan pedang-pedang dan senapang-senapang.
They are equipping themselves with swords and rifles.

198 *Ia bertongkatkan sebatang besi:* "He used an iron bar as a stick."
Here we have the prefix *ber-* and the suffix *-kan* added to a *noun*, the resulting word having a special meaning. This structure — *ber-*noun*-kan* — means "to use something (the object) as something (the noun)", and can be used with almost any noun that makes sense. For further examples see Section A above.

D. Exercises

Exercise 146 Translate into English:
1 Sebelum menyerang bandar itu, hendaklah kita melengkapkan tentera kita dengan senjata-senjata baharu.
2 Sepanjang malam itu ia bermimpikan seorang gadis cantik.
3 Selalulah ia duduk di serambi berangan-angan.
4 Tiba-tiba bilik saya dimasuki oléh lima orang bersenjata.
5 Permintaan-permintaan mesti diarahkan bertulis kepada Setia-usaha Tetap.
6 Dilihatnya akan seorang gadis yang berbaju sutera.
7 Akan surat tuan yang saya terima semalam, saya belum sempat menulis surat balasannya.
8 Buku ini berdasarkan Hikayat Hang Tuah.
9 Saya pergi ke dewan seni lukis untuk melihat gambar-gambar yang baharu.

10   Tolong berikan dia surat ini.

Exercise 147   Translate into Malay:
1   I hope that I shall get a letter from him today.
2   I have set my hopes on a letter from him today.
3   He dreams every night.
4   He dreamed about the pretty girl whom he saw at the exhibition.
5   As for the two sacks of rice — they were left behind in the shop.
6   Air force officers are not armed with rifles.
7   The national language course will begin on Friday; it is based on the language used in government offices.
8   I am going to the airport to inquire about the arrival of all aircraft from Singapore.
9   The rebels (*pemberontak-pemberontak*) armed themselves with stones and attacked the post office.
10   As for our native land — we must defend it with sticks and stones if we cannot get guns.

Exercise 148
Write down ten Malay sentences of your own composition using what you have learnt so far in the course.

Exercise 149
Tulislah satu karangan darihal *satu* daripada perkara-perkara yang berikut ini:
a   Tentera Udara Kita
b   Mempertahankan Tanahair
c   Cerita seorang Askar Malaysia.
d   Hari Raya Puasa
e   Tahun Baharu Cina

Minggu Yang Kelima Belas — Fifteenth Week
Pelajaran Yang Keempat Puluh Empat — Lesson 44

(a) Awalan Ber- dengan Akhiran -An; (b) Tekanan 1
(a) The Prefix Ber- with the Suffix -An; (b) Emphasis 1

A. Sentences

Sekarang sudah sepuluh tahun lebih mereka berkirim-kiriman surat.	*It is now more than ten years that they have been carrying on a correspondence with each other.*
Mereka bertangis-tangisan selepas kematiannya.	*They wept all over each other (or: they cried on each other's shoulders) after his death.*
Kedua-duanya bertémbak-témbakan.	*They both kept on shooting at each other.*
Kedua orang Perdana Menteri bersambutan dengan sukacita.	*The two Prime Ministers greeted one another with pleasure.*
Sudah lama mereka berkenalan.	*They had known each other (or: they had been acquainted) for a long time.*
Beras yang terjatuh dari atas meja itu sudah bertaburan.	*The rice which fell off the table was scattered about all over the floor.*
Jauh, jauh sekali di antara pokok-pokok kelihatan cahaya yang berkelip-kelipan.	*Far, far away between the trees could be seen a light which kept on flashing.*
Peluhnya turun bercucuran pada mukanya.	*The sweat trickled down his face.*
Ésok saya hendak pergi ke sana.	*I'm going there tomorrow.*
Semalam bapa saya sampai dari Ipoh.	*My father arrived from Ipoh yesterday.*
Ésoklah saya hendak pergi ke sana.	*I'm going there tomorrow; or: it's tomorrow that I'm going there.*
Semalamlah bapa saya sampai dari Ipoh.	*My father arrived from Ipoh yesterday.*

Bapa sayalah yang sampai semalam dari Ipoh.	*It was my father who arrived from Ipoh yesterday.*
Saya yang membaca buku itu.	*I'm reading that book.*
Kawan sayalah yang tidak mengundi; bukan saya.	*It was my* friend *who didn't vote; not me.*
Ahmad yang menutup pintu itu.	Ahmad *closed the door.*
Buku itulah kubaca semalam.	*It was* that *book that I read yesterday.*
Pintulah yang ditutup Ahmad, bukan tingkap.	*Ahmad shut the* door, *not the* window.
Kereta ini sudah kami beli semalam; kereta itu sudah kami beli tahun lepas.	*This car, we bought yesterday; that car we bought last year.*
Saya membaca sebuah buku yang sangat menarik hati.	*I am reading a very interesting book.*
Saya baca buku; bukan saya tulis buku.	*I'm reading a book, not writing one.*
Engkau membaca bukukah?	*Are you reading a* book?
Engkaukah membaca buku?	*Are* you *reading a book?*
Buku itukah kaubaca?	*Is* that *the book you're reading?*

B. Word List

Nouns

tekanan	*emphasis, stress*	tujuan	*policy*
peluh	*sweat*	cahaya	*light*
		muka	*face*

Verbs

berkirim-kiriman	*to correspond with one another*
bertangis-tangisan	*to cry on each other's shoulders*
bertémbak-témbakan	*to shoot at each other*
bersambutan	*to greet one another*
berkenalan	*to be acquainted with each other*

bertabur-taburan	*to be scattered about*
berkelip-kelipan	*to keep on flashing*
bercucuran	*to trickle*
tekankan (menekankan)	*to stress*
beratkan (memberatkan)	*to emphasise*

C. Grammar

199 *Sudah sepuluh tahun lebih mereka berkirim-kiriman surat:* "They have been carrying on a correspondence for more than ten years." The prefix *ber-* may be combined with a root-word and the suffix *-an* to form what may be called a reciprocal verb: that is a verb which implies that two or more people are doing the action *to each other*. In such formations the root-word is frequently, though not always, reduplicated. From *kirim*, "to send" or "to post", we get the form *berkirim-kiriman* meaning "to send or post to each other" and so "to carry on a correspondence with one another". Note these examples:

tangis (menangis)	*to weep*	bertangis-tangisan	*to cry on each other's shoulders*
témbak (menembak)	*to shoot*	bertémbak-témbakan	*to shoot at each other*
sambut (menyambut)	*to welcome*	bersambutan	*to greet each other*
kenal (mengenal)	*to know*	berkenalan	*to know each other*

200 *Beras ... itu sudah bertabur-taburan di lantai:* "The rice ... was scattered about all over the floor." Sometimes the reciprocal idea mentioned in 199 gives place to the idea of repetition or continuity of a series of similar actions. Examples:

bertabur-taburan	*to be scattered about*
berkelip-kelipan	*to flash continually*
bercucuran	*to keep on trickling*

201 *Ésok saya hendak pergi ke sana:* "I'm going there tomorrow." We must now consider more systematically the problem of emphasis *(tekanan)* in Malay. In English we have a very strong stress accent and we make great use of this, especially in speech, to indicate emphasis. Compare the following sentences in which the main stress has been marked with an acute accent (´):

Hé's going — He ís going — He's góing.

All the three sentences have a slightly different meaning because of the changes in the position of the stress accent. Malay stress is much less forceful than English stress, and although Malay does use this method to some extend in speech it prefers other methods of indicating emphasis.

The basic rule of emphasis in Malay is that the most important word or group of words normally comes at the beginning of the sentence. Adverbs and adverbial phrases, which are often emphasised — especially those indicating time — frequently come at the beginning in Malay for this reason. *Esok saya hendak pergi*, therefore, is more usual than *saya hendak pergi esok.*

202 *Ésoklah saya hendak pergi ke sana:* "It's tomorrow that I'm going there." If the emphasis is particularly strong the particle *-lah* is added to the emphasised word. This has much the same effect as introducing a sentence by "it is" or "it was" in English.

203 *Sayalah yang hendak pergi ke sana:* "It is I who am going there." When the word to be emphasised is a noun or pronoun — subject or object — it is often followed by the relative pronoun *yang,* or by both *-lah* and *yang* together.

204 *Saya yang membaca buku itu:* "I am reading that book."(i.e. not *you*). When the noun or pronoun to be emphasised is the subject, it is placed first in the sentence and is then followed by a verb, then the verb always takes the *me*-form if it has one. In such a case the stress is on the subject and not on the action itself.

205 *Buku itulah kubaca semalam:* "It is *that* book that I read yesterday." When the noun or pronoun to be emphasised and therefore placed first in the sentence is the object of the verb in English, then the verb does not take the prefix *me-* in Malay but remains in the simple form or, rather, the sentence goes into the

passive form. The basic difference between the *me*-form of a verb and its simple or passive form is, then, a difference of emphasis. In a normal sentence where the word order is *subject — verb — object —* the form we choose depends on the position of the emphasis. If the stress is on the verb rather than on the subject or object, we must use the simple or passive form without the prefix *me-*. Compare the following examples:

(a) Saya membaca sebuah buku.
   I am reading a *book*.

(b) Saya baca buku — bukan tulis surat.
   I am *reading* — not writing letters.

In example *(a)* the emphasis is on the object: "I am reading a book — not a newspaper"; or it may be on the subject: "I (i.e. not you) am reading a book". In example *(b)* the distinction is between two different actions: the verb is stressed and so cannot take the prefix *me-*.

206 *Engkau membaca bukukah?*: "Are you reading a *book?*" In questions the particle *-kah* is added to the most important word or word-group in the sentence: that is to the word or word-group about which we are really asking the question. Study the examples given in Section A above carefully.

D. *Exercises*

Exercise 150   Translate into English:
1   Surat itukah kautulis semalam?
2   Apa kaubuat? Aku baca buku.
3   Siapakah yang menutup pintu? Ahmad yang menutupnya.
4   Selepas ayah mereka bertolak ke Singapura, meréka pun mulai bertangis-tangisan.
5   Buku-bukunya bertabur-taburan di lantai biliknya.
6   Meréka bersambutan dengan tersenyum-senyum.
7   Bila encik hendak pergi ke Ipoh? Esoklah saya hendak pergi.

8 Semalam pada pukul empat petang saya duduk di dalam bilik saya membaca suratkhabar.
9 Bapa sayalah yang hendak membeli kereta baharu; bukan bapa dia.
10 Orang Melayu suka memulakan ayat-ayat meréka dengan perkataan-perkataan yang ditekankan.

Exercise 151   Translate into Malay:
1 This decision is based on the policy of the government.
2 The terrorists (*pengganas-pengganas*) and the policemen fired at each other for two hours.
3 Is it your father who sent this letter?
4 Is this the letter your father sent?
5 They have known one another for twenty years.
6 They are carrying on a correspondence with one another.
7 Outside the window of his room was a light which kept on flashing.
8 I am writing a letter, not reading a book.
9 I am writing a letter, not an essay.
10 It is an essay that I am writing, not a letter.

Exercise 152
Write down ten Malay sentences of your own composition.

Exercise 153
Tulislah satu karangan darihal salah *satu* perkara-perkara yang berikut ini:
   a *Kemerdékaan*
   b Suratkhabar-suratkhabar Malaysia
   c Singapura
   d Tugas Malaysia di Asia Tenggara (*tugas:* role, task, duty)
   e Syarikat-syarikat Kerjasama

Minggu Yang Kelima Belas
Fifteenth Week

Pelajaran Yang Keempat Puluh Lima
Lesson 45

Tekanan (-tah; juga; pula; pun) 2
Emphasis (-tah; juga; pula; pun) 2

A. *Sentences*

Apa lagi hendak dibuatnya?	*What else is he going to do?*
Apatah lagi hendak dibuatnya?	*Whatever will he do next?* or: *What on earth will he do next?*
Siapakah orang itu?	*Who is the man?*
Siapatah orang itu?	*Whoever is that man?* or: *Who can that man be?*
Ia bekerja kuat; tidak lulus juga.	*Although he worked hard, he didn't pass;* or: *he worked hard, (but) he didn't pass all the same.*
Ia bekerja kuat; tidak lulus pula!	*Although he worked hard, would you believe it, he didn't pass!*
Saya pun hendak belajar bahasa Melayu juga.	*I, too, am going to learn Malay.*
Bahasa Cina pun hendak saya pelajari juga.	*I'm going to study Chinese as well.*
Rokok sebatang pun tak ada lagi.	*There isn't even one cigarette left;* or: *there isn't a single cigarette left.*
Siapa pun tidak bercakap bahasa Inggeris di kampung ini.	*Nodody speaks English in this village.*
Apa pun tak ada dalam kotak itu.	*There is nothing in that box.*
Hamid sedang menulis surat; Yusuf pun mendengar radio.	*Hamid's writing a letter; Yusuf is listening to the radio.*
Yusuf mendengar warta berita; Hamid pun menulis beritanya sendiri kepada bapanya di Kuantan.	*Yusuf is listening to the news; Hamid is writing his own news to his father in Kuantan.*

Saya tinggal di dalam; ia pun keluarlah.	*I stayed inside; he went out.*
Hamid keluar makan angin; Yusuf pun tidurlah.	*Hamid went out for a stroll; Yusuf went to sleep.*

B. Word List

Noun
angin   *wind*

Miscellaneous
makan angin   *to go for a stroll, to go for a ride (*lit. *"to eat the wind")*

C. Grammar

207 *Emphasis: Further note on the prefix* me-: In this lesson we continue to study the various ways in which the various parts of a Malay sentence may be emphasised. So far we have said that the basic rule of emphasis is that the most important part of the sentence normally comes at the beginning and may be accompanied, according to circumstances, by either the particle -*lah* or the word *yang*, or by both. In questions the particle -*kah*, like -*lah* in statements, is added to the most important word or phrase.

We have also seen that the main distinction between the *me-*form of a verb and its simple or passive form is one of emphasis: the simple or passive form is used if the emphasis is on the verb and the *me-*form if the stress is anywhere else — with the exception that if the object is regarded as so important that it is placed at the beginning of the sentence (and this is much more common in Malay than in English) then the verb of which it is the object goes into the simple or passive form. There is a simple trick. which works in at least nine cases out of ten, and which you can try if you are uncertain whether to use the *me-*form of a verb or its simple or passive form in any given context. If you are trying to translate an English sentence into Malay, first of all read it *aloud* two or three times, making sure that you are using the intonation which gives the sentence the shade of meaning that you wish to convey. Then say it again, exaggerating your chosen intonation and taking careful note of the words on which the heaviest stresses fall. If any of these words are verbs which have to be rendered in Malay by verbs which *can* take the *me*-prefix then they will be in the simple or passive form, which might well be called the *emphatic form*. If the stresses fall on other words but not on the verbs, the verbs will, if they have one, go into the *me*-form, which we could well call the *unemphatic form*.

This opposition between emphatic (e.g. *tangkap*) and unemphatic (e.g. *menangkap*) forms is, I believe, why verbs used in the imperative (to give orders) practically never occur in the *me*-form. In a command the stress is almost always on the verb and for this reason Malay prefers the unprefixed form of such verbs in the imperative.

The main reason for my saying above that you should read the English sentence aloud before translating it into Malay is that in English we make such a great use of stress and intonation that, even when we read a text silently we mentally supply the correct stresses and intonations required by the context. In Malay, on the other hand, emphasis is actually shown even in writing by the use of the grammatical devices which we have been discussing, and by one or two others which we shall consider below.

208 *Apatah lagi hendak dibuatnya?:* "Whatever will he do next?" In addition to the particle *-kah*, which is used to make questions, there is another question particle, *-tah*, which can only be added directly to question words like *apa* (what), *siapa* (who) and *mana* (which); *-tah* is used with such words to indicate, sometimes, doubt or dubiousness, but more often to show surprise or astonishment, in which case it is very much like adding "ever " or "on earth" to the corresponding words in English.

209 *Ia bekerja kuat; tidak lulus juga:* "Although he worked hard, he didn't pass" or "He worked hard, (but) he didn't pass all the same." In "Speak Malay!", Lesson 48 (136), p. 162, this use of *juga* to express the English "although" was dealt with. This is an emphatic use of the word: *juga* in this sentence is really emphasising the verb (or phrase) it is attached to,

and at the same time gives the idea that the event was unexpected. If this unexpectedness is really surprising, then *juga* is changed to *pula*. Examples:

Ia bekerja kuat; tidak lulus pula!
Although he worked hard, would you believe it, he didn't pass!

210 *Bahasa Cina pun hendak saya pelajari juga:* "I'm going to study Chinese as well." *Pun* is another emphatic particle; when used together with *juga* it means "also" or "too". Notice, that in the examples given in Section A above the *pun* is attached to the most important word or phrase and that, normally, the whole group is then brought to the beginning of the sentence to emphasise it. The basic meaning of *pun* is probably something like "even", including the rather older meaning of "even", i.e. "also". This is very clear in negative sentences:

Rokok sebatang pun tak ada lagi.
There isn't even one cigarette (*or:* there isn't a single cigarette left).

211 *Hamid sedang menulis surat; Yusuf pun mendengar radio:* "Hamid is writing a letter; *Yusuf* is listening to the *radio*". *Pun* is used to focus attention on some topic of conversation, especially to introduce a *new* topic or a new subject or object for the next sentence. If we have been talking about Hamid, say, for a sentence or two, and then start saying something about Yusuf, for example, it is quite likely that Yusuf will have a *pun* tacked on to his name the first time it is mentioned. Later, if we want to re-introduce Hamid to the discussion, he will have to have a *pun* too. In this construction the verb is often accompanied by the particle *-lah*. In the corresponding English sentence the verb would, of course, just be heavily stressed. Examples:

Saya tinggal di dalam; ia pun keluarlah.
I stayed inside; *he* went *out*.

Hamid keluar makan angin; Yusuf pun tidurlah.
Hamid went out for a stroll; *Yusuf* went to *sleep*.

D. Exercises

Exercise 154 Translate into English:
1. Di manakah buku yang kubeli tadi itu?
2. Semalam saya makan di pekan; isteri saya makan di rumah.
3. Sudah sepuluh tahun ia tinggal di Malaysia; masih belum belajar lagu "Negaraku" pula!
4. Setelah Hang Jebat dibunuh, Hang Tuah pun baliklah.
5. "Sejarah Melayu" itu ialah sebuah buku Melayu yang termasyhur; "Hikayat Abdullah" pun masyhur juga.
6. Saya hendak menulis sebuah buku dalam bahasa Melayu; adik saya pun hendak menulis buku juga.
7. Encik kenal orang itukah? Tidak, orang itu tidak saya kenal.
8. Selepas pukul sebelas malam seorang pun tiada lagi di dalam dewan itu.
9. Ini dia buku yang saya beli pagi tadi. Mahukah encik baca?
10. Setelah encik membaca buku ini, buku itu pun patut encik baca juga.

Exercise 155 Translate into Malay:
1. *That's* the book I want to read.
2. I want to read it too.
3. Whatever is he going to do next?
4. He actually (use *pula*) wants to read that book!
5. While I was talking Yusuf went to sleep.
6. (Although) I waited for him for two hours, he didn't come all the same.
7. Whenever is he going to come? I have been waiting here for two and a half hours!
8. Where on earth have you put my shoes, Ahmad?
9. Chinese is a difficult language; so is Japanese.
10. Use the national language every day!

Exercise 156
Write down ten Malay sentences using what you have so far learnt during the course.

Exercise 157
Tuliskah satu karangan darihal *satu* daripada perkara-perkara yang berikut ini:
- a Bunga-bunga Kebangsaan (National Flowers)
- b Bangunan-bangunan Baharu di Pekan Tuan
- c Bahasa-bahasa dan Bangsa-bangsa Asia Tenggara
- d Mengambil Ujian Memandu Keréta
- e Satu Hari di Pantai

Minggu Yang Keenam Belas
Sixteenth Week

Pelajaran Yang Keempat Puluh Enam
Lesson 46

Cara-cara Menggunakan Akhiran -Nya
The Uses of the Suffix -Nya

A. Sentences

Ahmad telah membaca bukunya.	*Ahmad has read his book.*
Fatimah duduk di dalam biliknya.	*Fatimah is sitting in her room.*
Meréka selalu menyimpan keréta-kerétanya di belakang bangunan.	*They always park their cars behind the building.*
Surat ini ditulisnya semalam.	*This letter — he wrote yesterday.*
Ia mentutup bukunya lalu disimpannya dalam almari.	*He closed his book and put it away in the cupboard.*
Lepas itu ditulisnya surat kepada kawannya.	*And then he wrote a letter to his friend.*
Semalam saya melihatnya di pasar.	*Yesterday I saw him (or: her, or: them) in the market.*
Sayalah yang memberi hadiah kepadanya.	*I was the one who gave him a present.*
Almari ini besar; banyaklah buku-buku di dalamnya.	*This cupboard is big; there are many books inside it.*
Pagi tadi saya menerima surat daripadanya.	*This morning I received a letter from him.*
Sungai ini dalam benar; dalamnya tiga puluh kaki.	*This river is very deep; its depth is thirty feet (or: it is thirty feet deep).*
Besarnya keréta ini! Panjangnya lapan belas kaki!	*The size of this car! Its length is eighteen feet! (or: What a big car! It is eighteen feet long!)*
Datangnya pada pukul lapan menghairankan kami.	*His coming (or: his arrival) at eight o'clock surprised us.*

Datangnya Perdana Menteri di tengah-tengah percakapan meréka itu mengejutkan semuanya.	*The arrival of the Prime Minister right in the middle of their conversation startled them all.*
Buku itu warnanya hijau — ataupun warnanya buku itu hijau.	*The colour of that book is green — or — that book is green in colour.*
Bilik ini pintunya terbuka — ataupun — pintunya bilik ini terbuka.	*The door of this room is open.*
Ikan ini harganya lima puluh sen sekati — ataupun — harganya ikan ini lima puluh sen sekati.	*The price of this fish is fifty cents a catty — or — this fish costs fifty cents a catty.*
Semua tetamunya akan ditumpangkan di Istana Tetamu.	*All the guests will be accomodated in the Istana Tetamu.*
Di dalam maktab itu pengajarannya sangat baik.	*The instruction in that college is very good.*
Lepas itu kerétanya sampai; kami pun naiklah.	*Then the car (which we had been expecting) came and we got in.*

B. Word List

Nouns

dalamnya	*depth*	besarnya	*size*
panjangnya	*length*	datangnya	*arrival*
percakapan	*conversation*	warna	*colour*
ikan	*fish*	harga	*price*
sén	*cent*	kati	*catty (3 catties equal 4 pounds)*
pengajaran	*instruction*		

Adjective

dalam	*deep*	hairan	*surprised, astonished*
hijau	*green*	putih	*white*
mérah	*red*	biru	*blue*
kuning	*yellow*	hitam	*black*
kelabu	*grey*		

Verbs

simpan (menyimpan) keréta	*to park a car*
letak (meletak) keréta	*to park a car*
hairan (menghairankan)	*to surprise, to astonish*
kejutkan (mengejutkan)	*to startle*
tumpangkan (menumpangkan)	*to accommodate, to put up*

C. Grammar

212 *Summary of various uses of* -nya: During this couse we have made a great use of the suffix *-nya* and in this lesson we shall bring all its most important uses together under one heading. Basically *-nya* is a pronoun and is just another form of *ia* or *dia*. Unlike the latter, however, it is never used, except in dialect, by itself, but is always tacked on to the end of another word as a suffix. Furthermore, while *ia* and *dia* are usually only *singular*, *-nya* is used for the plural as well. It may therefore stand for "he", "she", "it" or "they" or any other forms of those English words.

(a) The most common use of *-nya* if probably as a *possessive* pronoun meaning "his", "her", "its" or "their" according to the context. Examples:

>*Ahmad membaca bukunya.*
>Ahmad reads his book.

>*Fatimah membaca bukunya.*
>Fatimah reads her book.

Ahmad dan Fatimah membaca bukunya.
Ahmad and Fatimah read their books.

(b) Another use of *-nya* is to express the third person subject in the passive construction. Examples:

Ahmad menutup bukunya lalu disimpannya.
Ahmad closes his book and (he) puts it away.

Fatimah menutup bukunya lalu disimpannya.
Fatimah closes her book and (she) puts it away.

Ahmad dan Fatimah menutup bukunya lalu disimpannya.
Ahmad and Fatimah close their books and (they) put them away.

(c) *-Nya* may also be the object of a verb or preposition. Examples:

Semalam saya melihatnya di pasar.
Yesterday I saw him (or "her" or "them") in the market.

Sayalah yang memberi hadiah kepadanya.
I was the one who gave him (or "her" or "them") a present.

(d) *-Nya* is often added to other parts of speech, especially to verbs or adjectives, to form a kind of noun (abstract or verbal). Examples:

Dalamnya sungai ini dua puluh kaki.
The depth of this river is twenty feet.

Besarnya keréta itu!
The size of that car! (*i.e.* What a big car!)

Panjangnya meja itu enam kaki.
The length of that table is six feet.

(e) In old-fashioned English we sometimes find expressions like "John his book" and "Thomas his house" instead of "John's book" and "Thomas's house". Malay has a very similar construction to this in which the possesser and the possessed may come in either order. Examples:

> *Buku itu warnanya hijau* (or: *warnanya buku itu hijau.*)
> That book is green in colour (*lit.:* "that book its colour").
>
> *Pintunya bilik ini terbuka* (or: *bilik ini pintunya terbuka*).
> The door of that room is open (*lit.:* "that room its door").

(f) Out of the use of *-nya* mentioned in *(e)* above comes another important one, viz. the use of *-nya* to define something in much the same way as the English definite article "the" is used. When added in this way to a noun, *-nya* indicates that the noun is the one we have been talking about or expecting to be mentioned. It has very much the meaning of "the something or other *in question.*" Examples:

> *Semua tetamunya akan ditumpangkan di Istana Tetamu.*
> All the guests will be accommodated in the Istana Tetamu.
> (The implication being that we have been discussing some celebration or other, or some public function, and this will naturally involve guests: and those guests *who are involved (-nya)* will be put up at the Istana.)
>
> *Lepas itu keretanya sampai; kami pun naiklah.*
> Then the car came and we got in.
> (The implication here is that we had been waiting for a particular car which finally arrived in accordance with our expectation.)

> *Note:* The only real difference between this use of *-nya* and the use of the English "the" in such contexts is that *-nya* could still be left out, whereas the English "the" could not.

D. Exercises

Exercise 158   Translate into English:
1. Berapa dalamnya sungai ini?
2. Bendéra kebangsaan warnanya mérah, putih, biru dan kuning.
3. Meréka membuka buku-bukunya lalu dibacanya.
4. Buku ini hendak saya berikan kepadanya.
5. Kecilnya budak ini! Berapa umurnya?
6. Selapas tetamunya sampai, keréta-kerétanya mesti diletak di belakang bangunan.
7. Bangunan itu tingginya seratus kaki.
8. Bilik saya tingkapnya empat.
9. Besarnya almari ini! Apa ada di dalamnya?
10. Meréka menyambut tetamunya di lapangan terbang lalu ditumpangkannya di Hotel Merlin.

Exercise 159   Translate into Malay:
1. This car has four doors (use *-nya*).
2. This college has six senior lecturers; so, the instruction is very good.
3. The road in which (*tempat*) we live is twenty-five feet wide.
4. How stupid this boy is! He can't even write his own name!
5. His going (like) that astonished them all.
6. These pens cost twenty-three dollars each.
7. How much is that beef? It costs three dollars a catty. How expensive!
8. When the car arrives, get in quickly and go to the airport.
9. She parked her car behind the post office and then went in to buy some stamps.
10. He took a new file and inserted the letters in it.

Exercise 160
Write down ten sentences of your own composition using what you have learnt so far during the course.

Exercise 161
Tulis karangan darihal *satu* daripada perkara-perkara berikut:
a Pelabuhan Pulau Pinang
b Lapangan Terbang Kuala Lumpur
c Sungai-sungai Malaysia
d Apakah pentingnya kedai-kedai kopi di dalam hidup orang Malaysia?
e Kerajaan Malaysia

Minggu Yang Keenam Belas
Sixteenth Week

Pelajaran Yang Keempat Puluh Tujuh
Lesson 47

(a) Awalan Si-; (b) Ayat-ayat Berlapis
(a) The Prefix Si-; (b) The Compound Sentence

A. Sentences

Di manatah si Ahmad? Sudah dua jam saya menantikannya.	*Wherever is that fellow Ahmad? I have been waiting for him for two hours.*
Si Yusuf selalu tidur; kerja sedikit pun tak buat.	*Old Yusuf is always asleep; he doesn't do a stroke of work.*
Si bodoh itu! Nama sendiri pun dia tak tahu tulis!	*Silly fellow! He can't even write his own name!*
Téngok si Gemuk itu! Selalulah dia makan nasi!	*Look at old Fatty! He's always eating!*
Dengarkan si Pandai itu! Selalu dia tahu jawapan.	*Listen to old Clever-clever! He always knows the answer.*
Perkataan-perkataan ini diarahkan kepada si pembaca.	*These words are addressed to the reader.*
Masa kita menyediakan satu siaran radio, patutlah kita mengingat si pendengar.	*When we are preparing a radio programme, we should remember the listener.*
Di manatah si Janggut tu?	*Where on earth is that fellow with the beard?* or: *Where's old Beaver got to?*
Ali dan Hamid pergi ke pekan.	*Ali and Hamid went to town.*
Ali dengan Hamid pergi ke pekan.	*Ali and Hamid went to town.*
Ia membuka bukunya lalu dibacanya.	*He opened his book and read it.*
Ia masak nasi lalu dimakannya.	*She cooked the rice and ate it.*
Ia duduk di serambi seraya minum téhnya.	*He sat on the verandah and drank his tea.*

Ia bercakap sambil menangis.	*He spoke and wept (at the same time);* or: *he spoke through his tears.*
Ia berdiri di depan darjah serta menyanyikan lagu kebangsaan.	*He stood in front of the class and sang the national anthem.*
Ia bekerja di perpustakaan seraya menjeniskan semua bukunya.	*He works in the library and classifies all the books.*
Ia belajar di maktab ini sambil mengajar di sebuah sekolah kebangsaan.	*He studies in this college and teaches in a national school.*
Saya singgah di rumahnya, tetapi dia tak ada.	*I called in at his house, but he wasn't in.*
Doktor bedah telah membedahnya; akan tetapi pembedahan tidak memuaskan hati, lalu ia pun matilah.	*The surgeon operated on him; but the operation was not satisfactory, and he died.*
Bukan Ali melainkan Hamid yang menutup tingkap.	*It wasn't Ali but Hamid who closed the window.*
Bukan saya melainkan dia yang tak mahu belajar bahasa Melayu.	*It's not me but him who doesn't want to learn Malay.*
Ia bukan ahli ubat, melainkan ahli kimia.	*He is not a pharmacist but a chemist.*
Orang itu bukan pelakon melainkan pengurus pentas.	*That man is not an actor but a stage-manager.*

B. Word List

Nouns

jawapan	*answer*	pembaca	*reader*
siaran radio	*radio programme*	pendengar	*listener*
darjah	*class*		

lagu kebangsaan	*national anthem*	lagu	*song*
ahli bedah	*surgeon*	pembedahan	*operation*
ahli ubat	*pharmacist*	ahli kimia	*chemist*
pelakon	*actor*	pengurus	*manager*
pengurus pentas	*stage-manager*		

Verbs

sediakan (menyediakan)	*to prepare*
nyanyikan (menyanyikan)	*to sing (trans.)*
jeniskan (menjeniskan)	*to classify*
bedah (membedah)	*to operate (surgically) upon*
puaskan (memuaskan)	*to satisfy*
puaskan (memuaskan) hati	*to be satisfactory*

Miscellaneous

dan	*and*	sekali lagi	*again*
sambil	*and*	dengan	*with, and*
bukan ... melainkan	*not ... but*	seraya	*and*
		serta	*and*
akan tetapi	*but*	tetapi	*but*

C. Grammar

213 *Di manatah si Ahmad?:* "Wherever is that fellow Ahmad?" We have had the prefix *si* before in the two expressions *si anu* and *si polan*, both of which mean "so-and-so". *Anu* by itself means "that", but is not much used outside dialect (it is very common in Kedah, for instance), and *polan* is from the Arabic word *fulan*, which also means "so-and-so". The addition of the prefix *si* to these two words has the effect of making them refer to persons. Now the prefix *si* may be added to almost any part of speech to give it a certain colour. It is frequently added, for example, to people's names, and then indicates a certain familiarity, if not a little contempt. It corresponds fairly well to "that fellow" or "old (George)" in English or to the German use of the definite article with Christian names: e.g. *"wo ist der alte Georg?"* ("Where's old George?") or *"hast du die Marie gesehen?"* ("Did you see Mary?").

214 *Si bodoh itu!:* "Silly fellow!" When added to an adjective *si* forms a slightly contemptuous noun. Examples:

Si Pandai	Old Cleversticks
Si Gemuk	Old Fatty

215 *Perkataan-perkataan ini diarahkan kepada si pembaca:* "These words are addressed to the reader." The prefix *si* is often used together with the agent-prefix *pe-*, and in this case is normally not contemptuous but simply acts as a kind of definite article, like the English word "the".

216 *Di manatah si Janggut tu?:* "Where on earth is that fellow with the beard?" When added to some nouns (e.g. *janggut*, "beard") *si* often gives the idea of a person who possesses the thing denoted by the noun. "Old Bluebeard" would probably be called *si Janggut Biru* in Malay!

217 *Co-ordination of Nouns and Verbs ("and" and "but"):* The most common word for "and" is, of course, *dan*, which in Modern Malay is used in much the same way as the English "and", i.e. it can join verbs as well as nouns, clauses as well as words. Strictly speaking, however, *dan* should not be used to join clauses or sentences. Its correct function in classical Malay is to join *nouns* only, and in this use it may be replaced by *dengan*, "with". In fact *dan* is probably just a shortened form of *dengan*.

Now, when "and" joins two sentences or clauses, there are in the more classical style several ways of putting it into Malay according to two main categories of meaning. Consider these English sentences: "he opened his book and read it" and "he sat on the verandah and drank his tea". In the first of these sentences the two actions — opening and reading — clearly form a *sequence*: he obviously could not read his book before he opened it. The reading took place *after* the opening. In this sentence, therefore, "and" really means "and then" or "and next". The best way of translating this meaning of "and" into Malay is to use the word *lalu*, which means something like "passing on to". Examples:

Ia membuka bukunya lalu dibacanya.
He opened his book and read it.

Ia masak nasi lalu dimakannya.
She cooked the rice and ate it.

In the other sentence — "he sat on the verandah and drank his tea" — the two actions — sitting and drinking — most probably happened *at the same time*. He sat on the verandah to drink his tea, because it was pleasant to sit there for that purpose. To render this meaning of "and" there are several words in Malay. The most common are *serta, seraya, sambil* and *lagi*. Examples:

Ia duduk di serambik seraya minum têhnya.
He sat on the verandah and drank his tea; *or:* he sat on the verandah *drinking* his tea.

Ia bercakap sambil menangis.
He spoke and wept (at the same time); *or:* he spoke through his tears.

The most common word for "but" is *tetapi* (colloquially, *tapi*) or sometimes *akan tetapi*. However, when "but" is used together with a negative to denote a strong contrast, then the usual construction in Malay is *bukan ... melainkan ...* (Cf. the distinction between *aber* and *sondern* in German, or between *pero* and *sino* in Spanish). Examples here will speak louder than words:

Bukan Ali melainkan Hamid yang mentutup pintu.
It wasn't Ali but Hamid who closed the door.

Ia bukan ahli ubat melainkan ahli kimia.
He is not a pharmacist but a chemist.

D. Exercises

Exercise 162   Translate into English:
1. Ia menjeniskan buku itu lalu disimpannya dalam almari.
2. Ia tersenyum lalu berkata, "Apa kaubuat?"
3. Ia tersenyum sambil berkata, "Sila masuk, tuan."
4. Bukan saya melainkan bapa saya yang hendak menjadi pegawai daérah.
5. Siapa yang membuat kerja ini? Bukan saya, melainkan dia.
6. Beliau bukan Perdana Menteri melainkan Menteri Pelajaran.
7. Ia menyanyi sambil menari selama dua jam.
8. Guru patut menunjukkan sebatang kalam seraya berkata, "Ini kalam."
9. Guru itu menunjukkan sebatang kalam lalu diangkatnya.
10. Tiba-tiba datanglah si Yusuf.

Exercise 163   Translate into Malay:
1. Where on earth is that fellow Krishna?
2. I want to classify these books but I can't read Jawi. — Tell old Ahmad to classify them.
3. The reader is advised to read the first book before trying to read the second.
4. Who on earth is that fellow with the beard?
5. They stayed in the coffee-shop and ate rice and curry.
6. He went into the coffee-shop and asked for a cup of coffee.
7. He studied chemistry (*ilmu kimia*) at the university for three years and became a chemist.
8. The stage-manager told the actors to come to the theatre at three o'clock, but three have not yet arrived.
9. He was operated upon by a famous surgeon, but he died all the same.
10. It wasn't Siti but Aminah who opened the door.

Exercise 164
Write down ten sentences of your own composition in Malay using what you have learnt so far in this course.

Exercise 165
Tulis karangan darihal *satu* daripada perkara-perkara berikut:
a Ceritakan sedikit darihal seorang pelakon Malaysia yang masyhur
b Panggung-panggung bandar tempat tuan tinggal
c Kepentingan bahasa Inggeris di dalam dunia sekarang
d Tulislah sepucuk surat kepada seorang sahabat Cina sambil menasihatkan dia manakah cara yang baik sekali belajar bahasa Melayu
e Perhubungan kebudayaan (*kebudayaan:* "culture") di antara Malaysia dan Indonesia

Minggu Yang Keenam Belas
Sixteenth Week

Pelajaran Yang Keempat Puluh Delapan
Lesson 48

Cara-cara Membentuk Katasifat
The Formation of Adverbs

A. Sentences

Keréta saya cepat.	*My car is fast.*
Keréta saya bergerak cepat.	*My car travels fast.*
Ia bercakap baik.	*He speaks well.*
Rumahnya cantik benar.	*His house is truly beautiful.*
Bila abangmu hendak sampai?	*When will your (elder) brother arrive?*
Ia mengulangkan soalannya sekali lagi.	*He repeated his question once more.*
Selepas itu ia pun keluarlah.	*After that he went out.*
Sebenarnya orang itu pandai bercakap bahasa Melayu.	*Truly that man is good a speaking Malay.*
Sesungguhnya dia tidak mahu pergi ke Singapura.	*He does not really want to go to Singapore.*
Kerja ini patut kaubuat sebaik-baiknya.	*You should do this work as well as you can.*
Kerétanya berjalan secepat-cepatnya tetapi terléwat sampainya.	*The car went as quickly as possible but they arrived too late.*
Ésok dia tidak boléh datang, agaknya.	*He probably won't be able to come tomorrow.*
Isterinya seorang ahli kecantikan, rupanya.	*His wife, apparently, is a beauty specialist.*
Suaminya seorang tukang ukir khabarnya; patung-patungnya telah dipertunjukkan di déwan seni gambar negara.	*Her husband is a sculptor, so they say; his statues have been exhibited in the national art gallery.*
Tiba-tiba kakinya tergelincir, lalu terjatuhlah ia.	*Suddenly his foot slipped and he fell down.*

Surat itu mesti kautulis baik-baik.	*You must write that letter carefully (or: properly).*
Ia bangun dengan cepat lalu pergi ke pejabat.	*He got up quickly and went to the office.*
Dengan hormatnya dipersilakan tuan melawat negeri ini.	*You are respectedly invited to visit this country.*
Kerja itu dihabiskannya dengan sebaik-baiknya.	*He finished the job as well as he could.*
Bukit-bukit ini akan diperiksa dengan baik-baik oleh dua orang ahli kajibumi.	*These hills will be properly examined by two geologists.*
Khabarnya ia akan mewakili negeri kita di Bangsa-bangsa Bersatu.	*It is said that he will represent our country at the United Nations.*
Bukan tiap-tiap orang ahli siasah yang boléh kita namakan negarawan.	*It is not every politician that we can call a statesman.*
Di maktab ia mempelajari politik dunia dan perékonomian.	*At college he studied world politics and economics.*
Gurunya seorang ahli sejarah yang termasyhur dalam dunia.	*His teacher was a world-famous historian.*

B. Word List

Nouns

kecantikan	*beauty*	pakar	*an expert*
ahli kecantikan	*beauty specialist*	patung	*statue*
		tukang ukir	*sculptor*
siasah	*politics*	ahli kaji bumi	*geologist*

negarawan	*statesman*	Bangsa-bangsa Bersatu	*United Nations*
sejarah	*annals, history*	siasah dunia	*world politics*
ahli siasah	*politician*	ahli sejarah	*historian*
ilmu bedah	*surgery*	keahlian	*skill*
bangsawan	*nobleman*	(seorang) berbangsa	*(a) nobleman*
pengelola	*organiser*		
pengurusan	*management*		

Adjectives

cepat	*quick, fast*	bersatu	*united*
berbangsa	*noble*		

Verbs

ulangkan (mengulangkan)	*to repeat*
tergelincir	*to slip*
habiskan (menghabiskan)	*to finish*

Miscellaneous

sekali lagi	*once again*	sebenarnya	*truly*
sesungguhnya	*really*	sebaik-baiknya	*as well as possible*
secepat-cepatnya	*as quickly as possible*	agaknya	*probably*
rupanya	*apparently*	khabarnya	*it is said*
		dengan cepat	*quickly*

C. *Grammar*

218 *Formation of adverbs:* In English we usually distinguish carefully between adjectives and adverbs. We say, for instance, "His singing is *good*", but few of us would ever say "He sings *good*". *Good* is an adjective and can only be attached to nouns or pronouns: the

corresponding adverb is "well". Adverbs are used to qualify or describe *verbs, adjectives,* or other *adverbs*; adjectives can only qualify *nouns* or *pronouns*. We say "His speech is quick" but "He speaks quickly", in which case the adverb is made by adding the suffix -*ly* to the adjective. We are not always so fussy in English, however, for we say both "His car is fast" and "His car goes fast". Malay is even less fussy than English can be, and there is no hard and fast rule about adverbs. Many adjectives can be used as adverbs without any change. Examples:

Keréta itu cepat.	The car is fast.
Keréta itu berjalan cepat.	The car goes fast.
Berita itu tidak benar.	That news is not true.
Rumahnya cantik benar.	His house is truly beautiful.

There are, however, quite a number of structural patterns which nearly always have an adverbial meaning, and although it is impossible to reduce them to definite rules it is just as well to have some idea of how they work, because they do occur quite frequently in all forms of Malay, spoken and written. One such structure is to place the short form of *satu*, "one" — viz. *se-* — in front of a root-word. Examples:

sekali	once
selepas	after
sesudah	after
sebelum	before

Another common structure is *se-* plus root-word plus *-nya*. Examples:

sebenarnya	truly
sesungguhnya	really

In the *se-*root-*nya* structure the *root* is often reduplicated and this often brings in the idea of possibility or of doing something to the best of one's ability:

sebaik-baiknya	as well as possible
secepat-cepatnya	as quickly as possible
selekas-lekasnya	as soon as possible

A very common adverbial structure is *root* plus *-nya*. We have already used quite a number of these. Examples:

agaknya	probably
rupanya	apparently
khabarnya	by all accounts (i.e. so they say)

Often mere reduplication alone is sufficient to make an adverb. Examples:

tiba-tiba	suddenly
baik-baik	properly, carefully

Adverbs are also often formed by adding the preposition *dengan* to an adjective or noun, or to any of the structures mentioned above. Examples:

dengan cepat	quickly
dengan hormatnya	respectfully
dengan sebaik-baiknya	as well as possible
dengan baik-baik	properly

221 *Tukang ukir:* "sculptor". In Lesson 41 (195) we saw that the word *juru* could be used to form compound nouns denoting people connected with certain actions: There are three Malay words which can be used like this: *tukang,* "workman", *juru,* "specialist" and *ahli,* "expert". *Ahli*, which also means "member (of a committee, etc.)", denotes considerably more expertise than *juru*, which, in its turn, denotes more skill or a higher social position than *tukang*. Examples:

tukang:

tukang kebun	*gardener*
tukang besi	*smith*
tukang gunting	*barber*
tukang daging	*butcher*

	tukang kasut	*shoemaker*
	tukang kayu	*carpenter*
	tukang emas	*goldsmith*
	tukang cap	*printer*
juru:		
	jurubahasa	*interpreter*
	jurubatu	*boatswain*
	jurucakap	*spokesman*
	jururawat	*nurse*
	jurutaip	*typist*
	jurutera	*engineer*
ahli:		
	ahli-ahli jawatankuasa	*committee members*
	ahli bahasa	*linguist*
	ahli bangunan	*architect*
	ahli bedah	*surgeon*
	ahli kaji bumi	*geologist*
	ahli ilmu bangsa-bangsa	*ethnologist*
	ahli negara, negarawan	*statesman*
	ahli patung	*sculptor*
	ahli pengetahuan	*scholar, savant*
	ahli radio, pakar radio	*radio expert*
	ahli sejarah	*historian*
	ahli teknik	*technician*
	ahli kimia	*chemist*
	ahli ubat	*pharmacist*

D. Exercises

Exercise 166   Translate into English:
1   Semua ahli-ahli jawatankuasa dipersilakan mengemukakan

cadangan-cadangannya sebelum akhir bulan ini.
2 Satu mesyuarat semua ahli-ahli bumi dan semua ahli-ahli ilmu bangsa-bangsa akan diadakan pada permulaan bulan depan di Dewan Besar Universiti.
3 Di manakah tukang kebun itu? Hari ini sedikit kerja pun tidak dibuatnya.
4 Seorang jurucakap kerajaan telah berkata bahawa Perdana Menteri akan tiba di lapangan terbang pada pukul lima setengah petang.
5 Sungguhpun ia menulis cadangannya dengan sebaik-baiknya, akan tetapi telah ditolak oleh jabatan Perdana Menteri.
6 Khabarnya suami dia yang menulis buku ini; suaminya ialah seorang jurutera yang masyhur.
7 Sungguhpun Perdana Menteri menulis surat itu sendiri tetapi telah ditaip oléh jurutaipnya lalu dikirimkan oleh kerani beliau.
8 Jurubahasa ialah seorang yang tahu bercakap dua bahasa, akan tetapi ahli bahasa ialah seorang yang mempelajari banyak bahasa supaya mengetahui dengan sebaik-baiknya.
9 Pada malam itu ia mendengar syarahan yang diberi oleh seorang pensyarah universiti. Setelah itu ia pun baliklah lalu tidur.
10 Radio saya sudah rosak; saya hendak memanggil seorang tukang radio supaya membaikinya.

Exercise 167   Translate into Malay:
1 On (*dalam*) the radio that last night I heard a very interesting lecture. It was given by Malaysia's representative at the United Nations.
2 According to a Ruritanian government spokesman all the rebels have been killed or arrested and put in jail.
3 Although he looked in four dictionaries (dictionary: *kamus*), he could not find the word he was looking for.
4 A man who sells medicine is called a pharmacist, and a man who sells meat is called a butcher.

5. My elder brother is studying Malay at the university; his teacher is a very famous Malay scholar.
6. This river is twenty feet deep; without (*tanpa* or *dengan tiada*) a boat (*sampan*) we cannot cross over.
7. Formerly my father was the headmaster of a national school, but now he has become an organiser of Malay schools.
8. Although he drove his car as fast as possible, he arrived too late. The train had already gone.
9. When you have finished reading this book, I hope that you will begin to study Malay literature.
10. If you want to be called a true Malaysian, you must learn the national language and use it as well as you can whether (*mahupun*) you are working or (*mahupun*) sitting at home.

Exercise 168
Write down twenty-five sentences using as much as possible of what you have learned during the course.

Exercise 169
Tulislah karangan darihal *satu* daripada perkara-perkara berikut:
a Bangsa-bangsa Bersatu
b Keadaan siasah di Malaysia
c Bahasa Melayu sebagai bahasa antarabangsa (international) di Asia Tenggara
d Peraturan Pelajaran di Malaysia
e Seorang tukang yang tuan kenal

Key To The Exercises

Exercise 1:
1. Hamid is fatter than I am.
2. Ahmad is the fattest of all.
3. This building is higher than that building.
4. The Malay language is the most useful.
5. I am more intelligent than he is.
6. This boy is less intelligent than Hamid.
7. This town is less big than (*or:* not as big as) Kuala Lumpur.
8. That table is the longest.
9. This table is the lowest.
10. This building is tall, but that building is the tallest.

Exercise 2:
1. Yusuf lebih berakal daripada ayahnya.
2. Bapa saya lebih gemuk daripada emak saya.
3. Keréta Ahmad kurang besar daripada keréta Hamid.
4. Negeri Perlis negeri yang kecil sekali di Malaysia.
5. Yusuf lebih gemuk daripada Ahmad, tetapi Ali yang gemuk sekali.
6. Di Kuala Lumpur bahasa Malaysia lebih berguna daripada bahasa Perancis.
7. Di Paris bahasa Perancis bahasa yang berguna sekali.
8. Ini kilang yang besar sekali di Malaysia.
9. Rumah saya lebih kecil daripada rumah dia.
10. Rumah Yusuf yang kecil sekali.

Exercise 4:
1. This one is smaller than that one.
2. This one is smaller.
3. Yusuf's father is very intelligent.
4. His mother is more intelligent.
5. Malay is a very useful language.
6. This building is very tall.
7. That building is taller.
8. This boy has no manners.
9. That box is very small.
10. Ahmad's car is too slow.

Exercise 5:
1. Bapa saya terlalu gemuk.
2. Bangunan ini lagi tinggi.
3. Budak ini kurang berakal.
4. Orang itu kurang ajar.
5. Yusuf lebih berakal daripada budak yang lain.
6. Ahmad gemuk, tetapi Said lagi gemuk.
7. Kilang ini amat besar; yang besar sekali di Malaysia.
8. Negeri Pahang negeri yang besar sekali di Semenanjung Malaysia.
9. Ipoh besar, tetapi Kuala Lumpur lagi besar.
10. Yusuf berakalkah? Kurang periksa.

Exercise 7:

Hamid:	We have arrived at the market. What are you going to buy first?
Yusuf:	I'm going to buy some durians. Durians are more tasty.
Hamid:	No. I don't agree. I think mangosteens are tastier than durians, but rambutans are the tastiest of all.
Yusuf:	Ah, that's correct! Rambutans are very tasty. I like eating them very much. The rambutan is the tastiest fruit in this country of ours.
Hamid:	We'd better buy the rambutans in this shop.
Shopkeeper:	What do you want to buy, gentlemen?
Hamid:	We want to buy some rambutans. Have you any big ones?
Shopkeeper:	Yes, I have. These are the biggest in the market.
Hamid:	Those? But those are too small. I want bigger rambutans.
Shopkeeper:	Bigger? Impossible! (*lit.* how can that be?) (You) can't get bigger ones anywhere. These rambutans are very big.
Yusuf:	All right. I'll buy ten. Here's the money.
Shopkeeper:	Thank you.

Exercise 8:

1 These rambutans are not very tasty.
2 Hamid is stronger than Ah Chong.
3 Ah Chong is very strong, but Krishna is the strongest.
4 His mother is younger than his father.
5 French is a very melodious language, but Malay is the most melodious of all.
6 English is more useful than French.
7 My younger brother is more active than my elder brother.
8 Noraini is bright, but Zainab is brighter.
9 The railway is swift but the aeroplane is the swiftest of all.
10 Kedah is bigger than Perlis.

Exercise 9:

1 Buah durian itu lebih besar daripada buah rambutan.
2 Kakak saya lebih muda daripada abang saya.
3 Bahasa Melayu itu bahasa kebangsaan Malaysia.
4 Apa encik nak beli di pasar? Buah manggis.
5 Yusuf kurang pantas — *or:* Yusuf tak berapa pantas.
6 Noraini sangat cerdik — *or:* Noraini cerdik benar.
7 Ah Kim amat pandai bercakap Melayu, tetapi bapa dia lagi pandai.
8 Bapa saya lebih tua daripada emak saya.
9 Yang ini terlalu kecil. Saya mahu yang lagi besar.
10 Kuala Lumpur bandar yang sangat besar.

Exercise 11:

1 melompat
2 membaca
3 menulis
4 mencuri
5 menyusun
6 mengganti
7 mengacau
8 mengupas
9 mendaftarkan
10 memukul

293

Exercise 12:
1. My elder sister does not like wearing pretty clothes.
2. He is looking for his father in the market.
3. That Chinese likes speaking Malay.
4. Encik Ali will represent our government.
5. My clerk will write that letter.
6. Hamid is drawing a picture of the post office.
7. He is going to put this letter in the new file.
8. My mother is reading a Malay newspaper.
9. His mother is now waiting for him outside the post office.
10. My elder brother is going to write a book in Malay.

Exercise 13:
1. Ali sedang menulis surat.
2. Ahmad hendak melukis gambar.
3. Guru akan menyatakan makna perkataan itu.
4. Orang akan memandang encik.
5. Saya hendak membeli buku Melayu yang baharu.
6. Kakak encik memakai pakaian cantik.
7. Ali hendak membuka pintu.
8. Saya akan menyimpan surat ini.
9. Orang India itu sedang membaca suratkhabar Inggeris.
10. Guru kita pandai menerangkan perkataan-perkataan yang baharu.

Exercise 15:
1. Hamid puts the cigarettes away in the box.
2. My elder brother has rolled up the carpet.
3. The Prime Minister is going to explain his policy to us.
4. He will not answer this question.
5. That man is always beating his dog.
6. We are going to buy a new carpet.
7. I have written three letters to him.
8. Your dog has damaged our carpet.
9. We are going to speak only Malay.
10. Our friends have bought a new house in Kuala Lumpur.

Exercise 16:
1. Saya sedang mencari emak saya.
2. Yusuf menyimpan buku dalam almari.
3. Ali tidak akan menjawab soalan itu.
4. Dia tidak suka menantikan orang.
5. Saya akan menghantar anak saya ke Kuala Lumpur.
6. Saya sudah datang mengambil buku saya.
7. Perdana Menteri sudah datang ke Kuala Lumpur menyatakan dasarnya yang baharu.
8. Saya sudah memasukkan surat encik ke dalam fail.
9. Anak saya sudah melukis gambar-gambar yang cantik.
10. Saya sudah menerima sepucuk surat sahaja.

Exercise 17:
Ali:	Hullo, how are you?
Ahmad:	I'm fine, thanks.
Ali:	What are you doing now?

Ahmad: I'm writing a letter.
Ali: Who are you writing to?
Ahmad: To my son. He has been waiting a long time for my letter. But I have had a lot of work, and up to now I have not had time to write to him. Only today am I able to write this short letter to him.
Ali: Have you had a letter from your son?
Ahmad: Yes. I have. Two weeks ago I got a long letter from him. In the letter he said he was waiting for me to write to him, but my letter had not yet arrived.
Ali: Where does he live?
Ahmad: He's living in London. He is representing the Malaysian government there.
Ali: Splendid! You'd better answer his letter, and I'd better not bother you any longer. I've got to go to the post office to register my two or three letters. Good-bye.
Ahmad: Good-bye.

Exercise 18:
1 The more he eats Malay curry the more he likes eating it.
2 I do not like reading such long books; that book is too long.
3 Malay curry is not as hot as Indian curry.
4 Indian curry is the hottest of all.
5 His father is as old as his mother.
6 Hamid is as big as an elephant.
7 The more intelligent the better.
8 He is not as intelligent as that.
9 The longer he stays in Malaysia the better he is at speaking Malay.
10 I think he likes eating hot curry.

Exercise 19:
1 Lagi ramai lagi seronok.
2 Bapa saya bukan setinggi itu.
3 Keréta saya sama besar dengan keréta encik.
4 Ah Kim sama malas dengan Yusuf.
5 Tong saya sama berat dengan tong dia.
6 Semakin berat semakin baik.
7 Makin dia bercakap makin dia mahu bercakap.
8 Rumah saya bukan sama besar dengan rumah guru besar.
9 Ibu saya bukan sama tua dengan bapa saya.
10 Saya ingat dia sampai semalam (*or:* kelmarin).

Exercise 21:
1 My son has entered the university in Kuala Lumpur.
2 I must read that book.
3 In front of my office is a "keep left" sign.
4 Use the national language!
5 French is very interesting.
6 Do you like driving a car?
7 Yesterday I read the Highway Code.
8 His car stopped outside the Government Secretariat.
9 If you want to register your child's name, you must go to the Education Office.
10 My younger brother is studying in a Malay primary school.

Exercise 22:
1. Panduan Jalan Raya itu buku yang sangat berguna.
2. Di mana encik bekerja? Saya bekerja di ibu pejabat.
3. Kalau kita membawa keréta di negeri Perancis, kita mesti mengikut sebelah kanan.
4. Sila masuk, tuan!
5. Apa makna isyarat itu?
6. Di tengah jalan ada isyarat "berhenti-lihat-jalan".
7. Bapa saya tidak suka memandu keréta.
8. Encik mesti mendaftarkan surat ini di pejabat pos.
9. Ah Kim selalu menulis surat dalam bahasa kebangsaan.
10. Marilah kita bercakap Melayu hari ini!

Exercise 24:
1. My elder brother is going to drive his car to Kuala Lumpur.
2. Where must I register my name? At the secretariat.
3. Chinese is a very interesting language.
4. He will open the office at nine o'clock.
5. Who will clean father's room?
6. The easier the better.
7. Have you learned all the road signs?
8. I have not yet learned all the signs.
9. Ahmad has not yet rolled up the carpet in my room.
10. That large building is the Government Secretariat.

Exercise 25:
1. Saya akan mengikut jalan raya ke Kuala Lumpur.
2. Apa makna perkataan yang susah ini?
3. Dia sedang memandu keréta.
4. Yusuf sama berakal dengan bapanya.
5. Kalau kita hendak memandu keréta, kita mesti belajar semua isyarat-isyarat jalan raya dahulu.
6. Kalau anak encik hendak masuk sekolah rendah, encik mesti mendaftarkan nama dia di pejabat pelajaran dahulu.
7. Di mana Pejabat Pelajaran? Pejabat Pelajaran ada di Ibu Pejabat Kerajaan.
8. Saya tidak boléh memandu kereta sejauh itu.
9. Saya belum membaca suratkhabar hari ini.
10. Marilah kita pergi ke pejabat pos; saya mesti menghantar surat ini kepada Ali.

Exercise 26:
A: What are you reading?
B: I am reading the "Highway Code".
A: The "Highway Code"? What's that?
B: The "Highway Code" is a very useful book. The government has compiled the book in order to help us to use the highway safely. Whether people drive cars, ride bicycles or walk, it makes no difference — we must all read the "Highway Code".

A: What's that picture?
B: This is a picture of the road signs. This picture is a picture of the "keep left" sign. When we see a "keep left" sign, we must drive our car to the left of it.
A: What is this sign? It has the words "stop – look – go".
B: When we see that sign, it means that we are about to enter the main road from a minor road. First, we must stop. Then we must look; (that) means we must wait for the vehicles in the main road to go past first. Only then can we proceed further.
A: That book is very useful. Where can I buy (one)?
B: (You) can buy it in any shop. It only costs fifty cents. Do buy one this very day. If you do not know the meaning of all the road signs, you certainly won't pass your driving test.

Exercise 27:
1 I have read that book.
2 We are going to go to Singapore.
3 Please come to my office at ten o'clock.
4 What time did you arrive here?
5 Come on, let's go to the pictures.
6 Where are you going to, madam? I'm going to Ipoh.
7 Who is going to teach me?
8 When are you going to write to him?
9 Are you the one who is good at speaking Chinese?
10 Is it you who opened the door?

Exercise 28:
1 Ke mana encik-encik hendak pergi? Kami hendak pergi ke pasar.
2 Kita mesti belajar bahasa Melayu.
3 Kami mesti belajar bahasa Inggeris, tetapi encik mesti belajar bahasa Perancis.
4 Tolong bagi saya suratkhabar.
5 Kereta kami ada di sini; di mana kereta tuan?
6 Tolong saudara pergi ke pejabat guru besar pada pukul sembilan.
7 Sayalah yang hendak belajar bahasa Melayu.
8 Di mana basikal aku? Kurang periksa.
9 Alikah yang menghantar surat itu kepada Perdana Menteri?
10 Puan pandai bercakap Melayu.

Exercise 30:
1 Today I have seen the Prime Minister at the airport.
2 He has visited our college.
3 My father teaches geography in a secondary school.
4 I am learning the national language in that school.
5 When will the government build a Day Training College in our town?
6 That man is the principal of a Teacher Training College.
7 Is it you who wants to get into this school?
8 My son is very fond of teaching history.
9 We must learn the history of this Malaysia of ours.
10 Tomorrow the Minister for Education will visit the National University in Penang.

Exercise 31:
1 Di sekolah menengah kita boleh belajar ilmu sains, ilmu alam dan bahasa Inggeris.
2 Meréka mesti pergi dengan bas, sebab meréka tidak ada kereta.
3 Saya ingat ilmu hisab lebih susah daripada ilmu alam.
4 Ya, tetapi ilmu sains sama susah dengan ilmu hisab.
5 Tahun depan anak perempuan saya hendak masuk Maktab Perguruan Bahasa; ia mahu menjadi guru bahasa Melayu.
6 Kalau engkau mahu menjadi guru sekolah rendah, baik engkau masuk Maktab Perguruan Harian.
7 Saya nampak dia, tetapi dia tidak nampak saya.
8 Di lapangan terbang Perdana Menteri negeri Ruritania berkata beliau hendak melawat Universiti.
9 Kampung aku kecil; kampung engkau pun kecil juga.
10 Tolong bagi saya buku itu; saya pun hendak baca juga.

Exercise 33:
1 He has told me to open the door.
2 The Prime Minister is waiting for his car.
3 The students of that lecturer enjoy listening to his lectures.
4 Students must write their essays before Saturday.
5 Your box is very heavy; what is in it?
6 Can you teach me to speak Malay?
7 His lecture is not very interesting.
8 This college is very large; who will run it?
9 Where are your books? In the cupboard, sir.
10 Are you going to sell him your car?

Exercise 34:
1 Di mana kerétaku? Keréta kau sedang menantikan kau di luar pejabat pos.
2 Di mana bapa kau bekerja? Dia pensyarah kanan di Universiti.
3 Dia bersyarah darihal bahasa Melayu; syarahannya sangat menarik hati.
4 Abangku bersyarah darihal ilmu pendidikan di Maktab Perguruan Harian.
5 Sebelum encik mendengar syarahannya, mestilah encik membaca buku ini.
6 Abangnya guru di sebuah sekolah kebangsaan.
7 Di mana dia membeli kerétanya yang baharu? Dia membelinya di Singapura.
8 Meréka sedang membaca bukunya yang baharu.
9 Di mana maktabnya? Di Kuala Lumpur.
10 Bapaku bekerja di Ibu Pejabat Kerajaan.

Exercise 36:
1 berkuda: to be on horseback, to ride.
2 berjalan: to go, to proceed, to walk.
3 berkasut: to wear shoes, to have shoes on.
4 berpagar: to have a fence, to be fenced.
5 bertingkat tiga: to have three storeys.
6 berkain biru: to wear a blue sarong.

Exercise 37:
1 That girl is wearing a black dress and white shoes.

2 A man on horseback entered the village.
3 Where does he work? He has a shop in the market.
4 This building has ten storeys.
5 I very much enjoy learning the national language.
6 Yesterday I saw a Malay wearing a white songkok.
7 Last night we spent the night in Kuala Langat.
8 He is very fond of walking.
9 The Concorde is an aeroplane which has no propellers.
10 This table has three legs.

Exercise 38:

1 Ia bersongkok hijau.
2 Méja itu berkaki empat.
3 Meréka berkuda.
4 Kita akan bermalam di Singapura.
5 Kakak saya akan berbaju putih dan berkain biru.
6 Rumah saya bertingkat dua.
7 Budak itu tidak berkasut.
8 Kapal terbang ini berkipas enam.
9 Ahmad belajar bahasa Inggeris di sekolah.
10 Ia berjalan kaki dari Ipoh ke Kuala Kangsar.

Exercise 39:

1 The Prime Minister will speak to the reporters at nine o'clock.
2 Who is that journalist in the black hat?
3 He arrived in a two-engined aircraft.
3 Tomorrow morning we are going to sunbathe on the beach.
5 Ahmad must put my clothes out in the sun.
6 He is going to go to the airport to welcome the Prime Minister.
7 Their cars went slowly.
8 Last night at the airport I saw a reporter with a long beard.
9 If he hasn't any money, the barber will not shave him.
10 In Kuala Lumpur there is a fourteen-storey building.

Exercise 40:

1 Saya selalu bercukur pagi.
2 Bapa saya sakit; dia mahu saya mencukurnya (or *mencukurkannya* if the implication is that the shaving is done as a favour). Cf. Gram. (148).
3 Saya berjemur di pantai.
4 Ahmad sudah menjemur hamparan.
5 Pemberita itu berkata bahawa kapal terbang Perdana Menteri akan tiba pada pukul lima.
6 Malam semalam saya telah melihat wayang gambar yang bernama "Orang yang Berbaju Putih".
7 Saya bekerja dalam sebuah bangunan yang bertingkat tujuh di Kuala Lumpur.
8 Siapa gadis cantik yang berbaju hijau itu?
9 Pegawai-pegawai berpedang; tetapi askar-askar bersenapang.
10 Siapa orang Melayu tua yang berkeris panjang itu?

Exercise 42:

1 Where does he work? He plants rice in Kedah.
2 When do the Malays plant their rice?

299

3 They plant their rice in the rainy season.
4 I am going to sell my car to his elder brother.
5 I am going to sell cars in Ipoh.
6 If you do not work, how are you going to pass the examination?
7 This morning he got up late (and) did not have time to shave.
8 The barber shaved him.
9 Who is the officer with the sword? He is my younger brother.
10 The Vickers Viscount is a four-engined aircraft.

Exercise 43:

1 Kami hendak berpindah ke Ipoh.
2 Burung itu hinggap di pagar.
3 Ia sangat berada.
4 Bapa saya berjual kuda.
5 Encik bercukurkah pagi tadi? Tidak; tukang cukur akan mencukur saya.
6 Encik melihatkah kapal terbang berkipas empat yang telah tiba di lapangan terbang pada pukul enam pagi tadi?
7 Ya, ada. Kapal terbang Perdana Menteri. Saya pergi ke lapangan terbang menyambut beliau.
8 Perdana Menteri berkata kepada pemberita-pemberita bahawa beliau akan bercakap dengan meréka ésok.
9 Saya sangat suka berjemur.
10 Tolong jemurkan pakaian saya. Cf. Gram. (148).

Exercise 44:

1 It does not look as if he will be elected.
2 An exhibition of pictures is being held now in Kuala Lumpur.
3 Who is that man in the songkok? He was not invited.
4 Mr So-and-So looks as if he will be elected by the people.
5 Apparently Mr So-and-So is an independent candidate.
6 Our college will be run by the government in future.
7 It seems that a general election will be held next year.
8 Ahmad was shaved by the barber.
9 The Prime Minister was welcomed by the Minister for Education.
10 All the carpets are being aired.

Exercise 45:

1 Calon ini sudah dipilih.
2 Suatu pilihanraya akan diadakan di seluruh Malaysia.
3 Encik Anu tidak akan dipilih; orang tidak percayakan dia.
4 Buku ini akan dibaca di seluruh negeri.
5 Keréta ini tidak boleh dijual sebelum ésok.
6 Surat ini mesti dihantar kepadanya hari ini juga.
7 Ia telah dipilihnya.
8 Surat ini telah ditulisnya.
9 Pintu ini telah dibuka oleh Yusuf.
10 Bilik saya sedang dicuci.

Exercise 47:

1 Where is my book? I have put it away in the big cupboard.
2 That candidate is a bad man. We shall not elect him.
3 The Prime Minister I have seen; the Minister for Education I have not (yet) seen.

4 This big car — where did you buy it?
5 I bought it in Singapore.
6 Such a long book I cannot read.
7 I have invited Ahmad; Hamid I have not yet invited.
8 Have you bought any rambutans? Yes, I have; I bought some this morning.
9 When are you going to write the letter? I *have* written it; here it is.
10 Have you visited the exhibition of pictures in the Tunku Abdul Rahman Hall? Yes, I visited it yesterday.

Exercise 48:
1 Keréta ini sudah kujual kepada bapa Ahmad.
2 Buku ini sudah kaubaca; buku itu belum kaubaca.
3 Pertunjukan itu telah digambar oléh Encik Polan.
4 Seorang calon bébas tidak akan saya undi.
5 Bila emak hendak membeli beras? Sudah emak beli (*or:* sudah kubeli).
6 Bila emak beli? Emak beli pagi tadi.
7 Agaknya, ia tidak akan dipilih.
8 Siapa yang menulis surat ini? Sayalah yang menulisnya, tuan.
9 Siapa yang melawat pertunjukan? Perdana Menteri yang melawatnya.
10 Minggu depan suatu pertunjukan akan diadakan oléh kerajaan di Dewan Tunku Abdul Rahman di Kuala Lumpur.

Exercise 50:
1 He peeled the rambutan and ate it.
2 He read the letter and put it into the file.
3 Ahmad wrote a letter and sent it to Hamid.
4 She washed her blouse and put it away in the cupboard.
5 He took his shirt and put it on.
6 I read the letter and showed it to Ahmad.
7 I welcomed Encik Hamid at the airport and took him to my house.
8 He met Ali and took him to his house.
9 He saw a new book and bought it.
10 They made coffee and gave it to their friends.

Exercise 51:
1 Nampaknya satu pilihanraya akan diadakan tahun depan.
2 Encik Polan akan menjadi Menteri Pelajaran, agaknya.
3 Tiap-tiap hari tiga buah keréta dijualnya.
4 Ia telah dijemput bersyarah kepada penuntut-penuntut maktab kita.
5 Dollah menggulung hamparan lalu diangkatnya.
6 Ia melukis gambar lalu ditunjukkannya kepada saya.
7 Lepas itu saya melukis gambar lalu menunjukkannya kepada dia.
8 Ia mencari bajunya lalu dipakainya.
9 Hamid yang menulis surat itu kepada Menteri Pelajaran.
10 Ayah Encik Ali yang berjual keréta di Singapura.

Exercise 53:
1 Suddenly I heard the voice of someone singing.

2 He ran over a boy and injured him.
3 That wicked man ran down a policeman and killed him (*or:* murdered him; i.e. he ran him over on purpose).
4 Two ships have collided in Singapore.
5 His car ran off the road and fell into a ditch.
6 One destroyer was sunk by a submarine.
7 What a lot of food! We'll never get through it!
8 Let us not forget this native land of ours.
9 Where's your book, Yusuf? I forgot to bring it, sir.
10 Suddenly I saw Ahmad working in his rice-field.

Exercise 54:
1 Ia tersenyum kepada saya.
2 Terkejutlah saya mendegar suaranya.
3 Saya tidak terjalan lagi (the *ter-* prefix is used in place of the *ber-* prefix to give the idea of impossibility).
4 Hati-hati! Awak nanti terjatuh tangga!
5 Ia dibunuh oléh sebuah keréta yang tersimpang lalu terjatuh ke dalam parit.
6 Dua buah keréta itu berlanggar lalu tersimpang.
7 Ahmad menémbak pegawai itu lalu melukakannya.
8 Surat ini tiada terbaca.
9 Buku ini tiada terbaca, tetapi mestilah saya baca sebelum peperiksaan.

10 Terkejutlah pegawai itu melihat tandatangan Perdana Menteri di bawah surat itu.

Exercise 56:
1 Encik Ali is writing a book in the national language.
2 The book which I bought yesterday was compiled by a very famous Malay author.
3 The officer who was carrying the drawn sword entered Yusuf's room and killed him.
4 He drew his sword and killed his enemy.
5 He killed his enemy with the sword which he had just drawn.
6 He was going to see a play in Kuala Lumpur, but he was too late.
7 He looked for hidden meaning in the letter, but he did not find any.
8 He laughed to see a book written by his son.
9 The "Story of Hang Tuah" is a very famous work in Malay literature.
10 The door is closed now; we cannot go in.

Exercise 57:
1 Pegawai kanan membawa pedang terhunus.
2 Tulisan dia hampir-hampir tiada terbaca.
3 Ia telah sampai terlambat.
4 Ia seorang wartawan yang termasyhur.
5 Pegawai itu memaksa dia menulis sepucuk surat.
6 Ia dipaksa oléh pegawai itu menulis sepucuk surat.
7 Saya terpaksa menémbak sebab dia hendak membunuh saya.

8 Bapa saya sudah membeli sebuah keréta yang terbesar.
9 Surat ini ditulis oléh seorang kawan saya; seorang kawan saya yang menulisnya.
10 Buku ini tertulis (*or:* **terkarang**) oléh guru saya yang lama.

Exercise 59:
1 While I was going to bed last night, I heard the voice of someone singing outside the window.
2 If we are going to learn the national language, we had better read books written by the most famous Malay authors.
3 Furthermore, we must listen to Malay plays on the radio.
4 While leaving the quayside in Singapore yesterday a very large steamship crashed into a Ruritanian destroyer and sank it.
5 The man who ran amok had a naked kris.
6 He took his kris and drew it in order to kill the policeman who was waiting for him outside the house.
7 But the policeman saw him coming and killed him with his rifle.
8 He cut a piece of bread and ate it with butter.
9 This book is too long; I can't read any more of it.
10 Ahmad took a piece of paper and wrote a letter to his father.

Exercise 60:
1 Jalan ini terlalu sempit.
2 Keréta dia terlanggar sebuah bas.
3 Terlihatlah ia bapanya keluar dari rumah.
4 Ada makna tersembunyi dalam perkataan-perkataan ini.
5 Kapal selam itu mengaramkan dua buah kapal musuh, tetapi akhirnya dilanggar sendiri oléh sebuah kapal pembinasa lalu di karamkan.
6 Ahmad bersembunyi di luar tingkap dan melihat Yusuf menyembunyikan wangnya dalam sebuah almari.
7 Ali tidak boléh mendapati makna tersembunyi dalam ayat itu.
8 Siapa membuka pintu ini? Kurang periksa; saya dapati terbuka bila saya sampai tadi.
9 Saya berharap bukan Hamid yang membukanya, kerana saya menyuruh dia semalam jangan buka pintu sebelum saya datang.
10 Nampaknya bukan Hamid. Hari ini dia tak ada, sebab isterinya sakit teruk. Dia dilanggar keréta malam semalam dan Hamid sudah bermalam di hospital.

Exercise 62;
1 If by any chance he is not at home, we shall have to look for him in town.
2 Although the destroyer rammed the submarine, she did not sink it.
3 If our suggestion is rejected by the government, we shall have to hold a special meeting.
4 If you get the opportunity, please support my proposal.
5 Even if he studied for ten years, he would certainly not speak the national language like a Malay.

6 It is clear that we ought to speak Malay every day with Malay friends.
7 Although he arrived at nine o'clock, the train had gone.
8 If father buys a new car, we'll be able to go to Singapore next month to visit Encik Ali.
9 Although the government's proposal was opposed by the opposition, it was passed by the House.
10 Although the matter was discussed for three and a half hours by the House of Representatives, I didn't understand a single word.

Exercise 63:

1 Walaupun encik membeli buku itu, tidak akan encik baca.
2 Sungguhpun cadangan itu telah dibangkang oleh pihak pembangkang, tetapi diluluskan oleh mesyuarat.
3 Walaupun tuan menyokong cadangan itu, tetapi akan ditolak.
4 Teranglah bahawa kita patut menyokong cadangan ini.
5 Sekiranya tuan pengerusi tidak hadir, mesyuarat akan diadakan oleh setiausaha.
6 Tuan pengerusi berkata kepada pemberita-pemberita bahawa satu mesyuarat khas akan diadakan minggu depan.
7 Ia berharap bahawa cadangan-cadangan kerajaan akan disokong oléh rakyat, walaupun ditolak oléh pihak pembangkang.
8 Meskipun perkara ini telah dirundingkan oléh Déwan Rakyat, tetapi belum dinyatakan kepada rakyat.
9 Jikalau sekiranya ia tiada di rumah, berilah surat ini kepada isterinya.
10 Teranglah bahawa tuan mestilah mendaftarkan nama anak di Pejabat Pelajaran, kalau dia hendak masuk sebuah sekolah menengah tahun depan.

Exercise 65:

1 After the submarine had been sunk, the destroyer finished its patrol and returned to its base.
2 With reference to your letter which I received yesterday, I shall reply after discussing it with the director.
3 After the minutes had been read by the secretary, the meeting discussed the proposals which were put forward by the opposition.
4 This work must be completed before 1982.
5 Formerly the doors of the office were always closed before half past four, but after Encik Ahmad became director the doors were not closed before five o'clock.
6 We should express our great gratitute to the secretary for the minutes which he has just read.
7 After reading the minutes of the special meeting, the secretary invited Encik Jamaluddin to explain the matters which ought to be discussed that day.
8 The general meeting will not be concluded before 10 p.m.
9 If by any chance the general meeting is not concluded before 12 midnight, how are we to get home?

10 Although the matter had been discussed in London, the opposition in this country did not agree with the government's action.

10 Tiba-tiba pegawai itu ternampak askar-askar musuh yang bersembunyi di sawah, tetapi terlambatlah ia lalu terbunuh kena sebiji bom tangan yang terjatuh di depannya.

Exercise 66:
1 Kami akan berunding tentang cadangan tuan ésok.
2 Kami akan merundingkan cadangan tuan ésok.
3 Sebelum mesyuarat ditamatkan, ia mengucapkan terima kasih kepada tuan pengerusi.
4 Dalam ucapannya ia berkata bahawa satu mesyuarat agung patut diadakan.
5 Sungguhpun pengerusi menamatkan mesyuarat pada pukul sepuluh malam, tetapi kita tidak keluar dari Déwan sebelum pukul sebelas setengah.
6 Dalam ucapannya kepada Déwan Rakyat, Menteri Pelajaran berkata bahawa lima puluh buah sekolah baharu akan dibuka sebelum akhir tahun 1980.
7 Pihak pembangkang berkata bahawa meréka hendak menyokong tindakan kerajaan dalam perkara ini.
8 Sebelum keluar ia menutup bukunya lalu disimpannya dalam almari, lepas itu ia mencari kunci keréta lalu didapatinya dalam bilik isterinya.
9 Sebelum menamatkan rondaan kapal selam itu mengaramkan sebuah kapal besar musuh yang membawa askar-askar ke negeri Ruritania.

Exercise 68:
1 In order that his amendment might be accepted by the special meeting, he discussed the matter with the chairman.
2 Because of the death of the Sultan all government offices will be closed on Wednesday.
3 After his car had crashed into the "keep left" sign, a policeman wrote his name in his book and reported it at the police station.
4 Provided that he can speak the national language, it will be easy for him to get work in a national school.
5 He said to his teacher, "If only I could speak Malay like a Malay!"
6 In order that his child could get into a secondary school, he went to the State Education Office in order to register his name.
7 After his child's name had been registered, the education officer asked what shcool his child wanted to enter.
8 After he had waited for two hours outside the office, he received his salary from the financial clerk.
9 If you can't buy the book which we were discussing just now, try and get it at Hong Tai's shop.
10 Although his car ran off the road and fell into the ditch at the side of the road, no one was hurt!

Exercise 69:

1 Jikalau sekiranya awak tidak boléh membeli buku itu hari ini, belilah ésok sebelum awak datang ke sekolah.
2 Sekiranya keréta kita terlanggar keréta orang lain, kita mesti melaporkan perkara itu di balai polis yang dekat sekali.
3 Selepas terjatuh tangga, saya berasa pening; jadi, isteri saya memanggil doktor.
4 Sebelum menamatkan syarahannya, pensyarah itu menyuruh penuntut-penuntut membeli sebuah buku yang baharu.
5 Oléh kerana pindaan yang kedua dikemukakan terlambat, tuan pengerusi berkata bahawa tidak boléh dirundingkan sebelum mesyuarat yang akan datang.
6 Dalam ucapannya Perdana Menteri berkata bahawa teranglah pindaan pihak pembangkang itu patut ditolak.
7 Sehingga pensyarah kanan kembali dari negeri Inggeris, pengetua maktablah yang akan bersyarah kepada penuntut-penuntut tentang kesusasteraan Melayu.
8 Pegawai daérah akan mengadakan satu mesyuarat hari ini untuk menyatakan berkenaan pilihanraya kepada orang daérahnya.
9 Asalkan encik bercakap lambat, tiap-tiap perkataan saya faham.
10 Hari ini di Déwan Rakyat Perdana Menteri berkata bahawa beliau telah dijemput melawat negeri Ruritania.

Exercise 71:

1 supporter (from *sokong*).
2 murder (from *bunuh*).
3 examiner, inspector (from *periksa*).
4 pointer, indicator, sign-post (from *tunjuk*).
5 voter, elector (from *pilih*).
6 barber, hairdresser, shaver (from *cukur*).
7 listener (from *dengar*).
8 reader (from *baca*).
9 writer (from *tulis*).
10 follower (from *ikut*).

Exercise 72:

1 pelawat (from *lawat*).
2 penjual (from *jual*).
3 pelukis (from *lukis*).
4 penanam (from *tanam*).
5 pemerhati (from *perhati*).
6 penolong (from *tolong*) or pembantu (from *bantu*).
7 pembeli (from *beli*).
8 penggali (from *gali*).
9 pemukul (from *pukul*).
10 pengajar (from *ajar*).

Exercise 73:

1 I am not very fond of (eating) fruit.
2 Where is the bottle opener?
3 If I haven't got a broom, how am I going to sweep the floor?
4 He went to the fruit market to buy durians.
5 The thief dug a big hole with a spade and buried the money which he had stolen.
6 Near the post office there is a fruit seller.
7 This door-handle is broken. Who broke it?

8 Tomorrow the chief examiner will hold a meeting of all assistant examiners.
9 Malay is the most useful language in the Malay Archipelago.
10 This author is very famous; he has many readers.

Exercise 74:
1 Gali-galian Malaysia termasyhur di seluruh dunia.
2 Di antara buah-buahan Malaysia buah durian yang sedap sekali.
3 Ramailah pengikut-pengikut Perdana Menteri di seluruh Persekutuan Malaysia.
4 Ia telah tiba di Malaysia supaya menjadi penanam getah. Sekarang ia bertanam getah di negeri Kedah dekat Sungai Patani.
5 Setelah menyapu lantai pejabat, Ali mengambil penyapu lalu disimpannya dalam almari di bawah tangga.
6 Calon pembangkang tidak dipilih oléh sebab ia tidak dipercayai oléh pemilih-pemilih.
7 Pembunuh itu ditangkap oleh polis lalu digantung di Penjara Pudu.
8 Pencuri itu mencuri wang itu lalu ditanamkannya dalam lubang di belakang rumahnya.
9 Ia menggali lubang dengan penggali lalu menanamkan wang itu di dalamnya.
10 Setelah pencuri itu ditangkap, polis pun cari wang itu lalu didapatinya di dalam lubang di kebun.

Exercise 76:
1 illustration (from *gambar*).
2 invitation (from *jemput*).
3 view, opinion (from *pandang*).
4 support (from *sokong*).
5 summons, call (from *panggil*).
6 merchandise for sale (from *jual*).
7 number (from *bilang*).
8 help, aid, assistance (from *tolong*).
9 drawing (from *lukis*).
10 reading (from *baca*).

Exercise 77:
1 tarian kebangsaan
2 suruhan
3 penyuruh
4 dalam pasaran dunia
5 berita harian
6 potongan pakaiannya
7 buku bacaan
8 perbincangan
9 kenalan lama
10 ingatan

Exercise 78:
1 We have no money to buy newspapers.
2 In which harbour will our ship drop anchor?
3 This magazine is a monthly.
4 When will the annual general meeting be held?
5 Malaysian minerals are famous in the world market.
6 The money for buying books has not yet been received from the government.
7 We ought to thank you for your invitation.
8 His pupils use two books: a reading book and a writing book.
9 Their teacher is a trainee teacher. He is inspected monthly by a visiting teacher.
10 Malaysian national dances are interesting.

Exercise 79:

1 Ini dia bilangan yang pertama sebuah majalah mingguan baharu yang bernama "Berita Mingguan".
2 Satu pertunjukan lukisan-lukisan ayah saya akan diadakan bulan depan di Dewan Tunku Abdul Rahman.
3 Ia membeli minuman sejuk lalu diminumnya sebelum keretapi bertolak.
4 Sesudah tuan menulis latihan ini, patutlah tuan menulis latihan delapan puluh.
5 Ia duduk di bilik bacaan lalu membaca buku tawarikh yang didapatnya dalam kutubkhanah maktab.
6 Patutlah saya mengucapkan terima kasih di atas sokongan tuan berkenaan dengan cadangan kami.
7 Encik Ibrahim telah disuruh oleh tuan pengerusi mengatur mesyuarat khas pada akhir bulan ini untuk merundingkan pindaan-pindaan yang dikemukakan oleh pihak pembangkang.
8 Setelah dua buah kapal itu berlanggar di luar labuhan mereka berlabuh lalu menunggu sehingga boleh diperiksa oleh pemeriksa kerajaan.
9 Keretapi itu bertolak tiap-tiap hari pada pukul sembilan.
10 Pembunuh itu membunuh mangsanya dengan pisau pembuka surat.

Exercise 81:

1 murder (*bunuh:* to kill).
2 enlightenment, illumination (*terang:* clear, bright).
3 income (*dapat:* to get).
4 conversation (*bercakap:* to speak).
5 theft (*curi:* to steal).
6 unity, union (*satu:* one).
7 registration (*daftar:* list).
8 hearing (*dengar:* to hear).
9 enmity, hostility (*musuh:* enemy).
10 transition (*menyeberang/seberang:* to cross over).

Exercise 82:

1 perbuatan (*buat:* to do).
2 perkembangan (*berkembang:* to blossom forth).
3 persembunyian (*bersembunyi:* to hide).
4 perjalanan (*berjalan:* to go).
5 perkapalan (*kapal:* ship).
6 persimpangan (*tersimpang:* to go off of a tangent).
7 perosakan (*rosak:* destroyed).
8 perhentian (*berhenti:* to stop).
9 pertanyaan (*bertanya:* to ask).
10 perhatian (*hati:* mind).

Exercise 83:

1 pengembalian (*kembali:* to return).
2 pemandangan (*pandang:* to look at).
3 pembangunan (*bangunkan:* to build).
4 penggantian (*ganti:* substitute).
5 pemindahan (*berpindah:* to move, to be transferred).
6 pembesaran (*besar:* large).
7 penerbangan (*terbang:* to fly).
8 penjadian (*jadi:* to become).
9 penyimpanan (*simpan:* to put away).
10 pembukaan (*buka:* to open).

Exercise 84:
1. In the opinion of my advisers, your proposal must be rejected.
2. I am not very fond of drinking cold drinks.
3. This broom has no handle.
4. The thief was caught by the police.
5. The registration of school children will be commenced next week.
6. Last night I talked to the Prime Minister; our conversation was very interesting.
7. The national language is a language of unity.
8. After the opening of the new building, the Prime Minister went back to his office.
9. Ahmad is waiting for his father at the bus stop.
10. He showed the enlargement of the picture to his wife.

Exercice 85:
1. Pendapatannya lima ratus ringgit sebulan.
2. Ia suka membeli permainan-permainan untuk anak-anaknya.
3. Pembangunan Bangunan Dewan Rakyat yang baharu telah dimulakan bulan lepas.
4. Selepas pelajaran ditamatkan, kanak-kanak pun keluarlah lalu mulai main sepak raga.
5. Pada fikiran saya, lukisan-lukisan dan gambar-gambar Cik Polan tidak berapa menarik hati.
6. Dalam surat ini ada dua perkataan yang tidak saya faham.
7. Dengan tolongan encik saya hendak memaksanya merundingkan perkara ini.
8. Perkembangan bahasa Melayu sebagai bahasa kebangsaan Persekutuan Malaysia sangat menarik hati rakyat negeri ini.
9. Saya menghantar surat ini untuk perhatian encik.
10. Suatu pertunjukan buku-buku sekolah akan dibuka esok oleh Menteri Pelajaran.

Exercise 86:
1. to finish (*habis:* finished).
2. to shorten, to abbreviate (*pendek:* short).
3. to clarify, to explain (*terang:* clear).
4. to calculate (*hisab:* calculation).
5. to free, to liberate, to release (*bebas:* free, independent).
6. to correct (*betul:* right, correct).
7. to strengthen, to reinforce (*kuat:* strong).
8. to sweeten (*manis:* sweet).
9. to unite, to unify (*satu:* one).
10. to allow, to permit (*benar:* true).

Exercise 87:
1. menguburkan (to bury, to entomb, to inter).
2. meneruskan (to go through with, to keep on with).
3. menyebabkan (to cause).
4. menyaksikan (to witness).
5. menetapkan (to fix).
6. menghangatkan (to heat).
7. mengutamakan (to put first, to pay special attention to).
8. menyediakan (to prepare).
9. menyelesaikan (to finish off, to attend to).
10. memecahkan (to break, to smash).

Exercise 88:
1. I have been invited to witness the opening of the new building.
2. Pay special attention to the national language! (*or:* put the national language first!)
3. We must keep on learning our national language.
4. The murdered man will be buried tomorrow morning.
5. Your essay must be shortened; I cannot read such a long essay.
6. The man who was arrested by the police last night will be released on Friday.
7. After his speech was finished, the Prime Minister sat down.
8. The students of this college are not allowed to go out after ten o'clock at night.
9. All lights must be put out at 11 p.m.
10. Before telling the story of Sang Kancil, out teacher explained the new words.

Exercise 89:
1. Gambar ini mesti dibesarkan.
2. Jalan kami hendak dilébarkan.
3. Surat encik telah dimasukkan ke dalam fail baharu.
4. Pelita sudah padam; siapakah yang memadamkannya?
5. Pembunuhan orang tua itu telah disaksikan oléh dua orang mata-mata.
6. Saya tak sempat membetulkan karanganmu sekarang ini juga.
7. Sebelum ia boleh digantung, pembunuh itu membunuh dirinya.
8. Makanan ini mesti dihangatkan sebelum dimakan.
9. Bahasa kebangsaan akan menyatukan semua orang Malaysia.
10. Perdana Menteri berkata bahawa beliau hendak menerangkan perkara ini sendiri.

Exercise 91:
1. His new book has not yet been issued.
2. At sunset the flag was lowered by a policeman.
3. He was invited to read the minutes to the committee members.
4. This unhappiness has been caused by the actions of the government.
5. Please lend me a hundred dollars.
6. The government ought to raise the price of rubber.
7. Last night I heard a Chinese reading a short story in Malay.
8. Make him a cup of tea and tell him to go to bed.
9. In this letter there are two words which I do not understand; please explain them to me.
10. This magazine is issued every Saturday.

Exercise 92:
1. Tolong tutupkan pintu.
2. Penuntut ini akan dikeluarkan.
3. Ia akan memberikan encik sebuah buku baharu.
4. Ia akan menamakan anaknya Rahmah.
5. Jangan naikkan bendéra sebelum matahari terbit.
6. Suruh Ahmad turunkan barang-barang saya sebelum pukul sepuluh.
7. Sebelum ayah saya pergi ke Singapura, ia memberikan saya sepatah nasihat.

8 Ia mengambil sehelai kertas lalu menulis surat kepada pengerusi jawatankuasa.
9 Kopi ini sudah sejuk; tolong hangatkan.
10 Ayah saya tidak membenarkan saya memberi seratus ringgit kepada Yusuf (or: memberikan Yusuf seratus ringgit).

Exercise 94:
1 When his aircraft began to descend, he was afraid.
2 The show will begin at 9.30 p.m.
3 Having gone up on to the stage he began his speech with the words "ladies and gentlemen".
4 We shall go to the Cathay Cinema to see the new Malay film.
5 He approached the theatre and stood outside until his friends came.
6 Ahmad brought down the big crate and put it away in the headmaster's room.
7 Last night my house was entered by a thief.
8 This table must be repaired by the carpenter.
9 Our government will be represented by Tuan Haji Ahmad.
10 Slowly the submarine neared the small island.

Exercise 95:
1 Rumah itu dimasuki oléh empat orang pegawai yang membawa pedang terhunus.
2 Butir-butir mesyuarat yang lepas belum dibacakan lagi.
3 Keréta saya sudah rosak; hendaklah dibaiki.

4 Ia mendekati sungai lalu terjun ke dalam air.
5 Jabatan Kerja Raya sudah mulai membangunkan sebuah bangunan baharu yang bertingkat lima di belakang Ibu Pejabat.
6 Ia naiki pentas lalu memulakan ucapannya.
7 Perlahan-lahan askar-askar musuh itu mendekati sungai.
8 Hendaklah kita membaikkan bangunan ini sebelum tahun depan.
9 Ia duduk di tebing sungai dan memandang kanak-kanak bermain di dalam air.
10 Tukang kayu mulai membaiki kerusi rosak itu dengan kayu yang dibeli Ahmad di pasar.

Exercise 97:
1 My greatest wish is to learn Malay.
2 My father will become the head of the department.
3 We are going to read the first story in this book.
4 All five of them are police officers.
5 In connexion with the new building there are two things which we must discuss: firstly, where shall we build it; secondly, where shall we get the money for it?
6 He bought those four books yesterday.
7 All four of them are written in the Jawi script.
8 All seven of them are Chinese who have just arrived in this country.
9 Our head of department will inspect the office at three o'clock.
10 Those three Japanese speak Malay well.

Exercise 98:
1. Keempat adik-beradik sedang bersekolah di Kuala Lumpur, tetapi tahun depan keempat-empatnya akan masuk universiti.
2. Kehendaknya ialah membangunkan sebuah bangunan baharu dekat pejabat pos.
3. Rumah besar ini ialah rumah yang kelima yang dibangunkannya di jalan ini.
4. Setelah keluar dari panggung, ketiga adik-beradik masuk ke dalam sebuah kedai kopi.
5. Ronggeng ialah satu tarian Melayu yang boléh kita lihat di seluruh Malaysia.
6. Bahasa Melayu ialah bahasa yang berguna sekali di seluruh Asia Tenggara.
7. Bahasa Malaysia ialah bahasa rasmi Malaysia dan berguna benar.
8. Ramaswami dan Krishnan ialah dua orang India; kedua-duanya bekerja di Pejabat Daérah.
9. Kelima orang penuntut ini tidak lulus di dalam peperiksaan.
10. Ayah saya baharu menjadi ketua kampung kita.

Exercise 100:
1. truth
2. ease, comfort
3. distance
4. goodness
5. laziness
6. unity
7. bitterness
8. beauty, prettiness
9. permission
10. cleverness, skill

Exercise 101:
1. kepeningan (*pening:* dizzy).
2. kesempitan (*sempit:* narrow).
3. keterangan (*terang:* clear).
4. kekuatan (*kuat:* strong).
5. kedalaman (*dalam:* deep, profound).
6. kerosakan (*rosak:* damaged).
7. kesalahan (*salah:* guilty).
8. ketentuan (*tentu:* certain).
9. keberatan (*berat:* heavy).
10. kemanisan (*manis:* sweet).

Exercise 102:
1. The progress of Malaysia and Singapore is of great interest to people all over the world.
2. The majority of the students in this college learn the national language.
3. There are many people who fear death.
4. His biggest difficulty is writing letters in the national language.
5. This boy's laziness cannot be tolerated any longer.
6. Ahmad asked permission to go out after dinner.
7. Our teacher talked interminably; in the end I went to sleep.
8. We cannot decide this matter before the general meeting.
9. He pulled the string and snapped it.
10. Clarification of these matters is no longer required.

Exercise 103:
1. Pegawai ini sangat bodoh; kebodohannya tidak tertahan lagi.
2. Pengetahuannya tidak berapa dalam.
3. Kebanyakan orang Cina di pejabat saya sedang belajar bahasa kebangsaan.
4. Ayah saya telah dihormati oleh kerajaan.

5 Itulah perkataan yang tidak diketahuinya.
6 Selepas keputusan-keputusan dikeluarkan, ia pun berkata dengan suara yang terputus-putus bahawa anaknya tidak lulus dalam peperiksaan.
7 Perkara ini akan diputuskan oléh Perdana Menteri sendiri.
8 Tali ini sudah putus; siapa yang memutusinya.
9 Para penuntut tidak dibenarkan membawa makanan sendiri ke dalam bilik makan.
10 Hari ini kami akan merundingkan kemajuan dua orang penuntut yang tidak lulus dalam peperiksaan.

Exercise 105:
1 Suddenly they heard the sound of a gun in the jungle.
2 Please leave that door open! Don't shut it!
3 The results of his examination are not very good.
4 He has lost all his money.
5 He wants economic independence.
6 Respected listeners! Our lessons are finished for this week.
7 His house cannot be seen from here.
8 Because of the shortage of water here, all the inhabitants of our village will move to another place.
9 Both of them died of hunger.
10 Suddenly the train departed. I was left behind.

Exercise 106:
1 Setelah kemerdékaan diterima, Ketua Menteri menjadi Perdana Menteri yang pertama.
2 Perdana Menteri akan berunding dengan para menteri di Déwan Tunku Abdul Rahman di Kuala Lumpur.
3 Sidang pembaca yang dihormati sekalian! Saya berharap bahawa buku ini akan menolong kamu belajar bahasa kebangsaan kita.
4 Pada bulan Ogos kita akan merayakan ulang tahun kemerdekaan.
5 Kebanyakan kawanku sedang belajar bahasa kebangsaan.
6 Semalam pengetua maktab kita menyuruh kita menulis sebuah karangan darihal pertunjukan yang diadakan minggu lepas.
7 Ketiga-tiganya hendak pergi ke England untuk belajar bahasa Inggeris.
8 Kejadian-kejadian bulan lepas telah menakutkan kerajaan Ruritania. Sekarang keadaan di sana sangat merbahaya.
9 Jangan takut menulis surat-surat encik dalam bahasa kebangsaan.
10 Meréka akan merayakan ulang tahun yang kedua puluh lima perkahwinan meréka pada tahun yang akan datang.

Exercise 109:
1 Early in the morning my uncle arrived to visit us.
2 In that pot there is not a single flower.
3 All day long he sat in the garden looking and looking at the flowers.
4 He talked and talked for three hours without stopping.
5 His books have been put away in the big cupboard.

6 Every day he sits just weeping and weeping because of the death of his child.
7 A magazine which is issued every month is a monthly magazine.
8 He kept on asking whether I could help him; at last I said "I suppose I can."
9 I waited and waited for him all that day; but he didn't come after all.
10 On the main road could be seen many vehicles.

Exercise 110:
1 Ia bertanya-tanya sudahkah ayahnya datang.
2 Pagi tadi saya tak boléh membeli apa-apa di pasar kerana satu sén pun saya tak ada lagi.
3 Kedai-kedai di Kuala Lumpur sangat menarik hati.
4 Kawan-kawannya hendak pergi ke negeri Perancis untuk belajar bahasa Perancis.
5 Adakah siapa-siapa duduk di serambi?
6 Bunga-bunga di dalam kebunnya sangat cantik.
7 Ia bangun pagi-pagi lagi lalu pergi ke pejabat.
8 Ia bertanya-tanya boléhkah ia pergi menéngok wayang gambar.
9 Tiap-tiap pagi saya bangun pada pukul tujuh lalu minum secawan téh.
10 Orang jahat itu memukul-mukul anjing itu sampai mati.

Exercise 113:
1 Some people do not like eating hot curry.
2 Some of them plant padi outside the village.
3 The district officer's wife is very pretty.
4 Two trestles are not enough to support such a big table.
5 Twenty per cent of the people of my village plant padi.
6 Three-quarters of them are rubber-tappers.
7 You must write that letter with great care.
8 She sat near the village well talking to the *penghulu's* wife.
9 In the final examination he got sixty-three per cent.
10 All the inhabitants of my village are Muslims by religion.

Exercise 114:
1 Kedua-dua penoréh getah di kebun getah bapa saudara saya.
2 Dua pertiga penduduk-penduduk kampung kita ialah peladang.
3 Dua puluh lima peratus orang ini tidak mengundi dalam pilihanraya yang lepas.
4 Orang-orang perempuan suka berdiri dekat telaga berbual-bual.
5 Anak-anak baru anak saya mahal-mahal.
6 Ia tidak lulus dalam peperiksaan: mendapat tiga puluh satu peratus sahaja.
7 Ia menunggu sejam setengah, tetapi kawannya tidak datang juga.
8 Ia tinggal empat tahun setengah di negeri China supaya belajar bahasa Cina.
9 Waktu sekarang pukul empat tiga suku petang.
10 Kerétapi akan bertolak pada pukul sebelas suku pagi.

Exercise 117:
1. He carried two buckets of latex back to the factory.
2. You must fill this bucket with the latex which was flowed into the cups.
3. On Fridays there are crowds of Malays praying in mosques.
4. Many, indeed, are the Indians who work as rubber-tappers on Malayan rubber-estates.
5. My grandfather, God have mercy upon him, passed away in 1948.
6. Before he went to his Maker he gave various advice to his wife.
7. His Majesty the first Paramount Ruler died in 1960.
8. When the meeting was over, Ahmad collected all the papers which had been left on the big table.
9. He hung a small cup on the rubber-tree to collect the latex.
10. His father is still alive, but his mother is dead.

Exercise 118:
1. Hari Jumaat yang lepas Ahmad sembahyang di surau di kebun getah tempat ia bekerja sebagai penoréh getah.
2. Abang Ahmad memang bertanam padi.
3. Sungguhpun datuk saya masih hidup lagi, tetapi sakit teruk.
4. Ah Chong berumur dua puluh tahun; kakaknya pun berumur dua puluh tiga tahun.
5. Emak sedang menyediakan makanan tengah hari di dapur.
6. Banyaklah pókok-pokok getah di keliling rumah kami.
7. Masa kakak saya mendukung kanak-kanak itu, adik pun masak nasi.
8. Bimbit timba ini balik ke kilang.
9. Getah itu hendaklah dipungut pagi-pagi.
10. Orang yang mengasihi tanahairnya, patutlah meréka belajar bahasa kebangsaannya.

Exercise 121:

27, Hill Road,
Happy Village,
Negeri Sembilan.
15th July, 1961.

My very dear Yusuf,

I have only just received this morning the letter which you sent to me from Penang. For this reason I am late in replying. Please excuse me.

I was very pleased to read in your letter that you can come to visit us in Happy Village at the end of this month. Please write another letter letting us know what time and what day you will arrive here. I shall wait for you at the railway station.

Yours sincerely,
AHMAD.

Exercise 122:

1 Ahmad menjilat setém lalu dilekatkannya kepada sampul surat.
2 Hendaklah saya mengirim surat ini kepada bapa saya sebelum pukul lima.
3 Saudaraku Ahmad: Saya menulis surat ini untuk menjemput saudara makan pada 28hb Ogos (dua puluh lapan hari bulan Ogos).
4 Tolong saudara beritahu saya bolehkah saudara datang. Yang benar: Yusuf.
5 Tolong pergi ke pejabat pos beli setem.
6 Bila surat itu sampai, lekaslah Ahmad membukanya lalu dibacanya.
7 Surat yang dihantar oléh saudara kepada saya pada 16hb Ogos itu belum sampai lagi.
8 Di dalam suratnya ia memberitahu bapanya bahawa baharulah ia mulai belajar bahasa kebangsaan.
9 Ia telah menulis surat untuk memberitahu saya bahawa ayahnya baharu meninggal dunia.
10 Ahmad memenuhi kalamnya dengan dakwat lalu menulis surat kepada sahabatnya.

Exercise 125:

1 This door must be used by office staff only.
2 I have the honour to request you to pay your tax before the end of this month.
3 I forward herewith two books just received from France.
4 Ahmad signed the letter and put it into the envelope.
5 The letter which the director wrote yesterday we must send by airmail.
6 I regret to inform you that your proposal has been rejected by the committee because of a shortage of funds.
7 I am pleased to inform you that you have passed the final examination.
8 With reference to your letter dated 13th May I regret to inform you that the permission which you request cannot be granted at this time.
9 Do not post this letter before it has been signed by the chairman.
10 I return herewith the sum of fifty dollars.

Exercise 126:

1 Tuan: Dengan hormatnya dimaklumkan adalah surat tuan yang bertarikh 18hb Mei telah diterima.
2 Surat-surat patut diarahkan kepada Setiausaha Tetap.
3 Bungkusan ini terlalu besar: tidak boleh dikirimkan dengan pos udara.
4 Dengan dukacita dimaklumkan adalah cadangan tuan telah ditolak oléh Tuan Menteri.
5 Berkenaan dengan surat tuan yang bertarikh 15hb Séptémber, dengan sukacita dimaklumkan adalah wang sebanyak enam ratus ringgit akan dihantarkan balik kepada tuan sebelum akhir bulan ini.

6 Tuan pengarah membaca surat itu lalu ditandatangannya.

7 Berkenaan dengan surat tuan yang tiada bertarikh, dengan dukacita dimaklumkan adalah anak tuan tidak boleh masuk sekolah menengah sebelum berumur dua belas tahun.

8 Dengan hormatnya dimaklumkan adalah kursus rasmi bahasa kebangsaan akan mulai pada 25hb Ogos.

9 Saya akan menghantar semua surat saya dengan pos udara.

10 Semua bungkusan-bungkusan mesti dikirim dengan kapal laut; pos udara terlalu mahal.

Exercise 129:

1 Write your address on this paper and give it to the clerk who sits behind the grille.

2 Where is the nearest post office? Next door to the Ministry of Finance.

3 Because he did not pass his law examination, he did not become a magistrate.

4 Because his letter was not addressed to the Permanent Secretary, it was sent back to the writer.

5 Please go to the post office and buy a 15 cent stamp for this letter.

6 Letters must be written in the national language.

7 His father is an education officer; he works at the Ministry of Education.

8 This morning I received a letter from the Minister for the Interior.

9 There is not a cent left; how are we going to pay our income tax before next month?

10 Lotteries will be run by the Department of Social Welfare to get money for the poor.

Exercise 130:

1 Bangunan baharu ini akan dibuka minggu depan oléh Pengarah Kerja Raya.

2 Dalam mahkamah pengadil ia dihukum tiga bulan penjara.

3 Tuan: Dengan hormatnya tuan dipersilakan membayar cukai pendapatan tuan sebelum akhir bulan ini.

4 Jabatan Perbendaharaan telah menolak permintaan kita untuk wang membangunkan sebuah bangunan bertingkat sepuluh yang baharu.

5 Ia menandatangani surat itu lalu dikirimnya kepada abangnya di pejabat pos yang dekat sekali.

6 Ia membeli sekeping setém sepuluh sén lalu dilekatkannya pada sampul surat.

7 Ia berharap mendapat kerja sebagai kerani di Kementerian Buruh.

8 Sesudah membaca surat itu ia pun menulis surat balasannya.

9 Di dalam perékonomian Malaysia perkara yang penting sekali ialah pembangunan luarbandar.

10 Menanam getah ialah satu daripada perusahaan-perusahaan Malaysia yang penting sekali.

Exercise 133:

1 dibelinya	2 kulihat
3 menulis	4 datang
5 diceritakannya	

Exercise 134:
1. The building in which his father works is a new one.
2. The building from the roof of which he jumped is an eleven-storey one.
3. The man with whom I was talking was his father.
4. It was the poor people to whom I gave the money.
5. The sound which I heard was the sound of her voice.
6. The man who wants to buy my car will come again at half past seven.
7. The shop in which you can buy that book is not open today.
8. The chair on which he was sitting just now is broken.
9. The person whom he invited was an old friend.
10. The book which I read yesterday was not very interesting.

Exercise 135:
1. Buku yang encik berikan saya semalam itu tidak berguna.
2. Rumah tempat dia duduk rumah besar.
3. Orang yang saya bercakap dengannya ialah seorang India.
4. Masa saya duduk di England, selalu saya bercakap bahasa Inggeris.
5. Di mana kedai tempat awak membeli buku ini?
6. Di mana awak mengirim surat yang kutulis semalam?
7. Orang yang saya membeli kereta ini daripadanya sudah pergi ke negeri Jepun.
8. Kertas yang saya menulis alamat tuan di atasnya sudah hilang.
9. Ini dia fail yang saya memasukkan surat tuan ke dalamnya.
10. Ini dia sekolah tempat saya belajar bahasa Melayu.

Exercise 138:
1. When he was representing the government in Egypt, he started learning Arabic.
2. When he goes to Japan next year, he will learn Japanese.
3. When I went into her room, she was sitting there weeping and weeping.
4. When I stay in that hotel, I always eat Chinese food.
5. He looked at me as if I were drunk.
6. When the train arrived at Kuala Lumpur Station, my father was waiting for me on the platform.
7. Since their father died, they have been poor.
8. All the time he was in France, he studied French at the Sorbonne.
9. When he got back from the market, there wasn't a cent left.
10. When are you going to sell that car?

Exercise 139:
1. Masa saya menulis surat, bapa saya pun masuklah.
2. Ia bercakap bahasa Melayu seumpama sudah lama ia belajar.
3. Kita hendak bercakap bahasa Melayu selama kita di Malaysia.
4. Siaran ini telah dirakamkan dalam studio-studio Radio Malaysia di Kuala Lumpur.
5. Waktu surat itu sampai, Ahmad membukanya lalu dibacakannya kepada isterinya.

6 Tiap-tiap tahun apabila saya melawat ibu bapa, selalulah saya membawa hadiah bagi meréka.
7 Bila awak hendak mulai belajar bahasa Melayu?
8 Bila dia sampai, beritahu dia sudah saya pergi ke pasar.
9 Tatkala saya duduk di London, selalu saya makan makanan Inggeris.
10 Asalkan awak bekerja kuat, tentulah awak akan lulus dalam peperiksaan.

Exercise 142:

1 All the time he was in Kuala Lumpur he studied Malay.
2 If you cannot speak Malay you will have to make use of an interpreter during your stay in Malaysia.
3 This national language of ours will unite the people.
4 That man is not trusted by the people; he always treats the public as children.
5 Having studied French for five years, he became an interpreter in Paris.
6 After the letter had been typed by his typist, Ahmad signed it and sent it off airmail.
7 Fatimah typed the letter and took it to the director.
8 People who are of the Islamic faith should not make a god of money.
9 Let us not treat the people as children.
10 A government spokesman said this morning that the new building would be opened by the Prime Minister next week.

Exercise 143:

1 Hendaklah kita mempergunakan makmal yang baharu.
2 Ia memperhentikan kerétanya di tepi jalan.
3 Bangunan ini hendaklah diperkuat; kalau tidak, hendak runtuh.
4 Orang ini tidak akan dipilih kerana ia memperbudakkan rakyat.
5 Bapa saya jurubahasa di mahkamah pengadil di Ipoh.
6 Anak lelaki saya hendak menjadi jurutera, tetapi anak perempuan hendak menjadi jururawat.
7 Hendaklah kita merakamkan siaran ini dengan pita.
8 Ia hendak merakamkan ucapan Perdana Menteri itu, tetapi permintaannya itu tidak diperkenankan.
9 Saya tidak suka pergi ke rumah Encik Ahmad kerana selalulah ia memperkatakan keadaan perékonomian di Asia Tenggara.
10 Ia mendapat ubat itu daripada jururawat lalu diminumnya.

Exercise 146:

1 Before attacking that town we must equip our army with new weapons.
2 All that night he dreamed about a pretty girl.
3 He always sits on the verandah dreaming.
4 Suddenly my room was entered by five armed men.
5 Requests must be addressed in writing to the Permanent Secretary.

6 He saw the girl wearing a silk blouse.
7 I have not yet had time to write a reply to your letter which I received yesterday.
8 This book is based on the Story of Hang Tuah.
9 I am going to the art gallery to see the new pictures.
10 Please give him this letter.

Exercise 147:

1 Saya berharap bahawa saya akan menerima sepucuk surat daripada dia hari ini.
2 Saya berharapkan sepucuk surat daripada dia hari ini.
3 Ia bermimpi tiap-tiap malam.
4 Ia bermimpikan gadis cantik yang dilihatnya di pertunjukan itu.
5 Akan kedua guni beras itu tertinggallah di kedai.
6 Pegawai-pegawai tentera udara tidak bersenjatakan senapang.
7 Kursus bahasa kebangsaan akan dimulai pada hari Jumaat; kursus itu berdasarkan bahasa yang digunakan di dalam pejabat-pejabat kerajaan.
8 Saya hendak pergi ke lapangan terbang untuk bertanyakan kedatangan semua kapal terbang dari Singapura.
9 Pemberontak-pemberontak telah bersenjatakan batu-batu lalu menyerang pejabat pos.
10 Akan tanahair kita hendaklah kita pertahankan dengan tongkat-tongkat dan batu-batu kalau tidak boléh kita mendapat senapang-senapang.

Exercise 150:

1 Is that the letter you wrote last night (*or:* yesterday)?
2 What are you doing? (what did you do?) I am reading a book (I read a book).
3 Who was it who shut the door? It was Ahmad who shut it.
4 After their father had left for Singapore, they began to cry on one another's shoulders.
5 His books were scattered all over the floor of his room.
6 They greeted each other with smiles.
7 When are you going to Ipoh? It is tomorrow that I'm going.
8 Yesterday afternoon at four o'clock I was sitting in my room reading the newspaper.
9 It is *my* father who wants to buy a new car, not *his*.
10 Malays like to begin their sentences with the emphasised words.

Exercise 151:

1 Keputusan ini berdasarkan tujuan kerajaan.
2 Pengganas-pengganas dan mata-mata bertémbak-témbakan selama dua jam.
3 Bapa encikkah yang mengirim surat ini?
4 Inikah surat yang dikirim oléh bapa encik?
5 Sudah dua puluh tahun mereka berkenalan.
6 Meréka sedang berkirim-kiriman.
7 Di luar tingkap biliknya ada cahaya yang berkelip-kelip.
8 Saya tulis surat, bukan baca buku.

9 Saya menulis surat, bukan menulis karangan.
10 Karanganlah saya tulis, bukan surat.

Exercise 154:
1 Where on earth is that book I bought just now?
2 Yesterday I ate in town; my wife ate at home.
3 Although he has been living in Malaysia for ten years, he still hasn't learnt (the song) "Negaraku" ("My Country").
4 Hang Jebat having been killed, Hang Tuah went home.
5 "The Malay Annals" is a very famous Malay book; also famous is the "Story of Abdullah".
6 I am going to write a book in Malay; my younger brother is going to write a book too.
7 Do you know that man? No, that man I don't know.
8 After 11 p.m. there wasn't a soul left in the hall.
9 Here is the book I bought this morning. Do you want to read it?
10 When you have read this book, you ought to read that book as well.

Exercise 155:
1 Itulah buku yang hendak kubaca.
2 Aku pun hendak baca juga (*or:* aku pun hendak membacanya juga).
3 Apatah lagi hendak dibuatnya?
4 Dia mahu membaca buku itu pula!
5 Sementara saya bercakap, Yusuf pun tidurlah.
6 Dua jam saya menantikan dia, dia tidak datang juga.
7 Bilatah dia hendak datang? Sudah dua jam setengah saya menunggu di sini!
8 Dia manatah Ahmad menyimpan kasut saya?
9 Bahasa Cina itu bahasa yang susah; bahasa Jepun pun susah juga.
10 Hari-harilah gunakan bahasa kebangsaan!

Exercise 158:
1 How deep is this river?
2 The colours of the national flag are red, white, blue, and yellow.
3 They opened their books and read them.
4 This is the book I am going to give him.
5 How small this boy is! How old is he?
6 After (*or:* when) the guests have arrived their cars must be parked behind the building.
7 That building is a hundred feet high.
8 My room has four windows.
9 What a big cupboard this is! What is inside it?
10 They welcomed the guests at the airport and put them up at the Merlin Hotel.

Exercise 159:
1 Kereta ini pintunya empat (*or:* kereta ini berpintu empat).
2 Maktab ini ada enam orang pensyarah kanan; jadi pelajarannya baik sungguh.
3 Jalan tempat kami tinggal lebarnya dua puluh lima kaki.
4 Bodohnya budak ini! Nama sendiri pun tak tahu tulis pula!

5 Perginya itu menghairankan semuanya.
6 Kalam ini harganya dua puluh tiga ringgit sebatang.
7 Berapa harganya daging lembu itu? Harganya tiga ringgit sekati. Mahalnya!
8 Bila kerétanya sudah sampai, lekas-la naik lalu pergi ke lapangan terbang.
9 Ia meletak kerétanya di belakang pejabat pos lalu masuk untuk membeli setém.
10 Ia mengambil fail baharu lalu dimasukkannya suratnya ke dalamnya.

Exercise 162:
1 He classified the book and put it away in the cupboard.
2 He smiled and (then) said, "What are you doing?"
3 He said with a smile, "Do come in, sir."
4 It is not I but my father who is going to be a district officer.
5 Who did this work? It wasn't me, but him.
6 He is not the Prime Minister, but the Minister for Education.
7 She sang and danced for two hours.
8 The teacher should point to a pen saying "this is a pen".
9 The teacher pointed to a pen and picked it up.
10 Suddenly Old Yusuf came.

Exercise 163:
1 Di manakah si Krishna itu?
2 Saya mahu menjeniskan buku-buku ini, tetapi saya tak tahu membaca tulisan Jawi. —Suruh si Ahmad jeniskannya.
3 Si pembaca dinasihatkan membaca buku yang pertama sebelum mencuba membaca yang kedua.
4 Siapakah si Janggut itu?
5 Mereka tinggal di kedai kopi sambil makan gulai dengan nasi.
6 Ia masuk kedai kopi lalu minta secawan kopi.
7 Selama tiga tahun ia mempelajari ilmu kimia di universiti lalu menjadi ahli kimia.
8 Pengurus pentas menyuruh pelakon-pelakon datang ke panggung pada pukul tiga, tetapi tiga orang belum tiba lagi.
9 Ia telah dibedah oléh seorang ahli bedah yang masyhur, akan tetapi dia mati juga.
10 Bukan Siti melainkan Aminah yang membuka pintu.

Exercise 166:
1 All committee members are requested to submit their suggestions before the end of this month.
2 A meeting of all geologists and ethnologists will be held at the beginning of next month in the great hall of the university.
3 Where on earth is that gardener? He hasn't done a stroke of work in my garden today.
4 A government spokesman has said that the Prime Minister will arrive at the airport at 5.30 p.m.
5 Although he wrote his proposal as well as he could, it was rejected by the Prime Minister's department.

6 By all accounts it was her husband who wrote this book; her husband is a famous engineer.
7 Although the Prime Minister wrote the letter himself, it was typed by his typist and posted by his clerk.
8 An interpreter is someone who speaks two languages, but a linguist is someone who studies many languages in order to know them as well as possible.
9 That night he listened to a lecture given by a radio expert at the university. After that he went home and went to bed.
10 My radio has gone wrong; I'm going to send for a radio mechanic to put it right.

Exercise 167:

1 Malam semalam dalam radio saya mendegar satu syarahan yang sangat menarik hati. Syarahan itu telah diberikan oléh wakil Malaysia di Bangsa-bangsa Bersatu.
2 Mengikut seorang jurucakap kerajaan Ruritania, semua pemberontak-pemberontak telah dibunuh ataupun ditangkap lalu dimasukkan ke dalam penjara.
3 Sungguhpun ia melihat dalam empat buah kamus, tetapi tidak boleh mendapati perkataan yang dicarinya.
4 Seorang yang berjual ubat dinamakan ahli ubat, dan seorang yang berjual daging dinamakan tukang daging.
5 Abangku sedang mempelajari bahasa Melayu di universiti; gurunya ialah seorang ahli pengetahuan Melayu yang termasyhur.
6 Sungai ini dua puluh kaki dalamnya; tanpa sampan tidak boleh kita menyeberang.
7 Dahulu ayahku ialah guru besar sebuah sekolah kebangsaan, tetapi sekarang ia sudah menjadi pengelola sekolah-sekolah Melayu.
8 Sungguhpun ia membawa keretanya dengan secepat-cepatnya, tetapi terlewatlah sampainya. Keretapinya sudahlah bertolak.
9 Sesudah tuan habis membaca buku ini, saya berharap bahawa tuan akan mulai mempelajari kesusasteraan Melayu.
10 Kalau sekiranya tuan hendak dinamakan seorang Malaysia yang betul, hendaklah tuan belajar bahasa kebangsaan lalu menggunakannya dengan sebaik-baiknya mahupun tuan bekerja mahupun duduk di rumah.

Appendix A
Malay-English Vocabulary

The following vocabulary contains all the words used in the course arranged alphabetically. The Arabic numerals in parentheses, e.g. (123), refer to the grammar sections in the body of the course. It is advisable to refer to the appropriate grammatical section before using any word which has such a number next to it.

A

abang elder brother
ada to be (to exist), to have
adakah . . .? (question former) (cf. French: *est-ce que . . .?*)
adakan (mengadakan) to hold (a meeting etc.), to set up
adalah that (conj.) (179)
adik younger brother, younger sister
adik-beradik brothers, sisters, brothers and sisters
adil just, fair
agaknya apparently (92)
agung general (adj.)
ahli member, expert (220)
ahli bahasa linguist
ahli bangunan architect
ahli bedah surgeon
ahli bumi geologist
ahli ilmu bangsa-bangsa ethnologist
ahli jawatankuasa committee member
ahli kaji bumi geologist
ahli kecantikan beauty specialist
ahli kimia chemist
ahli negara statesman
ahli pengetahuan scholar, savant
ahli radio radio expert
ahli sejarah historian
ahli siasah politician
ahli teknik technician, technical expert
ahli ubat pharmacist
ajar (mengajar) to teach
akan sign of future action (24); as for (196)
akan tetapi but (218)
akhir end (n.)
akhiran suffix
akhirnya in the end, finally
aku I, me, my (49)
alam world
alamat address
alir (mengalir) to flow
Allah God
almari cupboard
amat very (8)
ambil (mengambil) to take, to fetch
amuk (mengamuk) to run amok
anak child, son, daughter
anak lelaki son
anak perempuan daughter
anak-anak doll
anak-anak patung doll
angin wind (n.)
angkat (mengangkat) to lift, to pick up
angkut (mengangkut) to lift (heavy objects)
anjing dog
antarabangsa international
anu such-and-such (things)
apa what

apa-apa anything (167)
apa lagi? what else?
apabila when, whenever (189)
api fire
arahkan (mengarahkan) to direct
asalkan provided that (131)
Asia Asia
Asia Tenggara South-east Asia
askar soldier
ataupun or
atur (mengatur) to arrange, to organise
aturan arrangement, organisation
awak you, you (sing.) (74)
awal early (adv.)
awalan prefix
ayah father (cf. Lesson 1, Section E, note*)
ayat sentence (gram.)
ayat berkait complex sentence
ayat berlapis compound sentence

B

baca (membaca) to read
bacaan reading (n.)
bacakan read aloud
bagaimana how
bagi to give (co..); for (prep.)
baginda he, she (hon.) (164)
bagus fine, splendid
bahagia happiness
baharu (adj.) new
baharu (adv.) (to have) just (done)
baharulah only then
bahasa language
bahasa Arab Arabic (language)
bahasa Belanda Dutch (language)
bahasa Cina Chinese (language)
bahasa Inggeris English (language)
bahasa kebangsaan the national language (i.e. Malay)
bahasa Melayu Malay (language)
bahasa Perancis French (language)
bahasa Tamil Tamil (language)
bahawa that (conj.) (121)
baik good
baik (with vb.) had better
baik-baik (or *dengan baik-baik*) carefully, properly
baik jangan (with vb.) had better not
baiki (membaiki) to repair, to mend
baikkan (membaikkan) to repair, to mend
baiklah all right, O.K.
baju coat, jacket, shirt, blouse, dress
baju keméja shirt
bakar (membakar) to burn (tr.)
balai building (official)
balai polis police station
balas (membalas) to return (tr.), to give back
balasan reply (n.) answer (n.)
balik to return (intr.), to go back, to go home, to come back, to come home
bandar town
bandaran municipality; municipal
bangkang (membangkang) to oppose
bangkit to get up, to rise (from bed etc.)
bangsa race, nation, nationality; kind sort
Bangsa-bangsa Bersatu the United Nations
bangsakan (membangsakan) to classify
bangsawan nobleman
bangun to get up, to rise (from bed, etc.)
bangunan building
bangunkan (membangunkan) to build
bantu (membantu) to help, to assist
banyak a lot, much, many
bapa (or: *bapak*) father (cf. Lesson 1. Section E, note*)

bapa saudara uncle
barang goods
barang-barang luggage
bas bus
basah wet
basikal bicycle
batang cl. for stick-like objects
batu stone, mile
bawa (membawa) to take, to carry
bayar (membayar) to pay
bébas free, independent
bébaskan (membébaskan) to free, to liberate, to release
bedah (membedah) to operate (surgically) upon
begitu so, thus
bekerja to work
belanja expense, outlay
belanjakan (membelanjakan) to spend
beli (membeli) to buy
beliau he, she (59)
belum not yet (93)
benar true; very (8)
benarkan (membenarkan) to permit, to allow
bendang (cf. *sawah*) rice-field (North Malaysian Peninsular)
bendera flag
bentangkan (membentangkan) to spread out (tr.), to table (e.g. a motion)
bentuk form, shape
bentukkan (membentukkan) to form
berada well off, rich
berakal intelligent
beranda (cf. *serambi*) verandah (European-style)
berangan-angan to day-dream
berapa how much, how many
beras (cf. *padi, nasi*) rice (uncooked)
berasa to feel (intr.)
berat heavy
beratkan (memberatkan) to emphasise
berbaju to wear a jacket (shirt, blouse, etc.)
berbajukan to use as a jacket (shirt, blouse, etc.)
berbangsa noble (of high birth)
berbual to chat
berbuat to do (habitually), to make a habit of doing
bercakap to speak, to talk
bercucuran to trickle
bercukur to shave (intr.), to have a shave
bercuti to take leave, to be on leave, to have a holiday
berdasar to have as a basis
berdasarkan to be based on
berdiri to stand
berenang to swim
berguna useful
berharap to hope
berharapkan to set one's hopes on, to bank on
berhenti to stop (intr.)
berhormat honourable (162)
beri (memberi) to give
berikan (memberikan) to give
berikut following (adj.)
berita news, news-item
beritahu (memberitahu) to tell, to inform
berjalan to walk (44)
berjalan kaki to walk (44)
berjanggut (to be) bearded, to have a beard
berjemur to sunbathe (84)
berjual to sell (for a living) (86)
berjumpa (dengan) to meet (intro.) with
berkain to wear a sarong
berkait (cf. *ayat*) complex (gram.)
berkaki (empat, etc.*)* to have (four, etc.)

legs
berkasut to wear shoes
berkata to say
berkedai to keep a shop
berkembang to bloom, to flower
berkelip-kelip to keep on flashing
berkenaan (dengan) in connexion (with), with reference (to), with regard (to) (125)
berkenalan to be acquainted (with one another)
(tidak) berkeputusan uninterrupted, endless, interminable
berkeris to have a kris
berkipas to have a fan, to have propellers
berkipas-empat four-engined (80)
berkirim-kiriman to write to one another, to carry on a correspondence with each other
berkuda to be on horseback
berlabuh to anchor (intr.), to drop anchor
berlanggar (dengan) to collide (with) (104)
berlapis (cf. *ayat*) in layer, compound (gram.)
berlengkap to equip oneself, to get ready, to prepare (intr.) (197)
berlengkapkan to equip oneself with (197)
bermain to play
bermalam to spend the night
bermimpi to dream
bermimpikan to dream about
bermula to begin (intr.) (151)
bernama to have the name, to be named, to be called
berniaga to trade
berpagar to have a fence, (to be) fenced
berpedang to have a sword
berpindah to move (intro.), to be transferred
bersama-sama (dengan) together with
bersambutan to greet each other
bersatu united
bersawah to have a rice-field
bersekolah to go to school, to be at school
bersembunyi to hide (intr.)
bersenapang to have a gun
bersenjata to be armed
bersenjatakan to be armed with
bersetuju to agree
bersihkan to clean (dry)
bersongkok to wear a songkok
bersukacita to be happy
bersyarah to lecture
bertabur-taburan to be scattered about
bertambah to increase
bertanam to plant (86)
bertangis-tangisan to cry on each other's shoulders
bertanya to ask, to inquire
bertanyakan to ask about, to inquire about
bertarikh (to be) dated
bertémbak-témbakan to shoot at each other
bertingkat (dua, etc.) to have (two, etc.) storeys
bertolak to start, to see off, to leave, to depart (of ships, trains, aircraft, etc.)
bertongkat to have a stick
bertongkatkan to use a stick
bertopi to wear a hat (80)
bertulis written (adj.), in writing
berugama Islam to be Muslim by religion
berumah to have a house, to live in a house
berumur (lima tahun, etc.) to be (five years, etc.) old
berunding to have a discussion, to have

327

(a) talk(s) (125)
besar big, large, great
besarkan (membesarkan) to enlarge, to magnify
besarkan diri (membesarkan diri) to boast
besarnya size (212d)
besi iron
betul right, correct; really, very (8)
betulkan (membetulkan) to correct
biji seeds; cl. for small objects
bila when
bilang (membilang) to count (tr.)
bilangan number
bilik room
bilik makan dining room
bilik mandi bathroom
bimbit (membimbit) to carry in the fingers
biru blue
bodoh stupid
boléh can, to be able
bom bomb
bom tangan hand-grenade
bonda mother (cf. Lesson 1, Section E, note**)
botol bottle
buah fruit; cl. for large objects
buah-buahan fruit (collective)
buah cempedak jackfruit
buah durian durian
buah manggis mangosteen
buah rambutan rambutan
buang (membuang) to throw away, to discard
buat (membuat) to make, to do
buat-buat to pretend
bubuh (membubuh) to put (in or on something)
budak boy, girl, youngster
budak lelaki boy
budak perempuan girl

buka (membuka) to open, to switch on
bukan not
bukan . . . melainkan . . . not . . .but. . .
bukit hill
buku book
buku bacaan reading-book, reader
bulan moon, month
bulanan monthly (adj.)
bumbung roof
bumi soil, the Earth
bunga flower
bunga melur jasmine
bunga raya hibiscus
bungkusan parcel
bunuh (membunuh) to kill, to murder
bunyi sound (n.)
butir grain, pellet, particle
butir-butir minutes (of a meeting)

C

cabut (mencabut) to pull out, to extract
cadangan proposal, suggestion
cahaya light
calon candidate
calon bébas independent candidate
cantik pretty, beautiful
cara method, fashion
cari (mencari) to look for, to seek
cawan cup
cempedak jackfruit
cepat quick, fast, swift
cerdik bright, quick-witted
cerita story (cf. note in (144))
ceritakan (menceritakan) to tell (a story), to narrate
ceritera story (cf. note in (144))
ceriterakan (menceriterakan) to tell (a story), to narrate
cetera (royal) umbrella, (royal) sunshade (141)
cikgu teacher

Cina Chinese (adj.)
contoh example, specimen
cuba (mencuba) to try, to attempt
cuci (mencuci) to clean
cukai tax, duty
cukai pendapatan income tax
cukup enough, sufficient
cukur (mencukur) to shave (tr.)
curi (mencuri) to steal
cuti leave (n.), holiday

D

daérah district
daftar list
daftarkan (mendaftarkan) to register (tr.)
daging meat, flesh
dahulu first, formerly, ago (123)
dakwat ink
dalam (adj.) deep, profound
dalam negeri interior (of a country)
dalamkan (mendalamkan) to deepen (tr.)
dalamnya depth (212d)
dan and (218)
dan lagi and also, furthermore
dapat (mendapat) to get, to obtain
dapat to manage to
dapati (mendapati) to find
dapatkan (mendapatkan) to look for
dapur kitchen, stove
dari from
dari dalam from inside
dari mana? where from? whence?
darihal about, concerning
daripada from (people), than (2)
darjah class (in school)
darulbaka (**Arabic**) heaven, the Abode of the Eternal (174)
dasar policy, basis
datang to come

datangi (mendatangi) to come to, to arrive at, to attack
datangkan (mendatangkan) to bring, to bring about, to cause
datangnya arrival (212d)
datuk grandfather
dekat near
dekati (mendekati) to approach (tr.)
dekatkan (mendekatkan) to bring near
dengan with; as (29); and (218)
dengan baik carefully, properly
dengan cepat quickly
dengan selamat safely
dengan sendirinya of one's own accord, automatically (146)
dengan tiada without
dengar (mendengar) to hear, to listen to
deras swift, fast
déwa god
déwan council, board, hall
Déwan Bahasa dan Pustaka Language and Literature Agency (65)
Déwan Rakyat House of Representatives
déwan seni lukis art gallery
di in, at, on
di antara between, among
di atas on, above, over, for (126)
di bawah below, at the bottom (of)
di belakang behind, after (place)
di dalam in, inside
di depan before (place), in front of (123)
di keliling around
di luar outside
di mana where?
di mana-mana pun tidak nowhere, not anywhere
di pekan in town
di rumah at home
di sana there, over there
di seluruh throughout

di sini here
di situ there (near you)
di tengah in the middle (of)
di tengah-tengah right in the middle (of)
dia he, she, him, her, his (58)
diri self (146); personal (gram.)
diriku myself (146)
dirimu yourself, yourselves (146)
dirinya oneself, himself, herself, itself, themselves (146)
doktor doctor
dua two
duduk to sit, to sit down, to stay
duit money, cent (North Malaysian Peninsular)
dukacita sadness, regret
dukung (mendukung) to carry (a child astride on the hip)
dunia world
durian durian

E

ékor tail; cl. for animals
emak mother (cf. Lesson 1, Section E, note**)
enam six
encik you (sing.) (52)
encik-encik you (plur.) (52)
Encik Anu Mr. So and So
Encik Polan Mr. So and So
engkau you (62) (74)
erat close, tight, firm
ésok tomorrow

F

fail file, dossier
faham to understand
fikir to think

G

gadis girl (young woman)
gajah elephant
gaji salary, pay, wages
gali (menggali) to dig
gali-galian minerals
gambar (n.) picture, photograph, film
gambar (menggambar) to photograph, to film
gambaran illustration
ganti (mengganti) to substitute
ganti nama pronoun (gram.)
ganti nama diri personal pronoun (gram.)
gantung (menggantung) to hang
gemuk fat (adj.)
getah rubber, latex
gu (i.e. Cikgu) teacher (70)
gugus cluster (137)
gugusan cluster (137)
gugusan pulau-pulau archipelago (137)
Gugusan Pulau-pulau Melayu the Malay Archipelago (137)
gulai curry
gulung (menggulung) to roll up
gunakan (menggunakan) to use
guni sack
gunung mountain
guru teacher
guru besar headmaster, headmistress
guru pelatih teacher in training (140)
guru pelawat visiting teacher (140)

H

habis finished, all gone
habiskan (menghabiskan) to finish, to complete
hadiah present, prize
hadir present (adj.), in attendance

hairan surprised, astonished
hairankan (menghairankan) to surprise, to astonish
hakim magistrate
Hakim Besar Chief Justice
hamparan carpet
hampir-hampir almost, nearly
hangat hot, warm
hangatkan (menghangatkan) to heat, to warm up (tr.)
hantar (menghantar) to send
hantarkan (menghantarkan) to send
hantarkan balik (menghantarkan balik) to send back, to return (tr.)
harap hope (n.)
harapan hope (n.)
harapkan (mengharapkan) to set one's hopes on, to bank on
harga price
harganya it costs (212e)
hari day
hari-hari everyday
hari ini today
hari ini juga this very day
hari Jumaat Friday
hari Rabu Wednesday
harian daily (adj.) (65)
harimau tiger
hati liver (42)
hati-hati! be careful! look out!
haus thirsty
helai (pron. *lai*) cl. for items of clothing, sheets of paper, etc.
hendak (coll. *nak*) to want; sign of intended action (22) (23)
hendak ke to be off to
hendaklah...it is necessary to (that)...
hidup to live, to be alive; alive (adj.)
hijau green
hikayat story, romance, epic
hilang lost (adj.)
hinggap perch

hirau to care, to heed
hisab calculation
hisabkan (menghisabkan) to calculate
hisap (menghisap) to suck, to smoke (tobacco)
hitam black
hormat honour (162) (179)
hormati (menghormati) to honour (162)
hormatnya honour (162) (179)
hujan rain
hukum sentence (legal), judgement
hukumkan (menghukumkan) to sentence
hunus (menghunus) to draw (a sword), to unsheath
hutan jungle

I

ia he, she (58)
ialah to be (159)
ibu mother (cf. Lesson 1, Section E, Note**)
ibu bapa parents
ibu pejabat head office, secretariat, headquarters (38)
ikan fish
ikut by way of, via
ikut (mengikut) to follow (39)
ikut kiri! keep left!
ikut sini this way
ikut situ that way
ilmu knowledge, science, -ology
ilmu alam geography
ilmu bangsa-bangsa ethnology
ilmu bedah (science of) surgery
ilmu bumi geography
ilmu hisab arithmetic
ilmu kimia chemistry
ilmu pendidikan educational theory, education (as a study) (72)

331

ilmu sains science
India Indian (adj.)
ingat (mengingat) to think, to remember (33)
ingatan memory
ingati (mengingati) to remember, to think of (177); to remind, to admonish
Inggeris English (adj.)
ini this, these
ini dia ... this is ..., here is ...
istana palace
isteri wife
isyarat sign
isyarat jalan raya road-sign
itik duck
itu that, those

J

jabatan department
Jabatan Kerja Raya (J.K.R.) Public Works Department (P.W.D.)
Jabatan Parit dan Tali Air Drainage and Irrigation Department
Jabatan Perbendaharaan the Treasury
jadi so (conj.) (85)
jadi (menjadi) to become
jahat bad, naughty, wicked, evil
jalan road, way; to go (43)
jalankan (menjalankan) to set in motion, to run (tr.)
jalan raya main road, highway
jam hour; watch, clock
jamban lavatory, toilet
jambangan vase
janggut beard
jari finger
jatuh to fall (99)
jatuhkan (menjatuhkan) to let fall, to drop
jatuhkan hukum (menjatuhkan hukum) to pronounce sentence
jauh distant, far
jawab (menjawab) to answer
jawapan answer (n.)
jawatan office, position
jawatankuasa committee
Jawi Malay script, Arabic script
jemput (menjemput) to invite
jemputan invitation
jemur (menjemur) to dry (tr.) in the sun
jeniskan (menjeniskan) to classify
Jepun Japanese
jika if (114)
jikalau if (115)
jilat (menjilat) to lick
jual (menjual) to sell (86)
jualan merchandise (for sale)
juga (**usually with** *pun*) also (63) (209) (210)
Jumaat community, congregation; Friday
jumpa to find, to meet
juru expert (220)
jurubahasa interpreter
jurubatu boatswain
jurucakap spokesman
jururawat nurse
jurutaip typist
jurutera engineer
juta million

K

kacau (mengacau) to annoy, to stir
kadang-kadang sometimes
-kah question particle
kain cloth, sarong
kakak elder sister
kaki foot, leg
kakitangan employees, staff (182)
kalam pen
kalau if (113)

kali (e.g. *sekali, dua kali*) time, occasion (e.g. once, twice) (French *fois*)
kami we, us, our (51)
kampung village
kamu you, your (74)
kamus dictionary
kanak-kanak child, children
kanan right; senior (73)
kandar (mengandar) to carry (on a pole)
kapal ship
kapal api steamship, steamer
kapal laut (sea-going) ship
kapal pembinasa destroyer
kapal perang warship
kapal selam submarine
kapal terbang aeroplane, aircraft
karamkan (mengaramkan) to sink (tr.)
karang (mengarang) to compile, to compose, to write (books, etc.)
karangan composition, essay
kasih love (n.)
kasut shoe
kati catty (i.e. 1-1/3lb.)
kau- you (67)
kau you (67)
kawan friend
kayu wood (material)
ke to (a place)
ke mana? (to) where?; wither?
keadaan condition, situation
keadilan justice
keahlian skill, expertise
kebaikan goodness, advantage
kebajikan welfare
kebajikan masyarakat social welfare
kebangsaan national
kebanyakan the majority
kebebasan independence, freedom
kebenaran permission
keberatan heaviness, weight
kebodohan stupidity
kebudayaan culture; cultural

kebun garden
kebun getah rubber estate
kecantikan beauty, prettiness
kecil small, little
Kedah Kedah
kedai shop
kedai buku-buku bookshop
kedai bunga-bunga flower-shop
kedalaman depth, profundity
kedatangan arrival
kedelapan eighth
kedelapan belas eighteenth
kedengaran audible; to be heard (165)
kedua second (adj.)
kedua belas twelfth
kedua puluh twentieth
kedudukan situation, position
kedukaan unhappiness
keempat fourth
keempat belas fourteenth
keenam sixth
keenam belas sixteenth
kehendak wish, desire (n.)
kehendaki (menghendaki) to want, to require
kehilangan loss; to lose (165)
kejadian event
kejahatan wickedness
kejauhan distance
kejutkan (mengejutkan) to startle
kekasih darling, beloved
kekuatan strength, power
kekurangan shortage; to be short of (165)
kelabu grey
kelaparan hunger
kelihatan visible; to be seen (165)
kelima fifth
kelima belas fifteenth
kelmarin yesterday (35)
keluar to go out, to come out
keluarkan (mengeluarkan) to expel, to

dismiss, to issue (tr.)
kemajuan progress
kamalasan laziness
kemangkatan death, decease, demise (of kings, etc.) (127: note)
kemanisan sweetness
kemarin yesterday (35)
kemas (mengemas) to tidy
kemasukan to be entered (165)
kematian death
kembali to return (intr.)
kembali ke darulbaka to die (174)
kembali ke rahmatullah to die (174)
kemeja shirt
kementerian ministry (183)
kemerdekaan independence
kemudian then, next
kemukakan (mengemukakan) to bring forward, to put forward
kena must, to have to, to incur
kenal (mengenal) to know (a person) (French: *connaitre*)
kenalan acquaintance
kepada to (a person)
kepahitan bitterness
kepandaian cleverness, skill
kepeningan dizziness
kepentingan importance
keping piece, lump
keputusan result, decision
kerajaan government
kerana because, because of (127)
kerani clerk
keréta vehicle, car, cart, carriage
keréta lembu bullock cart
kerétapi railway train
keris kris, creese (Malay dagger)
kerja work (n.)
kerjasama co-operation
kerosakan damage (n.)
kertas paper
kertas tulis writing paper

kerusi chair
kesalahan guilt
kesatuan unit
kesebelas eleventh
kesembilan ninth
kesembilan belas ninteenth
kesempitan narrowness
kesenangan ease, comfort
kesepuluh tenth
kesihatan health
kesu̱ngguhan truth
kesusahan difficulty
kesusasteraan literature
ketahui (mengetahui) to know
ketentuan certainty
keterangan explanation, clarification
ketiga third
ketiga belas thirteenth
ketinggalan to leave behind, to get left behind (165)
ketujuh seventh
ketujuh belas seventeenth
ketua chief, head, headman
ketua jabatan head of (Govt.) department
ketua kampung village headman
ketua menteri chief minister
ketua pejabat head of department
Ketua Pos Negara Postmaster-General
kewangan finance
khabar news
khabarnya it is said that . . . by all accounts
khas special
kilang factory, mill
kipas fan, propeller
kiri left
kirim (mengirim) to send, to post (letters)
kirimkan (mengirimkan) to send, to post (letters)
kisah story (cf. note in 144)

kisi-kisi trellis, lattice, grille
kisi-kisi tingkap grille
kita we, us, our (50)
kotak box
koyak torn
koyakkan (mengoyakkan) to tear (tr.)
ku- I (66)
-ku me, my (66)
kuasa power
kuat strong
kuatkan (menguatkan) to strengthen, to reinforce
kuburkan (menguburkan) to bury, to inter
kucing cat
kuda horse
kuda-kuda trestle, clothes-horse
kuki cook
kuning yellow
kuntum cl. for flowers
kupas (mengupas) to peel, to pare
kurang less, not very (3) (6) (7)
kurang ajar ill-bred, bad-mannered (7)
kurangkan (mengurangkan) to decrease (tr.), to diminish (tr.)
kurang periksa I'm afraid I don't know (7)
kursus course (of study)
kurus thin (of people)
kutubkhanah library

L

labuhan anchorage, harbour
lagi still, yet, more (5); and (218)
lagi ... lagi the more ... the more ... (32)
lagi pula furthermore
lagi pun furthermore
lagu song
lagu kebangsaan national anthem
-lah (emphatic particle)
lain other, different
lakon play, drama
lakonan play, drama
lalu to pass by; and then (97) (218)
lalu (yang lalu) past, last (e.g. last week, etc.)
lama old (of things); for a long time
lambat slow, late
lamun provided that, if only (132)
langgar (melanggar) to run into, to run down, to ram (104)
langkah step
lantai floor
lapangan field
lapangan terbang airport
lapar hungry
laporkan to report
latih (melatih) to train
latihan training, pratice, exercise
laut sea
lautan ocean
lawat (melawat) to visit
lebar broad, wide
lebarkan (melebarkan) to widen, to broaden
lebih more (2), in excess
lebih kurang more or less, immediately
lekas quickly, swiftly, at once, immediately
lekat stick; to stick (intr.)
lekatkan (melekatkan) to stick (tr.)
lelaki male, masculine
lemari cupboard (also *almari*)
lembap moist, damp
lembapkan (melembapkan) to moisten
lembu ox, cow
lengkap complete, ready
lengkapkan (melengkapkan) to equip, to prepare (tr.)
lepas after (124); beyond, last, previous
lepas itu then, next, afterwards
lesen licence
letak (meletak) to put, to place (in a

lying position)
letak kereta (meletak kereta) to park a car
lidah tongue
lihat (melihat) to see, to look at
lima puluh fifty
lipat (melipat) to fold
lompat (melompat) to jump, to jump over
lompati (melompati) to jump on (to)
loteri lottery
loteri kebajikan masyarakat social welfare lottery
luar bandar rural
luar negeri external, foreign
lubang hole
lukakan (melukakan) to injure, to hurt, to wound
lukis (melukis) to draw, to paint (pictures)
lukisan drawing (n.)
lulus (**usually with** *dalam*) to pass (an examination)
luluskan (meluluskan) to accept, to pass (of a proposal, etc.)
lupa to forget (99) (100)
lupakan (melupakan) to forget (99) (100)

M

mabuk drunk, intoxicated
macam manner, kind, sort
macam mana how
mahal dear, expensive
mahkamah court (of law)
mahu to want
mahupun. . .mahupun . . whether. . or. . .
main to play
majalah magazine
majlis council, assembly
majlis bandaran town council, municipal council
maju progressive, making progress
majukan (memajukan) to prosper (tr.)
makan to eat
makan angin to go for a stroll, to go for a ride
makan malam dinner, evening meal
makanan food
makin. . .makin. . . the more. . .the more. . .
maklumkan (memaklumkan) to inform (179)
makmal laboratory, workshop
makna meaning
*maknanya. . .*it means (that). . .
maktab college, institute (65)
Maktab Perguruan Bahasa Language Institute (65)
Maktab Perguruan Harian Day Training College (65)
malam night
malas lazy
mana which, how
mana boléh? how can that be?
mana-mana any (167)
mana-mana pun any at all
manggis mangosteen
mangkat to die (of kings) (127) (174): note
mangkuk bowl, cup (without handles)
mangsa victim
manis sweet
maniskan (memaniskan) to sweeten
mari (**imperative of** *datang*, **q.v.**) come!
marilah kita . . . come on, let's . . .
markah mark (n.) (examination marks, etc.)
masa (conj.) while
masa (n.) time
masa yang akan datang the future
masak (memasak) to cook

masih still, yet
masuk to enter, to go in, to come in
masuki (memasuki) to enter (tr.)
masukkan (memasukkan) to insert
masyarakat society, community
masyhur famous
mata eye
mata-mata policeman
matahari sun
mati dead; to die (174)
méja table
melainkan but, except (218)
melanggar (langgar) to run into, to run down, to ram (104)
melaporkan (laporkan) to report
melatih (latih) to train
melawat (lawat) to visit
Melayu Malay (adj.)
melébarkan (lébarkan) to widen, to broaden
melekatkan (lekatkan) to stick (tr.)
melembapkan (lembapkan) to moisten
melengkapkan (lengkapkan) to equip, to prepare (tr.)
meletak (letak) to lay down
meletak keréta (letak keréta) to park a car
melihat (lihat) to see, to look (at)
melipat (lipat) to fold
melompat (lompat) to jump (up), to jump on to
melompati (lompati) to jump on, to jump on to
melukakan (lukakan) to wound, to hurt, to injure
melukis (lukis) to draw, to paint (pictures)
meluluskan (luluskan) to accept, to pass (of a proposal, etc.)
melupakan (lupakan) to forget (deliberately) (99) (100)
memadamkan (padamkan) to extinguish, to put out
memajukan (majukan) to prosper (tr.)
memakai (pakai) to wear, to use
memakan (makan) to eat (34)
memaklumkan (maklumkan) to inform (179)
memaksa (paksa) to force, to compel (108)
memandang (pandang) to look at, to stare at
memang of course, as you know
memanggil (panggil) to call, to summon
memaniskan (maniskan) to sweeten
memanjangkan (panjangkan) to lengthen
memanjat (panjat) to climb
memasak (masak) to cook
memasuki (masuki) to enter (tr.)
membaca (baca) to read
membacakan (bacakan) to read aloud
membaiki (baiki) to repair, to mend
membaikkan (baikkan) to repair, to mend
membalas (balas) to return (tr.), to give back
membangkang (bangkang) to oppose
membangsakan (bangsakan) to classify
membangunkan (bangunkan) to build, to erect
membantu (bantu) to help, to assist
membawa (bawa) to take, to carry
membayar (bayar) to pay
membébaskan (bebaskan) to free, to liberate, to release
membedah (bedah) to operate (surgically) upon
membelanjakan (belanjakan) to spend
membeli (beli) to buy
membenarkan (benarkan) to permit, to allow
membentangkan (bentangkan) to

spread out (tr.), to table (a motion, etc.)
membentukkan (bentukkan) to form
memberatkan (beratkan) to emphasise
memberi (beri) to give
memberikan (berikan) to give
memberitahu (beritahu) to inform
membesarkan (besarkan) to enlarge, to magnify
membesarkan diri (besarkan diri) to boast
membetulkan (betulkan) to correct
membilang (bilang) to count
membimbit (bimbit) to carry in the fingers
membuang (buang) to throw away, to discard
membuat (buat) to make, to do
membubuh (bubuh) to put
membuka (buka) to open, to switch on
membunuh (bunuh) to kill, to murder
memecahkan (pecahkan) to break, to smash
memegang (pegang) to hold
memendekkan (pendekkan) to shorten, to abbreviate
memenuhi (penuhi) to fill
memeriksa (periksa) to examine, to inquire into
memilih (pilih) to elect, to choose
meminjamkan (pinjamkan) to lend
meminta (minta) to ask for
meminta diri (minta diri) to take one's leave, to excuse onself
meminum (minum) to drink
memohon (pohon) to request (a person)
memotong (potong) to cut (off)
mempekerjakan (pekerjakan) to employ
mempelajari (pelajari) to study (194)
memperbaiki (perbaiki) to repair
memperbudakkan (perbudakkan) to treat as a child
mempercayai (percayai) to trust
memperdewakan (perdewakan) to treat as a god, to deify, to idolise (194)
mempergunakan (pergunakan) to make use of, to utilise
memperhatikan (perhatikan) to take note of, to pay attention to (194)
memperhentikan (perhentikan) to stop (tr.), to put a stop to
memperisterikan (peristerikan) to marry (of a man), to make a wife of, to take to
memperkatakan (perkatakan) to talk about
memperkenankan (perkenankan) to grant, to allow, to agree to
memperkuat (perkuat) to reinforce
memperlakukan (perlakukan) (sebagai) to treat (as), to regard (as)
mempersatukan (persatukan) to unite (tr.)
mempersilakan (persilakan) to invite, to request
mempertahankan (pertahankan) to defend
mempertunjukkan (pertunjukkan) to demonstrate, to exhibit
memuaskan (puaskan) to satisfy (tr.)
memuaskan (hati) satisfying, satisfactory
memukul (pukul) to strike, to beat
memulai (mulai) to begin (tr.) (151)
memulakan (mulakan) to begin (tr.) (151)
memungut (pungut) to collect
memutusi (putusi) to break off, to snap, to sever (tr.)
memutuskan (putuskan) to decide
menahan (tahan) to bear, to endure
menaiki (naiki) to ascend, to go up, to climb (tr.)

menaikkan (naikkan) to raise, to take up, to bring up
menaip (taip) to type
menakuti (takuti) to fear (tr.) to be afraid of
menakutkan (takutkan) to frighten
menamai (namai) to name, to call
menamakan (namakan) to name, to call
menamatkan (tamatkan) to terminate, to conclude, to close (tr.) (e.g. a meeting)
menanam (tanam) to plant
menanamkan (tanamkan) to bury, to inter
menandatangani (tandatangani) to sign (181)
menangis (tangis) to weep, to cry
menangkap (tangkap) to catch, to arrest
menanti (nanti) to wait
menantikan (nantikan) to wait for
menari (tari) to dance
menarik (tarik) to pull, to attract
menarik hati to interest, interesting
mencabut (cabut) to pull out, to extract, to uproot
mencari (cari) to look for, to seek
menceritakan (ceritakan) to tell (a story), to relate, to narrate
menceriterakan (ceriterakan) to tell (a story), to relate, to narrate
mencuba (cuba) to try, to attempt
mencuci (cuci) to clean
mencukur (cukur) to shave (tr.)
mencuri (curi) to steal
mendaftarkan (daftarkan) to register
mendalamkan (dalamkan) to depend
mendapat (dapat) to get, to obtain
mendapati (dapati) to get, to obtain
mendapati (dapati) to find
mendapatkan (dapatkan) to look for
mendatangi (datangi) to come to, to arrive at, to attack
mendatangkan (datangkan) to bring, to bring about, to cause
mendekati (dekati) to approach (tr.)
mendekatkan (dekatkan) to bring near
mendengar (dengar) to hear, to listen (to)
mendukung (dukung) to carry (a child on the hip)
menekankan (tekankan) to stress, to emphasise
menembak to shoot
menengah secondary (education)
menengok (tengok) to see, to look at
menerangkan (terangkan) to explain, to clarify
menerbitkan (terbitkan) to publish
menerima (terima) to receive
meneruskan (teruskan) to go through with, to keep going at
menetapkan (tetapkan) to fix
mengacau (kacau) to annoy, to stir
mengadakan (adakan) to hold (meeting, etc.), to set up
mengajar (ajar) to teach
mengalamatkan (alamatkan) to address
mengalir (alir) to flow
mengambil (ambil) to take, to fetch
mengamuk (amuk) to run amok
mengandar (kandar) to carry on a pole
mengangkat (angkat) to lift
mengangkut (angkut) to carry, to lift (heavy objects)
mengarahkan (arahkan) to direct
mengaramkan (karamkan) to sink (tr.)
mengarang (karang) to compile, to compose, to write (book, etc.)
mengatur (atur) to arrange, to organise
mengaum (ngaum) to roar (of lions, tigers, etc.)

menghendaki (kehendaki) to want, to require
mengejutkan (kejutkan) to startle
mengeluarkan (keluarkan) to expel, to dismiss, to issue
mengemas (kemas) to tidy
mengemukakan (kemukakan) to bring forward, to put forward
mengenal (kenal) to know (a person) (cf. French: connaitre)
mengetahui (ketahui) to know
menggali (gali) to dig
menggambar (gambar) to photograph, to film
menggantung (gantung) to hang
menggulung (gulung) to roll up
menggunakan (gunakan) to use
menghabiskan (habiskan) to finish, to complete
menghairankan (hairankan) to surprise, to astonish
menghangatkan (hangatkan) to heat, to warm up
menghantar (hantar) to send
menghantarkan (hantarkan) to send
menghantarkan balik (hantarkan balik) to send back, to return (tr.)
mengharapkan (harapkan) to set one's hopes on, to bank on
menghisabkan (hisabkan) to calculate
menghisap (hisap) to calculate
menghisap (hisap) to suck, to smoke (tobacco)
menghormati (hormati) to honour, to respect (162)
menghunus (hunus) to draw (a sword), to unsheath
mengikut (prep.) according to
mengikut (ikut) to follow, to go by way of
mengingat (ingat) to remember, to think (33)

mengingati (ingati) to remember, to think of (177)
mengirim (kirim) to send, to post
mengirimkan (kirimkan) to send, to post
mengoyakkan (koyakkan) to tear (tr.)
menguatkan (kuatkan) to strengthen
menguburkan (kuburkan) to bury, to entomb
mengucap (ucap) to pronounce, to express, to utter (126)
mengucapkan (ucapkan) to pronounce, to express, to utter (126)
mengulangkan (ulangkan) to repeat
mengundi (undi) to vote
mengupas (kupas) to peel, to pare
mengurangkan (kurangkan) to reduce, to diminish (tr.)
mengurus (urus) to manage, to arrange
menguruskan (uruskan) to manage, to arrange
mengutamakan (utamakan) to keep to the fore, to put first
meninggal (tinggal) to leave, to remain
meninggal to die (174)
meninggal dunia to die, to pass away (174)
meninggalkan (tinggalkan) to leave (165)
menjadi (jadi) to become
menjalankan (jalankan) to set in motion, to run (tr.)
menjatuhkan (jatuhkan) to let fall, to drop
menjatuhkan hukum (jatuhkan hukum) to pronounce sentence
menjawab (jawab) to answer, to reply
menjemput (jemput) to invite
menjemur (jemur) to dry in the sun (84)
menjeniskan (jeniskan) to classify
menjilat (jilat) to lick
mejual (jual) to sell (86)

340

menolak (tolak) to push, to reject
menolong (tolong) to help, to assist
menoreh (toréh) to tap (rubber)
mentéga butter
menteri minister
Menteri Pelajaran Minister for Education
menulis (tulis) to write
menumpangkan (tumpangkan) to accommodate, to put up
menunggu (tunggu) to wait
menuris (turis) to tap (rubber)
menuruni (turuni) to descend, to go down (tr.)
menurunkan (turunkan) to bring down, to take down, to lower
menutup (tutup) to close, to shut
menyaksikan (saksikan) to witness
menyambut (sambut) to welcome
menyanyi (nyanyi) to sing
menyanyikan (nyanyikan) to sing (tr.)
menyapu (sapu) to sweep
menyatakan (nyatakan) to explain, to clarify
menyatukan (satukan) to unite, to unify
menyebabkan (sebabkan) to cause
menyeberang to cross over
menyediakan (sediakan) to prepare (tr.)
menyelesaikan (selesaikan) to finish off, to attend to
menyembunyikan (sembunyikan) to hide (tr.)
menyépak (sépak) to kick
menyerah (serah) to surrender (tr.)
menyerah diri (serah diri) to surrender (intr.)
menyerahkan (serahkan) to surrender (tr.)
menyerahkan diri (serahkan diri) to surrender (intr.)
menyerang (serang) to attack

menyertakan (sertakan) to forward, to send on
menyimpan (simpan) to put away, to keep
menyimpan kereta (simpan kereta) to park a car
menyokong (sokong) to support
menyuruh (suruh) to order, to command, to tell
menyusun (susun) to arrange, to compile
mérah red
merajakan (rajakan) to make (into a) king
merakamkan (rakamkan) to record
merayakan (rayakan) to celebrate
merbahaya dangerous
merdéka independent
merdu melodious
merendahkan (rendahkan) to lower, to humble
merendahkan diri (rendahkan diri) to humble oneself
meréka they, their, them (60)
merosakkan (rosakkan) to damage, to destroy
merundingkan (rundingkan) to discuss (125)
mesin machine
mesin taip typewriter
Mesir Egypt
mesjid mosque
meskipun although (120)
mesti must (36)
mesyuarat meeting
mesyuarat agung general meeting
mewakili (wakili) to represent
mimpi dream (n.)
minggu week
minggu depan next week
mingguan weekly (adj.)
minit minute (n.)

minta (meminta) to ask for
minta diri (meminta diri) to take one's leave, to excuse oneself
minum (meminum) to drink
minuman drink (n.)
miskin poor
-mu you, your (68)
muda young
muka face, page
mula-mula first of all, to begin with
mulai to begin, (intr.) (151)
mulai (memulai) to begin (tr.) (151)
mulakan (memulakan) to begin (tr.) (151)
murid pupil
musim season
musim hujan rainy season
musim kemarau dry season
musuh enemy

N

naik to go up, to come up, to rise, to ride
naiki (menaiki) to ascend, to go up, to climb (tr.)
naikkan (menaikkan) to raise, to take up, to bring up
nak (coll. for *hendak*, q.v.) to be going to
nak ke (coll. for *hendak ke*, q.v.) to be off to
nama name
namai (menamai) to name, to call
namakan (menamakan) to name, to call
nampak to see, to be able to see, to be visible
nampaknya it seems, apparently (91)
nanti to wait
nantikan (menantikan) to wait for
nasi (cooked) rice
nasihat advice

negara state (adj.)
negarawan statesman
negeri country, state (n.)
negeri China China
negeri Inggeris England
negeri Jepun Japan
negeri Kedah Kedah
negeri Perancis France
negeri Perlis Perlis
nĕnĕk grandmother
ngaum (mengaum) to roar (of lions, tigers, etc.)
nya him, his, her, hers, it, its, them, their (69) (212)
nyanyi (menyanyi) to sing
nyanyikan (menyanyikan) to sing (tr.)
nyata clear
nyatakan (menyatakan) to explain
nyatalah bahawa... it is clear that...

O

oléh by (88) (89)
oléh kerana because (of) (127)
oléh kerana itu for this reason
oléh sebab because (of) (127)
oléh sebab itu for this reason
orang person, man woman
orang Cina a Chinese
orang gaji housemaid
orang India an Indian
orang Inggeris an Englishman
orang Jepun a Japanese
orang kedai shopkeeper
orang lain other people, someone else
orang lelaki man
orang Malaysia a Malaysian
orang Melayu a Malay
orang Perancis a Frenchman
orang perempuan woman
orang putih a European
orang ramai the public

P

pada at, on (45)
padam extinguished, out (of lamps, etc.)
padamkan (memadamkan) to extinguish, to put out
padang (open) field, (village etc.) green
padi (growing) rice
pagar fence
pagi morning
pagi-pagi early in the morning (169)
pagi tadi this morning (past) (71)
pahit bitter
pakai (memakai) to wear, to use
pakaian clothes, clothing
pakar an expert
paksa (memaksa) to force, to compel (108)
pandai clever, good at (25)
pandang (memandang) to look at, to stare at
pandangan view, opinion
pandu (memandu) to drive
panduan guide
Panduan Jalan Raya Highway Code
panggil (memanggil) to call, to summon
panggilan summons (n.), call (n.)
pangkalan (**also:** *pengkalan*) anchorage, landing place, base (mil.)
panggung stage, theatre, cinema (152)
panjang long
panjangnya length (212d)
panjangkan (memanjangkan) to lengthen
panjat (memanjat) to climb
pantas energetic, active
pantai beach, shore
para all, (plural sign) (162)
parit ditch, drain
pasar market, bazaar
pasaran market (abstract)
pasaran dunia world-market
pasif passive (gram.)
pasu flower-pot
patah broken, fractured
patah cl. for words, phrases, etc.
patung statue, image
patut ought, should (122)
payung umbrella, sunshade
pecah broken, smashed
pecahkan (memecahkan) to break, to smash
pedang sword
pedas hot (of pepper, curry, etc.)
pegang (memegang) to hold, to grasp
pegawai officer, official (n.)
pegawai daerah district officer
pejabat office (37)
pejabat pos post office
pekan town, market
pekerjaan profession, occupation, employment
pekerjakan (mempekerjakan) to employ
pelabuhan harbour, anchorage
peladang farmer
pelajar student
pelajaran education, lesson
pelajari (mempelajari) to study (194)
pelakon actor
pelatih trainee
pelawat visitor
pelita light, lamp
peluang opportunity
peluh sweat, perspiration
pelukis draughtsman
peluru bullet
pemandangan scene, scenery, view
pembaca reader
pembangkang opposer, opposing
pembangunan construction, development

pembangunan luar bandar rural development
pembantu assistant, helper
pembawa bearer (141)
pembawa cetera umbrella bearer (141)
pembedahan operation (surgical)
pembeli buyer, purchaser
pemberita reporter
pemberontak rebel (n.)
pembesaran enlargement
pembinasa destructive (cf. *kapal pembinasa*)
pembuka opener
pembukaan (act of) opening
pembunuh murderer
pembunuhan murder, killing
pemegang handle, holder
pemerhati spectator
pemeriksa examiner, inspector
pemilih voter, elector
pemindahan removal, transfer (n.)
pemukul hammer
penambat subordinate, subordinating (gram.)
penanam planter
penasihat adviser
pencukur shaver, barber, hairdresser
pencuri thief
pencurian theft
pendaftar registrar
pendaftaran registration
pendapatan income
péndék short, brief
péndékkan (meméndékkan) to shorten, to abbreviate
pendengar listener
pendengaran hearing
pendidikan education (72)
penduduk inhabitant
penerangan enlightenment, illumination
penerbangan flight, aviation
penerima receiver, recipient
pengadil judge
pengajar instructor
pengajaran instruction (teaching)
pengangkutan transport
pengarah director
pengarang author, writer
pengawal controller, comptroller
pengelola organiser
pengembalian restoration, restitution
pengerusi chairman
pengetahuan knowledge
pengetua principal (n.)
penggali spade
pengganas terrorist
penggantian substitution
penghabisan end, conclusion
penghulu district headman
pengikut follower
pengkalan (**also**: *pangkalan*) landing-place, anchorage, base (mil.)
pengurus manager
pengurus pentas stage-manager
pengurusan management
pening dizzy
penjadian formation
penjara jail, prison
penjual seller, salesman
penolong helper, assistant
penoréh tapper
penoréh getah rubber-tapper
pénsél pencil
pensyarah lecturer
pensyarah kanan senior lecturer
pentas platform, stage (152)
penuhi (memenuhi) to fill
penting important
penulis writer
penunjuk pointer, indicator, sign-post
penuntut student
penyapu broom
penyeberangan crossing, transition

penyimpanan store, depot
penyokong supporter
penyuruh commander
peperiksaan examination
perabot furniture
Perancis French
perang war
perasaan feeling, opinion
peratus (a) hundredth; per cent (172)
perbaiki (memperbaiki) to repair
perbandingan comparison
perbelanjaan expenditure
perbendaharaan treasury
perbudakkan (memperbudakkan) to treat as a child
perbuatan deed, action, verb
percakapan conversation
percaya to believe
percayai (mempercayai) to trust
percayakan to trust
perdagangan commerce, trade
perdana principal (adj.)
Perdana Menteri Prime Minister
perdelapan (an) eighth (172)
perdĕwakan (memperdĕwakan) to treat as a god, to idolise, to deify
perekat gum, glue
perĕkonomian economics; economic
perenam (a) sixth (172)
pergandaan reduplication
pergi to go
pergunakan (mempergunakan) to make use of
perguruan teacher-training
perhatian attention
perhatikan (memperhatikan) to take note of, to pay attention to (194)
perhentian station, stop, halt (n.)
perhentikan (memperhentikan) to stop (tr.)
perhubungan relationship, communication(s)

periksa (memeriksa) to examine, to inspect
peristerikan (memperisterikan) to marry (of a man), to take to wife
perjalanan journey, trip
perkahwinan marriage, wedding
perkakas furniture, equipment
perkapalan shipping, navigation
perkara thing, affair, matter, subject
perkataan word
perkatakan (memperkatakan) to talk about
perkembangan development, flowering
perkenankan (memperkenankan) to grant, to agree to, to allow
perkhidmatan service
perkuat (memperkuat) to reinforce
perkuatkan to reinforce
perlahan-lahan slowly
perlakukan (memperlakukan) (sebagai) to regard (as), to treat as
perlima (a) fifth (172)
Perlis Perlis
permainan game, toy
permintaan request
permulaan beginning (n.), commencement
permusuhan enmity, hostility
peronda (military) patrol
perosakan destruction, damage
perpuluhan (decimal) point (172)
perpustakaan library
persatuan unity, union, association
persatukan (mempersatukan) to unite, to unify
persekolahan schooling
persekutuan federation
Persekutuan Tanah Melayu Federation of Malaya (cf. Lesson 1, Section E, Note***)
persembunyian shelter, hiding-place

persilakan (mempersilakan) to invite, to request
persimpangan crossroads
pertahanan defence
pertahankan (mempertahankan) to defend
pertanian agriculture, cultivation
pertanyaan question, inquiry
pertiga (a) third (172)
pertujuh (a) seventh (172)
pertunjukkan (mempertunjukkan) to exhibit, to demonstrate
perusahaan industry
peti (large) box
peti surat letter-box
pihak side (in a contest, etc.)
pihak pembangkang the opposition (party)
pilih (memilih) to choose, to select, to elect
pilihan election, choice
pilihanraya general election
pindaan change (n.), amendment
pinjamkan (meminjamkan) to lend
pintu door
pita tape, ribbon
pohon tree
pohon (memohon) to request
pokok tree
pokok getah rubber-tree
polis police
pos post, mail
pos udara airmail
potong (memotong) to cut, to cut off
potongan cut (n.), style, shape
présidén president
puan madam, Mrs; you (54) (179)
puas hati satisfied (adj.)
puaskan (memuaskan) to satisfy
puaskan hati (memuaskan hati) to satisfy, to be satisfactory
pucuk shoot, bud; cl. for guns, letters
pukul o'clock (45)
pukul (memukul) to strike, to beat
pula actually (209)
pulau island
pun even, also (210) (211)
pun...juga also (63) (210)
pungut (memungut) to collect
pustaka book (65)
putih white
putus snapped, severed, broken
putusi (memutusi) to break off, to snap, to sever (tr.)
putuskan (memutuskan) to decide

R

Rabu Wednesday
radio radio
raga basket
rahimahullah (Arabic) may God have mercy on him (174)
rahmatullah (Arabic) the mercy of God (174)
raja king
rajakan (merajakan) to make (into a) king
rakamkan (merakamkan) to record
rakyat the people
ramai many (of people), crowded
rasmi official (adj.)
ratus hundred
raya public
rayakan (merayakan) to celebrate
rendah low, primary (education)
rendahkan (merendahkan) to lower, to humble
rendahkan diri (merendahkan diri) to lower oneself, to humble oneself
ribu thousand
ribut storm
ringkas brief
ringkasan summary

rokok cigarette
ронggéng ronggeng (a Malay dance)
rosak broken down, damaged, out of order
rosakkan (merosakkan) to damage, to destroy
roti bread
rumah house
rumah sakit hospital
rumahtangga home
Rumi Roman (adj.); Roman script
rundingan discussion
rundingkan (merundingkan) to discuss (125)
runtuh to collapse (of houses, etc.)
rupanya apparently

S

sahabat friend (176)
sahaja only (28)
sain (coll) to sign (181)
sains science (64)
sakit ill, sick (116) (117)
sakit teruk seriously ill
saksi witness (n.)
saksikan (menyaksikan) to witness
salah guilt, mistake, guilty, wrong
sama together with
sama ... dengan as ... as ... (2a)
sama sendirinya between ourselves, etc. (146)
sambil and (218)
sambut (menyambut) to welcome
sampai to arrive
sampan boat
sampul surat envelope (n.)
sangat very very much (8)
sapu to sweep, wipe
sapu tangan handkerchief
satu one
satukan (menyatukan) to unite, to unify
saudara friend (m.) colleague, you (55) (176)
saudari friend (f.) (176)
sawah (cf. *bendang*) rice field
saya I, me, my [South Malaysian Peninsular]
sayang darling, beloved
sayur (green) vegetable(s)
sayur-sayuran all kinds of (green) vegetables
se- one as (30)
sebab (n.) cause, reason
sebab (conj. and prep.) because, because of (127)
sebabkan (menyebabkan) to cause
sebagai as
sebaik-baiknya as well as possible
sebanyak as much as, to the extent
sebelah side
sebelum before, by (time) (123)
sebenarnya truly
secepat-cepatnya as quickly as possible
sedang (side of progressive action)
sedap tasty, nice
sedia ready
sediakan (menyediakan) to prepare (tr.)
sedikit a little (quantity of)
sehingga until (128)
sejarah annals, history
sejuta a million
sekali once
sekali lagi once again
sekalian all (162) the...-est (4)
sekarang now
sekiranya if, if by any chance (16) (17)
sekolah school
sekolah menengah secondary school
sekolah rendah primary school
sekolah tinggi, universiti university
selalu always
selam cf. kapal selam

selama as long as, all the while (conj.) (191)
selamat peace, safety
selamat jalan peace on the road
selamat tinggal stay in peace
semacam like (prep.) as if (192)
semakin...semakin... the more... the more... (32)
semalam yesterday, last night (35)
sembahyang to pray
sembunyikan (menyembunyikan) to hide (tr.)
semenjak since (180)
sementara while (189)
sempat opportunity
sempit narrow
semua all
semuanya all of them, all of it
semula again (as before)
sén cent
senang easy
senapang gun
sendikata conjunction (gram.)
sendikata penambat subordinating conjunction (gram.)
sendiri self
seni fine art (conjunction) (gram.)
seni lukis painting (as an art)
senjata weapon
seolah-olah as if (192)
sepak (menyepak) to kick
sepak raga Malay football
sepanjang the whole length of, as long as
sepanjang hari all day long
separuh (a) half, some, a few (172)
seperlima (a) fifth
sepuluh ten
serah (menyerah) to surrender (tr.)
serah diri (menyerah diri) to surrender (intr.)
serahkan (menyerahkan) to surrender (tr.)

serahkan diri (menyerahkan diri) to surrender (intr.)
serambi verandah (Malay-style)
serang (menyerang) to attack
seratus a hundred
seraya and (218)
Seri Paduka Baginda His Majesty (164)
seribu a thousand
seronok (adj.) enjoyable, merry, having a good time
serta and (218)
sertakan (menyertakan) to forward, to send on
sesudah after (conj.); after (prep. of time) (124)
sesungguhnya really
setelah after (conj.); after (prep. of time) (124)
setem stamp (postage)
setengah (a) half, some, a few (172)
setiausaha secretary
Setiausaha Tetap Permanent Secretary
seumpama as if (192)
si anu so-and-so
si polan so-and-so
siapa who
siapa-siapa anyone, anybody (167)
siaran broadcast (n.) programme (radio)
siasah politics
sidang session; (plural sign) (162)
sifatkata adverb (gram.)
sifatnama adjective (gram.)
sijil certificate
Sijil Persekolahan School Certificate
sila please (40)
simpan (menyimpan) to put away, to keep
simpan kereta (menyimpan kereta) to park a car
simpang crossroads
Singapura Singapore

soal question
soalan question
sokong (menyokong) to support
sokongan support (n.)
songkok Malay cap
studio studio
suami husband
suara voice
suatu one, a, an
sudah finished; (sign of perfect) (27)
suka to like
suka hati please, happy
sukacita happiness, joy
suku (a) quarter
sungai river
sungguh true; truly, very (8)
sungguhpun...tetapi... although (110) (119)
supaya in order to, in order that (130)
surat letter
surat balasan reply (to a letter) (n.)
suratkhabar newspaper
surau (Muslim) chapel
suruh (menyuruh) to order, to command, to tell
suruhan command (n.), order (n.)
susah difficult
susun (menyusun) to arrange, to compile
sutera silk
syarahan lecture (n.)
syarikat society, association
syarikat kerjasama co-operative society

T

tadi just now
-tah (emphatic question particle) (208)
tahan (menahan) to bear, to endure
tahu know (French: savoir)
tahun year
tahun depan next year
tahunan yearly (adj.); annual
taip (menaip) to type
tajam sharp, keen
tak not, no
tak apa it does not matter (cf. French: ca ne fait rien)
tak berapa not very (10)
tak dan (coll.) to have no time to
tak sempat to have no opportunity to, to have no time to
takut (to be) afraid
takuti (menakuti) to be afraid of
takutkan (menakutkan) to frighten
tali line, cord, string, rope
tali air canal
telekom telecommunications
telefon telephone
tamatkan (menamatkan) to terminate (tr.) to conclude (tr.)
tambahan addition; affix (gram.)
tanah land, earth, soil
Tanah Melayu Malaya (cf. Lession 1, Section E, Note***)
tanahair motherland, fatherland
tanam (menanam) to plant (86)
tanamkan (menanamkan) to bury, to inter
tanda sign, mark
tandatangan signature
tandatangani (menandatangani) to sign (181)
tangan hand, arm, sleeve
tangga ladder, stairs
tangis (menangis) to weep, to cry
tanpa without (prep.)
tapi (coll.) (cf. *tetapi*) but
tari (menari) to dance
tarian dance (n.)
tarik to pull
tarikh date (n.)
tatkala when (189)
taukeh towkay, Chinese businessman

349

tawarikh history
tebing bank (e.g. of a river)
téh tea
tekanan stress, emphasis
tekankan (menekankan) to stress, to emphasise
telaga well (n.)
telah (sign of perfect or past) (41) (93)
témbak (menémbak) to shoot
tembok wall (n.)
tengah hari noon, midday
tenggara south-east
téngok (menéngok) to see, to look at
tentang about, regarding (125)
tentera army, military force
tentera laut navy
tentera udara air force
tentu certain, sure
teori pendidikan educational theory
terang bright, clear
terangkan (menerangkan) to explain, to clarify
teranglah bahawa... it is clear that...
(tiada) terbaca illegible, unreadable (105)
terbang to fly
terbesar very big, very large (109)
(tiada) terbilang uncountable, countless (105)
terbit to rise (of the sun), to be issued, to be published
terbitkan (menerbitkan) to publish
terbuka open (adj.) (106) (107)
tergelincir to slip
terhunus drawn, unsheathed (106) (107)
terima (menerima) to receive
terima kasih thank you (126)
teringat to remember (suddenly)
terjatuh to fall (99)
terjatuh tangga to fall downstairs
terjun to jump downwards (intr.)

terkarang complied, composed (106) (107)
terkejut (to be) startled
terlalu too (much) (9) (111)
terlambat too late (109)
terlampau too much, excessively, too (9) (111)
terlanggar to crash into, to collide with to run over (104)
terluka to be injured, to be cut (wounded)
terlukis drawn, painted (106) (107)
terlupa to forget (99) (100)
termasyhur very famous (109)
ternampak to catch sight of, to spot
(tiada) terpakai unwearable, unusable
terpaksa to be forced, to be compelled (108)
terputus-putus broken, interrupted
teruk acute, severe, serious (of illness)
tersembunyi hidden, concealed (106) (107)
tersenyum to smile
tersimpang to go off at a tangent, to run off the road, to swerve
tertahan to be able to hear
(tiada) tertahan unbearable, intolerable
tertawa to laugh
tertinggal to leave behind, to get left behind (165)
tertulis written (106) (107)
tertutup closed (adj.) (106) (107)
terus straight (on), direct
teruskan (meneruskan) to go on with, to continue with
tetamu guest, visitor (82)
tetap definite, permanent
tetapi but (118-120) (218)
tetapkan (menetapkan) to make definite, to fix
tiada not (**tiada** or **tidak ada**)
tiang pole, post, pillar

tiap-tiap each, every
tiap-tiap hari daily (adv.), every day
tiap-tiap pagi every morning
tiba to arrive
tiba-tiba suddenly
tidak no, not (93)
tidak berapa not very (10)
tidak berkeputusan endless, interminable
tidak terpakai unwearable, unusable
tidak tertahan to be unable to bear
tiket ticket
timba bucket, pail
timbalan deputy
tindakan action (e.g. "for action" — **untuk tindakan**)
tinggal to stay, to remain, to live (dwell)
tinggalkan (meninggalkan) to leave, to leave behind (165)
tinggi high, tall, long (of noses)
tingkap window
tingkat floor, storey
tolak (menolak) to push, to reject
tolong (menolong) to help, to assist
tolongan help (n.) assistance
tong crate
tongkat stick
topi hat
toreh (menoreh) to tap (rubber)
tua old (of people)
tuan lord, sir, Mr; you (53)
tugas role, duty, task
Tuhan God
tujuan aim
tukang workman, artisan (220)
tukang besi blacksmith
tukang cap printer
tukang cukur barber, hairdresser
tukang daging butcher
tukang emas goldsmith
tukang gunting barber, hairdresser
tukang kasut shoemaker

tukang kayu carpenter
tukang kebun gardener
tukang masak cook-boy
tukang ukir sculptor
tulis (menulis) to write
tulisan writing (n.), script
tulisan Jawi Jawi script, Arabic script
tulisan Rumi Rumi script, Roman script
tumpangkan (menumpangkan) to accommodate, to put up
tunggu (menunggu) to wait
tunjukkan (menunjukkan) to point out, to show
turun to descend (intr.), to go down, to come down
turuni (menuruni) to descend (tr.), to go down (tr.), to come down (tr.)
turunkan (menurunkan) to take down, to bring down, to lower
tutup to close, to shut

U

ubat medicine
ucap (mengucap) to pronounce, to express, to utter (126)
ucapan (a) speech
ucapkan (mengucapkan) to pronounce, to express, to utter (126)
udang prawn
udara air, sky
ugama religion
ugama Islam Islam
ulang kaji revision
ulang tahun anniversary
ulangkan (mengulangkan) to repeat
umur age
undang-undang law
undi vote
universiti universiti
untuk for, in order to

urus to manage, to arrange
urusan business
uruskan to manage, to arrange

W

wakili to represent
waktu time
walaupun even if
wang money
warna colour
wartawan journalist

wayang puppet, puppet show
wayang gambar film, picture

Y

ya yes
yang which, who
yang akan datang future (adj.)
yang ini this one
yang lain the other one, the others
yang lalu last, past

Appendix B
English-Malay Vocabulary

The following vocabulary contains the English equivalents, arranged alphabetically, of all the Malay words used in the course. The Arabic numerals in parentheses, e.g. (123), refer to the grammar sections in the body of the course. It is advisable to refer to the appropriate grammatical section before using any word which has such a number next to it.

A

abbreviate, to pendekkan (memendekkan)
able, to be boléh
about (concerning) darihal, tentang (125)
accept (a proposal), to luluskan (meluluskan)
accommodate, to tumpangkan (menumpangkan)
according to mengikut
accounts, by all khabarnya
acquaintance kenalan
action tindakan (e.g. "for action" — untuk tindakan); *(deed)* perbuatan
active pantas
actor pelakon .
acute (of illness) teruk
address (n.) alamat
address, to arahkan (mengarahkan)
admonish, to ingati (mengingati) (177)
advantage kebaikan
adverb sifatkata
advice nasihat
advise, to nasihatkan (menasihatkan)
adviser penasihat
aeroplane kapal terbang
affair perkara
affairs perkara-perkara, urusan
affix tambahan
afraid takut

afraid I don't know, I'm kurang periksa (7)
afraid of, to be takuti (menakuti)
after lepas (124); *(behind)* di belakang; *(time)* setelah, sesudah, selepas (124)
afterwards lepas itu (124)
again sekali lagi; *(as before)* semula
Agency, Language and Literature Déwan Bahasa dan Pustaka (65)
ago dahulu
agree, to bersetuju
agree to, to perkenankan (memperkenankan)
agriculture pertanian
aid (n.) tolongan
air (n.) udara
air, to jemur (menjemur) (84)
air force tentera udara
aircraft kapal terbang
airfield padang terbang
airmail pos udara
airport lapangan terbang
all semua, sakalian (162)
all day long sepanjang hari
all gone (finished) habis
all of it semuanya
all of them semuanya
all right baiklah
allow, to benarkan (membenarkan), perkenankan (memperkenankan)
almost hampir-hampir

353

also pun ... juga (63)
also, and dan lagi
although sungguhpun (110) (119); meskipun (120), walaupun (118)
always selalu
amendment pindaan
amok, to run amuk (mengamuk)
among di antara
among (ourselves, etc.) sama sendirinya (146)
anchor, to (intr.) berlabuh
anchor, to drop berlabuh
anchorage pangkalan (pengkalan); labuhan; pelabuhan
and dan, dengan; lalu; seraya; serta; sambil; lagi (218) (97)
and also dan lagi
and then lalu (97)(218)
annals sejarah
anniversary ulang tahun
annoy, to kacau (mengacau)
annual (adj.) tahunan
annually tiap-tiap tahun
answer (n.) jawapan, *(letter)* balasan; surat balasan
answer, to jawab (menjawab)
anthem, national lagu kebangsaan
any mana-mana (167)
any at all mana-mana pun
anybody siapa-siapa, siapa pun (167)
anyone siapa, siapa pun (167)
anything apa-apa, apa pun (167)
apparently rupanya; agaknya (92)
approach, to (tr.) dekati (mendekati)
archipelago gugusan pulau-pulau (137)
architect ahli bangunan
arithmetic ilmu hisab
arm lengan; tangan
arm oneself with, to bersenjatakan
armed, to be bersenjata
armed with, to be bersenjatakan
army tentera

around (prep.) di keliling
arrange, to (compile) susun (menyusun); *(organise)* atur (mengatur); *(manage)* urus (mengurus), uruskan (menguruskan)
arrangement (compilation) susunan; *(organisation)* susunan; aturan
arrest, to tangkap (menangkap)
arrival kedatangan; datangnya
arrive, to sampai, tiba
arrive at, to datangi (mendatangi)
art (fine art) seni
art gallery dewan seni lukis
as (prep.) sebagai, semacam
as ... (as) se- (30)
as ... as ... sama ... dengan ... (29)
as if semacam, seumpama, seolah-olah (192)
ascend, to (tr.) naiki (menaiki)
Asia Asia
Asia, South-east Asia Asia Tenggara
ask (inquire), to bertanya
ask about, to bertanyakan
ask for, to minta (meminta)
assembly majlis
assist, to tolong (menolong); bantu (membantu)
assistance tolongan
assistant penolong, pembantu
association persatuan
astonish, to hairankan (menghairankan)
astonished (adj.) hairan
at di; pada (45)
attack, to serang (menyerang);*(metaphorically)* datangi (mendatangi)
attend to, to selesaikan (menyelesaikan)
attention perhatian
attention (to), to pay perhatikan (memperhatikan)
attract, to tarik (menarik) (42)
audible kedengaran (165)
author pengarang

automatically dengan sendirinya (146)
aviation penerbangan

B

back, at the di belakang
bad (wicked) jahat
bad-mannered kurang ajar (7)
bank (of river, etc.) tebing
bank (for money) bank (pron. béng)
bank on, to berharapkan; harapkan (mengharapkan)
barber tukang cukur, tukang gunting, pencukur
base (military) pangkalan (pengkalan)
based on, to be berdasarkan
basis dasar
basis, to have as a berdasarkan
basket raga
bathroom bilik mandi
be, to (exist) ada; *(copula)* ialah (159); *(become)* jadi (menjadi)
be able, to boléh
be going to, to hendak; (coll.) nak
beach pantai
bear (tolerate), to tahan (menahan)
beard janggut
beard, to have a berjanggut
bearded (adj.) berjanggut
bearer pembawa (141)
beautiful cantik
beauty kecantikan
beauty specialist ahli kecantikan
because kerana, oléh kerana; sebab, oléh sebab (127)
because of kerana, oléh kerana; sebab, oléh sebab (127)
become, to jadi (menjadi)
before (prep. and conj.) (time) sebelum; *(place,* i.e. in front of*)* di depan (123)
before (adv.) (formerly) dahulu (123)
begin, to (tr.) mulakan (memulakan); mulai (memulai) (151)
begin, to (intr.) bermula; mulai (151)
beginning permulaan
beginning, in (at) the mula-mula
behind (ad. and prep.) di belakang
believe, to percaya
beloved (n.) kekasih
better, had baik with vb.
better not, had baik jangan with vb.
between di antara
between (ourselves, etc.) sama sendirinya (146)
bicycle basikal
big besar
big, very terbesar (109)
bird burung
bit, a (a little quantity) sedikit
bitter pahit
bitterness kepahitan
black hitam
blood darah
bloom, to berkembang
blouse blaus
blouse, to wear a berbaju
blue biru
board (council) déwan, lembaga; *(plank)* papan
boast, to besarkan diri (membesarkan diri)
boat sampan
boatswain jurubatu
bomb bom
book buku; pustaka
bookshop kedai buku-buku
both kedua; keduanya; kedua-duanya (157) (158)
bottle botol
bottle-opener pembuka botol
bottom (of), at the di bawah
bowl mangkuk
box (small) kotak; *(large: crate)* tong; *(case)* peti

355

boy budak lelaki
bread roti
break (damage), to rosakkan (merosakkan)
break (smash), to pecahkan (memecahkan)
break (snap), to putuskan (memutuskan)
break off, to putusi (memutusi)
brief (adj.) ringkas
bright (clear) terang; *(intelligent)* cerdik
bring, to bawa (membawa)
bring (cause), to datangkan (mendatangkan)
bring about, to datangkan (mendatangkan)
bring down, to turunkan (menurunkan)
bring forward, to kemukakan (mengemukakan)
bring near, to dekatkan (mendekatkan)
bring up, to naikkan (menaikkan)
broad lebar
broadcast (n.) (radio) siaran
broaden, to lébar
broken (fractured) patah
broken (smashed) pecah
broken (snapped) putus
broken (of voices sobbing) terputus-putus
broken down (out of order) rosak
broom penyapu
brother (elder) abang
brother (young) adik
brothers (collective) adik-beradik
brothers and sisters adik-beradik
bucket timba
build, to bangunkan (membangunkan)
building bangunan
building (official or royal) balai
bullet peluru
bullock-cart keréta lembu
bury, to tanamkan (menanamkan)
bury (the dead), to kuburkan (menguburkan)

bus bas
business urusan (163)
but tetapi; tapi; melainkan (218)
butcher tukang daging
butter mentéga
buy, to beli (membeli)
buyer pembeli
by (agent) oléh (88) (89); *(time)* sebelum (123)
by way of ikut (39)

C

calculate, to hisabkan (menghisabkan)
calculation hisab
call (name), to namakan (menamakan); namai (menamai)
call (summon), to panggil (memanggil)
call (n.) panggilan
can (vb.) boléh
canal tali air
candidate calon
cap (Malay style) songkok
cap (Malay style), to wear a bersongkok
car keréta; motokar
care, to hirau
careful! (be careful!) hati-hati!
carefully (dengan) baik-baik
carpenter tukang kayu
carpet hamparan
carriage keréta
carriage (railway) gerabak
carry, to bawa (membawa)
carry (on a pole), to kandar (mengandar)
carry (in the fingers), to bimbit (membimbit)
carry (on the hip), to dukung (mendukung)
cart keréta
case (box) peti, tong
case (court) perkara
cat kucing

catch, to tangkap (menangkap)
catch sight of, to ternampak; terlihat
catty (1-1/3 lb.) kati
cause (n.) sebab
cause, to sebabkan (menyebabkan); datangkan (mendatangkan)
celebrate (tr.), to rayakan (merayakan)
cent sén; duit
certain tentu
certainty ketentuan
chair kerusi
chairman pengerusi
chapel (Muslim) surau
chat, to berbual
chemist (scientist) ahli kimia
chemistry ilmu kimia
chief (n.) ketua
Chief Minister Ketua Menteri
child (infant) bayi; kanak-kanak
child (offspring) anak
child, to treat as a perbudakkan (memperbudakkan)
China negeri China
Chinese (adj.) Cina
Chinese (n.) orang Cina
Chinese (language) bahasa Cina
choose, to pilih
cigarette rokok
cinema panggung (152)
clarification keterangan
clarify (explain), to terangkan (menerangkan)
class darjah
classify, to bangsakan (membangsakan); jeniskan (menjeniskan)
clean, to cuci (mencuci); bersihkan (membersihkan)
clear terang; nyata
clear that..., it is teranglah bahawa... nyatalah bahawa... (121)
clerk kerani
clever pandai (25)

cleverness kepandaian
climb, to panjat (memanjat); naiki (menaiki)
close, to tutup (menutup)
close (a meeting), to tamatkan (menamatkan)
closed (adj.) tertutup (106) (107)
cloth kain
clothes pakaian
clothes-horse kuda-kuda
clothing pakaian
cluster (n.) gugus; gugusan (137)
coat baju
coat, to wear a berbaju
Code, Highway Panduan Jalan Raya
collapse (of houses, etc.), to runtuh
colleague saudara (55)
collect, to pungut (memungut)
college maktab (65)
College, Day Training Maktab Perguruan Harian (55)
collide (with), to berlanggar (dengan) (104)
collide with, to terlanggar (104)
colour warna
come! (imperative) mari!
come, to datang
come back, to balik, pulang, kembali
come home, to balik, pulang, kembali
come in, to masuk
come on let's... marilah kita...!
come out, to keluar
come to (tr.), to datangi (mendatangi)
come up, to naik
comfort (n.) kesenangan
command (n.) suruhan
command, to suruh (menyuruh)
commander penyuruh
commence (tr.), to mulakan (memulakan); mulai (memulai) (151)
commence (intr.), to bermula; mulai (151)
commerce perdagangan
committee jawatankuasa

committee member ahli jawatankuasa
communications perhubungan
comparison perbandingan
compel, to paksa (memaksa) (108)
compelled, to be terpaksa (108)
compile, to susun (menyusun); karang (mengarang)
compiled (adj.) terkarang (106) (107)
complete (finish), to habiskan (menghabiskan)
complex (adj.) (gram.) berkait
complex sentence ayat berkait
compose, to karang (mengarang)
composed (adj.) terkarang (106) (107)
composition (essay) karangan
compound (adj.) (gram.) berlapis
compound sentence ayat berlapis
comptroller pengawal
concerning (about) darihal; tentang (125)
conclude (tr.), to tamatkan (menamatkan)
conclusion (end) penghabisan
condition (state) keadaan
congregation jumaat
conjunction (gram.) sendikata
connexion with, in berkenaan dengan (125)
construction (building) pembangunan
controller pengawal
conversation percakapan
cook, to masak (memasak)
cook-boy kuki
co-operation kerjasama
co-operative society syarikat kerjasama
cord tali
correct (adj.) betul
correct, to betulkan (membetulkan)
correspond with each other, to berkirim-kiriman
cost, it harganya (212e)
council déwan; majlis
count, to bilang (membilang)
countless tiada terbilang (105)

country negeri
course (of study) kursus
course, of mémang
court (of law) mahkamah
cow lembu; lembu betina
crash into, to terlanggar; langgar (melanggar (104)
cross over, to menyeberang
crossing (n.) penyeberangan
crossroads simpang; persimpangan
crowded ramai
cry (weep), to tangis (menangis)
cry on each other's shoulders, to bertangis-tangisan
cultural kebudayaan
culture kebudayaan
cup cawan
cup (without handles) mangkuk
cupboard almari
curry gulai
cut (n.) (style) potongan
cut (hurt), to be terluka
cut (off), to potong (memotong)

D

daily (adj.) harian (65)
daily (adv.) tiap-tiap hari
damage (n.) kerosakan
damage, to rosakkan (merosakkan)
damaged (adj.) rosak
damp lembap
dance (n.) tarian
dance, to tari (menari)
dangerous merbahaya
darling kekasih
date (n.) tarikh
dated, to be bertarikh
daughter anak perempuan
day hari
day, every tiap-tiap hari
day, this very hari ini juga

day-dream, to berangan-angan
Day Training College Maktab Perguruan Harian
dead mati
dear (expensive) mahal
death kematian
death (of kings, etc.) kemangkatan (127: Note)
decease (of Kings, ect.) kemangkatan (127: Note)
decision keputusan
decrease (tr.), to kurangkan (mengurangkan)
deed (action) perbuatan
deep dalam
deepen (tr.), to dalamkan (mendalamkan)
defence pertahanan
defend, to pertahankan (mempertahankan)
definite tetap
deify, to perdéwakan (memperdéwakan)
demise (of kings, etc.) kemangkatan (127: Note)
demonstrate, to pertunjukkan (mempertunjukkan)
depart, to (of ships, trains, etc.) bertolak
department jabatan
depot penyimpanan
depth kedalaman; dalamnya (212d)
deputy timbalan
descent (tr.), to turuni (menuruni)
desire (n.) kehendak
destroyer (ship) kapal pembinasa
destruction perosakan
development perkembangan; pembangunan
dictionary kamus
die, to mati; (**of kings**) mangkat; meninggal; meninggal dunia, kembali ke rahmatullah, kembali ke darulbaka (174) (127: Note)

different lain
difficult susah
difficulty kesusahan
dig, to gali (menggali)
diminish (tr.), to kurangkan (mengurangkan)
dining-room bilik makan
dinner makan malam
direct (adj. and adv.) terus
direct, to arahkan (mengarahkan)
director pengarah
discard, to buang (membuang)
discuss (tr.), to rundingkan (merundingkan) (125)
discussion (n.) rundingan
discussion, to have a berunding (125)
dismiss (sack), to keluarkan (mengeluarkan)
distance kejauhan
distant jauh
district daérah
district officer pegawai daérah
ditch parit
dizziness kepeningan
dizzy pening
do, to buat (membuat)
doctor doktor
dog anjing
doll anak-anak
done (finished) (adj.) selesai
door pintu
dossier fail
Drainage and Irrigation Department Jabatan Parit dan Tali Air
drama (play) drama
draughtsman pelukis
draw (pictures), to lukis (melukis)
draw (a sword), to hunus (menghunus) (106-108)
drawing (n.) lukisan
drawn (of pictures) (adj.) terlukis (106-108)

drawn (of swords) (adj.) terhunus (106-108)
dream (n.) mimpi
dream, to bermimpi
dream about, to bermimpikan
dress (n.) baju
dress, to wear a berbaju
drink (n.) minuman
drink, to minum (meminum)
drive (a car), to bawa (membawa)
drop (tr.), to jatuhkan (menjatuhkan)
drunk (intoxicated), mabuk
dry (in the sun), to (tr.) jemur (menjemur) (48)
duck itik
durian buah durian
duty (task) tugas
duty (tax) cukai

E

each tiap-tiap
ear telinga
early awal
early in the morning pagi-pagi (169)
Earth (the planet) bumi
earth (soil) tanah
ease (n.) kesenangan
easy senang
eat, to makan (memakan) (34)
economic perékonomian (163)
economics perékonomian (163)
economy (system of) perékonomian (163)
education pelajaran; **(as a science)** ilmu pendidikan (72)
Egypt Mesir
eight delapan, lapan
eigthteen delapan belas, lapan belas
eighteenth (adj.) kedelapan belas
eighth (adj.) kedepalan
eighth (n.), an seperdelapan (172)
elder brother abang

elder sister **kakak**
elect, to pilih (memilih)
election pilihan
election, general pilihanraya
elector pemilih
elephant gajah
emergency darurat
eminent utama
emphasis tekanan
emphasise, to tekankan (menekankan); beratkan (memberatkan)
employ, to pekerjakan (memperkerjakan)
employee pekerja (182)
employment pekerjaan
end (n.) akhir, penghabisan
end, in the akhirnya
endless tidak berkeputusan
endure (tr.), to tahan (menahan)
enemy musuh
energetic pantas
engineer jurutera
England negeri Inggeris, England
English (adj.) Inggeris
English (language) bahasa Inggeris
Englishman orang Inggeris
enjoyable seronok
enlarge, to besarkan (membesarkan)
enlargement pembesaran
enlightenment penerangan
enmity permusuhan
enough cukup
enquire (ask), to bertanya
enquire about, to bertanyakan
enquire into, to periksa (memeriksa)
enquiry pertanyaan
enter, to masuk
enter (tr.), to masuki (memasuki)
entered, to be kemasukan (165)
entomb, to kuburkan (menguburkan)
envelope (n.) sampul surat
epic (n.) hikayat
equip, to lengkapkan (melengkapkan) **(197)**

equip oneself, to berlengkap (197)
equip oneself with, to berlengkapkan (197)
equipped (adj.) lengkap (197)
-er (comparative suffix) cf. (1)
erect, to bangunkan (membangunkan)
error salah
essay (n.) karangan
-est (superlative suffix) cf. (1)
ethnologist ahli ilmu bangsa-bangsa
European (n.) Orang Putih
even (adv.) pun
even if walaupun (118)
event kejadian
every tiap-tiap
evil (adj.) jahat
examination peperiksaan
examine, to periksa (memeriksa)
examiner pemeriksa
example contoh
excuse oneself, to minta diri (meminta diri) (146)
exercise (n.) latihan
exhibit, to pertunjukkan (mempertunjukkan)
exhibition pertunjukan
expel, to keluarkan (mengeluarkan)
expenditure perbelanjaan
expense belanja
expensive mahal
expert (n.) ahli; juru (220)
explain, to terangkan (menerangkan), nyatakan (menyatakan)
explanation keterangan
express, to ucap (mengucap); ucapkan (mengucapkan) (126)
external (foreign) luar negeri
extinguish, to padamkan (memadamkan)
extinguished (adj.) padam
extract, to cabut (mencabut)
eye mata

F

factory kélang (or: kilang)
fair (just) adil
fall, to jatuh; terjatuh (99)
fall, to let jatuhkan (menjatuhkan)
famous, masyhur
famous, very termasyhur (109)
fan kipas
far jauh
farmer peladang
fashion (manner) cara
fast (adj.) deras, cepat
fat (adj.) gemuk
father bapa, bapak, ayah (cf. Lesson 1, Section E, Note*)
fault salah
fear (tr.), to takuti (menakuti)
federal persekutuan
federation persekutuan
Federation of Malaya Persekutuan Tanah Melayu (cf. Lesson 1, Section E, Note***)
feel (intr.), to berasa
feeling (n.) perasaan
fence (n.) pagar
fenced, to be berpagar
fetch, to ambil (mengambil)
field (open) padang
fifteen lima belas
fifteenth (adj.) kelima belas
fifth (adj.) kelima
fifth (n.) a seperlima (172)
fifty lima puluh
file (dossier) fail
fill, to penuhi (memenuhi); isikan (mengisikan)
film, to gambar (menggambar)
finally akhirnya
finance (n.) kewangan
financial kewangan
find, to dapat (mendapati)

361

finger jari
finish (tr.), to habiskan (menghabiskan)
finished (done; all over) sudah; habis; selesai
finish off, to selesaikan (menyelesaikan)
fire (n.) api
fire, to (dismiss) keluarkan (mengeluarkan)
first, (the) (yang) pertama
first (of all) (adj.) dahulu; mula-mula
first, to put utamakan (mengutamakan)
fish ikan
five lima
fix, to (make definite) tetapkan (menetapkan)
flag bendéra
flashing, to keep on berkelip-kelip
flesh (meat) daging
flight (aviation) penerbangan
flight (journey by air) penerbangan
floor (of a room, etc.) lantai
floor (storey) tingkat
flow, to alir (mengalir)
flower (n.) bunga
flower, to berkembang
flower-pot pasu
flower-shop kedai bunga
fly, to terbang
fold, to lipat (melipat)
follow, to ikut (mengikut) (39)
follower pengikut
following (adj.) berikut
food makanan
foot kaki
football (Malay style) sépak raga
for bagi; untuk (129); di atas (126)
force, to (compel) paksa (memaksa) (108)
forced (compelled), to be terpaksa (108)
foreign (affairs, etc.) luar negeri
forget, to lupa, terlupa (99); lupakan (melupakan) (100)
form (shape) (n.) bentuk

form, to bentukkan (membentukkan)
formation (creation) penjadian
formerly dahulu
forward, to (send on) sertakan (menyertakan)
forward, to bring (put) kemukakan (mengemukakan)
four empat
fourteen empat belas
fourteenth (adj.) keempat belas
fourth (adj.) keempat
fractured (adj.) patah
France negeri Perancis
free (adj.) (independent) bébas; merdéka
free, to bébaskan (membébaskan)
freedom kebébasan; kemerdékaan
French (adj.) Perancis
French (language) bahasa Perancis
Frenchman orang Perancis
Friday hari Jumaat
frighten, to takutkan (menakutkan)
from dari; daripada
from inside dari dalam
front of, in di depan
fruit (n.) buah
fruits (collective) buah-buahan (137)
fruit market pasar buah-buahan
function (duty, task) tugas
furniture perkakas
furthermore lagi pula, lagipun
future (adj.) yang akan datang
future (n.) masa yang akan datang

G

game permainan
gaol penjara
garden kebun
gardener tukang kebun
geography ilmu alam
geologist ahli bumi
general (adj.) agung

general election pilihanraya
general meeting mesyuarat agung
get, to dapat (mendapat)
get up, to bangun; bangkit
girl (child) budak perempuan
girl (young woman) gadis
give, to (coll.) bagi; *(lit.)* beri (memberi), berikan (memberikan)
give back, to balas (membalas)
glue (n.) perekat
go, to pergi; jalan (43); berjalan
go back, to balik; pulang; kembali
go down, to turun
go down (tr.), to turuni (menuruni)
go home, to balik, pulang, kembali
go in, to masuk
go out, to keluar
go through with, to teruskan (meneruskan)
go up, to naik
go up (tr.), to naiki (menaiki)
god déwa
god, to treat as a perdéwakan (memperdéwakan) (194)
God Allah; Tuhan
going to, to be hendak, nak (23)
goldsmith tukang emas
good, baik
good at pandai (25)
good time, having a seronok
goodness kebaikan
goods barang
gone, all habis
government kerajaan
grain, a butir
grandfather datuk
grandmother nénék
grant, to perkenankan (memperkenankan)
grasp, to pegang (memegang)
grave (n.) kubur
green hijau

greet (welcome), to sambut (menyambut)
greet each other, to bersambutan
grey kelabu
grille kisi-kisi tingkap
guest tetamu (82)
guide (book) panduan
guilt salah; kesalahan
guilty salah
gum (n.) (glue) perekat
gun senapang
gun, to carry a bersenapang

H

hairdresser tukang gunting, tukang cukur, pencukur
half, a setengah, separuh (172)
hall dewan
hammer pemukul
hand tangan
hand-grenade bom tangan
handkerchief sapu tangan
handle pemegang
hang, to gantung (menggantung)
happiness bahagia; sukacita
happy suka hati, bersukacita
harbour labuhan, pelabuhan
hat topi
hat, to wear a bertopi
have, to ada
have to, to kena
he ia, dia (58); beliau (59); baginda
head (part of body) kepala
head (chief) ketua
head of department ketua pejabat; ketua jabatan
head office ibu pejabat (38)
headman, district penghulu
headman, village ketua kampung
headmaster guru besar
headmistress guru besar
headquarters ibu pejabat (38)

363

health kesihatan
healthy sihat
hear, to dengar (mendengar); terdengar (102) (103)
hearing (n.) pendengaran
heat, to hangatkan (menghangatkan)
heaviness keberatan
heavy berat
heed, to hirau
help (n.) tolong
help, to tolong (menolong), bantu (membantu)
helper penolong, pembantu
her dia (58); beliau (59); -nya (66)
here di sini
here (hither) ke sini
here is (cf. French: voici) ... ini dia
herewith bersama-sama ini
herself sendiri; diri, dirinya (146)
hibiscus bunga raya
hidden (adj.) tersembunyi
hide (tr.) to sembunyikan (menyembunyikan)
hide (intr.), to bersembunyi
hiding-place persembunyian
high tinggi
highway jalan raya
Highway Code Panduan Jalan Raya
hill bukit
him dia (58); beliau (59); -nya (66): baginda (163)
himself sendiri; diri, dirinya (146)
his dia (58); beliau (58) -nya; (66); baginda (163)
His Majesty Seri Paduka Baginda (164)
His Majesty's Service, On (O.H.M.S.) Urusan Seri Paduka Baginda (164)
historian ahli sejarah
history tawarikh, sejarah
hither ke sini
hold, to pegang (memegang)

hold (e.g. meetings, etc.) adakan (mengadakan)
holder pemegang
hole lubang
holiday (leave) cuti
holiday, to take a bercuti
home rumahtangga
home, at di rumah
honour (n.) hormat (162); hormatnya (179)
honour, to hormati (menghormati) (162)
honourable, (the) (yang) berhormat (162)
honoured (adj.) dihormati (162)
hope (n.) harap; harapan
hope, to berharap
hopes on, to set one's harapkan (mengharapkan); berharapkan
horse kuda
horse, clothes- kuda-kuda
horseback, to be on berkuda
hospital hospital
hostility permusuhan
hot (warm) hangat
hot (of curry, etc.) pedas
hour jam
house rumah
house, to have a berumah
House of Representatives Dewan Rakyat
how macam mana; bagaimana
how can that be? mana boléh?
how many berapa
how much berapa
humble oneself, to rendahkan diri (merendahkan diri)
hundred ratus
hundred, a seratus
hunger kelaparan
hungry lapar
hurt (wound) (tr.), to lukakan (melukakan)
husband suami

I

I saya (47) (48); aku (49); ku- (66)
idolise, to perdéwakan (memperdéwakan) (194)
if kalau (113); jika (114); jikalau (115); sekiranya (116) (117)
if, even walaupun (118)
if only lamun (132)
ill sakit
ill, seriously sakit teruk
ill-bred kurang ajar (7)
illegible tiada terbaca, tidak terbaca (105)
illumination penerangan
illustration gambaran
immediately lekas
important penting, utama
in di; dalam; di dalam
inaudible tiada kedengaran, tidak kedengaran
income pendapatan
income tax cukai pendapatan
independence kemerdékaan; kebébasan
independent merdéka; bébas
independent candidate calon bébas
Indian (adj.) India
Indian (n.) orang India
indicator penunjuk
industry perusahaan
inform, to beritahu (memberitahu), maklumkan (memaklumkan ((179)
in front of di depan
inhabitant penduduk
injure, to lukakan (melukakan)
injured (adj.) terluka
ink dakwat
in order that untuk (129); supaya (130)
in order to untuk (129); supaya (130)
in the middle of di tengah-tengah; di tengah
inquire (ask), to bertanya
inquire about, to bertanyakan
inquire into, to periksa (memeriksa)
inquiry pertanyaan
insert, to masukkan (memasukkan)
inside di dalam
inspector pemeriksa
institute (n.) maktab (65)
Institute, Language Maktab Perguruan Bahasa (65)
instruction (teaching) pengajaran
intelligent berakal, cerdik
inter, to kuburkan (menguburkan)
interesting menarik hati (42)
interior (of a country) dalam negeri
interminable tidak berkeputusan
international antarabangsa
interpreter jurubahasa
interrupted (adj.) terputus-putus
into ke dalam
intolerable tiada tertahan, tidak tertahan)
intoxicated mabuk
invisible tidak kelihatan
invitation jemputan
invite, to jemput (menjemput), persilakan (mempersilakan) (180)
iron besi
iron bar, an sebatang besi
Islam ugama Islam
issue, to (tr.) keluarkan (mengeluarkan)
issued, to be terbit
it-nya (69)
its -nya (69)
itself sendiri (146); diri, dirinya (146)

J

jacket baju, jaket
jacket, to wear a berbaju (kan jaket)
jacket, to use as a berbajukan
jackfruit buah nangka
jail penjara

Japan negeri Jepun
Japanese (adj.) Jepun
Japanese (n.) orang Jepun
Japanese (language) bahasa Jepun
jasmine bunga melur
journalist wartawan (83)
journey perjalanan
joy sukacita
judge hakim
judgement hukum
jump, to lompat (melompat)
jump down, to terjun
jump on (to), to lompati (melompati)
jump over, to lompat (melompat)
jungle hutan
just (fair) adil
just, to have baharu with vb.
just now tadi
justice (abstract) keadilan
Justice, Chief Hakim Besar

K

Kedah negeri Kedah
keep, to simpan (menyimpan)
keep left (road-sign) ikut kiri (39)
keep on with, to teruskan (meneruskan)
kick, to sépak (menyépak)
kill, to bunuh (membunuh)
killing (n.) pembunuhan
king raja
king (of), to make (a) rajakan (merajakan)
kitchen dapur
*know, to (*French: saviour*)* tahu, ketahui (mengetahui); **(**French: **connaitre)** kenal (mengenal)
knowledge pengetahuan
kris keris
kris, to carry a berkeris

L

laboratory makmal
labour buruh
ladder tangga
lamp pelita
land, native tanahair
landing-place pangkalan (pengkalan)
language bahasa
Language and Literature Agency Dewan Bahasa dan Pustaka
Language Institute Maktab Perguruan Bahasa
large besar
large, very terbesar (109)
last (past) yang lalu, lepas
last night semalam; malam semalam (35)
late lambat
late, too terlambat
latex getah
lattice kisi-kisi
laugh, to tertawa
lavatory jamban
law undang-undang
lay down, to letak (meletak)
laziness kemalasan
lazy segan; malas
leave (n.) cuti
leave (tr.), to tinggalkan (meninggalkan) (165)
leave (intro.), to (to ships, trains, etc.) bertolak
leave, to take (to be on) bercuti
leave, to take one's minta diri (meminta diri)
leave behind, to tertinggal; ketinggalan (165)
lecture (n.) syarahan
lecture, to bersyarah
lecturer pensyarah
lecturer, senior pensyarah kanan (73)

left (adj.) kiri
left behind, to be tertinggal; ketinggalan (165)
leg kaki
legs, to have berkaki
lend, to pinjamkan (meminjamkan)
length panjangnya (212d)
lengthen, to panjangkan (memanjangkan)
less kurang (3)
lesson pelajaran
let fall, to jatuhkan (menjatuhkan)
letter surat
letter-box peti surat
liberate, to bébaskan (membebaskan)
library perpustakaan, khutubkhanah
licence (n.) lésén
lift, to angkat (mengangkat)
lift (heavy objects), to angkut (mengangkut)
light (n.) (lamp) pelita
like (prep.) sebagai, semacam
like, to suka
line (cord) tali
linguist ahli bahasa
list daftar
listen, to dengar (mendengar) (102) (103)
listener pendengar
listeners (radio, etc.) sidang pendengar (162)
literature kesusasteraan
Literature Agency, Language and Déwan Bahasa dan Pustaka (65)
little kecil
little, a sedikit
live (be alive), to hidup
live (stay, dwell), to tinggal; duduk
liver hati (42)
long panjang
long as, as selama (189)
long time, for a lama
look, to lihat (melihat), tengok (menengok)

look at, to pandang (memandang), téngok (menéngok)
look for, to cari (mencari)
looks as if, it nampaknya (91)
lord tuan
lose, to kehilangan (165)
loss (n.) kehilangan (165)
lost (adj.) hilang
lot, a banyak
lottery loteri
love (n.) kasih
low (adj.) rendah
lower, to (make) rendahkan (merendahkan)
lower, to (let down) turunkan (menurunkan)
luggage barang-barang

M

machine mesin
madam puan (54) (179)
magazine majalah
magistrate hakim
magnify, to besarkan (membesarkan)
Majesty, His Seri paduka Baginda
majority, (the) kebanyakan
make, to buat (membuat)
Malay (adj.) Melayu
Malay (n.) orang Melayu
Malay (language) bahasa Melayu
Malay Archipelago Gugusan Pulau-pulau Melayu (137)
Malay football sépak raga
Malaya Malaya, Tanah Melayu (cf. Lesson 1, Section E, Note***)
Malaya, Federation of Persekutuan Tanah Melayu (cf. Lesson 1, Section E, Note***)
Malayan (adj.) Malaya
Malayan (n.) orang Malaya
man orang lelaki

manage, to urus (mengurus; uruskan (menguruskan)
manage to, to dapat
management pengurusan
manager pengurus
mangosteen buah manggis
manners, to have no kurang ajar (7)
many banyak; *(crowded)* ramai
mark (sign) (n.) tanda
mark (examination) (n.) markah
market pasar; *(large or abstract)* pasaran
market, world- pasaran dunia
marriage perkahwinan
marry, to peristerikan (memperisterikan)
matter (affair) perkara
matter, it doesn't tidak apa, tak apa
me saya (47) (48); aku (49); -ku (66)
meaning (n.) makna
means (that ...), it maknanya ...
meat daging
medicine ubat
meet (tr.), to jumpa
meet (intr.), to berjumpa
meeting (committee, etc.) mesyuarat
meeting, general mesyuarat agung
melodious merdu
member ahli (220)
memory ingatan
mend, to baikkan (membaikkan); baiki (membaiki)
merchandise (for sale) jualan
merry seronok
method cara
midday tengah hari
middle of, in the di tengah; di tengah-tengah
mile batu
mill kilang
million juta
million, a sejuta
minerals gali-galian

minister (govt.) menteri
Minister for Education Menteri Pelajaran
Minister, Prime Perdana Menteri
ministry kementerian (183)
minute (n.) minit
minutes (of a meeting) butir-butir
mistake (n.) salah
moist lembap
moisten, to lembapkan (melembapkan)
moment, (at) that very pada waktu itu juga
money duit, wang
moon bulan
month bulan
monthly (adj.) bulanan
monthly (adv.) tiap-tiap bulan
more lebih (1); lagi (5)
more ... the more ..., the lagi ... lagi ... ; makin ... makin ... ; semakin ... semakin ... (32)
morning pagi
morning, this pagi ini; **(past only)** pagi tadi (71)
mosque mesjid
most, the yang ... sekali (4)
mother emak, ibu, bonda (cf. Lesson 1, Section E, Note**)
motherland tanahair
motion (in a debate) cadangan
mountain gunung
move (house), to berpindah
Mr Tuan
Mrs Puan
much banyak
murder (n.) pembunuhan
murder, to bunuh (membunuh)
murderer pembunuh
Muslim (n.) orang Islam
Muslim, to be a berugama Islam
must mesti (36); kena
my saya (47) (48); aku (49); -ku (66)
myself sendiri (146); diri, diriku (146)

N

name (n.) nama
name, to namakan (menamakan); namai (menamai)
narrate, to ceritakan (menceritakan); ceriterakan (menceriterakan)
narrow sempit
narrowness kesempitan
nation bangsa
Nations, the United Bangsa-bangsa Bersatu
native land tanahair
naughty jahat; nakal
navigation perkapalan
navy tentera laut
near (adj. and adv.) dekat
near, to bring dekatkan (mendekatkan)
nearly hampir-hampir
necessary to (that), it is hendaklah
new baharu
news khabar, warta berita (83)
newspaper suratkhabar
newspaperman (journalist) wartawan
newspaperman (reporter) pemberita
next (then) (adv.) kemudian
next week minggu depan
next year tahun depan
night malam
night, last semalam; malam semalam (35)
night, to spend the bermalam
nine sembilan
nineteen sembilan belas
nineteenth kesembilan belas
ninth kesembilan
no (adv.) tidak, tak; bukan; tiada
noble (adj.) (of high birth) berbangsa
nobleman bangsawan
not tidak, tak; bukan; tiada
note of, to take perhatikan (memperhatikan) (194)
not very kurang (7); tidak berapa, tak berapa (10)
not yet belum; belum lagi; tidak lagi
now sekarang
nowhere di mana-mana pun tidak
number bilangan, nombor
numeral bilangan
nurse (n.) jururawat

O

obtain, to dapat (mendapat)
occasion (**French:** fois) kali
occupation (work) pekerjaan
ocean lautan
o'clock pukul (45)
office (place of work) pejabat (37)
office (position) jawatan
office, head ibu pejabat (38)
officer pegawai
official (adj.) rasmi
official (n.) pegawai
off to, to be hendak ke (coll.) nak ke
O.G.S. (On Government Service) Urusan Kerajaan
O.H.M.S. (On His Majesty's Service) Urusan Seri Paduka Baginda
O.K. baiklah
old (of people) tua
old (of things) lama
old, to be (ten years) berumur (sepuluh tahun)
on di; di atas; pada (45)
once sekali
once, at lekas
once again sekali lagi
one satu, se-, suatu
one's own sendiri (146)
oneself sendiri (146); diri, dirinya (146)
only sahaja
only, if lamun (132)
only then baharulah

open (adj.) terbuka (106) (107)
open, to buka (membuka)
opener pembuka
opener, bottle- pembuka botol
opening (the act of) pembukaan
operate (surgically) on, to bedah (membedah)
operation (surgical) pembedahan
opinion pandangan
opportunity peluang; sempat
oppose, to bangkang (membangkang)
opposer pembangkang
opposition (political) pihak pembangkang
or ataupun
order, to (command) suruh (menyuruh)
order that, in untuk (129); supaya (130)
order to, in untuk (129); supaya (130)
organise, to atur (mengatur)
organiser pengelola
other lain
other people orang lain
ought patut (122)
our kita (50); kami (51)
out (of lamps, etc.) padam
outlay belanja
outside di luar
own (adj.) sendiri (146)
own accord, of its dengan sendirinya
ox lembu

P

pail timba
paint (pictures), to lukis (melukis)
painted (adj.) (pictures) terlukis (106) (107)
painting (as an art) seni lukis
palace istana
paper kertas
parcel bungkusan
pare, to kupas (mengupas)
parents ibu bapa

park (a car), to letak (meletak); simpan (menyimpan)
particle (grain) butir
pass (by), to lalu
pass (an examination), to lulus dalam
pass (a proposal), to luluskan (meluluskan)
passive (gram.) pasif
past (last) yang lalu
patrol (mil.) (n.) peronda
pay (n.) gaji
pay, to bayar (membayar)
peace selamat
peel, to kupas (mengupas)
pellet butir
pen kalam
pencil pensel
people orang
people, a bangsa
people, other orang lain
people, the rakyat
perch, to hinggap
Perlis negeri Perlis
permanent tetap
Permanent Secretary Setiausaha Tetap
permission kebenaran
permit, to benarkan (membenarkan)
person orang
personal (gram.) diri
personal pronoun ganti nama diri
pharmacist ahli ubat
photography (n.) gambar
photograph, to gambar (menggambar)
pick up, to angkat (mengangkat)
pick up (heavy objects), to angkut (mengangkut)
picture gambar; lukisan
picture (film) wayang gambar
piece keping
pillar tiang
plant (n.) pokok

plant, to tanam (menanam); bertanam (86)
planter penanam
platform pentas (152)
play (drama) lakon; wayang
play, to main; bermain
please (invitation) sila (40)
please (request) tolong (57)
pleased (adj.) suka hati
point (decimal) perpuluhan (172)
point (out), to tunjukkan (menunjukkan)
pointer penunjuk
pole tiang
police polis
policeman mata-mata
police station balai polis
policy dasar; tujuan
politician ahli siasah; ahli politik
politics siasah, politik
poor miskin
position (office) jawatan
position (place) tempat
position (state of affairs) keadaan
post (pillar) tiang
post (mail), (n.) pos
post (letters), to kirim (mengirimkan)
Postmaster-General Ketua Pos Negara
post office pejabat pos
pot (flower) pasu
power kuasa; kekuatan
practice latihan
pray, to sembahyang
prefix (gram.) awalan
prepare (tr.), to sediakan (menyediakan); lengkapkan (melengkapkan) (197); siapkan (menyiapkan)
prepare (intr.), to berlengkap (197); bersedia, bersiap
present (n.) (gift) hadiah
present (adj.) (in attendance) hadir
president presiden
pretend, to buat-buat

prettiness kecantikan
pretty cantik
previous (last) yang lalu
price harga
primary (educ.) (adj.) rendah
primary school sekolah rendah
prime (adj.) perdana
Prime Minister Perdana Menteri
principal (n.) pengetua
principal (chief) (adj.) perdana
printer tukang cetak; pencetak
prison penjara
prize hadiah
probably agaknya
profession pekerjaan
profound dalam
profundity kedalaman
programme (radio, etc.) siaran
progress, to make maju
progressive maju
pronoun (gram.) ganti nama
pronounce, to ucap (mengucap); ucapkan (mengucapkan) (126)
pronounce sentence, to jatuhkan hukum (menjatuhkan hukum)
propeller kipas
propellers, to have berkipas
properly (dengan) baik-baik
proposal cadangan
prosper (tr.), to majukan (memajukan)
provided that (conj.) asalkan (131); lamun (132)
public (adj.) raya
public, the orang ramai
Public Works Dept. (P.W.D.) Jabatan Kerja Raya (J.K.R.)
publish (tr.), to terbitkan (menerbitkan)
published, to be terbit
pupil murid
puppet-show wayang
pull, to tarik (menarik)
pull out, to cabut (mencabut)

purchaser pembeli
push, to tolak (menolak)
put, to bubuh (membubuh), taruh (menaruh)
put away, to simpan (menyimpan)
put down, to letak (meletak)
put first, to utamakan (mengutamakan)
put forward, to kemukakan (mengemukakan)
put out, to (extinguish) padamkan (memadamkan)
put up, to (accomodate) tumpangkan (menumpangkan)
P.W.D. J.K.R.

Q

quarter, a suku (172)
question (n.) soalan; pertanyaan
quick (immediate) lekas
quick (rapid) cepat, deras
quickly dengan cepat; cepat
quickly as possible, as secepat-cepatnya
quick-witted cerdik

R

race (of people) bangsa
radio radio
railway train keretapi
rain hujan
rainy season musim hujan
raise, to naikkan (menaikkan)
ram, to (of ships, etc.) langgar (melanggar) (104)
rambutan buah rambutan
read, to baca (membaca); bacakan (membacakan)
reader pembaca
reading (n.) bacaan
reading-book buku bacaan
reading-room bilik bacaan

ready sedia, siap; lengkap (197)
ready, to get (intr.) bersedia, bersiap; berlengkap (197)
really sesungguhnya
reason sebab
reason, for this oleh sebab itu, oleh kerana itu
rebel (n.) pemberontak
receive, to terima (menerima)
receiver penerima
recipient penerima
record, to rakamkan (merakamkan)
recording (n.) rakaman
recording-room bilik rakaman
red merah
reduplication (gram.) pergandaan
reference to, with tentang, berkenaan dengan (125)
regard (as), to perlakukan (memperlakukan) (sebagai)
regard to, with tentang, berkenaan dengan (125)
register, to daftarkan (mendaftarkan)
registration pendaftaran
registrar pendaftar
regret (n.) dukacita
regret, to cf. (179)
reinforce, to kuatkan (menguatkan); perkuat (memperkuat)
reject, to tolak (menolak)
relationship perhubungan
release, to (free) bēbaskan (membēbaskan)
religion ugama
remember, to ingat (mengingat); teringat
remind, to ingati (mengingati) (177)
removal (transfer) pemindahan
repair, to baikkan (membaikkan), baiki (membaiki), perbaiki (memperbaiki)
repeat, to ulangkan (mengulangkan)
reply (n.) (answer) jawapan

reply (n.) (to a letter) balasan; surat balasan
reply, to jawab (menjawab)
report, to laporkan (melaporkan)
reporter pemberita
represent, to wakili (mewakili)
representative (n.) wakil
Representatives, House of Dēwan Rakyat
request (n.) permintaan
request, to pohon (memohon); persilakan (mempersilakan) (180); minta (meminta)
require, to kehendaki (menghendaki)
respect (n.) hormat (-nya) (162) (179)
respect, to hormati (menghormati) (162)
restitution pengembalian
restoration pengembalian
result (n.) keputusan
return, to (tr.) balas (membalas); hantarkan balik (menghantarkan balik)
return, to (intr.) balik, pulang, kembali
revision ulangkaji
ribbon pita (127: Note)
rice (growing) padi
rice (uncooked) beras
rice (cooked) nasi
rice-field (South Malaysian Peninsular) sawah
rice-field (North Malaysian Peninsular) bendang
rice-field, to have a bersawah
rich kaya, berada
ride, to naik
ride, to go for a (pergi) makan angin
ride a horse, to berkuda
right (correct) betul
right (not left) kanan
rise, to naik
rise, to (of the sun) terbit
rise, to (get up) bangun, bangkit
river sungai
road jalan

road, main jalan raya
road sign isyarat jalan raya
roar, to ngaum (mengaum)
role (task) tugas
roll up, to gulung (menggulung)
Roman (adj.) Rumi
Roman script tulisan Rumi
romance (story) hikayat
roof bumbung
room bilik
rubber (material) getah
rubber estate kebun getah
rubber tapper penoreh getah
rubber-tree pokok getah
run, to (intr.) berlari
run, to (tr.) jalankan (menjalankan)
run amok, to amuk (mengamuk)
run down (over), to langgar (melanggar) (104)
run into, to langgar (melanggar); terlanggar (104)
run off the road, to (swerve) tersimpang
run over, to terlanggar; langgar (melanggar) (104)
rural luar bandar
rural development pembangunan luar bandar

S

sack (n.) guni
sack, to (dismiss) keluarkan (mengeluarkan)
sadness dukacita
safely dengan selamat
safety selamat
sail, to set bertolak
salary gaji
salesman penjual
sarong kain
sarong, to wear a berkain
satisfactory memuaskan hati

373

satisfy, to puaskan (memuaskan)
Saturday hari Sabtu
savant ahli pengetahuan
say, to berkata; kata
scattered about, to be bertabur-taburan
scene pemandangan
scenery pemandangan
scholar (savant) ahli pengetahuan
school sekolah
school, primary sekolah rendah
school, secondary sekolah menengah
school, to go to (to be at) bersekolah
science (school subject) ilmu sains
science (the sc. of; -ology) ilmu
script tulisan
script, Malay (Arabic) tulisan Jawi
script, Roman tulisan Rumi
sculptor ahli patung
sea laut
sea, by dengan kapal laut
season musim
season, dry musim kemarau
season, rainy musim hujan
second (adj.) kedua
secondary (educ.) menengah
secondary school sekolah menengah
secretariat ibu pejabat (38)
secretary setiausaha
Secretary, Permanent Setiausaha Tetap
see, to lihat (melihat), tengok (menengok); nampak
see, to be able to nampak
seed biji
seems, it nampaknya (91)
seen, to be kelihatan (165)
self (subject) sendiri; *(object)* diri (146)
sell, to jual (menjual); berjual (86)
seller penjual
send, to hantar (menghantar); hantarkan (menghantarkan); kirim (mengirim); kirimkan (mengirimkan)

send back, to hantarkan balik (menghantarkan balik)
senior kanan (73)
senior lecturer pensyarah kanan
sentence (gram.) ayat
sentence, complex ayat berkait
sentence, compound ayat berlapis
sentence (judgement) hukum
sentence, to pronounce jatuhkan hukum (menjatuhkan hukum)
serious (of illness) teruk
seriously ill sakit teruk
service perkhidmatan
Service, On Government Urusan Kerajaan (163)
Service, On His Majesty's Urusan Seri Paduka Baginda (163)
session sidang (162)
set in motion, to jalankan (menjalankan)
set off, to bertolak
set sail, to bertolak
seven tujuh
seventeen tujuh belas
seventeenth ketujuh belas
seventh (adj.) ketujuh
seventh, a sepertujuh (172)
sever, to putusi (memutusi); putuskan (memutuskan)
severed (adj.) putus
shall akan (24)
sham, to buat-buat
shape (form) (n.) bentuk
shape (cut of clothes) (n.) potongan
sharp tajam
shave, to (tr.) cukur (mencukur) (84)
shave, to (intr.) bercukur (84)
she ia, dia (58); beliau (59); baginda (163)
shelter (hiding-place) (n.) persembunyian
ship kapal
ship (sea-going) kapal laut

shipping perkapalan
shirt baju kemeja
shirt, to wear a berbaju
shoe kasut
shoemaker tukang kasut
shoes, to wear berkasut
shoot, to témbak (menémbak)
shoot at each other, to bertémbak-témbakan
shop kedai
shop, to keep a berkedai
shopkeeper orang kedai
short péndék
shortage kekurangan (165)
shorten, to péndékkan (memendekkan)
short of, to be kekurangan (165)
shot (bullet) (n.) peluru
should (ought) patut (122)
show (n.) pertunjukan
show, to tunjukkan (menunjukkan)
shut, to tutup (menutup)
sick (ill) sakit
side sebelah
side (in a contest, etc.) (n.) pihak
sight of, to catch ternampak, terlihat
sign (n.) isyarat; tanda
sign, to tandatangani (menandatangani), sain *(coll.)* (181)
sign, road- isyarat jalan raya
sign-post penunjuk
signature tandatangan
silk sutera
sing, to (intr.) nyanyi (menyanyi)
sing, to (tr.) nyanyikan (menyanyikan)
Singapore Singapura
sink, to (intr.) tenggelam; karam
sink, to (tr.) karamkan (mengaramkan)
sir, tuan; encik
sister (elder) kakak
sister (younger) adik
sisters (collective) adik-beradik
sit, to duduk

sit down, to duduk
sit on, to (tr.) duduki (menduduki)
situation keadaan; kedudukan
six enam
sixteen enam belas
sixteenth keenam belas
sixth (adj.) keenam
sixth, a seperenam (172)
size besarnya (212d)
skill kepandaian; keahlian
sky udara; langit
slip, to tergelincir
slow lambat
slowly perlahan-lahan
small kecil
smash, to pecahkan (memecahkan)
smashed (adj.) pecah
smile, to tersenyum
smith (blacksmith) tukang besi
smoke, to (tr.) hisap (menghisap)
snap, to (tr.) putusi (memutusi), putuskan (memutuskan)
snapped (adj.) putus
so (conj.) jadi (85)
so (thus) begitu
so-and-so si polan, si anu
social masyarakat
social welfare kebajikan masyarakat
society (association) syarikat
society (community) masyarakat
society, co-operative syarikat kerjasama
soldier askar
some setengah, separuh (172)
someone else orang lain
sometimes kadang-kadang
son anak lelaki
song lagu
soon as possible, as selekas-lekasnya
sound (n.) bunyi
south-east tenggara
South-east Asia Asia Tenggara
spade penggali

375

speak, to bercakap
special khas
specimen contoh
spectator penonton
speech, a ucapan
spend, to belanjakan (membelanjakan)
splendid bagus
spokesman jurucakap
spot, to (catch sight of) ternampak, terlihat
spread out, to (tr.) bentangkan (membentangkan)
staff (employees) kakitangan (182)
stage (n.) pentas; panggung (152)
stage-manager pengurus pentas
stairs tangga
stamp (postage) setem
stand, to berdiri
stare (at), to pandang (memandang)
start, to (of ships, trains, etc.) bertolak
startle, to kejutkan (mengejutkan)
startled, to be terkejut
state (adj.) negara
state (country) (n.) negeri
state (condition) keadaan
stateman ahli negara
station (railway, etc.) perhentian
statue patung
stay, to duduk
steal, to curi (mencuri)
steamship kapal api
step (pace), (n.) langkah
stick (n.) tongkat
stick, to use as a bertongkatkan
stick, to (tr.) lekatkan (melekatkan)
stir, to kacau (mengacau)
still (adv.) masih, lagi
stone batu
stop (bus, etc.) (n.) perhentian
stop, to (tr.) berhenti
stop, to (tr.) perhentikan (memperhentikan)
storage penyimpanan

store penyimpanan, stor
storey tingkat
storeys, to have (two) bertingkat (dua)
storm ribut
story hikayat, kisah, cerita, ceritera (cf. note in (144))
straight (on) terus
strength kekuatan
strengthen, to kuatkan (menguatkan)
stress (n.) tekanan
stress, to tekankan (menekan)
strike, to (hit) pukul (memukul)
string tali
stroll, to go for a (pergi) makan angin
strong kuat
student penuntut, pelajar
studio studio
study, to pelajari (mempelajari)
stupid bodoh
stupidity kebodohan
style (cut of clothes) potongan
style (manner) cara
submarine (n.) kapal selam
subordinate (gram.) penambat
subordinating conjunction (gram.) sendikata penambat
substitute, to ganti (mengganti); gantikan (menggantikan)
substitution penggantian
suck, to hisap (menghisap)
suddenly tiba-tiba
suffix (gram.) akhiran
suggestion cadangan
sum (of), the sebanyak
summon, to panggil (memanggil)
summons (call) (n.) panggilan
sun matahari
sunbathe, to berjemur (84)
sunshade (ordinary) payung
sunshade (royal) cetera (141)
supervisor penyelia
support (n.) sokongan
support, to sokong (menyokong)

supporter penyokong
sure tentu
surgeon ahli bedah
surprise, to hairankan (menghairankan)
surprised (adj.) hairan
surrender, to (tr.) serah (menyerah); serahkan (menyerahkan)
surrender, to (intr.) serah diri (menyerahdiri); serahkan diri (menyerahkan diri)
sweat (n.) peluh
sweet (adj.) manis
sweeten, to maniskan (memaniskan)
sweetness kemanisan
sweep, to sapu (menyapu)
swerve, to tersimpang
swift (adj.) deras, cepat, lekas
sword pedang
sword, to carry a berpedang

T

table méja
table, to (e.g. a motion) bentangkan (membentangkan)
tail ékor
take, to ambil (mengambil)
take down (carry down), to turunkan (menurunkan)
take up (carry up), to naikkan (menaikkan)
talk, to bercakap
talk, to have a (discussion) berunding (125)
talk about, to perkatakan (memperkatakan)
talk, to have (discussions) berunding (125)
tall tinggi
tangent, to go off at a tersimpang
tap (rubber), to toreh (menoreh)
tape pita
task (duty) tugas
tasty sedap

tax cukai
tax, income cukai pendapatan
tea téh
teach, to ajar (mengajar)
teacher guru, Cikgu (70)
teacher training perguruan
tear, to koyakkan (mengoyakkan)
technician ahli téknik
telecommunications telekom
tell (inform), to beritahu (memberitahu)
tell (narrate), to ceritakan (menceritakan); ceriterakan (menceriterakan)
tell (order), to suruh (menyuruh)
ten sepuluh
tenth (adj.) kesepuluh
terminate, to (tr.) tamatkan (menamatkan)
terrorist pengganas
test (examination) peperiksaan
thank you terima kasih (126)
that (demon. adj. and pron.) itu
that (rel. pron.) yang
that (conj.) bahawa (121); adalah (179)
that way (direction) ikut situ (39)
theatre panggung (152)
the . . . -est yang . . . sekali (4)
theft pencurian
their mereka; -nya (69)
them mereka; -nya (69)
the more . . . the more . . . lagi . . . lagi . . . ; makin . . . makin . . . ; semakin . . . semakin . . . (32)
the most . . . yang . . . sekali (4)
themselves sendiri; diri, dirinya (146)
then (next) kemudian
then, and lalu (97)
then, only baharulah
therefore oleh kerana itu, oleh sebab itu
these ini
they mereka, mereka itu
thief pencuri
thin kurus

377

think, to ingat (33); fikir (memikir) (177)
think, I agaknya (92)
think of, to ingati (mengingati) (177)
third (adj.) ketiga
third, a sepertiga
thirteen tiga belas
thirteenth ketiga belas
this ini
this is . . . ini dia . . .
this way (direction) ikut ini (39)
those itu
thousand ribu
thousand, a seribu
three tiga
throughout di seluruh
throw away, to buang (membuang)
thus begitu
ticket tiket
tidy, to kemas (mengemas)
tiger harimau
time (in general) masa
time (occasion) kali
time (point of time) waktu
time, for a long lama
time to, to have no tak sempat
to (places) ke
to (people) kepada
today hari ini
together with sama (dengan); bersama-sama (dengan)
toilet (W.C.) jamban
tolerate, to tahan (menahan)
tomb kubur
tomorrow ésok
tongue lidah
too (much) terlalu; terlampau (9) (111); sangat (9)
too many terlalu, terlampau (111)
too much terlalu, terlampau (111)
towkay (Chinese businessman) taukeh
town bandar, pekan
town, in di pekan

town council majlis bandaran
toy permainan
trade, to berniaga
train (rly.) keretapi
train, to (tr.) latih (melatih)
trainee pelatih
trainee-teacher guru pelatih
training latihan
Training College, Day Maktab Perguruan Harian
training, teacher- perguruan
transferred, to be berpindah
transition penyeberangan
transport pengangkutan
treasury perbendaharaan
Treasury, the Jabatan Perbendaharaan
treat (as), to perlakukan (memperlakukan) (sebagai)
tree pokok, pokok kayu
trellis kisi-kisi
trestle kuda-kuda
trickle, to bercucuran
trip (journey) perjalanan
troops askar-askar
true sungguh, benar
truly benar, sungguh (8); sebenarnya
trust, to percayakan; percayai (mempercayai)
try, to cuba (mencuba)
twelfth kedua belas
twelve dua belas
two dua
type, to taip (menaip)
typewriter mesin taip
typist jurutaip

U

umbrella (ordinary) payung
umbrella (royal) cetera (141)
umbrella-bearer pembawa cetera (141)
unbearable tidak tertahan

uncle bapa saudara
uncountable tiada terbilang (105)
undated tiada bertarikh
understand, to faham
unhappiness kedukaan
unify, to satukan (menyatukan)
uninterrupted tidak berkeputusan
union persatuan
unit kesatuan
unite, to (tr.) satukan (menyatukan) persatukan (mempersatukan)
united (adj.) bersatu
United Nations, the Bangsa-bangsa Bersatu
unity persatuan
university sekolah tinggi; universiti
unreadable tiada terbaca (105)
unsheath, to hunus (menghunus) (106-108)
unsheathed (adj.) terhunus (106-108)
until sampai, sehingga (128)
unusable tiada terpakai
unwearable tiada terpakai
us kita (50); kami (51)
use, to pakai (memakai), gunakan (menggunakan)
use (of), to make pergunakan (mempergunakan)
useful berguna
utter, to ucap (mengucap); ucapkan (mengucapkan) (126)

V

vase jambangan
vegetable(s) (green) sayur; sayur-sayuran (137)
vehicle kenderaan
verandah (Malay style) serambi; (European style) beranda
very sangat, amat, benar, sungguh (8)
very, not kurang (7); tidak berapa, tak berapa (10)

victim mangsa
view (opinion) pandangan
view (scene) pemandangan
village kampung
village headman ketua kampung
visible (adj.) kelihatan (165)
visible, to be nampak, kelihatan (165)
visit, to lawat (melawat)
visiting teacher guru pelawat
visitor pelawat, *(guest)* tetamu (82)
voice suara
vote, to undi (mengundi)
vote (n.) undi
voter pengundi

W

wages gaji
wait, to (intr.) nanti (menanti), tunggu (menunggu)
wait for, to nantikan (menantikan)
wall (structural) tembok
walk, to berjalan; berjalan kaki (44)
want, to mahu, hendak (23); kehendaki (menghendaki)
war perang
warship kapal perang
way (road) jalan
way, that (direction) ikut itu (39)
way, this (direction) ikut ini (39)
way of, by ikut (39)
we kita (50); kami (51)
wealthy kaya, berada
weapon senjata
wear, to pakai (memakai)
wedding perkahwinan
Wednesday hari Rabu
week minggu
week, next minggu depan
weekly (adj.) mingguan
weekly (adv.) tiap-tiap minggu
weep, to tangis (menangis)

welcome, to sambut (menyambut)
welfare kebajikan
well (n.) telaga
well as possible, as (dengan) sebaik-baiknya
well off kaya, berada
what apa
when bila; masa; tatkala; waktu; apabila (189)
whence dari mana
where di mana
where from? dari mana?
where to? ke mana?
whether ... or .... mahupun ... mahupun ...
which (rel.) yang
which (interrog.) mana
while (conj.) masa, sedang, sementara (189)
white putih
whither ke mana
who (rel.) yang
who (interrog.) siapa
whom (rel.) yang
whom (interrog.) siapa
wicked jahat
wickedness kejahatan
wide lébar
widen, to lébarkan (melébarkan)
wife isteri
will akan (24)
wind (n.) angin
window tingkap
wipe, to sapu (menyapu)
wish (n.) kehendak
with dengan
without tanpa, dengan tiada
witness (n.) saksi
witness, to saksikan (menyaksikan)

woman orang perempuan
wood (material) kayu
word perkataan
work (n.) kerja
work (literary) karangan
work, to bekerja
workman tukang
workshop makmal
world market pasaran dunia
write, to tulis (menulis)
write (books, etc.), to karang (mengarang)
writer penulis; *(author)* pengarang
writing (script) tulisan
writing, in bertulis
writing paper kertas tulis
written (adj.) bertulis; tertulis (106) (107); *(of books, etc.)* terkarang (106) (107)

Y

year tahun
year, next tahun depan
yearly (adj.) tahunan
yearly (adv.) tahun-tahun; tiap-tiap tahun
yellow kuning
yes ya
yesterday semalam, kemarin
yet lagi, masih
yet, not belum
you encik (52); tuan (53); puan (54); saudara (55); engkau (62) (74); kau-, kau (67)
young muda
younger brother adik lelaki
younger sister adik prempuan
youngster budak
yourself sendiri; diri; dirimu (146)
yourselves sendiri; diri; dirimu (146)

NOTES

NOTES

NOTES

TIMES LEARN MALAY

Malay in 3 Weeks *by John Parry and Sahari Sulaiman*
A teach-yourself Malay book that enables you to communicate in practical everyday situations.

Malay Made Easy *by A.W. Hamilton*
How to speak Malay intelligibly and accurately.

Easy Malay Vocabulary: 1001 Essential Words *by A.W. Hamilton*
A handbook to enlarge your vocabulary and to ensure effective communication in Malay on a wide range of topics.

Speak Malay! *by Edward S. King*
A graded course in simple spoken Malay for English-speaking people.

Write Malay *by Edward S. King*
A more advanced course on how to read and write good modern Malay.

Learn Malay: A Phrase a Day *by Dr. G. Soosai*
A simple but comprehensive way to learn Malay in 365 days.

Converse in Malay *by Dr. G. Soosai*
A compilation of the highly successful RTM *Radio Lessons* series, a programme which proved both popular and beneficial to thousands of listeners in mastering Malay.

Malay Phrase Book For Tourists *by Hj Ismail Ahmad & Andrew Leonki*
The indispensable companion, it helps tourists in everyday situations in a Malay-speaking world.

Standard Malay Made Simple *by Dr. Liaw Yock Fang*
An intensive Standard Malay language (bahasa Melayu baku) course designed for adult learners with no previous knowledge of the Malay language.

Speak Standard Malay: A Beginner's Guide *by Dr. Liaw Yock Fang*
An easy and comprehensive guide which enables you to acquire fluency and confidence in speaking standard Malay in only 3 months.

TIMES LEARN INDONESIAN

Standard Indonesian Made Simple *by Dr. Liaw Yock Fang with Dra Nini Tiley-Notodisuryo*
An intensive Standard Indonesian language course designed for beginners to gain mastery of the language.

Speak Standard Indonesian: A Beginner's Guide *by Dr. Liaw Yock Fang with Drs. Munadi Patmadiwiria & Abdullah Hassan*
An easy and comprehensive guide which enables you to acquire fluency and confidence in speaking Indonesian in only a few months.

Indonesian In 3 Weeks *by Dr. Liaw Yock Fang with Drs. Munadi Patmadiwiria*
A teach-yourself Indonesian book that enables you to understand what people say to you, and to make yourself understood in everyday situations.

Easy Indonesian Vocabulary: 1001 Essential Words *by Dr. Liaw Yock Fang*
A handbook to enlarge your vocabulary and to ensure effective communication in Indonesian on a wide range of topics.

Indonesian Phrase Book For Tourists *by Nini Tiley-Notodisuryo*
A handy reference for every traveller, it helps you in everyday situations during your stay in Indonesia.

DICTIONARY/THESAURUS

Times Comparative Dictionary of Malay-Indonesian Synonyms
compiled by Dr. Leo Suryadinata, edited by Professor Abdullah Hassan
For learners of Malay and Indonesian who want to know the differences that exist between the two languages.

Tesaurus Bahasa Melayu *by Prof. Madya Noor Ein Mohd Noor, Noor Zaini Mohd Ali, Mohd Tahir Abd Rahman, Singgih W. Sumartoyo, Siti Fatimah Ariffin*
A comprehensive A–Z thesaurus that enables you to master Malay vocabulary effectively.